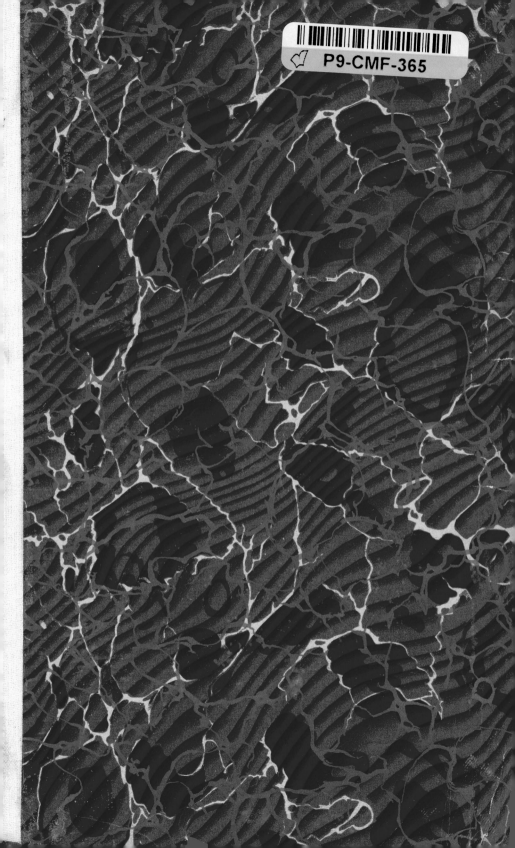

J. L. G. Ferris, Pinx.

THE
WORLD'S HISTORY
AND ITS MAKERS

BY

EDGAR SANDERSON, A. M.
AUTHOR "HISTORY OF THE BRITISH EMPIRE"

J. P. LAMBERTON, A. M.
AUTHOR "HISTORIC CHARACTERS AND FAMOUS EVENTS," "LITERATURE
OF ALL NATIONS," ETC.

JOHN McGOVERN
AUTHOR "THE GOLDEN LEGACY," "THE TOILERS' DIADEM," "FAMOUS AMERI-
CAN STATESMEN," ETC.

OLIVER H. G. LEIGH
COLLABORATOR ON "HISTORIC CHARACTERS AND FAMOUS EVENTS," "LITERA-
TURE OF ALL NATIONS" AND "LIBRARY OF AMERICAN LITERATURE;"
AUTHOR OF "HISTORY OF THE UNION LEAGUE
OF PHILADELPHIA," ETC.

AND THE FOLLOWING EMINENT AMERICAN EDITORS AND WRITERS:

JOSEPH M. ROGERS, A. M.; LAURENCE E. GREENE; M. A. LANE;
G. SENECA JONES, A M.; FREDERICK LOGAN;
WILLIAM MATTHEWS HANDY.

INTRODUCTION BY

MARSHALL S. SNOW, A. M.
PROFESSOR OF HISTORY WASHINGTON UNIVERSITY AND DEAN OF THE COLLEGE;
AUTHOR "CITY GOVERNMENT," "POLITICAL STUDIES," ETC., ETC.

TEN VOLUMES

VOL. IX

LITERATURE OF THE XIX CENTURY,

NEW YORK   CHICAGO

E. R. DU MONT

1902

CONTENTS

PHOTOGRAVURES

VOLUME IX.

INTRODUCTION

GENERAL VIEW OF MODERN HISTORY AND ITS RELATION TO LITERATURE

Centuries furnish convenient divisions for grouping great historical events and national movements, and thus marking the course of the world's progress in civilization. In modern history, the Fifteenth Century shows the capture of Constantinople by the Turks, but this loss to Christendom in the East was soon offset by the marvelous discovery of a New World in the West. The leading event of the Sixteenth Century was the Reformation, begun by an obscure German monk, and ending in the practical severance of the nations of northern Europe from their former obedience to the Pope. The Seventeenth Century was marked by the devastation of Germany in the Thirty Years' War and the struggle for civil and religious liberty in England, in which one King lost his life and another his throne, and the Revolution of 1688 made William of Orange King by the voice of Parliament. As a consequence of the same struggle the English settlement of the Atlantic Coast of North America was begun. In the meantime, through the consummate statecraft of Richelieu, France, though agitated by civil and religious wars, rose to a dazzling eminence, which she maintained in the splendid reign of Louis XIV. The Eighteenth Century was marked by the introduction of Western civilization into Russia by the half-savage Peter the Great, by the warlike career of Frederick the Great, which made Prussia one of the Great Powers, by the partition of turbulent Poland, and by two great revolutions. The American Revolution not only severed the English colonies from the mother country, but it proclaimed as a fundamental principle that all governments derive their just rights from the consent of the governed. The French Revolution, asserting the rights of man against the long-established oppression of the privileged classes, made its watchword "Liberty, Equality, Fraternity," and threatened to engulf the monarchies of Europe. It called to its aid the military genius of Napoleon Bonaparte, who soon directed its forces to new aims.

The Nineteenth Century opened with Napoleon as sole Consul of France, soon to be crowned Emperor by the Pope. With no military rival to endanger his supremacy, he sought to be the dictator of Europe. But his seizure of Spain was a blunder, his invasion of Russia proved to be a fatal mistake, and his astonishing career ended in irretrievable defeat at Waterloo. The allied sovereigns of Europe, still dreading revolution, used their efforts to baffle the desires of the people for constitutional freedom. The restored Bourbons had learned nothing and had forgotten nothing. But the revolutionary spirit, though harshly repressed, was not extinguished. In 1830 an Orleanist King was placed on the throne of France with the expectation of relief, and when this was disappointed another revolutionary crisis in 1848 brought in a republic. The wave of revolution again passed over Europe, threatening the stability of thrones and frightening monarchs from their propriety. But in a few years the French Republic was transformed into an empire under Napoleon III. In his brilliant reign of nineteen years Paris was again the most splendid capital of the civilized world. While France had thus been wasting its substance in vain show, Prussia, by severe discipline and rigid economy, had been renewing its moral and material strength. Its steady growth furnished to Bismarck and Moltke the means for its triumph over Austria in 1866 and over France in 1870, and made the Prussian King emperor of a remodeled Germany. France, crushed to earth, became again a republic, and so remains in spite of many reactionary attempts. Italy, long "merely a geographical expression," had, by the statesmanship of Cavour, the aid of France, and the enthusiasm of Garibaldi, been united under Victor Emmanuel, who made Rome his capital. England had borne the chief expense of the wars with the first Napoleon, and its people groaned under intolerable burdens. But from 1830 there was a series of constitutional and legislative reforms which gave needed relief in many directions and produced a wider diffusion of political power.

The United States, little concerned in the wars of Europe, rapidly developed the immense material advantages of its own vast territory. Though conflicts, chiefly due to the existence of negro slavery, brought on a bloody and costly civil war, it terminated in the restoration of the seceded States to the Union, and the constitutional prohibition of slavery. The political revolutions in Europe in the early part of the century gave Mexico and the South American dependencies of Spain and Portugal the opportunity to throw off their yoke, but their new governments have not been stable or prosperous. At the close of the century Spain has been compelled by the United States, after a remarkably brief war, chiefly naval, to relinquish the last of her possessions in the Western Hemisphere.

So far we have looked chiefly at the political history of the world. The manifest tendency has been to a larger admission of the people to a share in the government. Parliamentary institutions are found even in the monarchies inclined to despotism. In those countries where they have always flourished, the power of the lower house or popular branch has steadily increased, while that of the upper house or peers has been restricted to an occasional obstruction of legislation on which the Nation was not fully agreed. As a necessary support for the wide extension of suffrage popular education has been liberally promoted. This has not been confined to elementary branches, but has included all the courses of university teaching and various departments of industrial and mechanical training. This wider extension of education is undoubtedly due to the larger view of man's intellectual powers and to the better understanding of his relation to the world around him.

The Nineteenth Century has far surpassed its predecessors in mechanical inventions and scientific discoveries. This movement began with Watt's application of steam to stationary engines in the Eighteenth Century, but has increased in manifold proportion since its later application to land locomotion and ocean navigation. Other conspicuous triumphs are seen in the use of the mysterious power of electricity in the telegraph, the trolley car, and as an illuminant; in the invention of the sewing machine, the harvester, the telephone, the typewriter, the photograph, and the bicycle. The progress of science is attested by the wonders of the spectrum analysis, the ascertaining of the influence of microscopic organisms, the discovery of the Rœntgen ray and other forms of radiant energy, the detection of new chemical elements in the atmosphere. But the grandest results have been the two profound generalizations, which have effected not only the investigations of all scientists, but the thought of all studious men

—the conservation of energy, and the doctrine of evolution—the former showing that no force in the universe is ever lost, the latter proving the gradual adaptation of living creatures to their environment. The recent discovery of these fundamental principles of natural law and the simultaneous invention of numerous aids to human comfort seem to indicate the dawn of a new era of civilization.

Admitting then the superiority of the present age in material and scientific results, it is natural to ask, Has its intellectual and literary development been proportional to its mechanical progress? As we have taken a rapid view of the general movement of the modern centuries, we may add a similar survey of their relation to literature. The Fifteenth Century was distinguished by the invention of printing with movable metal types, which furnished an easy means of multiplying copies of all works. At first used for Latin Bibles, church-service books, and religious treatises, it was soon employed for works of all kinds. Invented in Germany, it was transferred speedily to France, Italy, England, wherever books were in demand. The Reformation of the Sixteenth Century called for translations of the Scriptures into the national languages, and thus gave a standard of prose style and orthography, which assisted in elevating the common speech. National enthusiasm stimulated the writers no longer cramped by efforts to express themselves in a dead language. The lusty vigor of youth is displayed in the lyrical and narrative poetry which found favor in royal court and baronial hall. Before the close of this century the drama became the popular form of entertainment. In England, where it was freed from the encumbering rules of classic tragedy, its success was greatest. There Shakespeare rose to a pre-eminent height as the unrivalled master of both tragedy and comedy. In France at the opening of the Seventeenth Century critics determined the rules of classicism which still to some extent regulate its poetry. In spite of these fetters Corneille and Racine achieved masterpieces, while Molière, by his comedies, won still more decided triumphs in overcoming the ecclesiastical prejudice against the stage. In England for a time the Puritans closed the theaters, but after the Restoration a more licentious form of comedy, imitated from the French, became popular. Yet at this time Milton, in poverty and blindness, set himself to compose the greatest English epic. Dryden, a poet of robust genius, yielded to the popular currents, and wrote licentious plays and poems of various degrees of merit.

At the opening of the Eighteenth Century everything, both in prose and verse, had been reduced to rule and measure. The French critics had become the acknowledged authorities in every form of literature. In Germany the native speech was neglected for literary purposes. Frederick the Great, much as he did for Prussia, wrote all his works in French. According to the principles then laid down, the chief aim of poetry was to be correct both in matter and form; to be natural was to be vulgar. Pope is the English examplar of this style, which long prevailed. In English prose, Addison held a similar place, and perhaps upon juster grounds. Later Dr. Samuel Johnson, a man of greater intellectual force, introduced a more artificial inflated style. His power lay in the sincerity and vigor with which he expressed his opinions, however prejudiced they might occasionally be.

But early in the same century there appeared two counter currents which were to increase in force and gradually overwhelm and sweep away the love of feeble correctness. The first was a new delight in the aspects of

wild nature and a desire to depict natural beauty as a
mental gratification apart from any human interest.
Thomson's "Winter" (published in 1727) is one of the
earliest evidences of this tendency in English poetry, and
it is notable that in it he employed blank verse rather than
the rhymed couplets then common. Combined with this
love of nature was a growing distaste for the prevailing
artificial civilization, and a desire to return to simpler
tastes and a more primitive mode of life. This tendency
was assisted by the publication of Bishop Percy's
"Reliques of Ancient English Poetry," the first important
collection of native ballads. These rude snatches of popular song infused new life and spirit into the poetic imagination.

A singular result of the uncritical revival of interest
in old forms of literature was a crop of literary forgeries.
A man named Ireland attempted to palm off a tragedy
called "Prince Vortigern" as a work of Shakespeare's.
The most pathetic case was the boy Chatterton's endeavor,
by the use of obsolete words and disguised spelling, to
pass some not unworthy composition of his own as poems
of a pretended monk, Thomas Rowley of Bristol. The
precocious genius was but eighteen when, to avoid starvation, he committed suicide. But the most noted of these
forgeries was James Macpherson's edition of the "Poems
of Ossian." They were founded on some fragments of
Gaelic traditional poetry, ascribed to Ossian or Oisin, a
bard of the Third Century, but modified in form and tone,
and filled with vague, sentimental gloom, which gave
them vogue throughout Europe, and affected French and
German writers of the beginning of the Nineteenth Century. The sturdy common sense of Dr. Samuel Johnson
was proof against the delusions of Macpherson.

Two new forms of literature sprang up in this century

—the periodical essay and the novel. The former, an adaptation of a French style of writing, was an outgrowth or department of the newspaper, which had begun in England about the middle of the Seventeenth Century. It flourished luxuriantly and became the favorite mode of prose-writing with professional authors. Although De Foe had written "The Adventures of Robinson Crusoe" and other fictitious biographies, not without merit, the origin of the novel is usually ascribed to the honest printer Richardson, who, in preparing a model letter-writer, tried to make it attractive by incorporating an entertaining story. The bulky book was called "The Story of Pamela; or, Virtue Rewarded." The witty and satirical Henry Fielding undertook to ridicule this moral story by relating "The Story of Joseph Andrews," in which Pamela's brother is made to pass through corresponding temptations to equivalent rewards. Both sober Richardson and gay Fielding persevered in their respective courses, producing new stories, superior to the first, but few other writers were induced to imitate them. The rollicking Smollett and the charming Goldsmith were the most successful in portraying ordinary life and character. The whimsical Laurence Sterne achieved unique but temporary success by his "Life and Opinions of Tristram Shandy, Gent.," in which he defied the conventions of society, and even of decency. His "Sentimental Journey" was written after a visit to France, in which he became acquainted with Rousseau's writings. The *dilettante* Horace Walpole published, in 1765, "The Castle of Otranto," and a few imitations of this romance were indications of reviving interest in mediæval history. But when we consider the overwhelming flood of novels which was to come on subjects of all kinds, domestic and historical, adventurous and analytical, it is astonishing that so few efforts were made in this direction in the Eighteenth Century, after the example was set. A more potent leader was required to smite the flinty rock and cause the streams of prose fiction to gush forth.

Modern France has been noted for its ready acceptance of formal rules in all matters of social observance. In the struggle which arose against the wanton tyranny of authority in church and state in the Eighteenth Century, there was no disregard of literary criticism. The witty, spiteful, mirth-provoking Voltaire, after having established his reputation as a versatile artist, as poet, satirist, critic, dramatist and philosophical writer, was ever ready to come forward as the champion of the oppressed. The peculiarity of his genius was shown in his boldness in attacking existing abuses and his success in escaping punishment from the powerful persons interested in them. The Swiss republican Rousseau, who was twenty years younger, was of entirely different temperament and tastes. While Voltaire was the favorite polished author of a cultured society, who appreciated the keenness of his wit and the vigor of his onset, the serious, moody Rousseau was simple in habit, a lover of nature, one who despised the supposed advantages of refinement, and wished to benefit mankind by proposing a return to barbarism. He rejected any positive rule of duty, and, insisting on the natural goodness of the heart, made sensibility the regulator of conduct. His own life was a wretched caricature of the ideal he proposed in his writings. Asserting that virtue was not compatible with wealth or dependence, he gave up an official position, discarded the customary dress of gentlemen, lived in concubinage with an illiterate woman, and bestowed his five children on foundling hospitals, because he was too poor to maintain them. And yet this selfish wretch who neglected the plainest dictates

of humanity, was able, by his plausible, deceptive eloquence, to fill the hearts of his readers with pity for
imaginary sorrows, with pardon for the basest seduction.
The germs of his works can be traced to English literature or to his observations during his brief residence in
England. Even "The New Héloise" owes much to
Richardson's "Clarissa Harlowe." His "Emile" advocated persuasively education in conformity with natural
inclination, rather than by compulsion. Its best principles have been adopted in later systems of education.
His "Social Contract" supplied a new theoretical basis of
government, and though entirely without historical proof,
has been a most effective argument in extending modern
democracy. No other writer of the Eighteenth Century
had vaster or more permanent influence on the social,
political, and literary movements of Europe. He dissolved
the bonds which had united the people in the existing governments, and resolved them into a loose aggregation of
atoms. And yet, by his sentiment and love of simple
nature, he seemed to satisfy the demands of the soul.
Rousseau created the intellectual atmosphere which was
essential to the terrific explosion of the French Revolution.

In other parts of Europe, in the beginning of that century, in spite of the almost universal acceptance of the
social fashions and literary decrees of the French court,
there were evidences of a struggle against this intellectual
bondage. The aspiration after the truth of life and natural feeling was not confined to France or England.
Strange to say, a most efficient instrument in this new
movement was "Robinson Crusoe," which was speedily
translated into German, and gave rise to numerous imitations. That familiar story led to further acquaintance
with English literature, and especially with Shakespeare
and Milton. Rival schools of critics were formed; the

pedantic Gottsched in Leipzig maintained the traditional
classicism, and made Milton a special object of attack;
while the more judicious Bodmer, who had been compelled to seek refuge in Switzerland, defended free nationality. The latter became a pioneer in the rescue of
the old German poems, especially of the "Nibelungenlied,"
since regarded as one of the chief glories of the Teutonic
race. In his defense of Milton, whom he translated
partly, he was aided by Klopstock, whose "Messias" is
the most successful imitation of the spirit of "Paradise
Lost," though more resembling an oratorio than an epic
or dramatic poem. The romantic Wieland and all the
literary youth supported the same cause, and the despotic
Gottsched was deposed from his literary dictatorship.
The liberal and learned Wieland passed through many
stages in his literary career. At first he was pietistic, like
the more earnest Klopstock, and imitated the English Dr.
Young, author of the "Night Thoughts." But later rationalism led him to lighter French models, and finally
his epicureanism was shown in romantic interpretations of
ancient Greek life. "Agathon" reveals many views of
Greek character in the Fourth Century before Christ.
In "The Abderites," on the other hand, there is, under a
veil of ancient names and manners, a burlesque of the
provincialism of petty German courts. But Wieland's
chief work is the brilliant romantic poem of "Oberon"
(1780) in which he exhibits changing pictures of rural
simplicity and Oriental splendor, city tumult and dismal
deserts, gay feasts and wretched shipwreck, and through
them all heroism and trusty friendship.

Greater than the cultured Wieland was the lofty idealist Lessing, who emancipated the German mind from
slavish imitation of foreign models. He not only led an
attack on the classic French drama but gave the

German stage beautiful models which still hold their place even beside Goethe and Schiller's master-pieces. His greatest work is "Nathan the Wise," in which he taught the duty of religious toleration. In his masterly treatise, "Laokoon," he investigated and demonstrated the ultimate principles of art, and its neces-sary limitations in its several departments of sculpture, painting and poetry. In his "Education of the Human Race" Lessing maintained that in all positive religions there is something of divine truth; that Providence is the teacher, mankind the pupil, and the successive religions or revelations the text books, but humanity, when fully de-veloped, will need no such external aids.

The intellectual agitation already produced in Ger-man by these and other native writers was intensified when the writings of the republican Rousseau began to appear. His urgent call to men to return to the state of primitive simplicity and to reject the pretended advantages of super-ficial civilization met with warm responses. All limita-tions to individual feeling, instinct and passion were to be removed. Sensibility was to be the universal rule of con-duct. This period is known as that of "Storm and Stress," from the title of a drama by Klinger in 1776, in which the hero's insatiable craving for activity leads him to run away to take part in the American Revolution. Many plays of this period indicate a rebellious state of society and threaten a speedy and inevitable revolution. Yet while there existed much distress and suffering, a corrupt aris-tocracy and disregard of humanity, there were also to be found domestic joys, pleasant lives in both city and coun-try. From the pictures of evil presented by the dramatists, or more probably from direct observation of their subjects, many of the rulers took warning and sought to avert the misery by initiating reforms, social and political. Both

Frederick II of Prussia and Joseph II of Austria were true benefactors of society, and rulers of smaller territories were not less devoted to the welfare of their people.

Goethe is considered by some to have initiated the "Storm and Stress" movement by his powerful national drama "Götz von Berlichingen," written when he was only nineteen years of age. Born in 1749, he owed much to his early acquaintance with English literature, especially with Goldsmith and Shakespeare. The long and steady growth of his powers, his determination to make every opportunity contribute to self-culture, his unsurpassed ability in combining the pure ancient Hellenic with the varied modern Teutonic spirit, gave his genius a universal sweep, making him truly cosmopolitan and rendering him eventually the foremost literary exponent of the Eighteenth Century. Schiller, ten years younger than Goethe, died at the early age of forty-five, having worn himself out with tireless industry. More true than Goethe to the limitations of the German spirit, Schiller is the beloved and typical poet of his race. His first drama, "The Robbers," is full of revolutionary fervor and boyish extravagance. It expressed the new spirit of the time, and was hailed with enthusiasm. Though punished for it by the Duke of Würtemberg, he obtained protection from others, and went on composing dramas of liberty and lyrics of philosophic idealism. He was made professor of history at Jena, and there became intimate with Goethe. This loving friendship had excellent effect upon both, stirring them to new displays of power. It was after consultation with the elder poet that Schiller decided to divide his play on the fate of Wallenstein into three parts, "Wallenstein's Camp," "The Piccolomini," and "The Death of Wallenstein." This trilogy is his masterpiece, and the hero's character is the most complex of his dramatic conceptions. His later plays are of high excellence, "William Tell" being the most admired as a highly romantic picture of a popular struggle for liberty. Schiller suffered from frequent illness, but never permitted his weak health to lower the joyful and inspiring tone of his poetry. His moral influence stimulated and encouraged the hearts of the German people in the period of their severe national trial.

The immediate effect of the outbreak of the French Revolution was to arouse youthful and enthusiastic minds with hopes and aspirations of a new ideal of humanity and fill them with dreams of a new golden age. Even the triumph of the baser elements and the bloody scenes of the Reign of Terror did not in all cases produce the revulsion which they did upon the philosophic statesman Burke and upon the poets Wordsworth, Coleridge, and Southey, turning them from ardent Revolutionists into staunch Conservatives. Byron and Shelley continued to war upon social order and their works propagated the spirit of revolution. Sir Walter Scott, whose feelings were strongly wedded to the past and to the established institutions of his country, had probably shown less sympathy with the destructive spirit of the age and yielded less to its illusions than any other man of genius in Europe. Goethe, who in his earliest writings had shown moderate revolutionary inclinations, had become justly conservative when the storm burst upon the Continent. These two great writers preserved the connection with the literature of the Eighteenth Century, and gave the impulse to much of that of the Nineteenth.

The broad characteristic of European literature at the opening of the Nineteenth Century is the reign of Romanticism. The settled result of the general agitation and many contradictory movements was an abandonment of the artificial and conventional stiffness produced by close adherence to rhetoricians' rules and pedants' notions. The spirit of life which breathed in the ancient classics was lost in the modern classicism. The new romantic spirit turned with fond regard to the faith and mysticism of early Christianity, to the pomp and ceremonies and sensuous religious worships of the days of chivalry, to the solemn cathedrals and ruined castles of the Middle Ages. It sought to recover the feelings of the knights and barons, priests and people of those ages of faith. It even went further abroad, seeking religious sentiment beyond dogma, and poetic beauty beyond myths. It found pleasure in the flowery poetry of the East, in the legends and traditions of Pagan mythology. The strange stories of the gods and goddesses of the Scandinavian North were studied and rehearsed with new zeal and eagerness. Though political events exercised disturbing influences in every country, yet the renovation of the human mind was made manifest in every department of literature. The poet's muse found fresh themes in the new revelation of the human heart and the beauties of nature. The satirist poured scorn on the shams of society and pedantry of the schools. Essayists, no longer confining themselves to tea-table miscellany, discussed philosophy and the science of government, and promulgated the doctrine of the equality of all men before God and the law. Soon great novelists undertook to paint the manners and characters of remote and foreign nations as well as those of their own time. Instead of the former rigid rules of expression, there was henceforth large variety both in matter and manner, and style became as capricious as human nature itself. The imagination was let loose to find in nature or history whatever could best illustrate the passions of the heart. This absolute liberty granted to writers is controlled by the approval accorded only to those who have expressed adequately the truth of nature and character.

In the following pages we shall endeavor to trace the development of each national literature in its principal representatives.

LITERATURE OF THE NINE-
TEENTH CENTURY

ENGLISH LITERATURE

FIRST OR PRE-VICTORIAN PERIOD—1800-1837

In the opening of the Nineteenth Century the virtuous but obstinate George III was King of England. His government, strongly backed by the people, was strenuous in resisting the ambition of Napoleon and the equally dangerous spread of French revolutionary ideas. William Pitt, who had been inclined to liberal reforms, had, under the stress of war, become severe and arbitrary in his home policy. But while the ruling classes were reactionary and were aiding the cause of despotism on the Continent, the great humanitarian movement which had given rise to the French Revolution was still in progress and manifested itself in manifold ways. The freedom of the press was invoked and maintained in its behalf. Poets and philosophers gave varied utterance to its spirit and delivered its message to the hearts of men. Not alone the oppressed and discontented listened and echoed its cries. The thoughtful, religious, and tender-hearted of all classes were moved and incited to action. The timid sought escape from evils of the present in dreams of a golden age, in stories of mediæval faith and feudal chivalry. But the bold were more eager and ardent in their passion for reforming the world. In the political field the revolutionary movement was repressed by William Pitt and the Tory party, but in the literary field it was soon overwhelmingly triumphant.

London has been the literary center of England fr[...] the golden age of Queen Elizabeth—not merely the [...] porium of books and publishers, but the residence o[...] frequent resort of all who have felt impelled to instruct or delight their fellow-men with the pen. There, in the reign of Queen Anne, Addison at Will's coffee-house gave his little Senate laws. There Pope and Swift and kindred spirits met and concocted the sayings and doings of the Scribler's Club. Not far off was the odious, noisy Grub Street, in which needy poets vainly strove to eke out a miserable existence. In his early years Dr. Samuel Johnson in his satire, "London," imitated Juvenal's famous description of Rome, but after drudgery had brought him fame, he ruled with imperious sway in the Club, which contained Sir Joshua Reynolds, Garrick, Goldsmith, and Burke. Great as was the gathering of intellect and genius in the English metropolis, its life was largely political and commercial, and it is justly called the modern Babylon. The fresh impulse that was to recreate parched English literature with the new century came from the North—from the hills and lakes of Scotland, and from the spirited debates of its picturesque capital.

The literary rivalship of Edinburgh is a prominent feature at the opening of the Nineteenth Century. The union of Scotland with England in 1707 had partly diminished the city's importance, yet it continued to be the residence of many of the Scotch nobility. It was the seat of a flourishing university, and the place of publication of many historical and philosophical works. The Scotch have always shown skill in compiling text-books, and encyclopedias and other works of reference have been wont to appear in Edinburgh. In spite of its nickname, "Auld Reekie," the town had an intellectual atmosphere, and its citizens were justified in giving it the surname of "the modern Athens." Notwithstanding political divisions, its general tendency has been Liberal. When the British government under Pitt was lavishing its wealth and bending its utmost energies for the overthrow of Napoleon, the citizens of the Northern capital were still discussing the principles and tendencies of the French Revolution. From this intellectual ferment came the new impulse which was to transform English literature.

About 1797 the witty English clergyman, Sydney Smith, started to go to Germany with a pupil, but was driven by the outbreak of war to take refuge in Edinburgh, and there officiated in a chapel. Forming the acquaintance of a number of talented young Whigs, who chafed under the repression of Liberal views, he persuaded them to start the "Edinburgh Review" in 1802. For its motto he proposed a line from Vergil, which he translated, "We cultivate literature on a little oatmeal," but as this statement was too close to the truth, a more severe sentence from an almost unknown classic was substituted. The first contributors were Francis Jeffrey, Henry Brougham, Francis Horner, J. A. Murray, and Smith, who edited a single number. Jeffrey, as the responsible editor from 1803 to 1829, exercised an immense influence on periodical literature and criticism. Soon the power of the "Edinburgh Review" was widely felt and acknowledged. It was due to the fact that its contributors were men of decided convictions. They were liberally paid for the candid expression of their opinions on new publications. Its judgment was looked for by authors with fear and trembling. In it Jeffrey castigated Byron's first volume, "Hours of Idleness," but called forth a fierce retort in his "English Bards and Scotch Reviewers." He was bold enough to condemn Scott's "Marmion" as childish. Jeffrey also persistently con-

demned and ridiculed Wordsworth's poetry, opening his
critique on "The Excursion" in 1815, with the memorable
words, "This will never do." In matters of taste Jeffrey
still adhered to the established ideas of the Eighteenth
Century. He was succeeded by Macvey Napier.

The "Edinburgh Review" was an independent ex-
positor of the principles of the Whig party. It advocated reforms in church and state, Catholic emancipation
and removal of disabilities from Dissenters, Parliamentary reform and extension of the suffrage. It reopened
questions of history as well as politics, and rendered new
verdicts according to new light. Many of its articles
were not merely reviews, but monographs on interesting
questions. Thus it furnished Macaulay the proper field
for the brilliant miscellanies which gave him much of his
fame, and prepared the way for his history. Sir Walter
Scott, though a Tory, contributed to the "Edinburgh
Review" until the vehemence of its Whiggism required
him to withdraw.

In opposition to the brave and vigorous "Edinburgh," the English Tories felt compelled to establish an
organ of their own. It was called "The Quarterly Review," and was first published in London in 1809, edited
by William Gifford, a satirist and translator of Juvenal.
It attained its best repute when under the control of John
G. Lockhart, son-in-law and biographer of Sir Walter
Scott. Among its early contributors were Canning,
Southey, Wordsworth, Scott, and John W. Croker. Besides its steady defence of the old principles and anom-
alies of the British Constitution, it was noted for its
ponderous learning.

But the Tories of the North, smarting under the
attacks of the "Edinburgh Review," were not fully satis-
fied with their new ally. It was too remote; its guns too

heavy and slow. Therefore William Blackwood, the Tory publisher of Edinburgh, began in 1817 to issue a monthly in their behalf. As regards politics it was fiercely conservative, defending monarchy, aristocracy and the Established Church; and briskly attacking all innovations; on its literary side it presented from the start brilliant stories and poems, and it overflowed with fun and animal spirits. An early number contained a pretended "Chaldee Manuscript," which gave in the style of the English Bible, a bitter satire on the Edinburgh notorieties of the time. This was soon followed by the "Noctes Ambrosianæ," a series of mirthful dialogues, interspersed with songs and poems, professed to be held by its chief contributors at Ambrose's tavern. These were mostly written by the brilliant Professor John Wilson, who, in his editorial capacity, bore the pseudonym of "Christopher North." He was a noted athlete and sportsman, a lover of the beautiful, a writer of pathetic tales and charming poetry, and was also professor of moral philosophy in the University of Edinburgh. His love of fun and display of it in "Maga" caused his more serious powers to be somewhat disparaged and neglected.

Beyond the Whigs of the "Edinburgh Review" there was a class of thinkers, urging Utilitarianism in philosophy and Radicalism in politics. These opposed the existing systems in church and state, and were severely criticized in the "Edinburgh" as well as in the "Quarterly." Jeremy Bentham was one of their leaders, and to defend and propagate their views, he founded in 1824 the "Westminster Review." Among its contributors were James Mill, and his greater son, John Stuart Mill, Sir John Bowring, and the philosophic historian, Buckle. As it led the way in removing the restrictions and legal disabilities of women, it is not surprising to find two eminent women writing for its pages—Harriet Martineau, and Marian Evans, who was to win fame as "George Eliot." It was long an object of curious dread in Conservative and Orthodox circles.

The literary success of "Blackwood's Magazine" led to the founding of other monthlies, some of which had no decided political bias. The "New Monthly Magazine" was edited by the poet Campbell, and numbered among its contributors Bulwer and Hood. Captain Marryat published in it some of his famous sea-stories. "Fraser's Magazine," started in 1830, was of high order, and gave cordial welcome to articles not readily accepted elsewhere. Thus Carlyle, who had done much writing, especially on German subjects, for the "Edinburgh Review," turned to "Fraser" when he wished to bring before the world his new fantastic clothes-philosophy in "Sartor Resartus." The "Dublin University Magazine," begun in 1832, was an outlet for the wit and learning which were cherished among the Irish Protestants of Trinity College, Dublin. It is remarkable that while scholars and graduates of the English Universities assisted in various reviews and magazines, no periodical was regularly issued in connection with either Oxford or Cambridge. The life of the English scholar was distinctly apart from the activity even of the literary world. But the reform movement began by the brisk, alert Sydney Smith in Edinburgh, eventually reached and agitated the quiet academic retreats on the Cam and the Isis. Then it took a new and strange form, and an Oxford movement, chiefly eccleciastical, passed around the English-speaking world. For a time it bore the name of Dr. Pusey, but the true leader was the preacher and theologian who became Cardinal Newman.

THE ROMANTIC SCHOOL

SCOTT

English literature in the Eighteenth Century had sunk into general monotony. The prevailing form of prose-writing was smooth didactic or reflective essays, except so far as some daring but incompetent novelists tried spasmodic, melodramatic tales. The established manner in poetry was the heroic couplet of Pope, whose aim was to be "correct" in matter and style. Thomson and Cowper had introduced a more varied and natural mode, but were more praised than imitated. Suddenly, with the opening of a new century, came a burst of freedom. Sir Walter Scott, Byron, Moore, Shelley, Keats, Southey, and Crabbe, displayed new varieties of metre, new wealth of subjects, new brilliance of description. Most of them published tales in verse or minor epics, some of them ballads and lyrical pieces. Wordsworth and Coleridge issued "Lyrical Ballads," and the former proclaimed the discovery of a new law of poetic diction, which he himself forsook in his better work. Foremost in popularity were the lilting lays of Scott, which revealed to the English the scenery, characters and traditions of North Britain.

Walter Scott, born in Edinburgh, August 15, 1771, had spent his childhood in the romantic Scottish Border, and been imbued with its traditions of warfare and superstition. After passing through the University of Edinburgh he had learned German, then a rare accomplishment. Filled with enthusiasm for its romanticism, he

23

translated ballads from Bürger and Goethe, and made a spirited version of the latter's youthful tragedy, "Götz von Berlichingen." Though slightly lame, Scott was active on foot and horseback, and when in 1799 he was made sheriff of Selkirkshire, he galloped around the country in search of ballads and legends. Thus were obtained three volumes of the "Minstrelsy of the Scottish Border," published in 1802. Its phenomenal success led the Countess of Dalkeith to request Scott to turn into verse the story of the goblin page connected with her family traditions. The result appeared in "The Lay of the Last Minstrel" (1805), which was received with universal acclamation and sank deeply into the popular heart. No English poem had ever sold so widely before, and Scott decided to give up practice at the bar for authorship. His official income, indeed, gave him ample means, and his generosity induced him to advance capital to James Ballantyne, the printer of his books. Ballantyne proved incompetent in business affairs, and eventually ruined himself and his trusting friend.

Scott in his "Lay" used octosyllabic verse, which, though founded on the metre of the Norman trouvères, had not previously been employed in English for serious poems. Its easy gallop and freedom from strict rules caused it to submit readily to the author's caprice. He varied it in passages expressing strong feeling or violent movement with an occasional short verse, while the longer lines rhyme sometimes in threes or fours. Scott wrote with great rapidity and did not pause to polish or correct, yet his flowing versification echoes well the sentiment of the moment. An admirable feature of his "Lay" is the framing of the story of sorcery and chivalric adventure—the description of the aged minstrel, his diffidence in the presence of the great lady, his gradual recall

of youthful inspiration, and the outbursts of poetic ex-
altation when his feelings are fully aroused. The most
striking scene is the opening of the tomb of Michael
Scott, and the taking of the book of gramarye from the
lifeless hand of the mighty wizard.

Scott followed up the unprecedented success of the
"Lay" by producing "Marmion," a somewhat similar tale,
in 1808. It related the visit of a valiant but unscrupulous
English knight to Scotland, and concluded with the fatal
field of Flodden (1513). A memorable tragic scene
describes the immuring of Constance before a grim tri-
bunal in the vaults of Lindisfarn Abbey. The battle is
also grandly produced with true Homeric directness, and
the death of conscience-haunted Marmion is an appropriate conclusion. Two years later appeared "The Lady
of the Lake," generally regarded as Scott's masterpiece.
It sets forth the conflict between the civilized Lowlanders
and the wild Highland clan, under the leadership of Roderick Dhu. Few scenes are more impressive than the
carrying of the Fiery Cross to summon the clansmen to
war, the battle of Beal' an Duine, and the death of Roderick.

Scott issued more metrical tales, but he seems to have
felt that he had exhausted the best of his poetic vein.
Later, with his notable generosity to the merits of other
writers, he acknowledged that the more dazzling and
forcible genius of Byron had surpassed his own, and he
quietly retired from the field of contest. But not to be
idle; on the contrary, to work more strenuously than ever
in the new realm of prose fiction. In 1814 appeared
anonymously, "Waverley; or, 'Tis Sixty Years Since,"
an attempt to recall the stirring events of 1745, when the
defeat of Culloden gave the death-blow to the hopes of
the Stuart Pretenders. The story was eagerly welcomed

by the people, many among whom could vouch for the truth of the picture. Scott, though full of enthusiasm for his native land and its people, had yet sufficient sympathy with English ideas to be able to treat his countrymen with the necessary aloofness for true perspective. He avoided the grossness and indecency which had prevailed in previous novel-writing and by his dignified self-respect commended his work to a wider circle of readers. Without disclosing his authorship, he soon issued "Guy Mannering," in which a young Englishman ventures into Scotland and becomes involved in the fate of some of its people. Among the striking characters presented were Meg Merrilies, the Gipsy seeress, and Dominie Sampson, the schoolmaster, overflowing with learning and kindness. A still more vigorous sketch of Scotch life and manners is found in "The Antiquary," in which he made friendly sport of the foibles of his friend, George Constable, and indeed of his own. Meantime, to keep up the mystification about "The Great Unknown," Scott prepared under his own name treatises on chivalry, romance, and the drama, edited the works of Dryden and Swift, issued new poems, and wrote much for an "Annual Register." He had bought land at Abbotsford in 1812, and entered upon vast schemes for building a mediæval castle. When the foolishness of his printer friend and partner threatened bankruptcy, the liberality of other publishers helped to tide over the crisis.

In "The Black Dwarf" and "Old Mortality" (1816) Scott entered on a new field of Scotch life, the struggles of the Covenanters, and when he was accused of treating them unfairly, he boldly reviewed his own novels in the "Quarterly," stated the principles and ideal of historical romance, and claimed high merit in truth of character for the works of the mysterious author. "Rob Roy," a spirited presentation of Highland life and manners, appeared in 1817, and then "The Heart of Midlothian," the pathetic tale of Jeanie and Effie Deans, perhaps the best of his novels in delineation of passion. It was followed by "The Bride of Lammermoor," a domestic tragedy of similar excellence; and "The Legend of Montrose," noted for the character of Major Dugald Dalgetty, pedantic soldier of fortune.

In 1819 the prolific author for the first time turned to England for the main scene of his story, and in "Ivanhoe" described that country in the time of lingering Norman and Saxon strife in the reign of Richard Cœur de Lion. The portrait of the Jewess Rebecca, one of his finest female characters, was suggested by Washington Irving's description of a lady of Philadelphia. "Ivanhoe," being free from the embarrassment of the Scotch dialect, and rich in pictures of feudal chivalry, has received wider popular approval than any other of Scott's works. "Kenilworth" is also a favorite, describing Queen Elizabeth's visit to the Earl of Leicester's castle in Warwickshire, and her interview with the beautiful and unfortunate Amy Robsart. "The Fortunes of Nigel" relate to London life, when the Scotch King had come to the English throne as James I. In "Quentin Durward" Scott at last ventured to cross to the Continent, and portrayed the strife between the crafty, superstitious Louis XI of France and Charles the Bold of Burgundy. In other stories of less merit Scott had returned to his native heath and presented both historic and domestic scenes. In 1825 he published the "Tales of the Crusaders," with Richard Cœur de Lion as a prominent personage.

Scott had for some years believed himself entirely freed from pecuniary embarrassments by the arrangements made by his partners in 1818. But the financial

crash of 1825 carried down the London and Edinburgh
houses with which the Ballantynes were involved, and
the silent partner was astounded to find himself legally
liable for not less than £130,000. Scott was now fifty-
four years old and might easily have taken advantage of
the bankrupt law, but his pride or high sense of honor
would not permit. Refusing all assistance, he determined to pay his debts or die in the effort. His wife soon
died, and he suffered other painful bereavements. Leaving the grandeur of Abbotsford, he took modest lodg-
ings in Edinburgh. The first novel written in the new
quarters was "Woodstock," a tale of Charles II's wanderings and restoration to the throne. It was written in
three months and brought £8,000. Within two years, as
the proceeds of some novels, including "The Fair Maid
of Perth," an elaborate but strongly prejudiced "Life of
Napoleon Buonaparte," and "Tales of a Grandfather,"
relating to Scottish history, Scott had accumulated
£40,000 for his creditors. But the steady drain on the
vital powers was too much for his endurance. Illness
began in 1829, and in the following February he had a
stroke of paralysis. Yet he worked on, and in spite of
friends and physicians would not take rest. His last
novels, "Count Robert of Paris" and "Castle Dangerous,"
show signs of failing powers. He became possessed of
the idea that his debts were paid, and then consented to
take a sea-voyage, recommended by his physicians. On
a government vessel he sailed for Naples and cruised
about the Mediterranean for some months. When he
felt that his end was near, he insisted on being taken back
to Abbotsford. There he died September 21, 1832.

Monuments have been erected to his memory in Edinburgh and other cities, but his true monument is Scotland
itself, nearly every province and town of which has been

made familiar by his magic pen.   He was "The Wizard
of the North" who conjured up the men and manners of
the past, "who bestowed upon Scotland an imperishable
name."   His works abound in wonderful variety of character and incident; while he excelled in delineating the
Scotch of both high and low degree, he was able from his
historical and antiquarian researches to present portraits
of other nationalities sufficiently individualized.   By his
skillful handling of subjects, he taught later historians
how to write, to give vivid effect to what would otherwise
be chronological details or philosophical abstractions.
Scott was an omnivorous reader, and no critic was more
generous in acknowledging the merits of his contemporaries.   Thoughtful critics confess his poetic excellence and admit his matchless power in turning back the
thoughts of men to the storied past, in giving a grand
impetus to the study of mediæval history and art.

BYRON

The genius and force of Lord Byron had powerful
effect not only on the youth of his own time in England,
but in France, Germany, Italy, and throughout Europe.
He was a stimulating propagator of Romanticism.   In
all his verse-stories he was his own passionate hero, and
that hero was recognized as the ideal of the youth of the
age.   Though regarded even in England as more original
and forcible than Sir Walter Scott, yet careful examination proves that Byron owed the general suggestion and
much of the success of his poetry to Scott.   Critics are
astonished at his voluminous output, for he was cut off
at the early age of thirty-six.

George Gordon Byron was born in London, January

22, 1788, but his early training was received at Aberdeen, where his mother, who had been deserted by her dissipated husband, went to live on a slender income. By an accident at birth one of his feet was deformed and caused a slight limp through life. When Byron was eleven years old, he succeeded to the title and estates of his grand-uncle, and removed to Newstead Abbey. He was sent later to Harrow School and Trinity College, Cambridge, but found delight in rude sports rather than study. Yet he scribbled verses and his first publication, "Hours of Idleness" (1807), was severely criticized in the "Edinburgh Review." The young poet retorted with furious vehemence on the whole literary craft in his "English Bards and Scotch Reviewers." But the attack was so absurd and unjust, that he afterwards endeavored to suppress it. When of age, he took his seat in the House of Lords, but had few acquaintances, and soon set out on a tour through Southern Europe. After two years' absence he brought back "Childe Harold's Pilgrimage" (1811), a poetical version of his travels, in Spenserian metre. The French wars had in great measure shut out the English people from the Continent; now a graphic poet presented them with brilliant pictures of scenery and countries almost unknown. But more than that, the traveler possessed a mysterious interest of his own; he was an outcast from his native land; he was consumed with melancholy, he sought distraction from himself. The immediate impression of the work is shown in Byron's exclamation: "I awoke one morning and found myself famous." At once the doors of the rich and noble were opened to the author. His pale melancholy features captivated women; his sweet voice and graceful form attracted every eye. He was flattered and idolized, but he did not yield to utter idleness. He added to his fame by poetical tales of the East, which had been drafted amid its scenery. These tales, whose metre was borrowed from Scott, were "The Giaour" (1811), "The Bride of Abydos" (1813), "The Corsair" (1814), "Lara" (1814), and "The Siege of Corinth" (1816). However different the story, there was but one hero in them all:

> "The man of loneliness and mystery,
> Scarce seen to smile, and seldom heard to sigh."

In these tales there are also constant references to a woman purely beloved, and there is reason to believe that an actual person is meant, who died in 1811. Her death is lamented at the end of Canto II of "Childe Harold," but her name is not given.

In January, 1815, Lord Byron married Miss Anne Isabella Milbanke, a lady of wealth and position, but a year later, after the birth of a daughter, she separated from him. The true reasons have never been published, but their tempers seem to have been incompatible; she was of severe morals and unsympathetic; he was licentious and of violent temper; she thought him actually insane. Public opinion in England condemned the husband, and he went abroad full of bitterness. At Geneva he wrote another canto of "Childe Harold," and "The Prisoner of Chillon." In 1817 he formed a liaison with the Countess Guiccioli, which was maintained through the rest of his life at Venice and other cities of Italy. His literary work was continued without intermission and included "Don Juan," "Mazeppa," the dramas "Marino Faliero" and "The Two Foscari," and the fierce satire, "The Vision of Judgment," in reply to Southey's absurd laudation of George III. In 1823 Byron was induced to take an active part in the Greek struggle for independence. He sailed from Genoa with arms, but the insurgents were insubordinate and not prepared for action.

He was seized with a fever at Missolonghi, and died April 19, 1824.

Immense as was the effect of Byron's personality and works on literature throughout Europe, the critical estimate of his ability has fallen greatly during the century. Shelley and Keats are ranked above him in artistic qualities and metrical effect. He was an admirer of Pope, and accepted Pope's rules of diction, but he practiced in various metres offered by contemporary poets, who are now forgotten. His mind was full of the stormy thoughts of his time, and thus he became the poet of revolution, able to stir mankind. His misanthropy and professed scorn for the world's opinion gave him power over that opinion. His descriptions are great and varied, and he was able to concentrate scenes in a line. The later cantos of "Childe Harold" are of greater value than those which gave him his first fame. "Don Juan" is perhaps the fullest exhibit of his character and poetical power; a splendid epic with an inglorious hero. It is full of sublime and exquisite descriptions, but does not hesitate to link these with vile and ignoble associations.

The meter and method of treatment are borrowed from the Italian burlesque poets, but in matter the poem is highly original; it is a succession of pictures of human life and society as he viewed them, with occasional satire or jesting comment. In spite of its lack of well defined plan, there is an artistic balance in its mixture of comedy and pathos.

MOORE

Thomas Moore, at one time eulogized as the most brilliant poet in England, is remembered chiefly by his popular "Irish Melodies," songs which have not lost all their charm. Besides his Celtic faculty of writing verses for singing, he was a lively conversationalist, and thus became a favorite with the Whig aristocracy at the beginning of the century.

Born in Dublin in 1779, he early showed his literary talent, and graduated at Trinity College in 1800. Going to London with a free translation of Anacreon, he obtained permission to dedicate it to the Prince Regent, afterwards George IV. A year later an original collection of licentious verse was published as "The Poetical Works of the Late Thomas Little," for the indecency of which he afterwards professed repentance. In 1803 an official post in the Bermudas was assigned to Moore, but he left it in charge of a deputy, and traveled in the United States. On his return to London he was welcomed by the world of fashion and satirized the Americans. His "Irish Melodies," adapted to ancient tunes, arranged by Sir John Stevenson, began to appear in 1807, and many additions were made in later years. These fascinating amatory and patriotic effusions rescued from vulgar associations the music of his native land, and are the best expression of his powers. His sparkling rhymes and varied measures so delighted the public that the Longmans offered him 3,000 guineas for an Oriental poem to be written in a year. Though he had never visited the East, he endeavored to steep his mind in Persian lore and imagery, and the result was the gorgeous "Lalla Rookh." It relates, in a frame-work of prose, the love-pilgrimage of the beautiful daughter of the Indian Emperor Aurungzebe, who, being betrothed to the Prince of Bucharia, set out from her royal home to meet him. The tedium of the caravan-march is beguiled by the charming recitations of a poet, with whom, ere she has reached her destination, she discovers she has fallen in love. But happily when she is presented at the Persian court, she beholds on the throne the poet who had won her heart. The poem is overloaded with tropical riches and tawdry ornament, but is redeemed also with many passages of pathos and quiet beauty. Moore's reputation was maintained for years, but after the advent of Tennyson it faded away, and recent critics have denied him real merit except that of improvisation.

His deputy in the Bermudas proved unfaithful, and Moore, being called on to make good his embezzlement, was plunged in pecuniary difficulties. He sought refuge on the Continent, and in "The Fudge Family of Paris" he satirized the boorishness of English travelers. In 1830 he published "The Life, Letters, and Journals of Lord Byron," whose friendship he had enjoyed. Some interesting documents which had fallen into his hands as editor, he destroyed, in order to spare the feelings of persons and families involved. In spite of some triviality of character, he was loyal to his native land, to his religion and his political party. Towards the close of his life his mental powers failed. He had suffered the loss of his five children, but his faithful wife survived him. He died in 1852.

SHELLEY

Even more than the passionate, erratic Byron the mild, philanthropic Shelley was the poet of revolt against the laws and forms of his age, yet he had much less influence in this direction. So refined and ethereal was his spirit, that his voice was lost on the multitude. But his poetry, apart from his philosophy, has been more and more admired by the best judges as time has passed on, and the later poets have resorted to him for instruction in their art. His lyrical faculty is almost without parallel in English poetry. Far beyond the light drawing-room songs of Moore, Shelley's lyrics, "The Skylark," "Ode to the West Wind," are buoyant and free and carry the spirit above the solid earth of every-day fact into the pure ether. He was a master of language as well as of melody. Beautiful and inspiring as is his poetry at its best, his life was a sad tragedy, full of grievous errors and useless rebellion.

Percy Bysshe Shelley was born in 1792, the eldest son of a wealthy baronet. He was educated at Eton and Oxford, but carried away by the infidelity of the French philosophers, he published a tract on "The Necessity of Atheism," and was therefore expelled from the University in 1811. The wild and fantastic poem, "Queen Mab," privately printed in 1813, expressed more boldly the same opinions. At the age of nineteen the impulsive Shelley, partly out of pity, married Harriet Westbrook, a girl of sixteen, daughter of an inn-keeper, and was denounced by his family, though his father granted him a moderate allowance. The youthful couple wandered on the Continent, but the marriage proved unhappy, and they were separated after the birth of two children. Before his first wife died in 1816, Shelley found more congenial companionship with Mary Godwin, who, as the daughter of William Godwin and Mary Wollstonecraft, had been trained in opposition to the ways of the world.

In 1818 he published "The Revolt of Islam," a poem which, under another title, had been prohibited by the authorities. It is a declamatory narrative, showing the triumph of his philanthropic theories over the tyranny and hypocrisy of established religious systems. The courts deprived Shelley of the custody of his children, and he went to Italy, where, during his few remaining years, he produced his best poetry. In "Prometheus Unbound" he attempted to solve the great problem of human free will, as suggested by the "Prometheus" of Æschylus. Shelley was a profound Greek scholar, and an ardent Platonist. His Prometheus is the personification of resistance to universal tyranny and priestcraft, which he always regarded as imposed on men by extraneous force, and not arising from internal causes. His strongest drama is "The Cenci," founded on one of the horrible stories of revolting crime in the Italian Middle Ages. In the elegy, "Adonais" (1821), he lamented in noble Spenserian verse the untimely death of the poet Keats. In his last poem, "Hellas," he expressed his hope of a grander and better golden age than that of ancient Greece. His death was singular and melancholy. While he was returning in a small yacht from Leghorn to Spezia, the vessel was caught in a squall, and Shelley, with two companions, perished. The poet's body was afterward cast on the shore, and was buried. But two weeks later Byron and a few friends burned it on a funeral pyre in the ancient manner.

Shelley, as a man, was mild, benevolent, temperate, his person was extremely delicate and refined; his poetry was full of tender, spiritual harmony; his diction choice and transparent; his power of imagination inexhaustible, carrying the mind far beyond the original idea, and introducing a perpetual interchange between the type and the things typified. In contrast with the serene philosophy of his real temperament he was too apt in writing to exaggerate the horrible and repulsive, and to use a fierce declamatory tone, which marred his early work. Posterity has learned to reject these extravagant outbursts and to dwell upon his sweet, graceful and ethereal lyrics as the true expression of his genius.

KEATS

John Keats was another remarkable manifestation of the poetic spirit of this period, though he had nothing of the revolutionary outburst. Born in humble circumstances in London in 1795, he was at fifteen apprenticed to an apothecary. His sympathy with the great English poets and with the Greek mythology, though he knew nothing of that language, led to his composing a narrative poem, "Endymion." It was published in 1818, inscribed to the memory of Chatterton, whom the new poet somewhat resembled. The ambitious epic was assailed severely by the "Edinburgh Review," and indeed all the critics, who lumped it with other poems as products of "the Cockney school." The poor consumptive Keats was wounded in spirit, yet, conscious of poetic power, he persevered in his chosen line. In 1820 appeared "Lamia," the pathetic "Isabella," the beautiful "Eve of St. Agnes," and the classical fragment, "Hyperion." The improvement in style and treatment won for them a more favorable reception than his first attempts. Keats, in expression and native melody, was of kin to Shelley, but he was free from the soaring philanthropy and passionate fierceness of the young aristocrat. He was content to live in the enjoyment of his poetic dreams without attempting to make an evil world better by savage denunciation. Gifted with fine fancy and a genuine predilection for Greek ideas, the slight errors due to his lack of careful culture are easily pardoned. Attacked with hemorrhage, he went to Italy, where he died in February, 1821, leaving as his epitaph, "Here lies one whose name was writ in water."

HUNT

Leigh Hunt is notable as an associate of most of the prominent English writers of the first half of the century. His father had been a Tory lawyer in Philadelphia, but left after the Revolution and took orders in England. Leigh was born in 1784 and educated at Christ Hospital, of which he has left a pleasing sketch. He began early to write verses, and was employed on newspapers. An incident in his editorship of "The Examiner" had a permanent effect on his career. It aimed to be independent in political and literary criticism, and published a sharp, but practically true, attack on the Prince Regent. For this Hunt was convicted of libel and sentenced to two years' imprisonment. This rendered him a martyr and brought him visits from Byron, Moore and other Radicals. But his cell was made a charming bower and abode of gayety, and his newspaper went on as before. Hunt's peculiar poetic talent was shown in "A Story of Rimini," a sprightly version of Dante's celebrated incident of Paolo and Francesca. He revived the natural style of Chaucer's tales, though he occasionally sunk into familiarity and flippancy. The new style was taken up by Shelley, Keats, and others. "Blackwood's Magazine" called them the "Cockney School of Poetry," but it was only Hunt that deserved the implied censure.

Hunt, careless and generous in money matters, through most of his career, suffered from pecuniary distress, and Shelley was a liberal benefactor. Hunt defended the poet when public opinion was against him, and a few years after Shelley went to Italy was induced to join him. A new periodical was projected, "The Liberal," to which Byron, Shelley, and Hunt were to contribute. But Shelley's sudden death and Byron's departure for Greece, destroyed the plan, though a few numbers appeared with poems from those authors.

The general demand for information about Byron led Hunt in 1827 to publish "Lord Byron and His Contemporaries." In this he took undue advantage of the opportunities he had enjoyed while living under Byron's roof, and sank in public esteem. He was condemned not merely as a man too ready to accept money obligations from those around him, but as willing to sell knowledge obtained in confidence. In spite of his diligent writing and many publishing schemes, Hunt was unable to retrieve his losses. At last Mrs. Shelley and her son settled an annuity on him and the government in 1847 gave him a pension.

The pitiable moral weakness of Hunt's character was generally known, and when Dickens caricatured him as Harold Skimpole in "Bleak House," the likeness was recognized, though the novelist afterwards endeavored to deny it. In many ways Hunt was a pleasant companion; his books abound in naive egotism and petty affectations, but also in correct criticism and genial fancy. His "Autobiography," published in 1850, is a truthful picture of himself, but reveals less about his distinguished friends than might have been expected. Though he wrote many pleasant pieces of verse, none has attained wider fame than the delightful "Abou Ben Adhem." He died in 1859.

THE LAKE SCHOOL OF POETRY

Two chief branches of the Romantic school of poetry which characterized the opening of this century, have been treated in brief outline—the first, comprising Scott, Byron, and Moore; the second, containing Shelley, Keats, and Leigh Hunt. It may be noted that the last of each group has gradually fallen in public estimation from the high rank once accorded to him, and might even be omitted without serious loss to literature, though the truth of history justifies his retention. The same is the case with the third class which remains to be mentioned— comprising Wordsworth, Coleridge, and Southey— often classed as the Lake School of Poetry, from their residence among the English lakes, and from some agreement in treating the aspects of nature. These writers really began to publish at an earlier date than some of those who have already been described, but they were slower in obtaining adequate recognition, and as regards fame they followed the others, though eventually they overtook and distanced them.

William Wordsworth was the chief leader in the movement which changed the direction of English poetry. In the Eighteenth Century a new love of nature had sprung up, which is exemplified in the works of Thomson and Cowper, but it hardly dared assert antagonism to the artificial poetry, inculcated by the precept and example of Pope. Then suddenly the peasant Burns stirred the hearts of the Scottish people with songs of love and patriotism and human equality. These lyrics, though in a rude, difficult dialect, reached the English stirred by the revolutionary spirit. Poets, who had been imitating old ballads, now began to discard rigid rules as worthless and stiff diction as cumbersome. Wordsworth deliberately attacked the artificial correctness of Pope, and demanded the expression of primal truth in natural manner. In his early utterances he was carried too far by his theory, but he finally brought his poetic phrase into harmony with his elevated sentiment.

William Wordsworth was born in 1770 in the County of Cumberland, where his ancestors had held land for centuries; to this perhaps was due his strong susceptibility for the beauty of nature. He was educated at Cambridge and traveled in France in 1791, when young men were filled with hope that the world was being made anew. Of this time he wrote long afterward:

> "Bliss was it in that dawn to be alive,
> But to be young was very heaven."

But lack of money compelled him to return, and for three years his prospects were uncertain. Then a legacy from a friend enabled him to pursue his natural bent. With his sister Dorothy he took a simple cottage and resolved to dedicate himself to poetry. He had already published two ventures, when he came in contact with the persuasive and stimulating Coleridge. The two poets published "The Lyrical Ballads" in 1798, to exemplify their theory of poetry. In the preface to the second edition (1800) Wordsworth declared that true poetry is "the spontaneous overflow of powerful feelings." Its language is therefore the simple, direct utterance of the heart. Its proper subjects are not strong passions, revenge, ambition, unbridled love, but the tranquil virtues, the development of the affections, and the effort of the soul to unite itself with God. In his "Lyrical Ballads," Wordsworth gave weight and dignity to themes, which the "Edinburgh Review" condemned as trivial and vulgar. But the self-centred poet was not to be swerved by the judgments of critics; he moved calmly on, composing his meditative and reflective poems on simple incidents of life, yet rising at times to lofty and impassioned utterances on the Divinity which he beheld in nature. He regarded external nature as a conscious expression of the Divine nature. His tendency was to a mysterious, sublime pantheism, but it was held in check by his profound belief in the Christian revelation.

Wordsworth lived from 1813 at Rydal Mount, sustained in steadfast devotion to his lofty purpose by the cheerful companionship of his sister Dorothy and his wife. His poems were received with ridicule and protest by nearly all the critics, yet gradually the tide turned; Oxford bestowed on him the degree of D.C.L. in 1839, and Sir Robert Peel made him poet laureate in 1843. He died in 1850 at the age of fourscore. English public opinion had come to recognize him as a poet of the second rank, above Pope and Dryden, Thomson and Cowper, and almost on a level with Milton. The drawback to his fame is that much of what he wrote is dull and unworthy, and that his theory of poetic diction spoiled his utterance, owing to his lack of humor. In his later work he discarded the extreme simplicity and puerility which offended the early critics.

His great merit lies in his power of delineating nature, and the poetic force which his tendency to pantheism adds to this gift. He is also successful in noble lines, which record his feeling at special times and places. In his "Tintern Abbey" and "Ode on Intimations of Immortality from the Recollections of Childhood," he rose to sublime heights, even above the limit reached in other valuable work. His longest poem, "The Excursion," is but a fragment of a projected epic, in which a Scotch pedlar, a clergyman, and a disappointed visionary discuss fundamental questions concerning God and man, the problems of human life and duties. "The Prelude," which was intended as an introduction to this, was published after the author's death. Wordsworth took up the sonnet, which had been long neglected by English poets, and gave it new vogue. Some of his examples, as "Westminster Bridge" and "The World Is Too Much with Us," rank among the best specimens in English literature.

COLERIDGE

Coleridge, who was most intimately associated with Wordsworth in his youth and stimulated his early poetical work, was yet of entirely different character. Though a writer of abundant prose and verse of many kinds, he was influential on the public rather as an astonishing and suggestive talker. He was one of the first to introduce German philosophy into English thought. In theology he assisted in the change which produced the Oxford movement, and he was also the suggester of what has become known as the Broad Church School. Yet with all his ability his intellectual work was fragmentary and his career a melancholy wreck.

Samuel Taylor Coleridge was the son of a clergyman, and was born in Devonshire in 1772. He was educated at the famous Charterhouse or Christ Hospital in London, where he formed a lasting friendship with Charles Lamb. Afterwards he went to Jesus College, Cambridge. Though a diligent scholar at first, he got into difficulties and enlisted as a dragoon, but by the assistance of friends obtained a discharge a few months later. He returned to college, but fell in with Southey, and the two became engaged to sisters at Bristol in 1794. Both were filled with Revolutionary ideas and formed vague schemes of renovating humanity by founding on the banks of the Susquehanna a community to be called Pantisocracy (equal government of all). Coleridge left the university and was married to Sara Fricker in 1795. He became a Unitarian preacher, published some poems, and started a weekly paper, called "The Watchman." At Stowey he was associated with Wordsworth, and contributed to the "Lyrical Ballads," "The Rime of the Ancient Mariner," but withheld other poems already written.

The kindness of friends enabled Coleridge to go to Germany, where he studied literature and philosophy for fourteen months. Returning in 1800 he settled with Southey and Wordsworth in the Lake district. The three Radicals now became Conservatives, and Coleridge gave up his Unitarian views. As poets they had mutual effect on each other's work. Coleridge translated freely Schiller's "Wallenstein," enriching the drama. For a time he was secretary to the Governor of Malta, and after his return he was busy in newspaper work, lecturing, and the publication of two dramas and some poems. In 1816 he published "Christabel," which, though incomplete, is one of his finest poems. His friends were ever ready to help him, but though he was fertile in schemes literary and philosophical, he was incompetent to execute them in a reasonable degree. "The Friend" was a periodical issued for two years; "Biographia Literaria" is full of judicious criticism. The explanation of his imperfect performance is that he was a victim of the opium habit. He was unable to keep house with his own family, but

was sheltered by those who had regard for his abilities.
Dr. Gilman is especially remembered for this service, and
at his house in Highgate, Coleridge discoursed eloquently to vistors. There, with the exception of occasional excursions, he resided till his death in 1834.

So far as his own literary productions are concerned,
Coleridge is remembered by a few exquisite poems—
"The Ancient Mariner," "Love, or Genevieve," and the
fragments, "Christabel" and "Kubla Khan." They all
exhibit wonderful command of metre, language, and the
power of exciting emotion. His other poems vary in
excellence, sometimes sinking to worthlessness. His
prose-writings were written piece-meal, and have been diligently collected by several editors, but though there are
occasional gems scattered among them, their general
value is diminished by their lack of connection or completion. Yet, while the bulk of his writing is out of proportion to its utility, probably no man of the century, except
Sir Walter Scott, had wider-reaching effect on the higher
thought, philosophy, and literature of England.

SOUTHEY

Southey in his youth seemed likely to be as radical
in opposition to English ways as Byron, yet he soon
settled down to steady work as a Quarterly Reviewer,
an unflinching supporter of Church and State. In 1813
he was made poet laureate, and held the position for
thirty years. His Oriental poems, as elaborate but not
as gorgeous as Moore's "Lalla Rookh," have fallen into
a more profound oblivion. As a poet he is remembered
by a few short pieces; as a prose-writer, by his biographies
of Nelson and Wesley, and by the whimsical rambling
work, "The Doctor," which was an improvement in

decency, though not in lively interest, on its model, Sterne's "Tristram Shandy."

Robert Southey was born at Bristol in 1774, and went to Balliol College, Oxford, but left without taking a degree. Infatuated with the wildest revolutionary doctrines, he published, in 1794, the drama of "Wat Tyler," and, with the aid of Coleridge, another on "The Fall of Robespierre." The Jacobinical poets became engaged to sisters, named Fricker, and also formed a Utopian scheme, learnedly called Pantisocracy. It was their dream to found a model community on the banks of the Susquehanna, a river of which they knew little except its romantic name. Here the golden age should be renewed in a Platonic republic from which vice and selfishness would forever be excluded. But alas! for want of the necessary money the beautiful vision was never realized.

Southey married Edith Fricker in 1795, yet went immediately alone to Lisbon, where his uncle was a British chaplain. This visit led to his thorough study of Spanish and Portuguese history and literature, which proved of service in later years. His epic "Joan of Arc" (1796) showed that change of scene had not yet altered his republicanism, but the need of steady employment sobered his fancies. He had nothing to do with Wordsworth's "Lyrical Ballads," but cherished poetic fancies of his own. In 1804 he settled at Greta Hall, near Keswick, in the Lake country, and thenceforward led a laborious literary life, assisted by the generosity of his friends, yet grinding away on topics of the time for daily bread. When Coleridge deserted his family, Southey took up the additional burden. He had now come to hate and detest Napoleon as a tyrant, and sustained the Tory government of England in its repressive policy. His most ambitious undertaking was to illustrate the mythologies of the world in a series of poems. "Thalaba the Destroyer," "the wild and wondrous song," is founded on Arabian traditions, and celebrates the victory of faith over the powers of evil. It was written in irregular verse without rhyme, and, in spite of some beautiful passages, was received with little favor. "The Curse of Kehama" was founded on the Hindoo mythology, whose extravagant fables and horrors overtaxed the powers of the poet and his readers. In it he admitted rhyme, but he had less expectation of success as the theme was beyond the range of human sympathies.

In his next epic, "Madoc," Southey made use of Welsh traditions in regard to an early discovery of America. It was the least successful of his long poems, while the most popular was "Roderick," the tragic story of the last Gothic King of Spain. For the Christian King's sin his people were defeated by the Moors, but Roderick, escaping, though supposed to be killed, became a hermit. Called by a vision to redeem his people, he wandered through the country in the garb of a priest, and rallied his friends to a new conflict with the Moors. In the battle he was recognized by his war-cry, but after the victory he disappeared. Centuries later a humble tomb with his name was discovered in a hermitage.

All of these poems required an immense amount of reading in order to gather the material and proper surroundings. In fact, Southey's writing, both in prose and verse, was based on the most painstaking investigation, and his wildest fancies wear a matter-of-fact shape. His library contained 14,000 volumes, gathered for use and systematically read, as his "Commonplace Book" and "Omniana" testify. Yet as a poet, though he won high praise, he never was popular; he received far less for his toilsome works than Moore and men of less note for airy fancies. Finding that his poetry became less salable, he confined himself to prose, though even in this he did not find time to accomplish the great works which he had planned. His domestic life had its tragedies; his only son and prettiest daughter died, and his wife was insane for two years before her death in 1837. Two years later the bereaved poet married Caroline Bowles, herself a poet, but after a short period of comfort, his brain gave way, owing to his excessive work. He sank into imbecility and died in March, 1843.

Southey had resolutely clung to hope of fame as a poet, but he was doomed to disappointment. Though early classed with Wordsworth as forming the Lake school of poetry, he justly protested against this mistake of the "Edinburgh Review." Whatever lawlessness was manifested in Southey's poems, it was not due to Wordsworth's theory of poetic diction. In spite of his quiet, retired life, Southey retained his vehement partisan spirit after he had changed his party. His ode written during the negotiations with Napoleon in January, 1814, is one of the strongest denunciations of the Emperor. His lively burlesque of "The March to Moscow" bears witness to the same feeling. His most deplorable piece is the "Vision of Judgment," in which, as poet laureate, he depicted the entrance of George III into Heaven. In the preface he attacked what he called "The Satanic School," and Byron, who had already become a personal enemy of the laureate, took revenge in a severe satire on this absurd deification of the unfortunate English sovereign. But Southey must always be remembered with respect for his unflagging industry, his varied learning, his excellent prose style, his genuine humor, and a few cherished poems.

Besides the men of genius who have already been described as giving new character to the first third of the Nineteenth Century, there were several contemporaries of fair repute and respectable performance. The eldest of these, who lived to the age of ninety-two, was Samuel Rogers (1763-1855)), a Whig banker. His best remembered works are "the Pleasures of Memory" (1792) and "Italy" (1822). The former is in rhymed couplets, the latter in blank verse, but both belong in spirit to the Eighteenth Century. They are the efforts of a *dilettante* rather than the composition of a true poet. Rogers, by his wealth, was able to be a patron of literature and a connoisseur in art. His life was devoted to the pleasures of society; his hospitality was enjoyed by all the celebrities of the time; his conversation was highly esteemed; though his wit was sharp, his actions were charitable.

"The Pleasures of Hope," which gave early fame to Thomas Campbell (1777-1844), was suggested by Rogers' poem, but was more directly an imitation of Goldsmith's "Traveller." In it Campbell, then but twenty-one, made a poetical survey of Europe. His spirited ballads on events of the time, "Hohenlinden" (1799), "Ye Mariners of England" (1800), and "The Battle of the Baltic" (1809), have retained popularity, when his longer poems have lost it. Campbell, having settled in London, was constantly and remuneratively employed as miscellaneous writer, editor of biographical and critical works, and collections of poetry. His "Gertrude of Wyoming" (1809) is a tragic story in the Spenserian stanza, but the scene is laid in Pennsylvania, with which the author had no direct acquaintance. It is a conventional English tale with foreign locality, and melodramatic accessories. Campbell added to his fame by "Lochiel's Warning" and "The Exile of Erin," but not by his longer narrative poems. In 1830 he was made editor of Colburn's "New Monthly Magazine." He died in 1844.

REVIEWERS, MAGAZINISTS AND MINOR POETS OF THE FIRST PERIOD

The judicious Scotch lawyer and the witty English clergyman who gave the chief impulse to the "Edinburgh Review" in its first quarter of a century, deserve a little further notice. Francis Jeffrey (1773-1850) was a struggling barrister when he, with some hesitation, accepted the editorship. It was his sterling honesty and resolute independence which made the Review respected. Though his politics were Liberal, his literary principles were of the old school, and his censure even of his friends' departure from the established ways, were emphatic. Hence his impartial condemnation of Byron and Wordsworth, Scott and Southey, Leigh Hunt and Keats. His judgment of poetry has been reversed by time, but in all other respects his control of the Review was admirable. In 1829, when he had become the acknowledged leader of the Scottish bar, he resigned his editorship and was made Lord Advocate. After a brief experience in Parliament, he was made a judge, and thenceforward, according to Scotch practice, was known as Lord Jeffrey.

Sydney Smith (1771-1845) who, by accident, was stranded in Edinburgh for five years, though he constantly quizzed the national foibles of his Liberal friends, did them the great favor of uniting their abilities in the

Review. He soon left the Scotch capital for a church in London, where he achieved success as a preacher and lecturer. In 1806, when his political friends got into power, he was presented with a living in Yorkshire. Though it was a practical banishment from congenial society, he showed his wonted cheerfulness in his new circumstances and won the hearts of his rustic parishioners. He continued to write for the "Edinburgh" for a quarter of a century. His range of subjects was wide, including educational and geographical topics, as well as political and ecclesiastical, enlivening all of them with unexpected fun without departing from instructive and orderly exposition. Though he attacked grave social questions with lively wit and humorous exaggeration, he never indulged in mere buffoonery. When he made his reader laugh it was at something observed in the arguments or position he was attacking. In "Peter Plymley's Letters" he ridiculed the opposition of the country clergy to Catholic emancipation. His reputation as a wit unfortunately prevented his being made a bishop, but he was made a canon of Bristol Cathedral in 1828, and a prebend of St. Paul's in 1832. In his "Letters to Archdeacon Singleton" (1837) he defended, in his usual witty manner, the arrangements of cathedrals, which it had been proposed to alter. In private life he was a mirthful companion, as specimens of his table-talk, which have been preserved, abundantly testify.

Walter Savage Landor (1775-1864) has been pronounced by many poets, from Coleridge and Shelley to Swinburne and Lowell, to have been a great poet, and by excellent critics to have been an exquisite prose writer. He set himself to be an artist in language, but he is too coldly intellectual ever to win the hearts of the people.

His epic poem, "Gebir," is an Oriental story of no great interest, but it has many passages of magnificent beauty. It has been declared to have "Tennyson's finish, Arnold's objectivity and the romance of Keats and Morris." Landor was a most eccentric, ungovernable person, married in haste, quarreled with his wife, and went to Italy. Aristocratic in tastes, he was a republican in principle, and gave vent to explosions of wrath against Kings, critics and cooks, who were all in the wrong. His most valuable work is "Imaginary Conversations," in the several volumes of which he reports discussions of important subjects by noted historic personages. He had returned to England some years before 1858, where he published caustic epigrams and satires, under the title "Dry Sticks Fagoted." This overwhelmed him with libel suits, from which he fled again to Italy, there to die in exile at the age of eighty-nine.

As "Christopher North," the versatile editor of "Blackwood's Magazine," John Wilson (1785-1834) has already been mentioned, but his career deserves more notice. He was born at Paisley, Scotland, and graduated at Glasgow University in 1803 and at Oxford in 1807. He had become proficient in pugilism and pedestrianism, and was prominent in the "town and gown" fights, without neglecting the classics. His wealth allowed him to devote himself to athletics on his estate of Elleray on Lake Windemere. His love of literature was shown in "The Isle of Palms," a volume of poems bearing evidence of Wordsworth's influence. In 1811 Wilson married Jane Penny, and spent four more happy years at Elleray. Then, most of his fortune being lost in his uncle's speculations, he removed to Edinburgh and became a lawyer. Jeffrey, observing his ability, had solicited his contributions for the "Edinburgh Review," but men of such opposite temperament could not long agree. In 1817, when "Blackwood's Magazine" was started, Wilson was called to assist, and soon became its controlling spirit. Its red-hot Toryism and general vehemence put vigor in its partisans. In 1820 the chair of moral philosophy in the University of Edinburgh became vacant and Sir Walter Scott and other Tories urged the town-council to appoint Wilson. They were successful, and Wilson honored their choice by his masterly conduct of his classes for thirty years. Having sufficient leisure for literary work, he devoted himself with ardor to the interests of "Maga." His pathetic powers were shown in "Lights and Shadows of Scottish Life," published under a pseudonym in 1822, and in later tales. He treated subjects of all kinds from athletic sports to classical criticism in a lively, exuberant style, varying from intense enthusiasm to wild burlesque, and making abundant use of italics, capitals, dashes and exclamation points. Several volumes of these articles have been collected, but his most famous work is "Noctes Ambrosianæ," unrivaled as convivial table-talk, full of life, humor and dramatic force. In 1835 Wilson suffered a severe blow in the loss of his wife, but did not give up his writing until stricken with paralysis in 1851. He died at Edinburgh in 1854.

Closely associated with "Christopher North" in "Blackwood's Magazine" was the Ettrick Shepherd, James Hogg (1770-1835). His ancestors had been sheep-farmers in Selkirkshire for generations, and he was thus employed when Sir Walter Scott was collecting ballads for the "Minstrelsy of the Scottish Border." Hogg, who had learned to read after reaching manhood, astonished Scott by his poetic talent and his wealth of ballad lore. The Ettrick Shepherd was introduced to the literary circles of Edinburgh, where his racy speech, rustic humor and poetic inspiration soon made him a favorite. He was one of the projectors of "Blackwood's Magazine" and suggested "The Chaldee Manuscript," its earliest explosive. "Christopher North" made Hogg a prominent interlocutor in the "Noctes Ambrosianæ," heightening his foibles and peculiarities, yet doing justice to his genius. Though Hogg in prose and verse received advice and help from his better educated associates, he preserved a unique originality. His best songs, such as "Donald Macdonald," "The Village of Balmawhapple," rank close with those of Burns; in his "Jacobite Relics" he interspersed some clever forgeries. His long poems, "The Queen's Wake," "The Pilgrims of the Sun," "The Mountain Bard," are plainly imitations of Scott, yet not unworthy of comparison with the master's work; the fairy poem of "Kilmeny" is perhaps his best. In his novels, also, he followed the author of "Waverley," but with unequal steps. Though perfectly acquainted with Scotch life, he was deficient in construction of stories. "The Brownie of Bodsbeck," "The Three Perils of Man," "The Three Perils of Woman" are his most successful attempts.

A stranger genius, who gave to "Blackwood's" part of its striking character, was William Maginn (1793-1842), an Irish wit, noted for his extensive scholarship, and still more for his reckless bohemianism. He composed Anacreontics in Greek and Latin, and wrote gay ballads in thieves' slang. He appears in the "Noctes Ambrosianæ" as "Morgan O'Doherty." He afterwards went to London and, after service on various Tory journals, he was one of the projectors of "Fraser's Magazine." In it appeared his "Homeric Ballads" and "Shakespeare Papers." His irregular habits caused his connection with it to be broken off, and reduced him to extreme poverty.

The "London Magazine," founded soon after "Blackwood's," was marked by certain English peculiarities; it was more inclined to Liberalism, though it had some Tory contributors. Charles Lamb, Thomas DeQuincey, and William Hazlitt were among its noted writers. The personal history of Charles Lamb (1775-1834) is an affecting tragedy, brightened by his genial character. He was educated at the famous Blue-coat School, and at an early age became a clerk in the East India House, where he remained for thirty years. The cloud on his life was the fact that his elder sister, Mary, was liable to fits of insanity, and that in one of these she stabbed her mother to the heart. For a time she was confined in an asylum, and when her sanity returned Charles was permitted to take her home. Mary was never made aware of her desperate deed, but afterwards when she felt the trouble recurring, she cheerfully accompanied Charles to the asylum. While she was in mental health, they lived happily "in double singleness," and had weekly gatherings of literary friends. The gentle Charles, precluded from marriage, was a diligent student of early English writers, while Mary amused herself with the current literature. Charles wrote a tragedy, "John Woodvil," in the antique style, but it was severely scored in the "Edinburgh Review." His farce, "Mr. H—," failed at Drury Lane. Then he issued "Specimens of the Old English Dramatists," with excellent brief introductions, and with the aid of his sister, prepared for children, "Tales from Shakespeare." But the "London Magazine" opened for the literary clerk the proper field for his peculiar powers. Taking the pseudonym "Elia," he poured forth his fanciful observations and crotchets without restraint. He was essentially a Londoner, and told

of curious characters and incidents he had remarked on
its streets. He was also a lover of curious half-forgotten
lore, and he delighted to recall it for entertainment of a
new generation. His quiet merriment and genuine pathos
are set off by his quaint, old-fashioned style. His conversation abounded in puns, the effect of which was height-
ened by his stuttering. His "Letters," which have been
carefully edited, are written in the same vein as the more
finished essays, and prove that habit of thought to have
been natural. At times he soars in the realms of the imagination, but generally he keeps close to the familiar
earth. His "Dissertation on Roast Pig" is a classical
piece of fun; "The Praise of Chimney-Sweepers" is full
of humorous kindness; his "Dream-Children" and "The
Child-Angel" reveal the tender heart of the writer. He
describes his sister fondly under the name of "Bridget
Elia," and tells of his bachelor's life and mental oddities
with playful frankness. The essays, written simply to
entertain his friends, were a recreation after his daily
drudgery at office work. One stroke more must be added
to the tragedy of his life. Ten years younger than his
unfortunate sister, he died thirteen years before her. His
friend Talfourd wrote his biography without mentioning
the central tragedy in order to spare her feelings, but after
her death revised the narrative.

Another writer in the "London Magazine" who had
considerable influence in this direction was William Hazlitt (1778-1830). He has been pronounced by competent
judges the greatest of English critics. He was the son
of a Unitarian preacher, and in early manhood, coming in
contact with Coleridge, was powerfully affected by him.
His inclination was to art, and for a time he practiced
painting, but he was drawn into newspaper work in London. He became a critic of art and the drama, lectured on

literature, and wrote essays. His variable temper made him difficult to get along with. His severity was shown not only to his political opponents, but to those who tried to be his friends. He quarreled with his first wife, who had brought him some property, and was discreditably divorced from her. Then came a violent passion for the daughter of a lodging-house keeper, and when she jilted him he told the whole story without reserve in his "Liber Amoris." He married a second wife, but she left him in a few years. Hazlitt was a man of wider experience of life, more robust and more fluent as a writer than gentle Charles Lamb. His miscellaneous essays are not so uniformly excellent, but they comprise many admirable sketches, as "Merry England," "Going a Journey," "The Indian Jugglers." But his most valuable work is seen in his literary criticism, in "The Characters of Shakespeare," "The Elizabethan Dramatists," "The English Poets," and "The English Comic Writers." His strong personality caused him to have intense prejudices, so that his opinions need to be watched, but whenever he is really judicial, he exhibits the highest excellence of criticism—proper and adequate estimate of the authors considered.

Among the papers which gave high literary value to the "London Magazine," none were more remarkable than "The Confessions of an English Opium-Eater," which appeared in 1821. The author, Thomas DeQuincey (1785-1859) was born at Manchester and educated at Oxford, but being under no restraint, he wandered at times to Dublin, London, and elsewhere. He also acquired the opium habit, and after he settled in 1809 at Grasmere, in the Lake district, in a house formerly occupied by Wordsworth, the use of opium, or rather laudanum, grew upon him. He was at this time wealthy, and was admitted at once to intimacy with the families of the poets already domiciled

there. He had previously bestowed, through a friend,
£300 on Coleridge, as an acknowledgment of some slight
favor shown him. Gradually his fortune was wasted, and
the strange genius had to resort to his pen for a living.
In his "Confessions," and still more in his portrayal of
scenes from his dreams, DeQuincey used an elaborate
semi-poetical style. It was partly founded on his study of
music, and is seen in "Our Ladies of Sorrow" and "The
English Mail-Coach." Although he did not begin to write
for publication till he was thirty-six, once started he kept
it up vigorously to the end of his life. It comprised critical, narrative, biographical and autobiographic sketches,
in some of which he has been charged with falsifying facts,
and excused on the plea that to him dreams and realities
were often interchangeable. For these and other reasons,
there remains much mystery about the curious little man.
He removed to Edinburgh in 1830, and made that his chief
place of residence for the rest of his life. But his habits
were uncertain; he was fond of night rambles, and appeared and disappeared without notice. As a writer, when
at his best, he has seldom been excelled in strength or
brilliancy. At times he indulged in a peculiar, grotesque
humor, and often he marred the effect of his writing by
excessive argumentation, wearisome trifling, or endless
digressions.   Apart from the collection of his Essays,
made to various magazines, his few books have little
value. When the enterprise of an American publisher had
first put his essays in book form, the grateful author issued
a revised edition, which forms an enduring monument to
his memory.

WOMEN WRITERS OF THE FIRST PERIOD

A marked feature of the Nineteenth Century has been the number and excellence of its women writers. The first of merit still acknowledged is Maria Edgeworth (1767-1849). Her "Castle Rackrent" (1801) is a lively picture of the recklessness and misconduct of Irish landlords. Her "Belinda" (1803) exhibits the female dissipation of the time. In "Ormond," a youth of impetuous character, whose education has been neglected, rises to true nobility. In "Helen," a story of thrilling interest, it is shown that deceit brings misery in its train. "The Absentee" reveals the wretchedness inflicted on the tenantry by unscrupulous agents while the gentry pursue their pleasures in London. When Miss Edgeworth visited Sir Walter Scott in 1823, he said that her stories had made him wish to do for Scotland what she had done for Ireland. But this may have been only the baronet's gallantry to a lady author. She treated only of Protestant society, and dealt but sparingly with the peasantry and middle classes, and hence was not thoroughly national. Her chief excellence is in sprightly dialogue and amusing scenes. Her short tales are better than her long novels, and her moral stories for children have not yet entirely lost their vogue. She did not fully attain the art of creating individual characters, but rather depicted a variety of types and set them off with humor.

Another woman, less popular in her day, but now regarded as having a higher genius, was the English Jane Austen (1775-1817). Her first publication, "Sense and Sensibility," was in 1810, but she is said to have written novels many years before. In spite of her secluded life, and slender knowledge of society, she succeeded in creating many real characters. Her skill lay in building them up with an infinity of detail. Her delicate irony is rare among women, and gives her a modern tone. Two of her six novels were published after her death.

The three novels of Susan Ferrier (1782-1854) were published anonymously,—"Marriage," in 1818; "The Inheritance," in 1824, and "Destiny," in 1831. Sir Walter Scott praised their clever portraiture of contemporary Scotch life and manners, and called her, with reference to their common anonymousness, his "sister shadow."

Even more popular than these novelists was the poet Felicia Dorothea Hemans (1794-1835), whose verses won praises from the leading poets and critics of the day. Being a woman of wide culture, she ranged over Europe, seeking subjects for pathetic dramas, romantic tales, and songs of the affections. She wrote too fluently and did not stop to correct. The religious tone of her poetry, which descanted on the transitoriness of this world and the assured hope of a better world, commended it to the favor of many readers. She had been unhappy in her marriage with Captain Hemans and was compelled to write for the support of her children.

Two other women who were for a time unduly esteemed and afterward entirely neglected were Joanna Baillie (1762-1851) who wrote "Plays on the Passions," containing both tragedies and comedies on hatred, fear, love, revenge; and Miss Landon (1802-1838), known as "L. E. L.," who dashed off sentimental and impassioned lyrics, and several prose romances.

SUMMARY OF THE PRÉ-VICTORIAN LITERATURE

In the first third of the Nineteenth Century, England underwent one of its periodic revolutions in thought, politics, and literature. The system of reaction and repression which prevailed during the wars with Napoleon and for

some time after his downfall gave way under the influence
of free discussion to a liberal tendency which was first
strikingly manifested in the political sphere in the Parliamentary Reform of 1832, abolishing many rotten bor-
oughs and admitting new cities to representation. Corresponding with this movement, and helping to produce
it, was the literary revolution, whose conspicuous features
have already been indicated and are here rehearsed.

1. Independent literary criticism, inaugurated by the
"Edinburgh Review," gave a new impulse to literature,
which was increased by the larger opportunity granted
to writers by the establishment of "Blackwood's" and
other monthly magazines.

2. The rise of romantic poetry, for which the repub-
lication of old ballads had prepared the way, was first exemplified in Sir Walter Scott's picturesque metrical tales,
whose success swept away the artificial barriers of classical poetry. These tales were objective presentations of
historical or semi-historical scenes, leading captive the imagination before the critical faculties were roused to per-
form their supposed duty.

3. Byron adopted this narritive style, but charged it
with his own powerful personality and passion. He thus
added the subjective element, which brought the poetry
home to the hearts of his readers.

4. Wordsworth scornfully rejected Pope's limitation
of the nature and diction of poetry. His defense of simple language and common incidents as proper for poetry,
though his practice carried this to an undue extreme, was
necessary to overcome the formalism which had stifled the
imagination.

5. Wordsworth elevated the idea of poetry by making its highest aim to be the recognition of the Divinity
in nature and the soul of man. His dedication of his life

to this purpose was an inspiring example to his own and future generations.

6. The revival of genuine lyrical poetry is the strongest proof of the profound change in English nature. As in the Elizabethan age this lyrical outburst was manifested in a great variety of metres.

7. Prose style underwent a similar enlargement, resulting in quaint and elaborate effects, as in Lamb, De Quincey, Wilson, and others.

8. This period is grandly characterized by the rise of the historical romance, in which Sir Walter Scott was the unrivaled leader. To him is due in large measure the wide revival of interest in the Middle Ages, and the consequent restoration of mediævalism in art and religion. As high artistic blendings of historic fact with a gorgeous imagination, the works of "the Wizard of the North" stand alone, in spite of all attempts to rival their charm. It is noteworthy that Scott's long concealment of his authorship of "Waverley" was partly owing to the belief that such work was unworthy of his professional dignity, and that it required his phenomenal success to raise the novel to fair recognition as a legitimate branch of literature.

9. It is of interest to observe that in the early years of this century, when cultured women were restrained by rigid notions of their proper sphere from venturing into print, a few women poets were encouraged by words of praise from the greatest writers, and that the women novelists were admitted to have improved upon the extravagant romancings of the end of the Eighteenth Century. These beginners were the harbingers of the great crowd of women who have conferred honor on the reign of Victoria by their achievements in literature.

SECOND OR EARLY VICTORIAN PERIOD—
1837-1870

Students of English history note that the fourth decade of the century (1831-40), in which Victoria came to the throne, marks broadly a definite stage of progress. Let us glance first at the social and political changes during her reign. Parliamentary reform, which had been held back during the Napoleonic wars and the ensuing period of repression, had won its first victory in 1832. The reactionary policy of the Government came to an end, and the people rejoiced in their newly obtained privileges.

Conspicuous in bringing about these changes was Henry (afterward Lord) Brougham. He assisted in founding the University of London, entirely free from sectarian distinctions, and the Society for the Diffusion of Useful Knowledge, which published instructive works at low prices. At his suggestion Mechanics' Institutes were formed in all leading towns. A thirst for knowledge seemed suddenly to have seized the Nation. Agitation for the repeal of the corn laws followed, and proved successful in the next decade, when in 1845 England definitely adopted the policy of Free Trade. Social reforms were urged by the Radicals, but did not enlist popular support until 1848, when a tide of revolutionary sentiment again swept over Europe. The Chartists had come forward with demands for manhood suffrage and annual elections to Parliament, but they were suppressed by force. Still, this agitation in behalf of the working classes led to various schemes for the improvement of their condition. The most prominent, under the name of Christian Socialism, was supported by some distinguished

63

clergymen and showed its influence on literature. The coöperative societies for trade and industry which they favored, were generally failures.

The middle of the Century seemed to create a change in the national outlook. The World's Fair in the Crystal Palace, London, in 1851, the first of the international exhibitions, was hailed with enthusiasm, as inaugurating an era of universal peace. This feeling also manifested itself in contemporary literature. Yet within a few years came the futile Crimean War, which Englishmen now find it difficult to justify. It had, however, important reflex action by bringing about an alliance between England and France and promoting their friendly intercourse. In the next decade the secession of the Southern States and formation of the Confederacy found unexpected favor in England, but the Government refrained from active interference, though it did not fully enforce its neutrality laws. Further Parliamentary reform, the disestablishment of the Irish Church and effective promotion of public education brought the seventh decade to a close. The same year (1870) witnessed the downfall of Napoleon III, speedily followed by the establishment of the new German Empire and the French Republic.

Let us turn now to consider the literary movement during the same period. The great impulse which had quickened every department of literature at the opening of the century spent its creative force in three decades. Sir Walter Scott died in 1832, in the same year as Goethe, the revered Jupiter of the German Olympus. Other creative masters had already passed away, or practically rested from their labors, their honors being won, and their fame established. In the fourth decade new stars were beginning to appear above the horizon—Macaulay, Carlyle, Hallam, Bulwer and Dickens, soon to be followed by

Thackeray. Some of the great poets who had opened new fields still lingered and were yet adding to their work. Tennyson had begun to sing, but the Brownings still remained obscure. In every department of literature there was vast activity, and in some there was unquestioned pre-eminence. Poetry did not so deeply stir the minds of men, who had fallen into contemplative mood. But there was new interest and vigor in history, and men of genius were studying with zeal the records of the past and preparing new works which should soon be accepted as standard. The result of their labors has been in many cases a pulling down of long established views of men and institutions. The prejudiced decisions which had been widely diffused by partisan writers unable or unwilling to examine the original documents relating to controverted points have been rudely shattered by earnest iconoclasts. Credit must be given for some of these alterations to the change which has come over the spirit of governments, even in the most despotic courts. The archives, long jealously guarded, have been opened to students, seeking only to ascertain the exact facts. Floods of light have thus been shed on mysterious events and disputed characters. The genius of new historians and biographers has been employed in formulating new judgments on the leaders of the world and in presenting them for public discussion.

Another change in intellectual activity is seen in the enlarged study of nature, its laws and resources. The great practical applications of physical science which had followed Watt's invention of the steam engine had necessitated a closer examination of the natural world and its elements. New discoveries were made and new theories advanced in chemistry, physics, geology, and other branches of science. Some of these scientists were able to present their labors and conclusions in works attracting general readers by their picturesque and finished style. On the borders of literature proper there were writers who treated philosophical subjects in a popular way. John Stuart Mill was for some years editor of the "London and Westminster Review," and the chief advocate of Utilitarianism and Radicalism. But the philosophic Radicals did not then so deeply affect the popular mind as did the theological controversy, known as the Oxford movement. It dates from 1833, when Newman, Keble and Pusey began to issue "Tracts for the Times." Intended to rouse the Church of England from its lethargic latitudinarianism, it yet boldly attacked the Evangelicalism which had been taught by the most active and pious of the clergy. It called for a return to the primitive doctrine of the Church, and this was declared to be pure Catholicism. Newman and other leaders eventually went over to the Church of Rome, but the movement continued and was largely literary as well as religious.

Another ecclesiastical controversy, which affected Scotland only, resulted in the withdrawal of more than four hundred ministers from the Established Church to form the Free Church of Scotland. In the subsidence of these controversies the teachings of Coleridge and his followers gave rise to the Broad Church movement, which had closer relations with literature than the Oxford movement. It was the result of the teachings of Coleridge, but was largely developed by Maurice, Kingsley and Dean Stanley. Being ethical and historical rather than dogmatic, it soon pervaded the literature of the time.

After 1860 the whole world of thought began to be revolutionized with the doctrine of evolution. Though put forth early in the century as a scientific theory, it was not generally accepted and had little practical influence until after the publication of Darwin's "Origin of Spe-

cies," and the philosophy of Herbert Spencer. Gradually
the new doctrine spread, and later its results, direct and
indirect, were seen in the growth of scepticism and materialism, agnosticism and pessimism.

But the most striking feature of Victorian literature
is the rich and overwhelming abundance of prose fiction.
The novel has become a necessity of modern society. Its
all-pervading power compels genius to yield to its sway,
and writers of all kinds seek thus to present their thoughts
to the public. The novel no longer deals merely with
heroic persons and perilous adventures. It is no longer
intended for mere amusement. It finds nourishment and
support in the common scenes and daily walks of life. It
is concerned with the development of character, the exhibition of the struggles and varieties of ordinary existence.
It may also be employed in the inculcation of new theories
of education, of religion, or society. It is the most effective means for the teacher of whatever views to reach
the public mind.

But back of all these forms of literary activity and
affording them substantial support is the immense structure of periodical literature, ever varying in its details,
yet permanent in its general effect. The Parliamentary
Reform of 1832 led directly to the extension of education by mechanics' institutes and societies for the diffusion
of knowledge. Charles Knight in England and the
Chambers in Scotland deserve grateful remembrance for
their cheap publication of useful knowledge and general
literature. Every advance in popular education has
brought forth new periodicals and enlisted new writers
of ability. While the world must still wait patiently for
the divine gift of convincing genius, the general average
of expression in poetry and prose has undeniably been
improved, rather than lowered, by the magazines.

NOVELISTS OF THE EARLY VICTORIAN PERIOD

BULWER

The novel is the leading element in the literature of
Victoria's reign. It had been prominent from the beginning of the century, but now, by its ever-increasing quantity and its higher artistic excellence, it commanded
attention and admiration from reluctant critics. A
writer who attained eminence in this field as early as the
third decade maintained his place by successive efforts
for half a century. He is commonly known as Bulwer,
his full name being Edward George Earle Lytton Bulwer,
changed afterward, on succeeding to his mother's estate,
to Sir Edward Bulwer-Lytton, and finally, on his admission to the peerage in 1866, to Baron Lytton. He was
born in 1805, his father being General Bulwer, and was
educated at Cambridge, where he won the Chancellor's
prize for a poem. Even earlier he had published some
juvenile poems. His first romance, "Falkland" (1827),
was in the fantastic German style, but his fame began
with "Pelham" (1828), in which he brought his gentle-
man-hero in contact with all the varieties of English life,
from the man of fashion to the retiring scholar, and from
the reckless rogue to the bustling statesman. The story,
written in his twenty-third year, displayed not only
vivacity of intellect, but maturity of judgment. Other
novels speedily followed—"The Disowned" (1828),
"Devereux" (1829), "Paul Clifford" (1830), a melo-

dramatic chronicle of a highwayman, and "Eugene Aram"
(1832), a revelation of the steps by which a fine moral
nature may sink to brutal crime. Then the brilliant
author turned to historical romance, and in "The Last
Days of Pompeii" (1834) gave a vivid picture of life
under the Roman Empire, and the struggle of Christianity with Paganism. In "Rienzi" (1835) he described
the attempt to restore the ancient republic in mediæval
Rome. His Spanish romances, "Leila" and "Calderon,"
were less popular. When the author returned to English ground in "Ernest Maltravers" and its sequel "Alice,"
he was censured for the low moral tone of his treatment
of social problems. From the first critics had satirized
his melodramatic scenes and ridiculed his highly rhetorical style, but these very faults probably contributed to his
marked success with the public.

Literature by no means absorbed Bulwer's energy.
He was active in politics, favoring social and parliamentary reforms, and in the House of Commons, from 1831
to 1841, supported the Whig policy. He was on friendly
terms with the leading Radicals, and accepted some of
their ideas, but his professed aim was to elevate the masses
to better education, courteous manners and an aristocratic
sense of honor.

In 1838 he turned his attention from novels to the
drama, and with the aid of the tragedian Macready,
produced three plays which still hold the stage—"The
Lady of Lyons," "Richelieu" and "Money." His later
dramatic attempts were unsuccessful. New novels followed, among them being the mystical "Night and Morning" (1841), and "The Last of the Barons" (1843), an
effective historical romance of Warwick, the King-
maker. Then the indefatigable writer turned to poetry and
executed fine translations from Schiller; a satire, "The

New Timon," which provoked a reply from Tennyson, and a romantic epic, "King Arthur." The last-named, on which he staked his reputation as a poet, fell flat. It was written in stanzas of six lines; the story, characters and incidents seemed feeble and ineffective. In 1848 the dauntless author published anonymously in "Blackwood's Magazine" a new form of story, "The Caxtons." It was really an admirable adaptation of Sterne's style to new circumstances, and captivated the public before the authorship was avowed. Of the same kind were "My Novel" (1853) and "What Will He Do With It?" (1858). In these he treated again the varieties of English life, but showed perhaps a less hopeful spirit.

When Sir Edward Bulwer-Lytton returned to Parliament, in 1852, he took sides with the Conservatives, having been opposed to the repeal of the corn-laws. For some years he was busy with official duties. In "A Strange Story" (1862) advantage was taken of popular interest in Spiritualism to present a melodramatic romance. His later stories were published anonymously and won success by their merits. "The Coming Race" was a predictive display of the new condition of mankind when women should be the rulers and electricity should give increased control over nature. In "The Parisians" and "Kenelm Chillingly" the effects of modern ideas on French and English society respectively were strikingly contrasted. The veteran author died in 1873, leaving unfinished another historical romance, "Pausanias the Spartan."

From the outset of his career Bulwer was a studious critic, as well as a prolific writer. He formed theories of his art and laid down general rules which he endeavored to observe, but in minor matters he was careless, and he made the great error of describing the thoughts and feelings of his characters instead of making them reveal themselves in speech. The lasting wonder is that his works put forth in extreme old age showed no diminution of inventiveness or disposition to repeat his earlier ideas. Besides his novels, poems and dramas, he wrote many essays and disquisitions, full of well-digested learning and sage philosophy.

The chief misfortune of his life was his disagreement with his wife, a high-spirited Irish woman, who carried the quarrel into public in every possible way, while he manfully bore all in silence.

DICKENS

Nearly ten years after the first success of the versatile aristocratic Bulwer, another novelist of humble origin and widely different genius sent the English world into fits of laughter. Charles Dickens was born in 1812 at Portsmouth, where his father was a government clerk. But soon the family removed to London, where for years they struggled with poverty. Young Dickens received little education, and was early compelled to earn his own living, while his father was lodged in a debtors' prison. Charles became a reporter of Parliamentary debates and, after reaching manhood, contributed to a daily paper sketches of humorous incidents. They attracted attention, and were published in two volumes as "Sketches by Boz." This nickname was due to his brothers and sisters comparing Charles to Moses, the simple-minded youth in the "Vicar of Wakefield," who traded the family horse for a gross of green spectacles. Moses was corrupted by the children to "Boz," and the young author gave this cognomen celebrity. In 1837 he was engaged to write

papers to accompany comic sketches of Cockney sports-
men by Seymour. But the artist died, and Dickens
changed the character of the publication. It became
"The Posthumous Papers of the Pickwick Club," in
which the kind-hearted Pickwick passes through strange
trials without losing a jot of his faith in human nature.
Other characters intervened—the poetic Snodgrass, the
susceptible Tupman, the amateur sportsman, Winkle,
the loquacious swindling Jingle, and, above all, the irresistible Sam Weller, whose wit and wisdom shine tri-
umphantly at every turn. The novel humor of the "Pickwick Papers," with their caricature of the absurdities of
elections, courts and common life, set the world of England wild with merriment. Henceforth Dickens wrote
monthly or weekly serials on such themes as he pleased.
With all his love of fun, he wished to be a social reformer,
and in novel after novel, rapidly composed, he attacked
with potent ridicule some glaring evil of that land.
Thus "Oliver Twist" reveals the woes of orphans in the
parish work-house and throws a flood of light on the
haunts of crime in London. In "Nicholas Nickleby" the
dreadful mismanagement of private boarding-schools
was exposed in Do-the-boys Hall, conducted by Wack-
ford Squeers. "Old Curiosity Shop" blends pathetic
pictures of Little Nell and her grandfather with the
gayety of the Marchioness and the boisterousness of
Dick Swiveller, while the hideous Quilp supplies the
malevolence. "Barnaby Rudge" is in part a historical
romance, depicting in sombre colors the Lord George
Gordon riots of 1780 and their sudden collapse.

In 1841 Dickens, tired of incessant weekly labor,
visited America, and was received with enthusiasm.
Accustomed to the snug inns of England, he was shocked
with the rawness of the new country and the rude accom-

modations and rough company on his travels. His "American Notes for General Circulation," by their caustic comment and depreciatory tone, provoked severe retorts from those who had shown him hospitality. But his next novel, "Martin Chuzzlewit," repeated the offense in aggravated form. Yet Americans have since admitted that much of the satire and ridicule was deserved, though a cheerful philosopher might have been expected to find better things deserving of notice. Dickens did labor to promote cheerful views of life, and one of his ways was in his Christmas stories, of which the "Carol" was issued in 1843. "The Chimes," "The Cricket on the Hearth," and "Marley's Ghost" followed in successive years, overflowing with good cheer and charity. After a year's residence in Italy, which furnished the descriptive papers called "Pictures from Italy," Dickens issued "Dombey and Son" in monthly numbers. It satirized the pompous pride of the British merchant and contrasted his disappointment in founding a family with the hearty good nature of half-witted creatures. "David Copperfield" has always been regarded as largely autobiographic, and the inimitable Micawber is, in part, drawn from the author's father. With it is interwoven the pathetic tragedy of the homely Peggotys and the alluring villain Steerforth.

In 1850 Dickens became editor of "Household Words," a weekly, which soon attained an enormous circulation. For it he wrote "Hard Times," a story protesting against the cramming system of education. He also continued his monthly serials and did much miscellaneous writing. In "Bleak House" the tedious chancery system and its waste of life is severely arraigned. "Little Dorrit" exposes the evils of imprisonment for debt. In 1836 Dickens had married Catherine Hogarth, who survived him, but in 1859 he separated from her.

In 1859, in consequence of a quarrel with his publishers, Dickens left "Household Words" and established "All the Year Round," a similar weekly. For it he wrote "A Tale of Two Cities," in which he exhibited a striking episode of the French Revolution. "Great Expectations" is a novel of contrasts, in which a transported convict tries to leave a fortune to a boy who did him a slight kindness. In "Our Mutual Friend" the satire is directed against the rage for rising in the social scale. Besides the large income Dickens drew from the sale of his publications, he drew more from public readings of his works. For this purpose he again visited America in 1867, and his tour proved a social and financial success. After his return "The Mystery of Edwin Drood" began to appear, but was not completed. He died June 8, 1870, and was interred in Westminster Abbey.

The general quality of Dickens' works remained the same from first to last, though animal spirits predominate in the earlier. His enormous humor and exaggerated sentiment gave immense popularity to his pictures of low and middle class life, especially in London. His sympathies were with the honest poor; he made all the world share in their joys and sorrows and privations. He ridiculed class pretensions, but he never really understood the upper classes. He was fond of the theater from childhood, and took part in private theatricals, but he wrote no dramas, probably because he was always kept too close at other writing. Yet in actual life he was a constant actor, eager for the world's applause. He was handsome, with waving brown hair, and dressed in gaudy style. He was hard-working, painstaking, fertile in schemes, and fond of novelty and excitement. The continued strain made him restless and irritable, and too exacting of those around him. The wonder is that none of this irritability escapes into his works. There he exhibits not precisely what he observed, but with artistic and humorous exaggeration the effect of that as transformed by his peculiar genius. In youth his exuberance of fun partly concealed his intolerance of wrong, but as he grew older, though his humorous characters are as abundant as ever, his serious moralizing becomes plainer and stronger. "David Copperfield" represents his powers at the best; the works before it still excel in popularity those that followed that masterpiece. For pure amusement we still go back to the "Pickwick Papers."

THACKERAY

Though Thackeray was born a year before Dickens, he was more than a decade later in reaching popularity, and even then it was by no means equal to his great competitor's. He belonged to a wealthy Yorkshire family, but first saw the light in 1811 in Calcutta, where his father was in the civil service. When seven years old he was sent to England for his education, and after some years at the famous Charter-House, he went to Cambridge. But he did not graduate; having a comfortable fortune, he studied painting and traveled on the Continent. When the fortune was lost by imprudent investments or folly, the half-taught artist sought employment as an illustrator. Among those to whom he applied was Dickens, then starting the "Pickwick Papers," but Hablot K. Browne, known as "Phiz," was chosen. Thackeray therefore began to write squibs for "Fraser's Magazine," just started, and later for "Punch," which first appeared in 1841. To the latter he contributed the "Snob Papers" and "Memoirs of Mr. Jeames Yellowplush," in which the Cockney footman's views of life are set off by bad spelling. Other pen-names of this period are "Michael Angelo Titmarsh" and "George Fitz Boodle," but the industrious humorist was still little esteemed. Yet he published some pretty Christmas books and "A Journey from Cornhill to Cairo."

At last, in 1846, Thackeray began, like Dickens, to issue a novel in serial numbers. It was called "Vanity Fair, a Novel Without a Hero." It was written in a sociable, conversational tone, but was a scathing exposure of the shams and follies of the upper classes. The interest centers in the adventures of the shrewd and clever Becky Sharpe, who has set her heart on making a grand match. Unfortunately, the man whom she marries misses the coveted estate; then she becomes entangled with an aged debauchee, and is crushed by her husband's unexpected return from a sponging house. After the surprising success of "Vanity Fair" Thackeray never returned to the trifling writing which had chiefly occupied his time.

In 1849 he began "Pendennis," the hero of which represents himself, though the adventures through which he passes are not similar. Arthur has his faults and foibles, but his regret and repentance evoke the sympathies of the reader. His sweetheart Laura is a model of patient endurance with waywardness. In 1851 Thackeray visited America, lecturing on "The English Humorists of the Eighteenth Century." That age was always his familiar hunting-ground, and he discussed Addison, Steele and Swift with sincere sympathy. Still further use was made of this knowledge in his next book, "The History of Henry Esmond," which professed to be autobiographic and was exact in its imitation of the style of "The Spectator." Among the historical characters presented were Queen Anne, the Pretender, the Duke of Marlborough, and Addison, but the interest centers in the gentlemanly Esmond and his hopeless suit for his beautiful but proud cousin Beatrix. Fully assured of his position, Thackeray next issued "The Newcomes," a charming novel of social satire and philosophy. The real hero is the retired Colonel Thomas Newcome, a perfect gentleman in his dealings with all the world, who yet is fated to lose his fortune and die a pensioner in the Charter-House in which he had been a pupil.

Thackeray visited the United States again in 1856, and lectured on "The Four Georges," unveiling their foolish and vicious characters, with due exception and regard for George III, the only honest, virtuous man among them, yet doomed to sad attacks of insanity. The income from these lectures provided a fund for Thackeray's daughters, to whom he was specially affectionate. His wife had become insane in 1841, but she outlived him without recovering her reason. Partly as a result of his visit to America, Thackeray wrote his "Virginians," a continuation of "Henry Esmond." Among the characters introduced is Washington as a young man. The American regard for the Father of his Country caused an outcry against this picture, but more recent criticism is disposed to accept it as probable. Objection has also been made to some of the English portraits, but the interest of the story does not depend on these incidental figures.

In 1860 Thackeray again followed Dickens' example and became editor of the "Cornhill Magazine," a monthly which soon attained the unprecedented circulation of 100,000. In it he published "Loved the Widower" and "The Adventures of Philip," which recalled "The Newcomes." Philip has a wicked father and a stupid wife, but is greatly helped by the kindness of the Little Sister. A new novel, "Denis Duval," had just been commenced in the magazine, when the author was interrupted by death on the day before Christmas, 1863.

Thackeray was tall and strongly built, with abundant waving hair, which early became white. He had, unfortunately, a broken nose, owing to some accident, and was sensitive about its being noticed. His ordinary style was in clear, idiomatic English, but, under various pseudonyms, he used an appropriate variety of speech. In verse he sometimes adopted a half-serious, half-comic tone, which suited his philosophic resignation to the changes of time. Being thoroughly acquainted with English society, he was able to satirize effectively its wickedness and follies. He was a genuine humorist, and skilled in dealing with human foibles. A notable feature of his novels is his discoursing aside with his readers, letting the story pause while he moralizes shrewdly on the vagaries of human nature. His scenes and characters are real, true to life, idealized only so far as to adapt them to literary purpose. The critical appreciation of his work has steadily risen since his death, and he is even pronounced by some the first novelist of the century.

DISRAELI

Perhaps the most unique figure in English literature is Benjamin Disraeli, who, after a remarkable political career, full of stormy fights and glorious victories, became Earl of Beaconsfield. He was of Spanish-Jewish descent, but his father, Isaac Disraeli, the quiet plodding author of the "Curiosities of Literature," withdrew from the synagogue. Benjamin, born in 1804, early displayed a widely different character from his father, and in 1826 astonished the world with his dashing political novel "Vivian Grey." It satirized briskly the leaders of the time, discussed political problems seriously, and even prefigured his own career. It quite eclipsed Bulwer's "Falkland" which appeared in the same year. After a tour in the East, the successful young author published "Contarini Fleming" (1832), which treats of the development of a poetic character and gives brilliant sketches of Italy and Syria. Then came the "Wondrous Tale of Alroy" (1833), a dithyrambic Oriental romance of a mediæval Messiah, and "The Revolutionary Epick" (1834), in which he eulogized tyrannicide in blank verse. Meantime, Disraeli had been trying to get into Parliament as a Radical, but being twice defeated, he turned round and gave splendid help to the disheartened Tory party by his "Runnymede Letters" (1836), defending the British Constitution. Yet he always retained much of his early Radicalism and even compelled the reluctant Tories to accept some of it in order "to dish the Whigs." Other books were issued before he reached Parliament—"Henrietta Temple," a very sentimental love-story, and "Venetia," in which he rehearsed the story of Byron's life.

At the age of thirty-two, the persevering Disraeli entered Parliament, but his maiden speech was a deplorable failure. When hooted down, he replied, "I have begun several times many things, and I have often succeeded at last. I shall sit down now; but the time will come when you will hear me." In 1839 he married the wealthy widow of his friend, Wyndham Lewis, whom he afterward praised as a perfect wife. He assisted in forming a political literary group known as "Young England," and expounded its principles in "Coningsby; or, the New Generation" (1844). In this, as in all his

political novels, which should be read by those wishing
to know the inside of English history, he drew the principal characters directly from prominent persons of the
day, and the public were delighted at tracing the resemblance.   In "Sybil" (1845) he treated of the Chartist agitation.   "Tancred; or, the New Crusade" (1847) was a
further exposition of the political views he was urging
on the Conservative party.   Disraeli had now become a
prominent speaker in the British legislature, and fiercely
assailed Sir Robert Peel for his adoption of Free Trade.
When the Tories returned to power in 1852, Disraeli
was made the leader in the House of Commons.   His
increased political duties prevented his giving much time
to literature.   He first became Prime Minister in 1868.
Two years later, while out of office, he published
"Lothair," a brilliant presentation of the religious as well
as the political tendencies of the time.   It was aimed particularly at Cardinal Manning and the Jesuits.   In 1872
he was called to mourn the loss of his wife, who had
gloried in his triumphs and lightened his reverses.   In
1874 he was again Prime Minister, and two years later he
accepted the peerage which had been offered to him long
before.   Still greater glory awaited him when he took
part in the Berlin Congress, which readjusted the results
of the Russo-Turkish War, and when he induced Parliament to confer on Queen Victoria the title of Empress of
India.   The veteran statesman died in April, 1881.   In
the same year was published his last novel, "Endymion,"
in which were presented, after his usual fashion, Lord
Palmerston, Louis Napoleon (as a young man), and
other celebrities.

The career of Lord Beaconsfield is more romantic
than his novels, brilliant as they are with epigram and
paradox.   His style was highly rhetorical and sometimes

tawdry. Plagiarism was occasionally proved against him, in speech and writing, and yet his overwhelming originality could not be denied. His frequent presentation of living characters under thin disguises piqued curiosity, yet the real value of his work lay elsewhere—in the discussion of the social and political problems of England. He treated them ironically, yet he stated a certain amount of permanent truth.

MARRYAT

In the early numbers of "Blackwood's Magazine" appeared two series of sea-sketches—"The Cruise of the Midge" and "Tom Cringle's Log." They were composed by Michael Scott (1789-1825), and contain some fine descriptions of sea-fights, tropical scenery, the flirtations, duels and dangers of West Indian life. This was seventy years after Smollett, who was a ship's surgeon, had already used his knowledge of sailors' lives in his fictions. But the writer who has won highest distinction by his tales of nautical adventure is Captain Frederick Marryat (1792-1848). As a boy, though the son of a wealthy Londoner, he had frequently run away to sea, and at the age of fourteen he was allowed to enter the navy. Serving under the daring Cochrane (afterwards Lord Dundonald) he witnessed fifty engagements in thirty months. He was highly commended for valor in war and humanity in peace, and was distinguished as post-captain in the Burmese war of 1824-5. After more than twenty years' experience of sea-life, Marryat began to describe it in 1829. His first novel, "Frank Mildmay," was but a thinly disguised rehearsal of the adventures of Cochrane and his crew, and had material for half-a-dozen stories. The second, "The King's Own," is more artistic, and contains, besides some playful writing, a powerful dramatic scene, in which the captain sacrifices the frigate Aspasia in order to wreck a French line-of-battle-ship on a lee shore.

Marryat, having discovered his literary gift, retired from the naval service in 1830 and produced in rapid succession "Newton Forster," "Peter Simple," "Jacob Faithful," "Japhet in Search of a Father," "Midshipman Easy," and "Snarley-yow, of the Dog Fiend." Of these "Peter Simple" is the most popular, on account of the lively succession of humorous incidents, though the wild hilarity of "Dignity Ball" may be too "briny" for serious people. But "Snarley-yow" has been ranked higher for humorous portraiture and richness of incident. From 1832 to 1836 Marryat was editor of the "Metropolitan Magazine," and he produced a dozen more stories, some relating to the land and some intended for juvenile readers. He died at the age of fifty-six. His biography has been written by his daughter, a novelist of ability. Marryat's books have the faults of other sea-stories, a certain ferocity and fondness for practical jokes, yet they are full of vivacity and vigor, and show the terrible hardships and heroic actions, as well as the light-hearted fun of the sailor's life. Marryat's sea-stories were directly imitated by Chamier and Captain Howard, but their books did not obtain the same success.

LEVER

The military novels of Charles Lever have a strong resemblance to the nautical novels of Captain Marryat. Both authors endow their characters with an exuberant flow of animal spirits and furnish a rapid succession of amusing and exciting incidents. But Lever changed his style of writing more than once in his career. He was the son of an English architect, but was born in Dublin in 1806; educated in Trinity College of that city, and afterward at Göttingen, he became a physician. He displayed courage and skill in several parts of Ireland during the cholera outbreak of 1832. Then marrying Miss Baker, he went to Brussels and practiced among the British residents. From his own experience and the entertaining stories of retired officers who had served in Spain, he gathered the material of "The Confessions of Harry Lorrequer," "The Adventures of Charles O'Malley," and "Jack Hinton." These novels are careless in plot, but full of boisterous good humor, and describe fighting and battle-scenes with vigor. All classes of military men figure in them, from the Duke of Wellington to the reckless Micky Free. Lever became editor of "The Dublin University Magazine" from 1842 to 1845, and published in it several Irish novels, as "Tom Burke," "The O'Donoghue," "The Knight of Gwynne." They exhibit the volatile side of Irish life, and a racy national humor.

In later life Lever resided on the Continent, at Carlsruhe, in the Tyrol, at Spezzia, and finally at Trieste, where he died in 1872. In the novels of this period he described English travelers or residents on the Continent. Among them are "The Daltons," "The Dodd Family Abroad," "Davenport Dunn." He wrote also for "Blackwood's Magazine" miscellaneous papers under the name of "Cornelius O'Dowd." His latest novels were the best constructed, but the vigor of his invention and humor had been already spent, so that they never reached the popularity of his early ones.

OTHER IRISH STORY WRITERS

There are other novelists who more truly or fully represent the Irish character. John Banim (1800-1842) in "Tales of the O'Hara Family" and "The Denounced" shows the passionate and tragic side of peasant life. Gerald Griffin (1803-1840) dealt with the middle classes, and showed both the pathetic and humorous features of their lives in his famous "Collegians," which has been adapted for the stage under the title "Colleen Bawn." He had just achieved success after a hard struggle, when he withdrew to a monastery two years before he died. No one has depicted more faithfully all the aspects of the Irish peasant than William Carleton (1794-1869). His "Traits and Stories of the Irish Peasantry" appeared in 1830, and from that time to his death his literary activity was incessant. The most powerful of his works is "Fardarougha the Miser," in which the beautiful character of the miser's wife is sketched from his own mother. "The Black Prophet" graphically describes the sufferings of the famine of 1846. Thomas Crofton Croker (1798-1854), who was an antiquarian rather than a novelist, is best known by his collection of "Fairy Legends of the South of Ireland." The most amusing pictures of the Irish peasant have been furnished by Samuel Lover (1797-1868), who was chiefly an artist and song-writer. Both the song and the story of "Rory O'More" came from his pen. But his most famous book is "Handy Andy" (1842), which relates the comical blunders of a droll, muddle-headed peasant of the lowest class, who yet becomes an Irish peer, with the title Lord Scatterbrain.

MINOR WRITERS

One of the earliest imitators of Sir Walter Scott was George Payne Rainsford James (1801-1860), who published his first and perhaps best novel, "Richelieu," in 1825. He flung off rapidly some two hundred stories, which bore a strong family likeness, but were cheerfully received by the uncritical public, who sought only diversion. James was for many years a British Consul in Italy and the United States, and wrote some respectable historical works.

William Harrison Ainsworth (1805-1882) was also a prolific novelist, who confined his attention to English historical subjects, but handled them in a melodramatic way. His most popular books are "Jack Sheppard" and "The Tower of London," but neither is well constructed.

KINGSLEY

Charles Kingsley was the apostle of muscular Christianity, but his life was singularly uneventful. He was born in June, 1819, at Dartmoor, Devon, where his father was an old-fashioned fox-hunting rector. He went to Cambridge, took honors, and was ordained in the Church of England. In 1841 he became curate at Eversley, Hampshire, and was afterwards rector there till his death in 1875. He had been appointed professor of history in Cambridge in 1861, canon at Chester, and at Westminster in 1873. He made some trips on the Continent and visited America.

Kingsley's first book was "The Saint's Tragedy" (1848), a drama on the story of St. Elizabeth of Hungary.   Being roused by the Chartist movement and the writings of Carlyle to the necessity of righting the wrongs of the oppressed, he joined with F. D. Maurice in an effort to put Christian life into the masses.   His sympathy with the working-classes was shown in "Alton Locke" (1850), the pathetic story of a London tailor who took part in the Chartist insurrection, and in "Yeast" (1851), which made the stir of the time appear as a struggle towards a better life.   His contributions to "Fraser's Magazine" treated of a variety of subjects from literature to fishing.   "Hypatia," his first historical novel, is a vivid panorama of Alexandria in the Fourth Century and the struggle of Christianity with Pagan philosophy and other foes.   These foes are virtually the same in all ages, notwithstanding the diversity of appearances.   Hypatia, slain by a fanatical Christian mob, was the martyr maid of philosophy.   Kingsley's next novel, "Westward Ho!" (1855) generally considered his masterpiece, recalled the Elizabethan adventurers, Raleigh and Drake. "Two Years Ago" (1857) dealt with the Crimean War. "Hereward the Wake" (1866) went back to the Saxon times.   Throughout these historical novels the landscapes and sea-scenes are lovingly depicted, and the more remote they are, the more care is taken to render them pictorial.   "Andromeda" (1858) has been pronounced the most successful attempt at the use of hexameter verse in English.   It treats of the Greek myth of Perseus. "The Water Babies" (1863) is a charming fairy tale for children, yet contains satire for adults.   His short poems, such as "The Three Fishers," are full of freshness and grace.   An incidental remark of Kingsley's in 1864, which seemed to charge Newman with excusing disregard of truth, drew from the latter his famous "Apologia pro Vita Sua." This controversy was one of many which gave color to Kingsley's life.

His younger brother, Henry Kingsley (1830-1876), was also a vigorous novelist, though he never reached the same general recognition. Having lived in Australia five years, he made that land the scene of his best stories, "Geoffrey Hamlyn" and "Ravenshoe."

TROLLOPE

Among the severe British criticisms of America none was more deeply resented than Mrs. Frances Trollope's "Domestic Manners of the Americans." It was written after three years' residence, during which she was in business in Cincinnati. Being left a widow at thirty-five, she was obliged to support her family and became an industrious writer of lively books of travels and novels of some merit. Her eldest son, Thomas Adolphus Trollope (1810-1892), lived more than half his life in Italy, and wrote historical sketches and novels, chiefly relating to that country. But the younger son, Anthony Trollope (1815-1882), was perhaps the most prolific and popular novelist of his time, yet he was late in beginning to write. His first book, "The Warden" (1855), in which the chief character is a simple-minded, conscientious clergyman, was the beginning of a series comprising "Barchester Towers," "Doctor Thorne," "Framley Parsonage," "The Small House at Allington," and "The Last Chronicle of Barset." In these certain characters and whole families appear again and again, so that the reader keeps watching for old acquaintances or their relatives. They all belong to England of his day and range from the lower middle to the upper class, including especially clergymen and their wives. The stories contain the ordinary incidents of life, and the conversation is sprightly. In "Phineas Finn" and some other books Trollope entered the region of politics, giving sketches of Gladstone and Disraeli under other names. He wrote a few books of a different class, but not successfully. He had an official connection with the Post-Office, which, however, did not occupy much of his time. The public were surprised to learn from his "Autobiography" that he did his writing almost mechanically, so many words an hour, and were disposed to underrate the value of what they had previously prized.

READE

Perhaps one of the most eccentric English authors was Charles Reade (1814-1884). He was born at Ipsden, near Oxford, graduated at that University, and was elected a Fellow of Magdalen College. This gave him independence, so that he was slow in beginning to write. After some unsuccessful attempts at drama, he published in 1852, "Peg Woffington," a brilliant short story. His "Griffith Gaunt" is a powerful but disagreeable picture of life in the Eighteenth Century. "It Is Never Too Late to Mend" (1856) is a tale of his own times, exposing the ill treatment of prisoners and describing mining life in Australia. "The Cloister and the Hearth" (1861) is his longest and greatest work, professing to relate the story of the father of Erasmus in the Fifteenth Century. Though he borrowed much from Erasmus himself, he added romance, passion and pathos. He used to accumulate newspaper clippings of strange facts and incidents, which he arranged and indexed in huge scrap-books, and then drew from these sources such details as he required for his powerful stories of modern life. Yet it was rather his own genius than this patchwork that enabled him to reveal the gloom of prisons, the horrors of mad-houses, the outrages of trade-unions, the perils of the sea. His stories show him a man of strong likes and dislikes. He assisted in dramatizing some of his stories, and had lawsuits and newspaper controversies about the copyrights.

Wilkie Collins (1824-1889) was a prominent member of Dickens' staff in the "Household Words," and was noted for his skill in constructing intricate plots. The reader of the serial was kept in anxious suspense from week to week until the elaborate tangle should be un-raveled. This sensation was especially produced by the "Woman in White" (1860), in which was presented his most life-like character, the plausible, fat Italian, Fosco, adventurer and villain.

Judged by his books, George Borrow (1803-1881) was a man of roving and adventurous temper, fond of the Gipsies and their wild life, yet he was also a thorough Englishman, devoted to his country and its institutions. For a few years he wandered over many lands and mingled with strange folk, yet he spent the last half of his life quietly in his native place. He was born at Nor-folk, the son of a soldier, and went to London, where he was employed in obscure literary work until, in 1833, he was selected by the British and Foreign Bible Society as a traveling agent in Russia and the East, and afterwards in Spain. Returning to England in 1840 he married a lady of some wealth and published the books by which he is known. The first was "The Gipsies in Spain" (1841), soon followed by "The Bible in Spain" (1842) a wildly romantic book of travels, whose fanciful coloring makes them seem like the phantasms of a dream. His powerful novel, "Lavengro" (1851) partly autobiographic, tells the story of a man who joins the Gipsies and is full of fascination for a select class of readers. Its sequel, "Romany Rye" (1857), is of less interest. Besides these, Borrow issued some dictionaries and translations from strange tongues, and "Wild Wales," a book of travels in his former style.

The most successful attempt at portraying school-boy life is "Tom Brown's School Days" (1856), by Thomas Hughes (1823-1896), who afterward became a member of Parliament. The title page of his book correctly described him as "An Old Boy." Throughout his life, devoted to earnest endeavors to benefit workingmen and others, he retained much boyishness of spirit and interest in boys' affairs. He was really Tom Brown himself, while his friend, little Arthur, was afterwards Dean Stanley. The book was a tribute to Dr. Arnold and his system of education at Rugby. It was followed by "Tom Brown at Oxford" (1861), written with studious accuracy, but not the native force of the Rugby book. His other books were popular discourses on practical religion.

WOMEN WRITERS OF THE EARLY VICTORIAN PERIOD

BRONTË

Women have held a conspicuous place among the writers of Victoria's reign. Prominent among the novelists was Charlotte Brontë (1816-1855), the eldest of three sisters, daughters of an eccentric Irishman, who had become parson of a moorland parish in Yorkshire. Brought up amid poverty in this dreary wilderness, they had intense longings for advantages beyond their reach. They were intended to be governesses, and for this purpose Charlotte and Emily spent a year at Brussels. After their return the three sisters published a volume of poems, under the assumed names, Currer, Ellis, and Acton Bell, each retaining her own initials. The literary instinct was strong, and they resolved to write each a story. Charlotte's attempt, "The Professor," could not secure a publisher. Then she set to work on "Jane Eyre," which, after being refused by several publishers, was at last accepted and issued in 1847. It is the story of a plain orphan girl, educated by charity, who enters the household of Edward Rochester, an ugly, domineering master, whose insane wife is kept in concealment. This man, who had been sated with the excitements of the world, finds himself, to his own surprise, becoming interested in the little, plain, but intelligent woman, who evidently tries to avoid his attentions. The book revealed with circumstantial detail much of the author's experience, and also the deepest feelings of her heart. Its truthfulness captured the reading world, and Char-

lotte was summoned to London to meet the literary mag-
nates, but the shy little woman soon returned to her
moorland home. Her second book, "Shirley" (1848),
was more labored than the first, and shocked some readers
by making her heroine seek too eagerly for the man of her
choice. In "Villette" (1852) she made use of her experiences in Brussels, and won a new success in the love
of the vivacious French professor, Paul Emmanuel, for
the modest little English girl, Lucy Snowe. In 1854
Charlotte was married to her father's curate, Mr. Nich-
olls, but she died within a year. Her sister, Emily
(1818-1848), had written a fiercely tragic novel, "Wuth-
ering Heights," and some short poems of strong feeling.

The strange biography of the Brontë family was written by Mrs. Elizabeth Gaskell (1810-1865), herself a
novelist of merit. Her first story, "Mary Barton"
(1848), was a pathetic delineation of some scenes of
Manchester life. "Ruth" (1850) was a story of the redemption of a too trusting girl who had been seduced by
a villain. But the most noted of Mrs. Gaskell's works is
"Cranford," a pleasing chronicle of the simple events of
a quiet little village.

One of the most highly esteemed women-novelists
was Dinah Maria Muloch, afterwards Mrs. Craik (1826-
1887). Her most noted work is "John Halifax, Gentleman" (1857), a quiet story of a pure love. She had
written some novels before this, and many more after it,
but none quite equal to this delicate master-piece.

GEORGE ELIOT

In the sixth decade of the Century a new name appeared in imaginative literature, to which at once high
rank was awarded. This was George Eliot, the pseu-

donym of Mary Ann (or Marian) Evans, who was then living with George Henry Lewes as his wife, though they had not been legally married. Marian Evans was born at Nuneaton in Warwickshire in 1819. Her parents were respectable, religious, narrow-minded people, but after her mother's death she came in contact with persons of somewhat wider culture, who held extreme Unitarian views. Influenced by the culture, she quickly adopted their views, and at their request translated Strauss's "Life of Jesus." After a year of study in Geneva, she settled in London, contributing to the "Westminster Review" and making more translations. Thus she was introduced to George Henry Lewes (1817-1878), a versatile but not very successful writer, though an able critic. Mr. Lewes had separated from his wife, and he induced Miss Evans, who had little regard for the conventions of society, to take the vacant place. At first they were utterly condemned by the London world, but after her genius was manifested, they were practically forgiven. The lowness of their fortunes led Mr. Lewes to suggest that his consort should use her ability for social description in fiction. The first result appeared in "Blackwood's Magazine" as "Scenes of Clerical Life," of which "The Sad Fortunes of the Reverend Amos Barton" attracted the most attention. Her first novel, "Adam Bede" (1859) is the finest literary report of the spirit of Methodism. The Quaker preacher, Dinah Morris, was drawn from the author's aunt. The book was the first adequate study of English country life apart from the gentry. "The Mill on the Floss" is a more tragic story, in which Maggie Tulliver is the victim of her own trustfulness. In "Silas Marner" (1861) Methodism again played an important part. These books were the natural, unaffected outpouring of the author's genius. Mr. Lewes, who had discovered and fostered her abilities, drew around her a remarkable circle of worshipers. The constant applause, seldom tempered by criticism, and her own love of philosophical study, led her to yet more arduous efforts. In "Romola" (1863) she treats of Florence in the time of Savonarola, but while the preaching monk is carefully portrayed, the interest lies in the other characters — Romola, the idealized school-girl, and the attractive, yet remorseless, villain Tito.

Then the great author, now recognized as a supreme analyst of character, returned to English ground. Yet "Felix Holt, the Radical" (1866) was her least successful work. "Middlemarch" (1817), however, retrieved her fame and presented a memorable picture of literary failure in the scholar Casaubon, said to be drawn from Mark Pattison, and of woman's devotion to a fading ideal in the lovely Dorothea. In "Daniel Deronda" (1876) she embodied a noble conception of the modern Jew, and commended his aspirations on behalf of his race. But stubborn English opinion declined to be moved. Still less did it care for "The Impressions of Theophrastus Such" (1878), a volume of essays. Mr. Lewes died in 1878, and in May, 1880, Miss Evans was formally married to John Walter Cross, but died in the following December. Mr. Cross published her biography, but it gives an inadequate idea of this woman of genius. Her earliest books were faithful delineations of characters that had been familiar to her youth, and abounded in genuine humor. Her later books were more ambitious studies of the complex characters of a larger society, highly philosophical, but not finally satisfying. Her poems never enjoyed public favor.

ROMOLA AND HER FATHER

After the great and sudden outburst of song in the early years of the Century there came a season of comparative lull. No thrilling voice was added to the concert, but some of the older songsters were still heard. It was hardly until Tennyson was made poet laureate on the death of Wordsworth (1850) that his popularity began. He had shown himself a disciple of Keats, worshiping beauty, and had been charged by the critics with effeminacy. But "Locksley Hall" (1842), "The Princess" (1847), and the grand elegy, "In Memoriam" (1850), testified to his original power. Henceforth his utterances became the acknowledged poetic expression of English feeling. Browning, three years younger, was still slower in obtaining popular recognition. Though he early won a few earnest devotees, his name and works did not become familiar to the public until 1869, when "The Ring and the Book," perhaps partly by its size, forced attention. Thenceforth he wrote constantly, was read with new interest and loving care, and the very obscurity of his verse gave occasion for a cult, which still prevails. But for twenty years before he had reached his fame, his wife had been well known and was regarded as the greatest female genius of her country. Her fluent verses, picturesque romanticism, religious sentiment, humanitarian feeling, strong pathos, and perhaps her own sad story, brightened by love, had given her an assured place in the affections of the people.

In this period there was a notable movement, known as Pre-Raphaelitism. It belonged chiefly to art, but extended into literature, beginning about 1840 or earlier. It was a return to the spirit of the Middle Ages, and had grown out of the Romanticism of the beginning of the Century, fostered by the ecclesiastical Oxford movement. It affected many poets, but its chief representative is Dante Gabriel Rossetti (1828-1882), the son of an Italian exile who had settled in London. Rossetti was both a painter and a poet, and endeavored in his poems to express pictorial ideas. "The Blessed Damozel," his first published poem, is a typical example of his school. His gifted sister, Christina Georgina Rossetti (1830-1895), also belonged to this school, and her work was deeply colored by her religious feelings.

A poet who, though he published but little, had great effect upon subsequent poets, was Edward FitzGerald (1809-1883). This effect was produced by his remarkable translation or paraphrase of the Persian astronomer-poet, Omar Khayyam, which first appeared in 1859. By its ridicule of asceticism and self-denial, and its mystical materialism, it has done much to render an epicurean pessimism popular.

Matthew Arnold (1822-1888) is more famous as a critic than as a poet, yet he showed considerable power in his poems, in which he endeavors to restrain the tendency to ornament and to return to the simplicity of Wordsworth, or rather of Greek.

About 1850 there was a stir of poetic feeling which was chiefly manifested in what was ultimately condemned by its name, the Spasmodic School. The leaders were the English Sydney Dobell (1824-1874) and the Scotch Alexander Smith (1829-1867). Dobell, who was afflicted with ill health, wrote two dramas, one of which, "Balder" (1853), has been compared to Ibsen's later work. Smith published "A Life Drama" (1853), which had a phenomenal, but only temporary success. The two poets, excited by the Crimean War, published together, "Sonnets on the War" (1855), and Dobell continued in the same strain in "England in the Time of War" (1856). Smith published "City Poems" (1857), and afterwards confined himself chiefly to prose description. During their vogue the young poets were extravagantly praised, but judicious critics pointed out their heaping up of imagery and sentiment and excess of passion. They were in fact heirs of the spirit of Byron, but transferred their heroes' struggles from the world of action to the world of thought. Their dramatic efforts were effectively burlesqued by W. E. Aytoun in his "Firmilian, a Spasmodic Tragedy," which silenced them.

An older poet, belonging to the same school, was Philip James Bailey, born in 1816, whose "Festus" (1839) for a while took the world by storm. It was a long poetical and philosophical colloquy between God, Lucifer, angels and men. Some admirers regarded it as a Christian reply to Goethe's "Faust." But in spite of some fine passages, it was soon neglected, and the author's later poems did not revive his reputation.

TENNYSON

Alfred Tennyson distinctly devoted his life to poetry, and though, without fortune, waited patiently for recognition by the world. He was forty-two when he was made poet-laureate and thereby helped to wealth, which he lived long to enjoy. He was the son of a clergyman and was born at Somerby in Lincolnshire in 1809. He was educated at Trinity College, Cambridge, and published "Poems, Chiefly Lyrical" in 1830. These poems were fresh and sweet and musical, but were severely at-

tacked by the critics.   The poet afterwards rejected some
and amended others.   In 1833 came a second volume,
containing "The May Queen," "The Lotos-Eaters," and
"A Dream of Fair Women."   The first became a universal favorite, the others showed a singular power of
dreamy fancy, which was often exercised afterwards.   In
1842 another volume was published, which some early
admirers thought he never excelled.   It contained "Lady
Clara Vere de Vere," "The Talking Oak," and the weird
soliloquy of "Locksley Hall."   "Morte D'Arthur" was
the germ from which was to be developed the long series
of the "Idylls of the King."   In 1847 came "The Princess," a narrative poem in blank verse, treating pleasantly
of woman's rights.   It told how a Princess, eager to assert woman's equality, had gathered a court, from which
men were carefully excluded, and how her plans were
thwarted and she herself became a victim to love.   A few
of the poet's finest lyrics were interwoven—"The Splendor Falls," "Tears, Idle Tears," and "The Bugle-Song."

In contrast with this was "In Memoriam" (1850), the
wonderful elegy in which the poet laments the loss of his
friend, Arthur H. Hallam, who had been betrothed to his
sister.   It consists of 130 poems, each of several stanzas,
representing all the varying moods of his thought on his
affliction, recollections of the past, and hopes of the
future.   Though all the stanzas are of the same peculiar
form, the poet's mastery of music and diction has prevented unpleasant monotony.   Again, in contrast with
this song of grief came in 1855 "Maud," a poem of love
and marriage, with many happy lyrics.   But its too cloy-
ing sweetness was not so well relished.   The author
afterwards amended it.

In mature life Tennyson took up again the favorite
story of King Arthur and sought to make it an English

epic. The four poems of the original "Idylls of the King" (1859) are named from four women, prominent in the story—Enid, Vivien, Elaine, and Guinevere. The contrast of style and subject in these idylls was carefully wrought out. But the epic was steadily enlarged by the poet until it comprised fifteen separate poems. Founded originally on Sir Thomas Malory's prose romance, it was largely reconstructed with aid from the Welsh and French chronicles, and even modernized in tone. How far the later additions are improvements is disputed by critics.

Meantime Tennyson had written many other poems, some of which were on events of the time, as the noble ode on the funeral of the Duke of Wellington; "The Charge of the Light Brigade," a battle lyric of Balaklava in the Crimean War; and "The Defence of Lucknow," one of the Sepoy Mutiny. "Enoch Arden" is a touching idyll of common English life; "Rizpah," a tragic idyll from Scripture narrative. "The Voyage of Maeldune" was a rarely successful reproduction of the spirit of old Celtic poetry. In 1875 the poet began a series of dramas with "Queen Mary," and continued it with "Harold," "The Falcon," "Becket," and "The Foresters," some of which were put on the stage. In 1880 he issued a volume of "Ballads," worthy of his fame. "Locksley Hall, Sixty Years After" is a fitting companion to the thoughtful poem of his youth. In the last volume appearing in his life-time was "Crossing the Bar," which was taken as his dying song. He died at Aldworth in October, 1892, and was buried in Westminster Abbey.

Tennyson from the beginning of his career was noted for the exquisite music of his verse, the exactness of his rhymes, the attention to sound as well as sense. This faculty he undoubtedly learned from Keats, though he improved it and made it thoroughly his own. He profited by the criticism of his earliest work, but without submitting unduly to the arbitrary decisions of others. To the end of his life he continued to correct and improve his work, making it more clear and harmonious. He has been censured for lack of profundity, but he does not avoid expressing thought on the great problems of existence, though he refuses to rave and gesticulate about them. His strength lay in his thorough understanding of the simple elements of life, and his ability to express their full meaning. His versification is the most perfect in the English language, and has been the model to his successors, as it was indeed to his contemporaries.

ROBERT BROWNING

Browning was in almost everything in direct contrast with his great contemporary, Tennyson. From his first utterance the latter was recognized as a sweet singer, long before he was found to be an interpreter of the human heart. The former, if listened to at all, was regarded as a speaker of dark sayings, an unintelligible discourser. But after he had unexpectedly burst into snatches of melody, attention was given to his enigmatic torrents of words, and he was discovered to be a profound analyst of souls and motives. Then the wide-spread interest of this age in the study of character caused him to be esteemed a prophet, and led to the formation of societies to observe his wonderful experiments. In the end, as Tennyson was quoted with affection, Browning was worshiped with awe. Yet he never lost his self-poise, but cheerfully kept his place in society and watched with continual interest the doings of his fellow-men.

Robert Browning was born in London in May, 1812. He belonged to the middle class, was the son of a Dissenter, and was educated privately. His first book, "Pauline" (1833), was an immature attempt to describe a philosophic life; it had, like some later poems, dramatic qualities without dramatic form. After a year's travel on the Continent he published "Paracelsus" (1835), in which the hero seeks infinite wisdom, but comes to see that knowledge without love is vain. The tragedy of "Strafford" (1837) was written for the stage, and had some success in spite of the complicated involved style which characterized all his early work. In "Sordello" (1840) he filled up the meager outline of a story suggested by Dante, and made the Italian troubadour overcome the temptation of lending himself to a faction that he might accomplish great good for mankind. In all of these works there was a certain egotism, the heroes being indeed but shadowy projections of the author's soul. But people refused to take the trouble to understand them. The series of "Bells and Pomegranates" (1846) opened with the beautiful lyrical drama of "Pippa Passes," and contained lyrics which won general praise. A friendly allusion to them by Miss Elizabeth Barrett in one of her poems led to the acquaintance of the two poets, which ripened into love and marriage. They went to Italy and resided chiefly in the Casa Guidi Palace in Florence fifteen happy years, until his wife's death in 1861. In that time Browning published "Christmas Eve and Easter Day" (1850) and "Men and Women" (1855), dedicated to his wife as "the Moon of Poets." In 1869 he boldly challenged the world with his long, complicated mediæval Italian story of "The Ring and the Book" in four volumes, containing 20,000 lines. The kernel is that a middle-aged husband, jealous of his child wife, so tormented her with ill treatment that she fled under care of a young priest, who afterwards is brought to trial before the Pope.   The case is told over and over again by the various participants, good and bad, from their several points of view, their own souls and motives being revealed in the telling.   Strange as is the form of this poem, its power must be acknowledged.

Later Browning found pleasure in skillful translations from the Greek tragedians—"Alcestis," "Agamemnon," and afterwards from the great comic poet in "Aristophanes' Apology."   But he was not merely a scholar; he was a favorite in London society.   There he found subjects of his own time in "Mr. Sludge the Medium," "Prince Hohenstiel-Schwangau," and "Bishop Blougram's Apology."   These are apologetic poems, tending to prove that a man's character is determined not by what he thinks but by what he does.   Other works continued to flow from his pen, mostly in his peculiar blank verse, sometimes narrative, sometimes dramatic monologue. His last work, "Asolando" (1889), named from Asolo, a favorite village near Venice, is thought to be one of his best, as it contains some fine lyrics.   Just after it was published he died, on December 12, 1889, at his only son's residence in Venice.

Browning deliberately set at naught the rules and usages of English speech; he used strange words, odd phrases, bad rhymes; he seemed to be in so great a hurry to deliver his message that he could not pause to select the proper terms.   Many personages in his poems used the same broken style.   In his early works he expressed through characters partly drawn from history, rather the tumult of his own soul, but as years brought the philosophic mind he became a realist and studied the characters of others as seen in life or gleaned from reading records.   All readers are constrained to admit his power of turning souls inside out, and to feel the humor and pathos of these revelations. While he took most delight in delineating character, he described external nature with freedom and force, painting it in grand outlines, with felicity of color. Considerable part of his work was dramatic, and besides the one already mentioned, "The Blot on the 'Scutcheon" and "Colombe's Birthday," were presented on the stage. He was indeed a master of dramatic character, though perhaps not of construction. But for the general public his power lies in his shorter pieces, in the spirited and beautiful lyrics; even into these he sometimes thrust his queer expressions and fantastic phrases. Perhaps "The Last Ride Together" is the most perfect, but others are more widely known.

MRS. E. B. BROWNING

By universal consent Mrs. Browning is the first of England's women poets. She had reached fame before her husband seemed ever likely to do so. Born Elizabeth Barrett at Carlton Hall, in Durham, in 1806, she was taught Greek early and wrote poetry. But the breaking of a blood-vessel weakened her frame and when sent to the sea-shore she was shocked by the drowning of her brother. Unable to be removed, she lay there a year, and when at last taken to her father's house in London, she was a confirmed invalid, doomed to a darkened room. Yet she studied in many languages and composed poems, full of feeling. "The Seraphim and Other Poems" (1838) and "The Romaunt of the Page" (1839) showed her classic taste and bore some resemblance to Shelley. The two volumes of "Poems" (1844) were more original. In "A Vision of Poets," seeking to set forth the relation of suffering to genius, she gave brief description of "the dead kings of melody" from Homer to Byron.

The public, who loudly welcomed the woman singer, gave preference to the romantic "Rhyme of the Duchess May," the pathetic "Bertha in the Lane," and the grand sacred lament of "Cowper's Grave." A report of the condition of children in the factories stirred the weak invalid to rouse the slumbering humanity of England with "The Cry of the Children." The long narrative of "Lady Geraldine's Courtship," in which she alluded flatteringly to Browning's "Pomegranates," had a romantic sequel in fact. The robust young poet called to express his thanks, was permitted to see the invalid on her sofa, became a frequent visitor, and persuaded the prisoner to marry him even against her family's wishes. Restored by love to unexpected strength, she went with him to Florence. Full expression of her passionate love to her husband was given in her pretended translations, called "Sonnets from the Portuguese :"

> A mystic shape did move
> Behind me and drew me backward by the hair,
> And a voice said in mastery, while I strove :
> 'Guess now who holds thee ?'—'Death !' I said. But there
> The silver answer rang : 'Not Death, but Love !'

The revolutionary movements in Italy excited the poet's interest, and her feeling at what she witnessed is expressed in "Casa Guidi Windows." Other political poems followed, but more labor was devoted to the long novel in blank verse, "Aurora Leigh" (1856). The chief characters are an Italian girl, highly endowed by nature, but trained in the English method, and an English gentleman compelled to forfeit her love because of his guilt toward a young countrywoman. In spite of its fervid energy, the poem could not long maintain its hold on popular sympathy. The gifted author died in June, 1861.

While Mrs. Browning by her pathetic sentiment early won general favor, critics who admired her poetic genius could not overlook her faults.   She possessed an original metrical faculty and must have been a careful observer of nature before she was confined to her sick-room.   But she allowed her fluency to carry her poems to excessive length, and used strange and superfluous words.   She was careless about rhyme, not only using mere vowel rhyme, but compelling vulgar or ridiculous pronunciation.   Her greatest failure was her attempt to put a whole novel into verse.   Yet Swinburne has lately in his energetic fashion, declared again his high admiration for "Aurora Leigh." But this and many of her shorter pieces are forgotten by the public, while memory lingers on her lyrical and narrative poems.

MINOR POETS

Caroline Elizabeth Sarah Norton (1808-1877), often called the Hon. Mrs. Norton, was a granddaughter of the famous Richard Brinsley Sheridan.   At the age of nineteen she was married to the Hon. George C. Norton, but in 1840 the union was dissolved after she had been subjected to shameful persecution for alleged infidelity. From her childhood she had written verses, and in 1831 she published "The Undying One," a poem on the Wandering Jew.   After her separation from her husband she published many tales and poems and contributed frequently to periodicals.   She was pronounced by the "Quarterly Review" "the Byron of our modern poetesses."   This indicates the intense personal passion and forceful expression of her work.   She is best known by the favorite piece for recitation, "Bingen on the Rhine."

Another woman who later touched the popular heart

with her poems was Jean Ingelow (1830-1897). She had published some tales before her reputation was gained by her "Poems" (1863). The most noted of them are "High Tide on the Coast of Lincolnshire" and "Songs of Seven," exhibiting seven stages in woman's life. Other poems and stories did not increase the popularity she had obtained as an exponent of woman's feelings.

HOOD

The contrast between the hard life struggle and the mirth-provoking works of Thomas Hood (1798-1845) is truly pathetic. He was the jester and punster of his generation, and an exquisite song writer, yet he is best remembered by two sorrowful poems, "The Song of the Shirt" and "The Bridge of Sighs," the pitiful wail of the poor seamstress and the heart-breaking lament for the drowned outcast of society. These verses awoke the popular heart to a deep sympathy with suffering and a remorseful horror for complicity in crime. Hood was the son of a poor bookseller and had learned a little of engraving before he began to write for the press. The "London Magazine," "Punch," and other periodicals published his wares, but the remuneration was scanty. For his serious poems, excellent as are "The Plea of the Midsummer Fairies" and "The Haunted House," he got so little that he was compelled, as he expressed it, to be "a lively Hood for a livelihood." Various misfortunes deprived the poor consumptive of enjoyment of his small earnings, and he had to flee to the Continent to escape the debtors' prison. When enabled to return, he edited more than one periodical with unflagging diligence and gayety in spite of the inroads of the dread disease of which he died. Shortly before the end, Sir Robert Peel awarded him a pension.

Much more cheerful, yet even shorter, was the life of a similar genius, Winthrop Mackworth Praed (1802-1839), who also died of consumption. He was educated at Eton and Cambridge, and at both displayed his talent for verse writing. He was called to the bar, served in Parliament, and held a government office. But he is remembered by his bright poems, which mingle spice, humor, and tender sentiment, or touch off gracefully social trifles. The best of his exquisite pictures is "The Vicar;" his "Speaker Asleep" is a keen thrust at Parliamentary practice.

Less popular than Hood, yet even more full of fun, was Richard Harris Barham (1788-1845) who, strange to say, was a clergyman, strictly attentive to his parochial duties. In spite of a crippled right arm, he was a diligent writer. His early charges were in smuggling districts, which furnished materials for his later "Ingoldsby Legends." He removed to London in 1821 and there became active in journalism, while not neglecting the church. In 1834, under the pseudonym "Thomas Ingoldsby," he began to contribute to the newly established "Bentley's Miscellany," the humorous stories in prose and verse, which made him famous. They were founded on old legends of mediæval saints and miracles or other discoveries of his antiquarian studies. The poetical stories were a loose, rambling metre, with unexpected doggerel rhymes, which helped the fun of the narrative. Morals, equally unexpected, were often attached. Barham was a matter-of-fact Englishman and rampant Protestant of the old High Church style. Regarding the old stories as superstitions, he found in them excellent material for his wit and fancy, and still fancied he was doing good service.

Ebenezer Elliott (1781-1849), a Yorkshire man, who won fame as "the Corn-law rhymer," was a dull boy at school, and was early put to work in an iron foundry with which his father was connected. His poetic genius was awakened by his brother's reading to him Thompson's "Seasons," and was confirmed by the bequest to his father of a curate's library, containing other poetry of a high order. His first poem, "The Vernal Walk," and many others, testified his strong love for country scenes. But his deepest feeling was stirred by the sufferings of poor mechanics and their families, and in his "Corn-Law Rhymes" (1831) he gave voice to their hatred of the tax on bread. Yet Elliott himself knew these sufferings rather by observation than experience. After carrying on the business of an iron-founder at Sheffield for twenty years he retired with a competent fortune.

"The Angel in the House," an idyl of domestic love, is the chief performance of Coventry Patmore (1823-1897). It was issued in four parts, "The Betrothal" (1854), "The Espousal" (1856), "Faithful for Ever" (1860), and "The Victories of Love" (1862). Never was the perfect blessedness of married life more sweetly or chastely sung than in this quietly beautiful and somewhat mystical poem. Patmore was a native of Essex, and for over twenty years was an assistant librarian at the British Museum. In 1877 he published anonymously "The Unknown Eros and Other Poems," indicating unabated vigor, but not adding to his fame.

Arthur Hugh Clough (1819-1861) appeared to his friends capable of accomplishing better things than his actual work. He had distinguished himself at Rugby and Oxford, but the Tractarian controversy first attracted and then repelled him. His "Bothie of Tober-na-

Vuolich" relates in hexameters the aspirations and adventures of some English students with their tutor in the Highlands. Losing his religious faith, Clough resigned his Oxford fellowship, but engaged in educational work through most of his life. "Amours de Voyage" gave his impressions of Rome, as seen in a vacation. "Dipsychus" (double-minded) is a serious poem, with fine descriptive passages. "Mari magno" (on the great sea) contains homely tales of love and marriage. Clough's scepticism mars his work both in spirit and in execution, but when he forgot it, he showed genius. Matthew Arnold lamented him in "Thyrsis."

Frederick Locker-Lampson (1821-1895) was one of the modern troubadours, touching in elegant verse the whims and fancies of society. His "London Lyrics" (1857) stand at the head of this class. As a companion volume he collected from other poets "Lyra Elegantiarum (1867) and to these added a miscellany of prose and verse, partly original, called "Patchwork."

OWEN MEREDITH

Owen Meredith is the name in literature of Robert, first Earl of Lytton (1831-1892) only son of the novelist Bulwer. He was an indefatigable writer of verse, beginning with "Clytemnestra" (1885). He belonged to the diplomatic service, and, by the favor of Lord Beaconsfield, reached the high posts of Viceroy of India in 1876, and Ambassador to Paris in 1887. His most popular works are "Lucile" (1860), an animated narrative of modern high life, and "Tannhäuser" (1861), the story of a German mediæval minstrel, who fell into the snares of Lady Venus, but repented and was saved. While residing in Constantinople, Lord Lytton translated many songs from the Servian. He had, indeed, a fine lyrical faculty, which was shown in most of his works. He had also a peculiar power of suggestive narration and of symbolism. The latter appears in his "Fables in Song" (1874), the former in "Chronicles and Characters" (1869). His "Glenaveril" (1885) is a long narrative in rhyme, more serious than "Lucile." One of his last works was a fantastic romance, "King Poppy." He died while writing the last words of a poem. Though endowed with original powers, he sometimes experimented in the style of other writers, thus bringing on himself the charge of plagiarism.

HISTORICAL LITERATURE OF THE EARLY VICTORIAN PERIOD

The literature of the Nineteenth Century has been distinguished by large and valuable additions to history. The tremendous upheaval of the French Revolution compelled men to consider from new points of view the foundations of government, and led them not only to examine more closely the process of the construction of the existing state of society, but to compare with it the remains of former civilizations. From consideration of dynasties and family compacts of sovereigns they turned to the condition and welfare of the people. "History is philosophy teaching by examples," said Bolingbroke early in the Eighteenth Century. Historians were stimulated by the later events of the same century to draw from the records of the past the proper lessons for the conduct of the present. The people were coming to assert their power and needed to be instructed in what direction to do so. After a time enlightened governments began to admit the people to their confidence; they opened the treasuries of their archives, and arranged state papers for consultation by students.

The reviews and other periodical literature furnished new opportunities for historical writers to gratify the desire of the public for information on the past as well as the present. Historians could thus make essay of their powers and trial of the public taste. Many authors who were chiefly devoted to other departments of literature not only made such occasional contributions to history, but wrote one or more volumes. Sir Walter

Scott, besides his "Life of Napoleon," retold and vivified the annals of his country in his delightful "Tales of a Grandfather." Southey prepared an elaborate "History of Brazil." His "History of the Peninsular War," though well written, was eclipsed by the more brilliant work on the same subject by the enthusiastic warrior, Sir William Napier (1786-1860), which has been pronounced "the finest military history in the English language." Dickens, in the midst of his labors as editor and novelist, found time to write a "Child's History of England." G. P. R. James compiled histories of Charlemagne and Louis XIV, which are now esteemed more highly than his novels. But attention is here given only to the great writers who have in this age reconstructed the history of the past and erected enduring monuments.

It is singular that the history of ancient Greece, told admirably in its own language by Herodotus, Thucydides and Xenophon, should in recent times have become a favorite field of exercise for historians. William Mitford (1744-1827) was the first to give zest to the study of antiquity by infusing into it his hatred of democracy. His "History of Greece" (1784-1818) is vigorously written, but is often inaccurate. It is remarkable that there should have been two restatements of that history from the Liberal side, one by Bishop Connop Thirlwall (1797-1875), which began to appear in 1835, and the other, still more radical, by George Grote (1794-1871) who was a banker and member of Parliament. Though he had not attended a university, Grote displayed accurate scholarship and gave new life to the old texts of the Greek authors. He is an ardent pleader for the Athenian democracy, and even for the sophists and demagogues. Thirlwall's "History" is more dignified and judicial in tone, but never attained the same degree of popularity.

The early history of Rome also attracted the attention of investigators as needing reconstruction on account of its fabulous character. The German scholar Niebuhr had shown the improbability of the traditions which had long been accepted, and had endeavored to extract whatever truth was concealed in them. Dr. Thomas Arnold (1795-1842), the great schoolmaster of Rugby, followed in his footsteps and retold the "History of Rome" from its foundation to the time of Hannibal. Still further valuable labor was confidently expected from him when he was made professor of modern history at Oxford, but after delivering one course of lectures, he died suddenly. Charles Merivale (1808-1894), dean of Ely, afterward undertook in his "History of the Romans Under the Empire" to bridge the gap between the end of Arnold's and the beginning of Gibbon's great history. He also prepared for the "Students' Series" a smaller "General History of Rome."

BUCKLE

A most remarkable historical monument is the incomplete "History of Civilization" by Henry Thomas Buckle (1823-1862). He had been privately educated, was wealthy and learned, but he had imbibed strong prejudices against religion and the church. With a view of expounding ultimately English civilization, he undertook first to discuss European civilization, and to show that the differences in it depended on geographical conditions and on the forms of government, civil and ecclesiastical. As examples he treated at great length Spain and Scotland; his facts are capriciously selected to suit his theory, and his arguments are one-sided. Nevertheless the clearness of his style and the aggressive force with which he pleaded his position gave his work a brief popularity, which, however, it did not retain. As it followed the French method of excessive generalization and propagated Voltaire's views, the sober English mind rejected the curious work.

HALLAM

Three great historical works form the monument of Henry Hallam. They are distinguished by their judicial impartiality, and are referred to as authorities by men of all parties. Hallam was born in 1777, the son of a dean of Bristol, and was educated at Eton and Christ Church, Oxford. He was called to the bar, but early obtained an official position which allowed him plenty of leisure for authorship. After contributing some articles to the "Edinburgh Review," he published "A View of the State of Europe During the Middle Ages" (1818), to which he added a supplemental volume thirty years later. Meantime he had issued in 1827 his "Constitutional History of England," and in 1837 his "Introduction to the Literature of Europe in the Fifteenth, Sixteenth, and Seventeenth Centuries." The two later works are really continuations of the first, though in different directions. The "Middle Ages" is a comprehensive survey of European history from the Fifth to the Fifteenth Century. The author carefully avoids generalization on the movements of society. The "Constitutional History" brought the English part down to the reign of George II. It was confined to changes in the organization of the state, and omitted personal history as much as possible. Hallam considered that the modern Whig constitutionalism was the ideal standard to which all questions should be referred, and may therefore have been too severe on Charles I and some statesmen of his century. His "Literature of Europe" is rigidly an account of the books of the period, arranged according to the dates of publication and the nature of their subjects. Biographical notices of the authors were excluded, thus diminishing the general reader's interest. But the critic's conscientiousness and accuracy are as conspicuous as his patient industry and wide range of reading. No mere display of erudition is made, but results are given as compactly as possible. His style is clear and uniform, and in the "Literature" there are passages of special beauty. Hallam died in 1859, having outlived his wife and two sons. One of the latter, Arthur Henry Hallam (1811-1833), was of most brilliant promise, and has been lamented by his friend Tennyson in the most exquisite elegy in the English language.

ALISON

Sir Archibald Alison (1792-1867) was the son of a clergyman of the same name, whose "Essay on the Principles of Taste" was long admired. The son was educated at the University of Edinburgh, was called to the bar, and was appointed sheriff of Lanarkshire. He was a strong Tory and contributed to "Blackwood's Magazine" on a variety of subjects. After thirty years of preparation he published, from 1839 to 1859, a "History of Europe" from the commencement of the French Revolution to the accession of Napoleon III. It occupied altogether eighteen volumes, yet it proved popular. But the critics condemned it for its turgid and diffuse style, for the clumsy arrangement of the material, and the poor portraiture of characters. The author's partisan prejudices often prevented him from stating cases fairly, yet the work is not so inaccurate as it has sometimes been represented. The real trouble is that it is difficult to read, as both friends and foes of his principles have admitted.

MILMAN

Henry Hart Milman (1791-1868) was distinguished as a poet and even dramatist before he became a church historian. He was educated at Eton and at Brasenose College, Oxford, and wrote several plays, of which the best, "Fazio," was acted in 1815. Then, taking orders, he became vicar at Reading, where he still wrote poetry, including some fine hymns. In 1821 he was made professor of poetry at Oxford, but the tragedy of "Anne Boleyn" (1826) closed his career as a poet. After contributing several articles to the "Quarterly Review," Milman published a "History of the Jews" (1829) which called forth censure by its tendency toward the later critical views of the Old Testament. He went on with a "History of Christianity to the Abolition of Paganism" (1840) and finally issued his ablest work, "History of Latin Christianity" (1854). This grand subject was handled with adequate erudition. The author edited Gibbon's great "History of Rome," correcting errors and adding new information. In 1849 Milman had been advanced to the deanery of St. Paul's, which is considered the highest literary preferment in the Church of England.

LINGARD

Turning now to the history of England itself, the earliest name encountered is that of John Lingard (1771-1851). His "History of England" has been praised by critics of all classes for its accuracy and fairness, in spite of his professional predilections and prejudices. He was a Roman Catholic priest, having been educated at the English college at Douay and at Crook Hall near Durham. He was professor of philosophy at Ushaw, but in 1811 withdrew to Hornby, where he composed his history. In 1817 he visited Rome to make researches in the Vatican Library, and in 1821 Pope Pius VII made him doctor of divinity. His historical work began with "The Antiquities of the Anglo-Saxon Church" (1806) which was afterward considerably enlarged. His "History of England" appeared in eight volumes, from 1819 to 1830.

MACAULAY

In popular esteem the foremost historian of the century is still the brilliant partisan Macaulay. He gives to events of the past, not too remote for general interest, a perennial freshness. He tells an entertaining or thrilling story in full detail, without delivering a philosophical lecture. His style is pointed, vigorous, and full of allusions, which add to its weight.

Thomas Babington Macaulay was born at Rothley, in Leicestershire, in 1800. He was the son of a Liverpool merchant and remarkably precocious. Sent to Trinity College, Cambridge, he distinguished himself as a debater and won prizes for poems. He had just been called to the bar in 1825 when his well-known radical article on Milton appeared in the "Edinburgh Review." This opened his literary career, and he soon obtained political rewards for his services to the Whig cause. When elected to Parliament in 1830, his first speech on Reform established his fame as an orator. In 1834 he was sent to India as a member of the Supreme Council, and prepared a code of laws for that country, which, however, was not adopted. He was returned to Parliament in 1839 as a member for Edinburgh, but in 1847 he was defeated, his support of a grant to Maynooth College having shocked the Protestantism of his constituents. During these years he had steadily contributed to the Review brilliant essays on historical, critical and miscellaneous subjects. He had also published his spirited

"Lays of Ancient Rome" (1842). He had long cherished the intention of writing the history of England from the accession of James II. To this work his time was now devoted, and in 1848 two volumes were issued. They won instant popularity and increased his fame. The electors of Edinburgh, in 1852, returned him again to Parliament without exertion on his part. In 1857 he was raised to the peerage as Baron Macaulay of Rothley. He died of heart disease in December, 1857. His personal reputation was much enhanced by the excellent biography published by his nephew, Sir George Trevelyan, which revealed his admirable private character.

Macaulay had a brilliant classical prose style which won the admiration and even the envy of his contemporaries for its effectiveness. His "Essays," dealing chiefly with the great men of English history and literature, yet including Frederick the Great and Machiavelli, have become familiar to all readers. The particular book which furnished the subject of discussion was usually briefly dismissed, while the essayist gave his own views at length. These views were stated in the most positive terms, so that his heroes became angels, and his villains almost devils who should be driven from the world. In his "History" his wide range of reading and firm grasp of results were yet more remarkably displayed. His view of the state of England at the death of Charles II is a marvelous compilation from a thousand sources, yet presenting a consistent, perfectly intelligible picture. Macaulay has been accused of suppressing or distorting the evidence in regard to some characters, but it has hardly been proved, except in the case of William Penn. In general, he took the utmost pains to be accurate, not only reading all the records of important events, but visiting the actual places. The example thus set has been followed by later historians to the great gain of truth.

CARLYLE

Like a rugged peak towering grandly above the undulations of a mountain range, stands Thomas Carlyle among the great writers of the century. He wrote histories with the inspiration of a poet, biographies with the choice precision of an artist, essays and pamphlets which combine the solemnity of a seer with the scurrility of a buffoon. Nearly forty years were requisite to raise him from the obscurity of his native corner to his predestined place among the leaders of his age, and then for forty years he swayed the minds of men or growled contemptuously at their neglect. His manifest sincerity and intense earnestness compelled respect for his repellant individuality. Beneath his savage moroseness dwelt a tender human heart, with an unshaken belief in the eternal verities.

Thomas Carlyle was born on the 4th of December, 1795, at Ecclefechan, in Dumfriesshire, Scotland. His father was a stonemason and a stern Covenanter. Thomas was sent at fifteen to the University of Edinburgh to study for the ministry, but his conscience forbade him the pulpit. He taught school for a time, and in 1822 became tutor in the Buller family. He wrote also for Brewster's "Encyclopædia" and contributed to the magazines. His special acquaintance with German was shown in his excellent translation of Goethe's "Wilhelm Meister" and his admirable "Life of Schiller." In 1826 he married Jane Welsh, a woman of brilliant intellect, who is said to have hesitated in choice between him and the gifted preacher, Edward Irving. They lived for some months in Edinburgh, but the unpolished rustic was not admitted to its literary circles. Then he resolved to retire to a small moorland farm which his wife owned at Craigenputtoch in Dumfriesshire. In this wilderness Carlyle fought his

great spiritual battle and emerged triumphant.   For earthly living he wrote for the "Edinburgh Review" many
articles on German literature, Burns, Dr. Johnson, etc.
It was a bright gleam of sunshine when Emerson made
his pilgrimage to this remote spot to honor one whose
greatness he was among the first to discern.   He had been
attracted by the fantastic essays on Clothes-Philosophy,
which were appearing in "Fraser's Magazine" under the
title, "Sartor Resartus" (The Tailor Done Over).   Their
importance was disguised by representing them as an-
notations on a book by a German professor, Diogenes
Teufelsdrökh (God-born Devilsdung).   It was really
Carlyle's autobiography, summary of philosophy and confession of faith.   By Emerson's favor the papers were
gathered into a book and published at Boston two years
before an English edition was printed.   Carlyle received
his share of the American profits.

After six years' residence at Craigenputtoch, Carlyle
removed to London and took the little house at Chelsea,
which has now been made a memorial and place of pilgrimage.   Here he completed his work on the French
Revolution, already commenced in the Scotch farm-house.
John Stuart Mill borrowed the first volume in manuscript
and lent it to his friend, Mrs. Taylor, whose housemaid
used it to kindle a fire.   Mill insisted, against Carlyle's
proud refusal, on paying for the loss, but the terrible task
of rewriting the manuscript had to be performed.   This
work, which first gave Carlyle fame, is memorable for its
creation of a prose epic style, as well as for its new mode
of viewing and interpreting history by vivid pictures.   The
"French Revolution" came out in 1837, and in spite of
furious outcries against its style and temper, gave its
author rank among the great historians of the world.
Carlyle now lectured on "German Literature," on "His-

tory" and on "Heroes and Hero-Worship," the last being printed in 1841 and becoming one of his best-known books. He discussed the political problems of the time in "Chartism" (1839), and in "Past and Present" (1843), which greatly stirred the thoughtful public. In 1845 he published his "Letters and Speeches of Oliver Cromwell," in which he did much to explain the character and deeds of that extraordinary leader.

The revolutions of 1848 filled Carlyle with indignant scorn for the weakness and stupidity of governments that did anything but govern, and henceforth he insisted on the submission of the common herd to the Strong Silent Man. In "Latter-Day Pamphlets" (1850) he discussed the "nigger" question and other political problems. In contrast with this came his "Life of Sterling" (1851), which was written as a reply to Archdeacon Julius Hare's sketch of their friend, and exhibited distinctly Carlyle's attitude towards the Church. The "History of Frederick the Great" was next undertaken, and fourteen years were spent as Mrs. Carlyle expressed it, "in the valley of the shadow of Frederick." The historian was drawn to the Prussian King by his admiration for strong individual will. Yet he became conscious of the demerits of his hero, and explained that he was called Great only "because he managed *not* to be a liar and a charlatan as his century was." Carlyle did not appreciate the making of a strong Prussia as preliminary to the formation of a new German Empire. So also he had no sympathy for the North during the American Civil War, yet, long after it was over, on reading the "Harvard Memorial Biographies," which a friend had sent him, he exclaimed in thoroughly Scotch style, "I doubt I have been wrong." He was chosen Lord Rector of Edinburgh University in 1866, and his address to the students had great success. The only drawback was that his wife was unable to attend; she died before his return to London. Carlyle poured forth the bitterness of his anguish in his "Reminiscences," which he marked to be revised before publication. Unfortunately, his executor, the historian Froude, published them without reservation, and thus brought deep reproach upon the philosopher. Carlyle survived his wife fifteen years, but did no important work in that time. "The Early Kings of Norway" was his last history. He died in 1881, aged eighty-six.

Carlyle's works are chiefly historical or biographical, though like a Hebrew prophet, he delivered many messages to his countrymen on the social and political sins or duties of the time. He denounced Disraeli's Reform bill of 1867 as "Shooting Niagara," and predicted deplorable consequences. It was well said of him, "Carlyle comprehends only the individual; the true sense of the unity of the human race escapes him." Hence he turned history as far as possible into biography of heroes. Hence, too, he insisted that the duty of each age and country is to discover its hero, and, having discovered the fated leader, to commit control of everything to him. Beyond this, the duty of every man is to work, to employ usefully for himself and others whatever talents he possesses. With loud vociferation Carlyle denounced speech, and clamored for silence, yet appeared unconscious of the self-contradiction. His peculiar style was partly due to his study of German, especially Richter, but it is more largely due to his giving vent to his native Scotch fervor, and expressing in print the twists and turns of his own thought and speech. There is great variety in his style, which changes readily from sober statements to fierce denunciation or quaint humor, to glowing enthusiasm or pathetic lamentation. His aim is always to lead men to live and act as in the presence of an eternal righteous ruler.

THEOLOGICAL WRITERS

Few writers of theological works can be treated in a history of general literature. Yet some have had such wide effect on the public mind and have given occasion for so much discussion that they claim special mention. Perhaps no one has a stronger claim than John Henry Newman (1801-1890) who, after leading the movement which gave new life to the Church of England, abandoned it for the Church of Rome, in which he was made a Cardinal. He was born in London and educated at Oxford. He held various positions in his University, and in 1827 became vicar of St. Mary's Church, which gave him opportunity by his sermons to direct the minds of the students. He had originally been an Evangelical, but his studies of the early Church led him to adopt views generally considered Roman Catholic. These were justified by his theory of development. In 1833 he began to publish "Tracts for the Times," in which he was assisted by Keble and Dr. Pusey. When Tract No. XC was condemned by the bishops the series stopped. In 1843 Newman resigned St. Mary's, and two years later he was admitted to the Church of Rome. In its communion he worked quietly. He assisted in the attempt of 1854 to establish a Catholic University in Dublin, but spent most of his time in educational work at Edgbaston, near Birmingham. In 1864, taking advantage of a charge made against him by Kingsley, he issued his famous "Apologia pro Vita Sua" as his defense. By its masterly style and careful argument it turned the public mind in his favor. In 1872 he entered into controversy with Gladstone on Vaticanism. In 1879

Pope Leo XIII advanced him to the Cardinalate, for which he visited Rome.   When he died, in August, 1890, men of various positions spoke in praise of his character.

Newman's works comprise nearly 40 volumes, and from these he had edited a selection in his later years.   Good judges reckon him among the best English prose writers. His "Sermons" are in this respect much superior to his "Development of Christian Doctrine" and "History of the Arians in the Fourth Century."   Their characteristics are simple but impressive language, moderate sentences, sparing use of illustrations and metaphors, perfect clearness, and through them a deep seriousness and solemnity.   Newman's few poems are also excellent, the best being the familiar hymn, "Lead, Kindly Light," written in 1833. "The Dream of Gerontius," a vision of death and judgment, was a product of his old age.   Soon after his admission to the Roman Church, he published two religious novels: "Callista," a story of the persecution of Christians in North Africa in the Third Century; and "Loss and Gain," a story of his own time.

Newman's early associate in the Tractarian controversy, Edward Bouverie Pusey (1800-1882) remained in the Anglican Church, and lived to see his party become dominant in it.   He edited the "Oxford Library of the Fathers," translations of early Christian writers.   His "Sermons," not so attractive in style as Newman's, were well adapted to University students.   The most notable work of his old age is the "Eirenicon," a plea for the reunion of the great Christian Churches.

In sacred verse John Keble (1792-1866) was the successor of the saintly George Herbert of the Seventeenth Century.   His "Christian Year" (1828), a series of hymns on the church festivals, elevated the religious feelings of the country and assisted the Oxford movement, which a sermon of his in 1833 started. He had a brilliant course at Oxford, taking many prizes, and in 1831 was made professor of poetry there. He wrote several of the celebrated "Tracts for the Times," but his life was chiefly spent in his country church at Hursley. Besides the "Christian Year" he published "Lyra Innocentium," hymns for children, and "Miscellaneous Poems." All are characterized by perfect taste as well as high spirituality, careful diction and melody.

One of the effective promoters of the Broad Church movement, which grew out of resistance to the extreme views of the Tractarians, was Frederick Denison Maurice (1805-1872). He had been educated at Cambridge, but being then a Unitarian, could not obtain a degree. Under the influence of Coleridge, his views were changed, and he went to Oxford, got his degree, and was ordained in 1834. His rejection of the doctrine of eternal punishment caused him to lose a professorship in King's College, Cambridge. Others who were charged with heresy found in him an able defender, but he refused to form a party. He was a promoter of Christian Socialism, and of plans for the benefit of workingmen. His longest work is "History of Moral Philosophy," of which branch he was made professor at Cambridge in 1866. His writings were numerous and had great influence on other clergymen rather than on the public directly.

More widely known and more prominent in literature was Arthur Penrhyn Stanley (1815-1881) commonly called Dean Stanley, from his position in Westminster Abbey. He was the son of a bishop and became the son-in-law and biographer of his teacher, Dr. Arnold, of Rugby. After a distinguished course at Oxford, he held various preferments in the Church and was from 1856 to 1863 professor of ecclesiastical history at Oxford. Church history was the chief field of his studies and writings. Among his works are "Sinai and Palestine" (1854), the result of a tour in the Holy Land; "Lectures on the Greek Church" (1861), derived from a visit to Russia; "History of the Jewish Church" (1843), a volume on "The Church of Scotland," and "Christian Institutions" (1881). Regarding the Church as an historical society, necessarily subject to variations in different ages, he delighted to trace its growth and development. But he sought also to promote in his own day a more comprehensive spirit of Christianity, and took every opportunity to show his recognition of it in other men. Hence he frequently entered into controversy to protect those whom he considered unjustly attacked. The term Broad Church was originated by him to indicate the proper attitude of the English Church towards clashing opinions and doctrines. When canon of Canterbury he prepared the interesting "Memorials of Canterbury" (1855), and later he prepared the still more valuable "Memorials of Westminster Abbey" (1867). In 1878 he visited the United States and afterwards published "Addresses and Sermons" delivered there. The leading characteristic of his speaking and writing was the universality of his religious sympathies, finding good in all men.

SCIENTIFIC LITERATURE OF THE EARLY VICTORIAN PERIOD

Science has occupied a prominent and steadily increasing place in the publications of the Nineteenth Century. Most of these are not considered to belong to literature, yet some, from being addressed to the general public rather than scientific experts, and from the excellence of the style in which they are presented, are allowed at least honorable mention. Among the earlier writers were the chemist Sir Humphry Davy, the Scotch encyclopædist, Sir David Brewster, the astronomer, Sir John Herschel, the geologist, Sir Charles Lyell. But none of their writings attracted so much attention as one which appeared anonymously in 1844, "The Vestiges of Creation," but which was eventually known to be the work of Robert Chambers, distinguished both as publisher and editor. It was, as he said, "the first attempt to connect the natural sciences into a history of creation." It treated of the formation of the solar system, then of the earth in its geological periods and the kinds of life found in each, the origin of animals and of man. Although the author tried to show that the order of creation indicated by scientific research agreed with the Biblical account, the book was strongly condemned by the theologians. But fifteen years later, a bolder speculator, more thoroughly equipped with scientific knowledge, by publishing "The Origin of Species," revolutionized the whole world of thought.

DARWIN

Charles Robert Darwin, the greatest man of science of his time, was born at Shrewsbury in 1809. He was the son of Dr. Robert W. Darwin, a physician, and grandson of Dr. Erasmus Darwin, who wrote a didactic poem called "The Botanic Garden." Charles went to Glasgow to study medicine, and afterwards to Cambridge, where, under the influence of Prof. Henslow, he acquired a liking for zoölogy and botany. On taking his degree in 1831, he received an appointment without pay on the Beagle, a vessel about to sail for South America on a scientific cruise. Five years were spent in the Pacific Ocean, during which Darwin laid the foundation of his theory. When he returned the Government granted him £1,000 to prepare a full account of his observations and discoveries. The first result was a very entertaining "Narrative of the Surveying Voyages," which was followed by the "Zoölogy" and some geological treatises, including one on "The Structure of Coral Reefs" (1842). Darwin's health was much impaired by his voyage. In 1839 he married his cousin, and having a moderate fortune, he selected a house at Down, in Kent, where he was able to carry on his ingenious experiments in regard to pigeons and domesticated animals. In 1844 he wrote a sketch of his conclusions on the formation of species by natural selection. Later he communicated a paper on his views to a few scientists, but in 1858 he was surprised at receiving a letter from Alfred R. Wallace, then in the East Indies, containing the same theory. By the advice of friends, Mr. Wallace's letter and Darwin's paper were read to the Linnæan Society in 1858. In the next year Darwin's "Origin of Species" was published, and at once scored a success. The sensation and discussion extended far beyond scien-

tific circles. The argument was so clear and so well supported by experiments that most readers were convinced
that in the struggle for existence and survival of the fittest
there was adequate explanation of the facts of the animal
world.

The author went steadily on with his experiments and
gathered material for an enlargement of his theory. In
"The Variation of Plants under Domestication" (1868),
new arguments were added, and finally, in "The Descent
of Man" (1871), the conclusion which had been anticipated was formally reached. The doctrine of evolution
was completely formulated. The non-scientific world had
loudly protested against the first work, but able controver-
sialists had defended its conclusions, so that the later met
with much less opposition. Darwin himself was always
cautious in his experiments and careful not to draw un-
warranted inferences from them. His clear and pleasing
style went far in winning attention to his arguments. His
sincerity in declaring his views and his generosity in
acknowledging the help of others made all scientists his
friends. To the end of his life he continued adding to his
scientific discoveries. His "Expression of the Emotions
in Man and Other Animals" emphasized the connection
extending through animated nature. One of his latest
treatises was "The Formation of Vegetable Mould
Through the Action of Worms" (1881). He died April
19, 1882.

HUXLEY

Thomas Henry Huxley (1825-1895) was not only a
scientist, but a ready writer on many topics. He was born
at Ealing, studied medicine, and became a doctor in the
navy. While off the coast of Australia natural history
occupied much of his time, and his discoveries procured

for him admission to the Royal Society on his return in
1851. He then began to lecture at the Royal School of
Mines, and soon became one of the directors of the official
side of scientific life in London. Already noted as a comparative anatomist, palæontologist and microscopist, he
became an ardent defender of Darwinism. He wrote for
the London Times its review of the "Origin of Species."
His own work on this question is "Man's Place in Nature"
(1863). Visiting the United States in 1876, he lectured
on evolution, and on his return published his "American
Addresses." One of his noted works was "The Crayfish"
(1877), commended as a model scientific treatise. In
1880 Huxley was appointed inspector of fisheries, but five
years later he retired on account of ill health. In 1883 he
had been made president of the Royal Society, and in 1892
a member of the Privy Council. Throughout his career
he took an interest in philosophical discussion, as was
shown in his treatises on Descartes and Hume. At its
close he stated his main object to have been "to promote
the application of scientific methods of investigation to all
the problems of life." Believing that knowledge of God
is beyond the reach of man, he opposed theological speculation, and, objecting to the name "skeptic" (doubter),
he invented the term "agnostic" (one who does not know)
to indicate his position. His "Essays" were collected in
nine volumes in 1894. After his death in June, 1895, his
scientific publications were collected in four volumes.

TYNDALL

Another scientist who claims attention by felicity of
style is John Tyndall (1820-1893). He was born near
Carlow, Ireland, and became an assistant in the Ordnance
Survey in 1839. Afterwards he was a railway engineer

at Manchester and taught physics in Queenwood College. He pursued special studies in magnetism in Germany, and in 1857 obtained the degree of Doctor at Marburg. He had already been professor of natural philosophy at the Royal Institution in London, and in 1867 he was made its superintendent. His noted works are "Heat Considered as a Mode of Motion" (1863), "On Radiation" (1865), "Dust and Disease." He spent many vacations in Switzerland studying the glaciers, and published some books on mountain-climbing. In 1872 he lectured in the United States, and gave the proceeds for the promotion of scientific study in this country. In 1874, at the meeting of the British Association at Belfast, he delivered an address defending the cause of science, claiming for it complete freedom in its own domain, and excluding religion from the field of knowledge, but allowing it exercise in the region of emotion. In his explanation of evolution, he said: "I discern in . . . matter . . . the promise and potency of all terrestrial life," yet he also said: "The whole process of evolution is the manifestation of a Power absolutely inscrutable to the intellect of man," and declared himself not a rank materialist. He did much to popularize science by his lucid expositions. His "Fragments of Science" are full of entertaining reading.

PERIODICAL LITERATURE AND CRITICISM

Dickens, who was much more than a novelist, gave a new impulse to periodical literature by starting "Household Words" on lines of his own devising. Charles Knight and others had in the thirties issued weekly journals which made popular instruction their chief aim. Dickens sought to meet the public who had shown their approval of his novels, to give them rational entertainment by lively and picturesque descriptions of places, travels and whatever was of general interest. While he wrote much himself, and obtained novels from Bulwer and Lever, he gathered around him a staff of younger men whom he specially trained for this work. The plan proved successful, not only in the first form, but in "All the Year Round."

In 1859 "Macmillan's Magazine" was started with the design of giving for a shilling (instead of 2 1-2 shillings, the price of older monthlies), a supply of literature by the Kingsleys and writers of equal excellence. Almost immediately the rival "Cornhill Magazine" appeared with Thackeray as editor, and with illustrations from some of the best artists. It maintained a high literary tone, Matthew Arnold and Ruskin being among its contributors. Its success was seen in its unprecedented sale of 100,000 copies. The desire to reach the widest possible audience prevented these magazines from taking distinct sides in politics.

Weekly newspapers had for a long time been published whose chief object was to comment on public affairs. "The Examiner," founded in 1808 by Leigh Hunt and his brother, had a brilliant career of nearly seventy years, un-

der various editors, as an advocate of the Liberal cause.
"The Spectator" was founded in 1828 to represent the
attitude of more orthodox Liberals towards the questions
of the day. It attained a high reputation for its unswerv-
ing honesty. In recent years it has represented the Broad
Church attitude in regard to public affairs. It departed
from Gladstone's policy when he began to advocate Home
Rule for Ireland. The "Saturday Review," founded about
1840, as an independent Tory paper, has always been imbued with classical culture. Avoiding the scandalous per-
sonalities of earlier satirical papers, it commented freely
and sharply on the public utterances and records of prominent men, and waged relentless war on folly and igno-
rance. It was written "by gentlemen for gentlemen," and
became the highest critical authority in politics, literature
and social matters. It still pursues its well-marked course,
brilliant in execution, but critical rather of evil, than inspiring to good.

Sir Arthur Helps (1813-1875) was respectable as a
historian and essayist, and was honored by being chosen
by Queen Victoria to edit the speeches of her husband and
her own "Journals of Life in the Highlands." He was
educated at Eton and Cambridge, where he was a friend
of Tennyson. Afterwards he was secretary to several
ministers, and of the Privy Council, and used his leisure
in essays and historical writing. His most popular work
is "Friends in Council" (1847), which reports the discussion of ethical and æsthetic questions by a group of well
educated persons. Occasionally a slight story is introduced
to illustrate the attitude of a disputant. Helps had already
published biographies of Columbus and the Spanish Con-
querors of the New World, and he combined these studies
in his "History of the Spanish Conquest in America"
(1855-61). The latter, though accurate and carefully

written, has not superseded Prescott. Helps, having won
a wide circle of readers, published more dialogues and
essays and one mildly philosophic romance, "Realmah."
For his editorial services to the Queen he was knighted in
1872.

MATTHEW ARNOLD

Matthew Arnold (1822-1888) was distinguished as
both poet and critic, but especially in the latter capacity.
He was the eldest son of Dr. Thomas Arnold, of Rugby,
and was educated at Oxford. For most of his life he was
a government inspector of schools.   His first book of
poems, "The Strayed Revellers" (1849) was published
anonymously; his second, "Empedocles on Etna" (1853)
was recalled after a few copies were sold. Then he issued
a collection from these with a preface discussing poetry.
He maintained that true poetry depends on the subject
and its appropriate treatment, not on occasional bursts
of beautiful thought. Arnold was professor of poetry at
Oxford from 1857 to 1867. Though strongly influenced
by Wordsworth, his high culture disposed him to go back
to Greek literature for form and models. He was the
poet of thought rather than of life. Hence he was the
poet of the Universities, but did not reach the people.
Among his longer poems the most notable are "Sohrab
and Rustum," a tragic narrative from Persia; "The Sick
King in Bokhara;" "The Scholar-Gipsy," which describes
finely the country around Oxford; and "Thyrsis," a noble
elegy on his friend Clough. Many of his short poems are
full of romantic grace, expressed in a classical style.

A new era was opened in his career when he began
to publish "Essays in Criticism," which were collected in
1865. They noted and satirized English lack of culture,
and pointed out what the French Academy had done for

common writing. The ordinary Briton, absorbed in practical and material things, indifferent to art and intellectual pleasure, was held up to scorn as a Philistine—an enemy of light—a term borrowed from the German universities. Criticism was declared to be "a disinterested endeavor to learn and propagate the best that is known and thought in the world." The essays had considerable effect on the professional critics, as well as on the public. Henceforth the long reviews were more animated, the short ones less flippant.

Arnold being encouraged to go on, entered the theological field, for which he was less qualified by knowledge and training. Yet his "Literature and Dogma," "God and the Bible," "St. Paul and Protestantism" were none the less popular. With keen wit and a lordly air he attacked the crude notions and palpable inconsistencies of common beliefs. He insisted that the language of the Bible is not fixed and scientific, but fluid and literary. To interpret its phraseology as precise leads to absurdities. But the new definitions he proposed deserve little favor. He dwelt on the name God, and defined it as "the Eternal not-ourselves which makes for righteousness;" salvation is "a harmonious perfection only to be won by cultivating many sides in us." His earnest desire was for "sweetness and light." He taught that the way to gain a higher life is by self-renunciation.

After some years Arnold returned to pure literary work, varying it with political discussion. He never meddled with art. For books of selections from Byron, Shelley and Wordsworth he wrote introductions of varying value, that on Wordsworth being his best. He made two visits to the United States, lecturing in the principal cities, but offended the Bostonians by his verdict on Emerson, pronouncing him neither a poet nor a philosopher, but acknowledging him as a seer. His "Discourses in America" contained several utterances as little likely to be acceptable to his hearers. Yet he won credit by having the courage of his convictions. Hardly had he returned to England, when he died suddenly in April, 1888.

RUSKIN

The greatest master of English prose is John Ruskin, who after setting out to be an artist, became an art-critic, and thence proceeded to be a critic of everything pertaining to human life. He was born in London in 1819, the only son of a wealthy wine merchant. After a strict religious training at home, he was educated at Oxford, and journeyed on the Continent. After some years' study of art he published, in 1843, the first volume of his "Modern Painters. By an Oxford Graduate." It was a revelation of a new world to art-neglecting, dim-eyed England, immersed in business and politics. In that country æsthetics had not been cultivated; few paintings were publicly exhibited, private collections were small and limited. The new critic, or rather prophet of art, deeply imbued with the Romantic revival, and devoted to Sir Walter Scott, found in the splendid nature-painting of J. W. M. Turner a noble realization of his own ideas, and became the herald of his genius. But he had to teach an ignorant, hostile crowd, and he assailed names hallowed by tradition. He issued a second volume in 1846, and the fifth in 1860, having remodeled the plan on which he started. Meantime his "Seven Lamps of Architecture" (1849) applied to another department the principles on which he insisted, that true art involves the highest morality. The seven lamps are sacrifice, truth, power, beauty, life, memory, obedience. The "Stones of Venice" (1853) treated of sculpture in the same grand way, working ethics into essential relation with æsthetics. In his enthusiasm for art he insisted that beauty is utility, and in the "Political Economy of Art" (1858) he sought to combine what had been considered opposing elements.

Ruskin's views on art, presented with splendid rhetorical force, made constant headway. Though for a while derided, his influence as an art-teacher rose. He was the inspirer of the Pre-Raphaelite movement, which flourished about 1850, but afterwards dissolved. Ruskin was made Slade professor of fine arts at Oxford in 1870, and gave £5,000 to endow a master of drawing. Meantime he had issued a great number of small works with fantastic titles, often in Latin. Among these were "Unto this Last" (1862), opposing common views of political economy; "Sesame and Lilies" (1865), treating of female education; "The Crown of Wild Olive" (1866); "Queen of the Air" (1869). He came to advocate socialistic views, and advanced impracticable projects for the benefit of working men. Though his theories were almost universally rejected, particular applications were adopted. Art and art-literature became popular. But among the new generation of artists there was opposition to his teaching. They insisted on art for art's sake only. Ruskin's royal dogmatism on all subjects provoked revolt, yet his works were eagerly read. For many years (1871-1884) he published at irregular intervals rambling papers called "Fors Clavigera." When it was pointed out that he sometimes contradicted himself, his answer was easy: "I never met with a question yet, which did not need, for the right solution of it, at least one positive and one negative answer, like an equation of the second degree. Mostly, matters of any consequence are three-sided, or four-sided, or polygonal; and the trotting round a polygon is severe work for people any way stiff in their opinions."

In 1885 Ruskin began to issue his charming, frank, complacent autobiography, "Præterita," full of his usual digressions into all manner of subjects. Many of his essays were collected in "Arrows of the Chace." His later writings are often colloquial in style, though sometimes rising into passages of grand eloquence. From the first he had been master of a grand ornate style, surpassing in evenness of power "Christopher North" and DeQuincey. It was sometimes unduly florid, tending to become blank verse in prose. Yet this tendency was held somewhat in check by regard for the beauties of nature and art which he aimed to describe. He excelled Kingsley in his gorgeous descriptions of scenery. As regards matter, his works abounded in childish crotchets and feminine dislikes. In ideas he was an unsafe guide, full of visionary notions. His ample fortune has been largely diminished by his liberal gifts to various schemes for promoting art and benefiting workingmen. His most remarkable self-sacrifice was his relinquishing his wife to the painter Millais when he found that they had fallen in love with each other.

THIRD OR LATER VICTORIAN PERIOD—
1870-1899

The period from 1860 to 1870 was the heyday of Liberalism and Reform. A willing ear was lent to all who had proposals for the welfare of mankind. So complete was the tendency in popular sentiment that the astute Disraeli, always awake to the stirring of the social breezes, persuaded the reluctant Tories to adopt Parliamentary reform extending popular suffrage, and thus take the "leap in the dark"—"shooting Niagara," as Carlyle vigorously phrased it. Liberalism won new political victories, including the disestablishment of the Irish Church and the Educational Reform of 1870. It looked steadily ahead for new triumphs.

Literature reflected this spirit of hopeful confidence. Perodical literature put forth new ventures as at the beginning of the Century. Writers abounded, and newcomers were eagerly welcomed. The public listened readily to new claimants for its regard, whether their subject was society or philosophy, science or religion, the times before the flood or the topics of to-day. In this era of free discussion a new tendency sprang up alongside of the prevalent, progressive, hopeful spirit. The doctrine of Evolution, put forth scientifically by Darwin, and extended philosophically by Herbert Spencer, was at first stoutly opposed, after a time cautiously admitted as a possible or probable theory, and still later almost universally affirmed. So far reaching was this theory that as soon as it was fairly considered it had its effect not only on natural science but on history, the record of human development. It had its effect on religion, on ethics, on poetry, on essays, on fiction, on social life, on politics. New publications and new writers rose to advocate and apply it in every direction. For many it removed the firm basis of past beliefs and led to doubt and pessimism. Some it turned to study of remote races and times. It gave importance to hitherto neglected customs and superstitions and roused curiosity respecting savage tribes.

That period inaugurated a new era of travel and exploration. The Suez Canal opened a new route between east and west. Darkest Africa was brought to light. Japan was opened to Western civilization. Every great nation had its expedition to make a dash for the North Pole. In every part of the world there was running to and fro and knowledge was increased. All this activity was reflected in the pages of literature. It gave new theories to the journalist, to the light essayist, to the sober statistician, to the thoughtful philosopher, and to the soaring poet. It was the germ of imperial expansion, which was soon to prevail in Great Britain, and has, to the astonishment of all, taken firm hold on the American mind to-day.

During this period writers have come more than ever to look to the people for remuneration of their services of instruction, entertainment, moral and intellectual uplifting. The immense circulation of newspapers and periodicals has caused a demand for the labors of talented writers which has proved more remunerative than the gifts of sovereigns and noble patrons in former centuries. Nor has this reward been carelessly, or unwisely distributed. Compare the list of the poets laureate of England from Ben Jonson to Alfred Austin with the leading names on the catalogues of publishers of to-day. The pensions bestowed by the British government to-day are regulated by the Prime Minister, who is guided by the enlightened

criticism of the press. The literary pension list of the
past sixty years is a roll of honor, every one borne on it
has done something to elevate, instruct or entertain his
fellowmen.

It is not because Queen Victoria has had any special
interest in literature or has given marked encouragement
to authors that this period bears her name. She has published some books of personal interest, and she has enlisted the services of a graceful writer in behalf of her husband's memory. But her name is stamped on this literature as her effigy is stamped on the coins of the realm,
because she is, in her station, the accepted embodiment of
the unity of the empire. During the early part of this
period she maintained a seclusion, perhaps too strict, out
of respect for her consort's memory. Later she has
occasionally discharged the public functions belonging to
her exalted place. At all times she has borne well the
"fierce white light which beats upon a throne." But it has
belonged to a mightier power to direct the varying course
of English literature.

The reviews, which did much to stimulate and elevate
literature at the opening of the Century, had fallen into
the background toward its close. The "Edinburgh,"
"Quarterly," and "Westminster" are still issued regularly
and contain able articles, but they no longer exert the
power and command the obedience which once they did.
Of the monthlies, "Blackwood's" still holds its own, main-
tains the same political views, and furnishes reading of
the same quality as of yore. "Fraser's," which for a time
was edited by Froude, and had brilliant success, declined
from its prestige under his successor. It was bought by
Longman, who, finding it difficult to restore its fortunes,
changed it in 1882 to "Longman's Magazine," lowered its
price, and sought to please less critical readers. "Mac-

millan's Magazine" continues to be marked by the fine
style and correct taste which characterized it at the start.

A new impulse was given to periodical literature by
the establishment of the "Fortnightly Review" in 1865.
The popular monthlies, seeking to reach all classes of readers, had tabooed politics and accepted only comparatively
light literature. But there was a large number of thoughtful persons who wished for careful statement and sober
discussion of the questions of religion and politics constantly brought forward. The "Fortnightly," intended
for this class, seemed to take the "Revue des Deux
Mondes" for its model. It was edited at first by George
H. Lewes, and afterwards by John Morley, but in 1882
passed into the charge of T. H. S. Escott, and again in
1887 to that of Frank Harris. At first, as its name indicated, it was published every second week, but afterward
became a monthly without change of name. It was Liberal
in politics, but on other questions it solicited contributions
from leading thinkers without regard to their special
views. Yet as a fact, it favored agnosticism by giving
prominence to its advocates.

This agnostic bias of the "Fortnightly" led to the
establishment of the "Contemporary Review" in 1866.
It had the same general features, was Liberal in politics,
but Christian in tone. It was edited at first by Dean
Alford, but in 1870 passed to James Knowles. In 1877
the latter being denied by the publishers the freedom which
he deemed essential to the welfare of the Review, left it
and founded the "Nineteenth Century," which also proved
successful. These three Reviews still flourish, and furnish to their readers discussion of all important questions
by able writers. The names of the contributions are in
nearly every case given. In 1883 the "National Review"
was established to support the Conservative cause. It is

attempted new Parliamentary reform. But the crafty Disraeli outwitted him, persuading even the Tory party to adopt more radical measures and take "a leap in the dark." But the Liberals were soon restored to power, and Gladstone first became Prime Minister in 1868. In contradiction of the arguments of his own early book, he soon brought about the disestablishment of the Irish Church. The Education Bill of 1870 did much to popularize instruction. The advocates of every advance movement appealed to Gladstone to take up their cause, but the body of Parliamentary supporters fell off. Being defeated at the polls in 1874, he soon announced his retirement from political strife. No competent successor was found in the Liberal party. The Bulgarian atrocities of 1877 rekindled the zeal of the Grand Old Man, and in 1880 by a memorable campaign he not only carried the district of Mid-Lothian but returned to Parliament with a splendid majority at his back. Desiring to settle the troublesome Irish question, Gladstone granted, in 1881, a new land law for that island. Great as this relief was, more was demanded. Coercion failed to restore quiet. The Home-Rulers steadily obstructed Parliamentary business. Finally, in 1886, Gladstone, in a supreme oratorical effort, introduced a measure granting Ireland autonomy, but the bill divided the Liberal party, a large section becoming Liberal-Unionists. Yet in 1892 Gladstone's followers won at the polls, and he again became Prime Minister, pledged to the same policy. The Home Rule bill passed the House of Commons, but was rejected by the Lords in September, 1893. In the following March the veteran statesman finally retired from political life. He died May 19, 1898, having suffered much from cancer in the face.

Gladstone was a great Parliamentary leader, a master of finance, and after he had fairly entered on his career, a steady advocate of reform in English government and of liberty and progress in other nations. The hostility which he encountered in the later years of his activity was due not merely to his advocacy of Home Rule for Ireland, but to his resistance to the growing desire for the expansion of the British Empire. He had special gifts as an orator— a grand presence, a clear, ringing voice, a brilliant eye, a thorough sincerity, and an overpowering enthusiasm. But he had faults of speech which appeared still more in his writing and were pointed out by Macaulay even in the review already quoted: "His rhetoric, though often good of its kind, darkens and perplexes the logic which it should illustrate. Half his acuteness and diligence, with a barren imagination and a scanty vocabulary, would have saved him from almost all his mistakes. He has one gift most dangerous to a [philosophical] speculator—a vast command of a kind of language, grave and majestic, but of vague and uncertain import."

It was his work on "The State in Relation to the Church" (1839), which gave Macaulay the opportunity for this criticism. Gladstone had early acquired fondness for Greek literature, and in the intervals of his political career he published "Studies on the Homer and the Homeric Age" (1858), and other similar books, including a "Homeric Primer," in which he maintained very conservative views about that poet. Still insisting that the truest relaxation is to be found in change of employment, the statesman frequently contributed to leading reviews on literary and miscellaneous topics. Many of these articles were collected in his "Gleanings of Past Years" (8 vols., 1879), but many more were written subsequently. Perhaps his most interesting essays are those of a biographical character—as on Bishop Patteson, Leopardi, Daniel O'Connell. Americans are attracted by his "Kin Beyond Sea."

After he had retired from political life, he amused himself by translating Horace, and toward the close of his life, as a pious tribute to the great philosophical defender of religion, he edited "The Works of Bishop Butler."

MORLEY

John Morley is well known as a Liberal statesmen, and has been frequently mentioned as a possible leader of his party in the House of Commons, yet he is really and essentially a literary man, and has done more for literature than for politics. He was born at Blackburn, Lancashire, in 1838, graduated at Oxford and was called to the bar. He became editor of the "Literary Gazette," and in 1867 of the "Fortnightly Review," which owed its success to his efforts. To this he joined charge of the "Pall Mall Gazette" in 1880. But in February, 1883, he was elected to Parliament from Newcastle-upon-Tyne as an advanced Liberal. He now withdrew from editorial duties except those of "Macmillan's Magazine," whch he held until 1886. In Parliament he soon rose to be an effective debater, and on the platform he became one of the chief speakers. Gladstone, in 1886, and again in 1892, made him Chief Secretary for Ireland. Morley has since shared the fortunes of the Liberal party, while remaining steadfast to the policy of Home Rule for Ireland.

To literature Morley has contributed a number of biographical studies of the highest value—"Edmund Burke" (1867), "Voltaire" (1872), "Rousseau" (1876), "Richard Cobden" (1881), and "Diderot and the Encyclopædists" (1878). His essays on historical, literary and social topics were collected in "Critical Miscellanies" (1871 and 1877). Morley was drawn to the French biographies by his interest in the rise of the democratic, socialistic and sceptical views which in modified forms have come to prevail in his own time. He is a sympathetic interpreter of the views and suggestions of those reformers for the amelioration of society, however vague and impracticable their schemes might be. In spite of the audacity of his utterances on religious questions, Morley, by his clearness of style and skill in presentation of opinions and arguments, won the regard of his readers. In his later works he is more restrained and yet equally effective. Besides the writings already mentioned be published two excellent treatises "On Compromise" (1874) and "Aphorisms" (1887).

The Conservative leader of the House of Commons, Arthur James Balfour, nephew of Lord Salisbury, is an able writer on philosophical subjects. His most important treatises are "The Foundations of Belief" and "An Apology for Philosophic Doubt."

HISTORICAL LITERATURE OF THE LATER VICTORIAN PERIOD

More than 130 years ago the historian Robertson wrote: "The universal progress of science during the two last Centuries, the art of printing, and other obvious causes, have filled Europe with such a multiplicity of histories and with such a vast collection of historical materials that the term of human life is too short for the study or even the perusal of them." If this was true in his day, how much more true is it at the present time. In spite of all the labor-saving inventions, the historical student is more than ever overwhelmed with the countless issues of the press, the publications of governments, societies, antiquarians and fellow laborers. The result is that for his main work he is compelled to renounce vast ambitions, and to restrict himself to single epochs. In slight essays he may take a rapid survey of great regions or important events apart from his chosen field. The reviews and magazines give ready admission to such sketches and they help to give him necessary practice in writing and supply the needy student with means for his more important work. Hence we have Freeman's "Historical Essays" and Froude's "Short Studies," which are more attractive to the general reader than their more solid work. But the vast learning and minute research which went to form the latter were equally requisite in the former. Still that genius may find a way to accomplish what common sense pronounces impossible, is perhaps proved by the labor of John Richard Green.

FREEMAN

Although blessed with an ample fortune, Edward
Augustus Freeman (1823-1892) wrote diligently as for
daily bread, not merely the great histories which bring
him solid fame, but monographs and articles for reviews,
magazines and newspapers, on almost all manner of subjects. Yet through them all one spirit is easily traced.
"History," said he, "is past politics; politics is present history." These two subjects, which he pronounced one and
the same, dominate nearly all his writings. He was born
at Harbourne, in Staffordshire, in 1823, and was educated
at Trinity College, Oxford. His earliest writing was on
architecture, treating of church restoration and the cathedrals of England. The general interest in the Crimean
War first drew him into his larger field, leading him to
prepare a "History of the Saracens." When the American
Civil War was raging he began a "History of Federal
Government from the Achæan League to the Disruption
of the American Republic." But the work was suspended
when only one volume was completed. The title of this
work shows his too great confidence in his own judgment
as to results, yet he was passionately fond of truth, and
spent much time not only in ascertaining facts for his own
works, but in controverting the incorrect statements of
others. The architectural studies which led to the detection of some of these errors, probably gave him a bent
in this direction, and his writing for the "Saturday
Review" helped it. His greatest work is the "History of
the Norman Conquest" (6 vols., 1867-76), written in a
graphic style and abounding in evidence of careful
research. In fact, the research and consequent discussion
are too fully displayed, often occupying in notes and
appendixes more than the rest of each volume. In this

work the attention is confined to public men and leading events, to William and Harold, and the battles between them; the actual condition of the people, Saxon and Norman, is not regarded. But the characters are carefully portrayed and the story is told with animation. As part of his passion for accuracy he insisted on spelling Anglo-Saxon names in the old style, while he Anglicized the French names in a queer fashion. A "Short History of the Norman Conquest" (1880) was afterward prepared, and the larger one was extended in the "Reign of William Rufus" (1882). Meantime, from the numerous contributions to reviews were collected "Historical Essays" (3 series, 1875-80). Several of his works treated of the Turks and their government, to which he was bitterly opposed. Others related to the growth of the British constitution, and to various forms of government. In 1881 Freeman visited America, lecturing in the principal cities; these lectures on the development of the English race were published, as were also his "Impressions of the United States" (1883). His latest great work was a "History of Sicily" (3 vols., 1888-92), which was left incomplete. Freeman died at Alicante, in Spain, in March, 1892.

FROUDE

The greatest historian of recent times, most brilliant if not absolutely accurate in details, was James Anthony Froude. His character and career afford many contrasts with those of Freeman, who frequently took occasion to point out Froude's mistakes, yet without much diminishing the regard felt for his history. Froude was born in 1818, the son of a clergyman, and was educated at Westminster and Oxford. Coming under the influence of Newman, he took part in the Tractarian movement, and assisted in writing "Lives of the English Saints." But when Newman entered the Roman Church, Froude recoiled and, falling into scepticism, wrote "The Nemesis of Faith" (1849), which was severely censured. Carlyle now became his adviser. From conscientious motives Froude gave up his college fellowship, and sought to make a living by literary work, writing for "Fraser's Magazine" and the "Westminster Review," the essays that were afterward collected in "Short Studies." But his chief work is the "History of England from the Fall of Wolsey to the Defeat of the Spanish Armada" (12 vols., 1856-70). It was founded on original research, on a careful examination of the documents of the period, especially the acts of Parliament. These, he insisted, must be correct in fact, while narratives would partake the prejudices of the writer, especially if an ecclesiastic. Froude endeavored to restore life to the past, to render the personages introduced more than mere lay-figures. And he succeeded in presenting Henry VIII, Queen Catharine, Mary Queen of Scots, Mary of England, and Elizabeth as actual human persons, though whether they preserved exact resemblance to the originals was keenly disputed. Froude was possessed not only with artistic sense, but with intense patriotic feeling, which made him believe and assert that in the main England had acted right in the momentous crisis of the Reformation. He regarded ecclesiasticism as injurious to genuine morality. These were undoubtedly the motives of his selection of this epoch as his theme. Another subject fruitful in controversy was next handled in "The English in Ireland" (3 vols., 1871-74). This strongly partisan work, which supported the general course of the alien rulers, offended the Irish Nationalists without satisfying English readers. Froude was then sent by the British Government to visit and report on the colonies. The result is seen in his "Oceana," a general sketch, and "The English in the West Indies." The author's reports and recommendation to the Government called forth angry replies from the colonists, and were never acted upon. Froude was appointed by Carlyle his literary executor, and as such gave to the world the reproachful "Reminiscences," which the writer had marked not to be published without revision. The result was to expose the bickerings of the Carlyle household, and exhibit the philosopher as a chronic faultfinder, snarling at everybody. His admirers were intensely displeased and threw the blame on Froude for not suppressing or discreetly editing the papers put in his charge. But the bold writer went steadily on his course. Eventually when Freeman, his severest critic, died, Froude was appointed to succeed him as professor of history at Oxford. He delivered three courses of lectures, which were published in "The Life and Letters of Erasmus," "English Seamen of the Sixteenth Century," and "Lectures on the Council of Trent." They give further example of the qualities seen in his previous historical works—lively picturesque style, skill in rendering characters and incidents as real. Froude died in October, 1894.

MAINE

Still another great writer in the historical field was Sir Henry Sumner Maine (1822-1888), whose special department was the development of law and the organization of society. Educated at Christ's Hospital and Cambridge, he graduated in 1844, and became Professor of Civil Law. In 1862 he was called to India to take part in legislative reform. On his return, in 1870, he was knighted and was appointed Professor of Jurisprudence at

Oxford, and was made member of the Council for India. In 1877 he was chosen Master of Trinity Hall, Cambridge, and Professor of International Law. Maine early undertook to correct the theory of organized society maintained by Blackstone. He showed in his "Ancient Law" (1861) that social institutions were developed by custom, and that society moves from status to contract, that is, from regarding everything as fixed by class usage to allowing special arrangements to be made by individuals. His views were supported by what he observed in India, as reported in his "Village Communities in the East and West" (1871), and were further developed in his "Early History of Institutions" (1875). His lucid style and fine literary power promoted the general acceptance of the new theory. His "Popular Government" (1890) is a severe arraignment of democratic institutions and tendencies.

LECKY

Prominent among the philosophic historians who discuss social movements rather than events, ideas rather individuals, is William Edward Hartpole Lecky. He was born at Dublin, Ireland, in 1838, and graduated from Trinity College in 1859. His first work, published anonymously in 1861, was "Leaders of Public Opinion in Ireland," treating of Dean Swift, Flood, Grattan and O'Connell. Its flowing style and wide sympathy won for it general favor. After extensive travel on the Continent, Lecky settled in London, and published his "History of the Rise and Influence of the Spirit of Rationalism in Europe" (2 vols., 1865). Rationalism was defined to be that cast of thought which leads men to subordinate dogmatic theology to the dictates of reason. Its influence makes men regard the successive systems of theology as

varying expressions of the universal religious sentiment;
in ethics, it makes them regard duty as depending on conscience only; in history, it causes them to attribute
phenomena to natural causes rather than supernatural.
The progress of this mode of thought was held not to
depend directly on the teaching of great thinkers, but to
be slow and indirect, gradually rising from the mass of
the laity to the clergy. The peculiar nature of this philosophic work, treating of magic, witchcraft, miracles, persecution, and the separation of politics from the church,
drew to it special attention. The "History of European
Morals from Augustus to Charlemagne" (2 vols., 1869)
is a parallel work. Lecky rejects utilitarian ideas, and con-
siders morality as intuitive. He contrasts the Stoic and
Epicurean systems with Christian morality, and finds the
cause of the conversion of the Roman Empire in the ade-
quacy of the latter to the wants of the age. The causes
alleged by Gibbon are pronounced helpful, but not sufficient. The rise of asceticism and monasticism is traced to
evils for which they were temporary remedies.

Lecky had now established his reputation as an original
thinker on historical and moral problems. In his next
work he came closer to the questions of his own time.
His "History of England in the Eighteenth Century"
(7 vols., 1878-88) is not a history in the ordinary sense,
but a collection of essays on the prominent facts and features of the nation's life. It discusses separately the nature
of monarchy and aristocracy, the growth of democracy,
the increasing power of Parliament and the press, religious liberty, the rise of Methodism and the causes of the
French Revolution. Besides these, considerable space is
given to Irish affairs, and later this part was printed separately as a "History of Ireland." It relates chiefly to the
rebellion of 1798, and is markedly impartial. The part

relating to the American Revolution has also been issued separately in this country. Lecky had been elected to Parliament as a Liberal, but in 1886 he refused to follow Gladstone in the movement for Home Rule, and was afterwards defeated for re-election.

BRYCE

Of the English philosophic historians none has been better known in the United States than James Bryce. His "American Commonwealth" (1888) was a revelation to Americans themselves of the true significance and value of their institutions. James Bryce is of Scotch-Irish descent, and was born in Belfast, Ireland, in 1838. He was educated at Glasgow University and at Oxford, graduating in 1862 with high honor. His prize essay on "The Holy Roman Empire" (1864) raised him at once to high rank among historians. This valuable treatise first fully explained the importance of the imperial idea in the Middle Ages, and its lasting effect upon Italy and Germany. Bryce was made professor of civil law at Oxford in 1870. He spent his vacations in foreign travel, which gave him abundant material for contributions to magazines. In 1880 he was elected to Parliament as a Liberal, and in 1886 he was made Under-Secretary of Foreign Affairs in Gladstone's cabinet. His valuable work on the United States was the result of careful observation during three visits to this country. Compared with DeTocqueville's "Democracy in America," published fifty years earlier, it exhibits not only the astonishing growth of the nation, but its power of readjusting its institutions and laws to meet emergencies. Excellent as was the Frenchman's report, Bryce's work surpasses it in broad views and wealth of information. While he does not hesitate to point out defects, his general tone is that of admiration and sympathy. A curious result followed its publication. Having allowed Seth Low to write the chapter on Tammany rule in New York City, he was afterward prosecuted for libel by A. Oakey Hall, who had been mayor of New York, but was then resident in London. Bryce was convicted, and obliged to pay damages and cancel the offensive chapter.

SYMONDS

Another noted historian, who gave attention, however, to art, literature and criticism instead of politics, was John Addington Symonds (1840-1893). He was born at Bristol, educated at Harrow and Oxford, and was a Fellow of Magdalen College. Though wealthy, he had inherited consumption, and was obliged to reside at Davos-Platz, in Switzerland, for benefit of the climate. His culture was of the highest order, and to promote it among men was his chief aim. Culture he defined as "the raising of intellectual faculties to their highest potency by means of conscious training." His greatest work, "History of the Renaissance in Italy," in five volumes (1875-86), treats fully of the revival of learning in the Fourteenth and Fifteenth Centuries, the flourishing of the fine arts and literature, and the Catholic reaction which followed. The great characters, Dante, Petrarch, Boccaccio, Michael Angelo, Raphael, are described sympathetically. During his loving labor in this monumental work, many essays, critical and speculative, were prepared. His "Studies of the Greek Poets" are not only valuable contributions to classical scholarship, but are full of freshness and vigor, which commend them to the reader unacquainted with the originals. His interest in the rise of modern literature led to studies of Shakespeare's predecessors, and biographies

of Sir Philip Sidney and Ben Jonson.   He was also fully
awake to the literature of his own time, as is seen in his
criticisms of Walt Whitman and Zola, both of whom he
regarded as having helped man to understand himself.
His essays treat of a variety of other subjects connected
with art and literature.   His original poems are light, elegant and romantic; his translations are chiefly from his
favorite Italians.

GREEN

Among the few historians that have the faculty of
making history entertaining, Green holds a foremost place.
His "Short History of the English People" won more
readers than any other work of its class, while its originality obtained credit from the ablest critics.   Yet the author
had not set out to be an historian, but rather was drawn
by circumstances to his task.   John Richard Green was
born at Oxford in 1837, and educated there without
obtaining distinction.   On graduating he entered the
Church, and in 1865 became Vicar of Stepney in East London.   Holding High Church views, he was active in
parochial duty and in charity organization.   To eke out
his slender income he wrote for the "Saturday Review"
articles on historical and social topics, which were afterward collected as "Stray Studies in England and Italy."
Part of them were derived from his winter visits to Italy
on account of his delicate lungs.   When his health was
broken down by parish work, and his former rigid church
views abandoned, he retired from active clerical work.
Archbishop Tait made him librarian at Lambeth, where
Green began his "Short History of the English People."
Published in 1874, it was at once received with enthusiasm.   His aim was to entertain as well as instruct, to
exhibit the life of the people in successive stages rather

than recount the doing of Kings and Courts. His vivid, picturesque style brought distant times and places close to view. Some errors in minor particulars evoked criticism, but these were soon corrected. The gratified author then enlarged his work to four volumes (1878-80), still retaining the methods and style which had given the original popularity. Then he sought to go more deeply into the origin of England's greatness, and in "The Making of England" (1882) treated the early Anglo-Saxon period. This was to be followed by "The Conquest of England," but the work was interrupted by his death at Mentone, Italy, in March, 1883. His wife had faithfully watched over his precarious health, and helped him as amanuensis. Since his death she has superintended special editions of his works. The distinguishing merits of Green's work are his wide human sympathy and his power to make the past real to the imagination. He steadily refrained from injecting into the past the party spirit, political and ecclesiastical, of the present.

KINGLAKE

The prodigious scale on which modern history is often constructed is exemplified in Kinglake's "History of the Crimean War," which occupies seven volumes, though the war lasted but two years. Alexander William Kinglake (1811-1890) was educated at Eton and Cambridge. His travels in the Levant furnished material for "Eothen" (1844), a gem of literary art. His rollicking adventures were related in a lively, humorous style, smart and sometimes flippant. Kinglake was elected to Parliament, but was never prominent as a member. From love of adventure he visited the Crimea during the war and received kindness from Lord Raglan, which he abundantly repaid.

At the request of Raglan's family he undertook the history and then made most careful study of all the details of the war. Accounts of these he arranged in the most orderly fashion, so that an affair of ten minutes may be spread over seventy pages. A volume is given to the battle of Inkermann. His partiality toward Lord Raglan and other British generals is offset by his prejudice against Napoleon III and the French commanders, yet he is full of admiration for the Russian defender of Sebastopol, Todleben. His style is too brilliant for history, and the entire work was condemned by Matthew Arnold as an example of British bad taste.

Samuel Rawson Gardiner, born in 1829, was professor of modern history in King's College, London. He devoted himself especially to the history of the Seventeenth Century, and has published the "History of England from the Accession of James I to the Restoration" (12 vols). Apart from this he has published an excellent "Student's History of England" and several books describing epochs and characters of the period of his chief work.

Justin McCarthy, born at Cork, Ireland, in 1830, has been an active politician and journalist, and has written some novels of merit. His chief historical work is "A History of Our Own Time" (1879-97), notable for its fairness in treating political questions still in dispute. The success of this work led him to write a "History of the Four Georges" (1889) and a "History of Ireland," which show the same excellent qualities.

POETS OF THE LATER VICTORIAN PERIOD

Down to the last decade of the Century the two great poets who are the literary glory of the Victorian era survived in revered old age, and still sent forth poems worthy of their fame. But their lives and works have already been discussed and others claim attention. A general characteristic of these later poets, as indeed of nearly all poets of the Century, is the tendency to recur to the past for themes of their important works. This is partly an imaginative escape from the recognized ills or prosaic monotony of the present, just as poets of former days sung of the Golden Age. But it is partly due to the increased knowledge of history, which, in these days of books and universal education, is forced upon everybody. Hence latter-day poets revert to King Arthur and the knights of the Round Table, to the quest of the Holy Grail, to mediæval legends, to classical mythology and Icelandic sagas.

Another characteristic is the frequency of imitation, the distinct following of an earlier poet, or of Wordsworth, Tennyson, or even Browning, as a master. This is due to the spread of criticism and the careful study of the thought and art of those who have been awarded admission to high station in the temple of the Muses. The beauty of their work being acknowledged, it is regarded as the duty of others to learn wherein it consists, then follows imitation, conscious and unconscious. Even Matthew Arnold, a poet of ability, was overborne by his critical spirit and study of his predecessors. Such poets remember too much of what others have sung, and waste their own talents in striving to reproduce the effect of the songs hallowed by associations.

The greatest poets of this time, except the first two, are Swinburne and William Morris, both highly educated, and both decidedly musical. Swinburne, indeed, is the greatest musician in English verse, the most complete master of both words and meter. His work is chiefly lyrical, but he has also composed excellent dramas. Morris was an epic poet, but chose to present his narrative poems in rhyme, with occasional lyrics interspersed. Besides these there have been several poets who have introduced new forms and measures from old French verse. Some of them have gone on to more serious work in poetry, others have turned to writing light essays. The period has been full of experiments, and taken altogether, poetry has declined. This was proved, perhaps, when Tennyson died, for three years passed before one was found worthy to take his place. The two mentioned above were, of course, excluded for their pronounced political opinions, Swinburne being a Republican, and William Morris a Socialist. So the highest official honor which can be given to an English poet passed after a long pause to Alfred Austin, who then, at the age of sixty, first became known to the world.

A curious but exquisitely pleasing mixture of old fashions and modern style is found in the work of Austin Dobson. His poems have been chiefly *vers de société* and imitations of old French meter. In prose he has written biographies of English literary men, and studies of four French women, all belonging to the same period as his "Eighteenth Century Vignettes." Austin Dobson was born at Plymouth in 1840, studied civil engineering, and has held office in the Board of Trade. He began writing in 1868, but published no volume till 1873, when his

"Vignettes in Rhyme" were collected. Another collection is called "At the Sign of the Lyre" (1885).

His friend, Edmund Gosse, born in 1849, was in youth an assistant librarian at the British Museum, and wrote poems and essays for the periodicals. He afterward became translator to the Board of Trade. Poems collected in several volumes "On Viol and Flute" (1873), "Firdausi in Exile" (1885), show his skill as a lyrist. In many of them Old French metrical forms are used. His "Studies in the Literature of Northern Europe" (1879) are the result of travels in Sweden and Norway. Other books treat of English literature in the Seventeenth and Eighteenth Centuries, in which he is an acknowledged authority. Thorough knowledge of his subject and delicate skill in handling mark all his work.

WILLIAM MORRIS

Although at first a product of the Pre-Raphaelite movement, William Morris developed a true originality of poetic idea and expression. Well trained in the Greek classics, and ever retaining warm affection for them, he yet gave the wealth of his genius to the wild sagas of the Norsemen, until he himself became an inventor of sagas undistinguishable from the originals. But Morris's energy was not confined to the poetic field. Entering into business as a designer of household decoration, he forced that department of art on the public attention until he revolutionized the interiors of all buildings of any pretentions. Similarly, he revived the quaint art of the early printers of books. But more than this, though a wealthy man, he was active in propagating Socialism as the panacea for human woes.

William Morris (1834-1896) was born near London,

and was educated at Exeter College, Oxford.   He studied
painting before he turned to literature and house decoration.   His first poem was "The Defence of Guinevere"
(1858), showing that he had been attracted by the Arthur-
ian Legend, as was Tennyson, whose "Idylls of the King"
began to appear in the same year.   His next was the "Life
and Death of Jason" (1867) in which the Greek myth was
told at great length in romantic style.   Then came his
distinctive work, "The Earthly Paradise" (1868), which
is a cycle of twenty-four narrative poems of different
lengths, all in rhyme, but in various meters.   Mariners
of Norway seeking Paradise but baffled in their quest,
happen upon a land occupied by descendants of the ancient
Greeks, and a year is spent in alternate tales from Greek
and Norse mythology.   Here are recited by one party the
stories of Atalanta, Cupid and Psyche, Pygmalion and
Galatea; while the others tell of Ogier the Dane, Gudrun,
and Tannhäuser.   They are picturesque and full of a subtle
musical charm, the classical spirit still predominating.
Morris went on to "The Story of Sigurd the Volsung and
the Fall of the Niblungs" (1876), in which he tells in his
own inimitable way the famous German epic of the
"Nibelungenlied."   This work he regarded as his best, but
readers generally prefer the earlier poems.   Translations
of three great epics, Virgil's "Æneid" (1876), Homer's
"Odyssey" (1887) and the Saxon "Beowulf" (1895),
testified his devotion to former poets.   Yet the translator
used his opportunity freely, seeking to render these masterpieces into poems of his own style.   From the Icelandic
several prose translations were made, Professor Magnus-
son assisting in the "Saga Library," of which five volumes
were issued, including the "Heimskringla."   But besides
these translations Morris published other things of his
own, as "Hopes and Fears for Art" (1881) and "Aims of

Art" (1887) and Socialist treatises and hymns. Finally came his own romances in the form of old sagas, "The House of the Wolfings" (1889), "The Story of the Glittering Plain" (1891), "The Wood Beyond the World" (1894), and "The Well at the World's End" (1896). These prose poems go back to the primitive age of the Teutonic race, telling of noble warriors and their heroic deeds, of lovely women and splendid feasts. This ever-increasing devotion to dreams of a world which has long passed away, if it ever actually existed, prevents Morris from obtaining the wide recognition which is necessary to true fame. Subjects totally out of our knowledge cannot satisfy the desire of the mind for intellectual gratification.

There is another Morris, a poet somewhat popular, but by no means of the fame of William. This is Lewis Morris, who was born at Carmarthen, in Wales, in 1834. He was educated at Oxford and was called to the bar in London. In 1880 he was made Justice of the Peace for his native county, and went to reside there. His "Songs of Two Worlds" appeared in three series (1871-75); "The Epic of Hades" (1877) is poetical drama, describing the punishment and purgation of spirits. Though censured by the critics, it enjoys favor with the masses. Among his latter works are "Songs Unsung" (1883) and "Songs of Britain" (1887).

SWINBURNE

Swinburne has been recognized from his first appearance as a poet unmatched in the mastery of rhythm and melody, and in the serious beauty of his descriptions. In spite of his continuous writing, he has not attained a higher place than he reached by his first effort. But that place was high, so that he was even regarded by some as superior to Tennyson and Browning. He still remains next to these among the poets of the later Victorian era.

Little is known of the life of Algernon Charles Swinburne. His father was a British Admiral, his mother a daughter of the Earl of Ashburnham. He was born in 1837 near Henley on the Thames. He was educated partly in France, partly in Eton, and then went to Balliol College, Oxford, but left in 1860, and went to Italy. He afterward lived in London with Rossetti, and later at Wimbledon. He entered literature as a dramatic poet, publishing "Rosamond" and "The Queen Mother" in 1860, "Atlanta in Calydon" in 1864, and "Chastelard" in 1865. Of these "Atalanta" attracted most attention, as being a noble imitation of Greek tragedy. But in 1866 the public were amazed and shocked by his "Poems and Ballads," which displayed his wonderful poetical powers, but in some instances dwelt on forbidden subjects. The objectionable pieces are said to have been written in protest against conventional morality. The American edition bore the title "Laus Veneris." After a time Swinburne issued more "Poems and Ballads," full of sweetness and beauty, and free from the sins of his youth; then "Songs Before Sunrise," dedicated to Mazzini, and hailing the revolution in Italy; "Songs of Two Nations," in which the "Song of Italy" is conspicuous; "Songs of the Spring-tides," and other volumes. As the titles of these indicate, Swinburne is above all a musician, who elicits, even from the harsh and crabbed Saxon tongue a wonderfully sweet and unprecedented harmony. "Tristram of Lyonesse," though a narrative in rhyme, is strongly dramatic; "The Tale of Balen" (1896) is derived from Sir Thomas Malory's "Morte d'Arthur." To his former dramas several others have been added. "Erechtheus" is another Greek tragedy; "Bothwell" and "Mary Stuart" treat the story of the beautiful Queen of Scots, but with bitter prejudice against her. "Marino Faliero" is from Venetian history.

Besides his poetical work, Swinburne has done much in prose, critical, controversial and miscellaneous. The work of the Elizabethan dramatists has been examined and expounded with exhaustive skill in monographs and essays. Swinburne's eulogies are often extravagant, his controversial writings are sometimes rabid. His prose style is vehement and often obscure from his recondite allusions and strange use of words. Though an aristocrat by birth and training, he is a Republican by conviction, and has given unqualified utterance to his views. Even his poetry is marred by the fierceness of his hatred to Napoleon III, whom he regarded as the betrayer of liberty.

SIR EDWIN ARNOLD

By a sympathetic revelation of the principles of Buddhism in "The Light of Asia," Edwin Arnold won wide fame for himself and favor for the religious system which moulds the lives of one-fourth of the human race. He was born in Sussex, England, in 1832, and after graduating at Oxford, engaged in teaching at Birmingham. As principal of a Sanskrit college at Poonah, India, from 1857 to 1861, he acquired that special familiarity with the religions of Asia which is displayed in his later work. Returning to England for a vacation, chance led him to an important editorial position on the London "Telegraph." After some translations from Greek and Sanskrit, he issued, in 1879, his poetical paraphrase of the life and teachings of Buddha. By its brilliant local color and gorgeous imagery, as well as the interwoven resemblance to the Christian Gospels, this epic captivated the world. Then in 1881 came "Indian Idylls," taken from the Hindu epic, Mahabharata, and in 1883, "Pearls of the Faith; or Islam's Rosary," which was intended to do for Mohammedanism what his former poem had done for Buddhism. Next the author turned to Persia, and translating from Sadi's poems, published, in 1888, "Sadi in the Garden; or the Book of Love." Taking up the story of Jesus, he wrote "The Light of the World" (1892), but none of his later works attained the success of that on Buddha. His visit to Japan in 1892 furnished material for his prose work "Japonica," and led to his marriage with a Japanese lady. His former wife was an American. Arnold has been a diligent and versatile journalist as well as poet. His friendly exposition of non-Christian religions has brought high honors from the King of Siam, the Sultan of Turkey, the Shah of Persia, and the Emperor of Japan. Queen Victoria also, in 1888, created him Knight Commander of the Indian Empire. These honors are undoubtedly deserved, as Arnold's works have done much to make the adherents of various religions better acquainted with each other's views. But his merits as a poet are not so highly esteemed as formerly. The poetry is picturesque, the meter graceful, but the embellishment too lavish to suit the Western mind, and the introduction of foreign terms, hardly to be understood, fatigues the reader.

WILLIAM WATSON

When Lord Tennyson died in 1892, the question of the succession in the laureateship was widely discussed, and many critics urged the claims of William Watson. Unfortunately a mental trouble about that time required his removal to an asylum. He afterwards entirely recovered. Watson was born at Wharfdale, in Yorkshire, in 1850. His father was a Liverpool merchant. On account of delicate health, the boy was educated privately.

He became passionately fond of Shelley, Keats and Wordsworth. He had published two volumes before his "Wordsworth's Grave" (1892) brought him into general recognition. His tribute to Tennyson's memory "Lachrymæ Musarum" (1892) secured for him, through Gladstone, a government pension of £200. "The Purple East," which was afterward enlarged into "The Year of Shame," was a series of sonnets, upbraiding the English for their neglect of the Armenians in 1896. These ringing sonnets recall Milton's vehement denunciation of the persecution of the Vaudois. Watson's later volumes are "The Tomb of Burns" and "The Father of the Forest."

AUSTIN

When it was announced in 1895 that the poet laureateship left vacant since the death of Lord Tennyson had been bestowed by Lord Salisbury on Alfred Austin, most Americans were astonished; they did not know the man, had never heard of his poetry. Yet Austin was then sixty years old, and had been active in literature for many years. He was born near Leeds in 1835, of Roman Catholic parents. He was educated at Stonyhurst College and St. Mary's, Oscott. His early poems were satires, among which "The Golden Age" had the most success. Afterward came dramatic, lyric, and narrative poems, fairly good but not striking, the best being "The Human Tragedy," "Rome or Death" (1873), and "Savonarola" (1881). The laureate's later poems have had no striking merit. He is simply a respectable minor poet, with strong patriotic feeling, which is well shown in "England's Darling," a eulogy of Alfred the Great. His fondness for quiet country scenes appears in many poems, as "The Garden I Love."

PHILOSOPHERS AND SCIENTISTS

HERBERT SPENCER

The philosophical writer who has had the widest and most penetrating influence upon the intellect of the Century is Herbert Spencer, the apostle of evolution, even beyond Darwin. He was born in 1820 at Derby, where his father was a schoolmaster of especial note for his skill in teaching geometry. Herbert, at the age of seventeen, became a railway engineer and soon contributed papers on technical subjects to engineering journals. In 1842 he published a pamphlet on "The Proper Sphere of Government," and in 1848 was made sub-editor of the "Economist," which position he held five years. He had in the meantime published "Social Statics; or the Conditions Essential to Human Happiness Specified, and the First of Them Developed," which was in 1892 abridged and revised in connection with his later "Man and the State." In 1852 Spencer contributed to the "Westminster Review" an article on "Manners and Fashion," showing that political, religious and ceremonial forms are protective envelopes within which a higher humanity is gradually developed, but are cast aside when they become hindrances. In 1855 he published his "Principles of Psychology," which was afterward incorporated in his "Synthetic Philosophy." In 1860 his prospectus of this system was issued, announcing that it would be complete in ten volumes. The next twenty-five years were spent in carrying out this elaborate programme with immense labor and phenomenal ability. The doctrine of evolution, toward which he had been moving even before Darwin had published his "Origin of Species," was now made the basis and guide in all human affairs as in the world of nature. Evolution he defines to be "an integration of matter and concomitant dissipation of motion, during which the matter passes from an indefinite, incoherent homogeneity to a definite, coherent heterogeneity." After the introductory treatise on "First Principles" (1862), came "Principles of Biology," of "Psychology," of "Sociology," "Ceremonial Institutions," "Political Institutions," "Ecclesiastical Institutions." The "Data of Ethics" was issued among these, out of its proper order on account of its importance. The sciences relating to the inorganic world he omitted as sufficiently treated in other ways. The aim of his philosophy is to encourage the scientific study of life and society as the practical means of attaining the highest good The absolute and infinite is regarded as unknowable, though the exercise of trying to find it out may not be altogether unprofitable.

Before this grand work was fairly commenced, Spencer issued his valuable treatise on "Education—Intellectual, Moral and Physical," from which a few principles are here briefly stated. Science is compared to Cinderella, the household drudge, who has been despised by her haughty sisters, but is now to be advanced to the highest station. Knowledge must be made attractive to the pupil if he is to be benefited. The aim of moral education is to make self-governing beings. The preservation of health is a primary duty for the discharge of which the laws governing the body must be known. All of these principles have been approved and put in practice by the leading teachers of to-day.

The next in popularity of Spencer's work is "The Study of Sociology" (1874) which sets forth the means of ascertaining the principles by which human society should be regulated.   His political views are presented in "The Man *versus* the State" (1884), in which he opposes the later tendency of Liberalism to compulsory laws, making it indeed a new form of Toryism; he also objects to the belief in the divine right of Parliament as the great political superstition of the present time, as the belief in the divine right of Kings was of the past.   The only proper function of government, as he has always held, is to protect life, property and order, leaving the settlement of the general relations of society to individual action.   Spencer has thus been a determined foe of Socialism and an advocate of individualism.   He has not hesitated to enter into controversy on behalf of his views.   Herbert Spencer was also the editor of a series of volumes called "Descriptive Sociology," in which it was intended to bring together a repertory of facts concerning the physique, habits and customs of several sections of the human race.   Eight volumes had been issued when the work was suspended on account of the enormous expense involved.   In spite of ill health, which threatened to prevent the conclusion of his proposed great "Synthetic System of Philosophy," Spencer worked steadily and systematically till it was completed in 1897.   He persistently refused to join scientific societies or accept university honors or do anything which might distract him from his self-appointed work.

Spencer's idea of evolution was gradually worked out through diligent study of scientific facts, and was eventually extended till it embraced the whole universe.   Then in explication of his system he reversed the process, applying his theory to the basic conditions of the world, and showing its agreement with recorded facts.   This requires that immense amount of illustration from every department of science, with which his work seems to some to be overloaded.   His philosophical system, the only strictly inductive one in the world, has quickly been accepted by students of science, and has gradually won its way among philosophers. Its far-reaching effects are felt in every department of thought.

DRUMMOND

In the borderland of literature between science and religion no writer has obtained more readers than Henry Drummond. He was born at Stirling, Scotland, in 1851, and was educated at the University of Edinburgh and at the Free Church Divinity Hall. During his course at the latter he was an active assistant to Messrs. Moody and Sankey in their evangelistic tour in Great Britain and Ireland. On being ordained he was appointed to a mission chapel in Malta, but in 1877 was made professor of natural science in the Free Church College at Glasgow, where he also took charge of a mission church. During one of his vacations he made a geological expedition to the Rocky Mountains with Professor Geikie. His lectures and other addresses furnished his "Natural Law in the Spiritual World" (1883), but before it was published he had gone on a journey to the heart of Africa. The brilliant presentation of new views of the old spiritual truths gave the work immediate success. Drummond returned to take up religious work among college students, and later in its behalf visited Australia. In 1893 he traveled through the United States, addressing college students and lecturing in the large cities. Several of these addresses, as "The Greatest Thing in the World," "Pax Vobiscum," were widely circulated. "The Ascent of Man" (1893) is an able reply to extreme Darwinian views, showing that nature includes struggle for others as well as for self. Another publication was "Tropical

Africa," which gives the clearest view of the condition of that region yet published. Africa, however, had implanted the seeds of disease in his system and the brave, hard-working Christian professor after two years of struggle with ill health, died in March, 1897.

ESSAYISTS AND MISCELLANISTS

MALLOCK

A singular fate has overtaken William Hurrell Mallock. It is his misfortune to be almost entirely excluded from serious consideration, not by the future, but by the very success of his first book. The jest of his satire was so piquant that he can hardly afterward be regarded as in earnest. He is a nephew of the historian Froude and was born in Devonshire in 1849. He was educated at Oxford and won the Newdigate prize by his poem. "The Isthmus of Suez." His satrical ability was shown in "The New Republic" (1876), a modern dialogue in imitation of Plato's "Republic." The speakers represent, under thin disguises, the leaders of modern thought—Matthew Arnold, Huxley, Tyndall, Ruskin, and others. They severally propose to dismiss from their New Republic imagination, poetry, superstition, religious belief, serious convictions, the middle classes, but are driven out in confusion when Mr. Herbert (Ruskin) banishes the upper classes as well. The parody on the style of thought and writing of the speakers is perfect, and the success of the skit was complete. The author followed it up by "The New Paul and Virginia; or, Positivism on an Island" (1878), but this had little effect. Mallock then turned to serious writing, and discussed "Is Life Worth Living," in which the emptiness of this life, if there be no future, is forcibly presented. His numerous essays on social topics have been collected in several volumes, among them being "Property, Progress, and Poverty" (1884), and "Classes and Masses; or, Wealth and Wages" (1896). He is a strong reactionary, seeking to go back to mediævalism in social organization and religious belief. But into all his writing a bitter mixture of doubt and mockery is infused. Mallock has also published some sentimental romances which receive but little attention.

Among the writers noted for elegance and even daintiness of style, Walter Pater (1839-1894) holds the chief place, though he wrote but little. He was educated at Oxford and became a Fellow of Brasenose College. To him the chief object of life was to extract the utmost of pleasure from living in a refined way, especially from education and art. The study of Greek pervaded Pater's life and writings. Nor was his first book, "Studies in the History of the Renaissance" (1873), untrue to this principle, since it had reference to the revival of Greek culture in modern society. This next, "Marius the Epicurean" (1885), is a story of ancient Rome in the time of Marcus Aurelius, when the Stoic philosophy dominated the higher classes, and Paganism and Christianity touched and blended. An important character is the celebrated Apuleius, to whom Pater shows favor. In "Imaginary Portraits" (1887) and "Appreciations" (1890) the style is not so perfect as in his former works. At his best his style is less exuberant than Ruskin's, more finished and exquisite, never overloaded with ornament. It aims at well modulated harmony, and excels in the construction of paragraphs to this end.

In modern times there have been a few writers who won fame by giving such accurate descriptions of nature as attested their loving feeling for it, and drew others to share, at least while reading, this love. Such was Gilbert

White, of Selborne, in the last Century, and such is John
Burroughs in our own time and country. The only recent
English representative of this class, which may be called
nature-essayists, was Richard Jefferies, whose life was
cut off before he knew his fame. The son of a farmer, he
was born near Swindon, in Wiltshire, in 1848. Self-
educated, he began writing for local newspapers at
eighteen, and in 1877 went to London to engage in journalism. His first book was "The Gamekeeper at Home"
(1878). This was followed by "The Amateur Poacher"
(1879), "Hodge and His Master" (1880), "Round About
a Great Estate" (1880), and "Life of the Fields" (1884).
These were highly praised by observant critics for both
matter and style. They are breezy books, which make
men and boys fond of out-of-door rural life. The author
wrote also some novels, which were of little value. For
several years he was an invalid and, brooding on his
troubles, he became a mystical pessimist. His "Story of
My Heart" (1883) was a remarkable autobiographic
sketch, which was hardly heard by the public till after his
death, in August, 1887. A strange fame then set in and
gave value to his writings, which had before but slight
appreciation by the public.

LANG

A most pleasant writer of light verse and graceful
essays, an able translator of Homer and French lyrics, a
judicious exponent of anthropology, and many other important matters is found in the gifted Scotchman, Andrew
Lang. He was born at Selkirk in 1844, and was educated
at St. Andrews University and Balloil College, Oxford.
He soon began to write for periodicals, and in 1872 published "Ballades and Lyrics of Old France." With some

friends he began to imitate the forms of old French verse, introducing ballads, rondeaus, and villanelles.   His "Ballades in Blue China," "Ballades and Verses Vain," "Rhymes Old and New," indicate by their titles their general light, airy quality, yet sometimes he attempts something of a higher kind, and performs it well.   "Helen of Troy" (1882) is his most ambitious poem and should have led to something still grander.   In the field of anthropology and comparative mythology he has been an earnest worker, as is shown by his volumes, "Custom and Myth" (1884) and "Myth, Ritual, and Religion" (1887).   He proves that many myths, long held to be of Aryan origin, are practically found among savage tribes in various parts of the earth.   Lang is a fine classical scholar, as he has shown not only in his excellent prose translations of Theocritus and Homer, but also in numerous lively essays by quotation and allusion.   Yet he is by no means so wedded to the ancients as not to have regard for the modern classics.   From foreign lands he has brought into English some fine collections of fairy tales, as in the "Blue Fairy Book" and the "Red Fairy Book."   His essays on French literature are valuable contributions to that department. "The Mark of Cain" (1886) is a caricature of the sensational story, which was then largely in vogue.   But he has also seriously attempted historical romance in "The Maid of Fife" (1895), which has Joan of Arc as the central figure.   He has written some excellent biographies, as the lives of Lord Iddesleigh (better known as Sir Strafford Northcote) and of Lockhart.   He has also edited many selections of standard literature, writing excellent introductions.

NOVELISTS OF THE LATER VICTORIAN PERIOD

MACDONALD

The earliest of the novelists of Scottish life, with marked religious purpose, was George Macdonald. He was born at Huntly, in the North of Scotland, in 1824. After graduating at Aberdeen University, he studied theology in the Independent College, Highbury, London. For some years he was a preacher to Scotch Congregationalists in London, then resigned his ministry and joined the Church of England. He became principal of a seminary, but has been chiefly engaged in literary work, and has resided much in Italy. His first publications were poems, which were followed by "Phantastes, a Faerie Romance" (1858). His first novel, "David Elginbrod," appeared in 1862, and was the harbinger of a large number of the same class. His motive is to present to his fellow-men "the common good, uncommonly developed," as being more true to humanity than pictures of evil or failure. This strong moral purpose, faithfully carried out, does not prevent him from showing power in his carefully wrought plots, life-like characters, and dramatic incidents. Among his best novels are "Alec Forbes of Howglen," "Annals of a Quiet Neighborhood," "Wilfrid Cumbermede," "The Marquis of Lossie," and especially "Sir Gibbie." Peculiarly attractive are his stories for children, "At the Back of the North Wind" and "The Princess and Curdie." He has also published some sermons and religious treatises. His poems are pure and spiritual.

BLACKMORE

Although Richard Doddridge Blackmore has written many novels, he is known as the author of one—"Lorna Doone," a semi-historical romance, which has given fame to a Devonshire valley. He was born in Berkshire in 1825, graduated at Oxford, studied law, practiced as a conveyancer, and when his health failed, became a market-gardener near London. His first literary ventures were poems. He did not attempt novel-writing till he was nearly forty, nor did he secure much attention for some time after his best work was published in 1869. Slowly its merits were recognized and at last the melodramatic romance attained popularity. "Lorna Doone" is a story of the time of King Charles II. The Doones were a family of outcast nobles, living as robbers in Bagworthy forest, the wild road to their home being strictly guarded against intruders. But young John Ridd, the stout and valiant son of a simple yeoman, who keeps sheep on the Downs, chances to meet Lorna Doone, the fair queen of the wild band, falls in love with her, undertakes wild and desperate adventures for her sake, and rescues her and himself out of perils by his native shrewdness. Among Blackmore's other stories are "The Maid of Sker," "Cripps the Carrier," "Erema; or, My Father's Sin," "Sir Thomas Upton." He depicts with much skill the peasants and fisher-folk of the West of England, hardy, slow of speech, yet keen-witted. His stories are told in a quaint, meditative way, are full of adventure and dramatic situations. His heroes are gallant, and his heroines sweet, but the other characters, parsons and rustics, or even highwaymen, usually excite more interest.

Perhaps the most prolific writer of books in the present day is the Rev. Sabine Baring-Gould. He was born at

Exeter in 1834, graduated at Cambridge twenty years later, and entered the Church. He became rector at Lew Trenchard, Devonshire, in 1881. Part of his youth was spent in Germany and France, and from the literature of these countries he has drawn for his numerous writings. His easy conversational style has enabled him to treat English rural life, Ireland, theological topics, mediæval myths, folk-lore, comparative mythology, and German history in an equally interesting way. The best known of his books is "Curious Myths of the Middle Ages" (1866). Of more than thirty novels may be mentioned, "Red Spider," "Mehalah; a Tale of the Salt Marshes," "Gabrielle André," "In Exitu Israel." Wide information and powerful imagination are shown in these, but the striking characters often drawn from English peasant life, are not attractive. Much more pleasant is his biography of the Rev. R. S. Hawker, "The Vicar of Morwenstow."

Henry Rider Haggard is a fine story-teller, whose accounts of wild adventures gave him for a time extraordinary success. He was born in 1856 and had been on Government service in South Africa. After publishing an account of "Cetewayo and His White Neighbors" (1882) he used his knowledge of strange lands in romances of adventure. Among the most noted of his books are "King Solomon's Mines" (1886), "She" (1888), and "Allan Quartermain" (1889). In "The World's Desire" he was associated with Andrew Lang.

BLACK

The Scotch Highlands and the rocky islands to the West are the region which William Black has made familiar by several fine stories, but he is quite as much at home in London drawing-rooms. He was born at Glasgow in 1841 and went to London in 1864. In 1875 he gave up journalism for fiction, in which he had already made some ventures. His first really successful novel was "A Daughter of Heth" (1871), in which a gay Southern girl, full of innocent wiles, is sadly bewildered and tragically misunderstood by the grim, sober folk among whom she has thoughtlessly been lured. In the "Princess of Thule," the proud and beautiful heroine by her feminine witchery and skill in sailing, captivates the summer tourist. "The Strange Adventures of a Phaeton" (1872) describes a tour through Great Britain, interweaving a love-story. "White Wings" (1880) is a yachting romance. "Shandon Bells" (1883) is an Irish story, telling the struggles of a literary man. Black is an enthusiastic lover of outdoor sports, of fly-fishing, yachting, and deer-stalking, and describes all these in his stories. He is equally skillful in delineating the wild scenery of rocky islands, the grandeur of sunsets, the terrors of ocean storms, and the melancholy temperament and peculiar humor of the Highland chief and clansmen.

HALL CAINE

As Black has given prominence to the Hebrides, Hall Caine has given his native Isle of Man a place in literature. He was born in 1853 and became an architect in Liverpool. He had, however, an inclination to literature, which was fostered by his friendship with Dante Gabriel Rossetti, with whom he went to live in London in 1880. His first book was "Recollections of Rossetti," and in 1885 he published his first novel, "The Shadow of a Crime," which was written with prodigious pains. "The Deemster" (1887) obtained more favor, "The Scapegoat" (1891) still more, and "The Manxman" (1894) completed his group of pictures of Manx life. Yet for each of these he has declared that he drew the primary idea from the Bible —from the story of Joseph and his brethren, from David and Uriah, and from David and Jonathan. Mr. Caine visited Russia in 1892 in behalf of the persecuted Jews, and in 1895 lectured in the United States. His novel, "The Christian" (1897), presents, according to his view, the religious question of to-day. John Storm, a religious fanatic, is yet in love with Glory Quayle, a friend of his childhood, who has become a famous actress, and tries to draw her from demoralizing associations. When she refuses, his frenzy makes him seek to kill her, but her words restore him to sounder mind. Storm, who has been a High Churchman, finally becomes a Salvation Army preacher, and after a meeting is assaulted by a mob in the streets. Glory hastens to him and they are married while he is lying on his death-bed. The scenes of the story are highly realistic, but the whole is wildly improbable.

BESANT

Sir Walter Besant had been a worker in other fields before James Rice, editor of "Once a Week," took him into partnership in novel-writing. Good as their joint efforts were, Besant's chief fame is due to his later independent output. An astonishing material response to his "All Sorts and Conditions of Men" was the People's Palace, built and liberally furnished to provide recreation for the poor but honest inhabitants of East London. This in turn brought the philanthropic author his knighthood. Walter Besant was born at Portsmouth in 1838, and was educated at King's College, London, and Christ's College, Cambridge. He became professor in the Royal College of

Mauritius for seven years. Then, returning to England, he published "Studies in Early French Poetry" (1868) and "French Humorists" (1873). He was secretary of the Palestine Exploration Fund and, with Professor Palmer, wrote a "History of Jerusalem" (1871). Meantime, his acquaintance with Rice had ripened into their well-known partnership, the results of which were "Ready-Money Mortiboy," "With Harp and Crown," "The Golden Butterfly," and "The Chaplain of the Fleet." The latter relates to the Fleet prison, into the foul atmosphere of which an innocent country girl, niece of the chaplain, brings an air of purity. After the death of Rice in 1882, Besant issued his famous novel, depicting the ordinary, dreary life of East London, which his hero and heroine undertake to relieve with a palace of pleasure. In other stories, as "The Children of Gibeon" (1884) and "The World Went Very Well Then" (1885) Sir Walter Besant pursued his philanthropic schemes. But in many more he treated a wide range of subjects and characters, sometimes the woman question or other problems of the time, sometimes a miser or whimsical individual, sometimes the wrongs of the poor, and sometimes the sufficiency of a little for life's wants. Some of them are tragical or melodramatic, but most of them are pervaded with a cheerful humor, which is seen even in their titles, as "Call Her Mine" and the "Wapping Idyll."

HARDY

Far different in aim and effect is the stern realist, Thomas Hardy, loving painter of rural scenery, but grim pessimist in his delineation of character and fate. Born in Dorsetshire in 1840, he studied architecture, but at the age of thirty turned to novel-writing and soon proved sig-

nal ability.   "Under the Greenwood Tree" (1872) showed
him a master of rural life and of the English rustic, whose
homely dialect talk reveals an unconscious humor.   In "A
Pair of Blue Eyes" (1873) the heroine, Elfride, when a
girl, trifles a little with a village youth, who pines and dies,
leaving his mother to avenge his wrongs.   A slight im-
prudence of Elfride's with another is magnified into a
scandal which drives off her true lover.   In "The Return
of the Native" the lofty pride of the dainty Eustacia Vye
destroys the ambition of Clym Yeobright without granting
him love.   In "Jude the Obscure," the hero wishing to
become a student at Oxford, is tricked into marriage with
the sensual Arabella.   Later, when his early hope seems
likely to be realized, he meets his intellectual cousin, Sue,
who is so highly educated that she is too pure to think of
marriage, yet in too intimate association with Jude, falls
into sin.   In "Tess of the D'Urbervilles" a fair country
maiden had been betrayed, but had gone to tend a dairy a
short distance away, where her fault was unknown.
Angel Clare, a gentleman's son, falls in love with the dairy-
maid, but on their marriage-day he feels bound to confess
a previous love-affair.   Tess then tells her own story, and
Clare, horrified, repulses her as unclean, and she is swept
downward to her wretched fate.   These powerful but
gloomy novels show Hardy's stern, fatalistic view of
human life, regarding the causes and chances leading to
failure and misery as more numerous and powerful than
those tending to success.   In parts of these stories and
still more in his short tales, the charms of the country are
finely depicted, and in this Hardy excels all other novelists.

GEORGE MEREDITH

George Meredith is unique among English novelists. He can never become popular, for he disdains elaborate plots and cares little for dramatic scenes. His design is to reveal character as it is exhibited in real life in a succession of apparently unimportant incidents. All subjects are treated with philosophic calmness, yet with patient study. The minds and thoughts of men, and still more of women, are the objects of his searching analysis. Meredith was born in Hampshire in 1828, and spent much of his childhood in Germany. He studied law, but soon devoted himself to literature. He married a daughter of Thomas Love Peacock (1785-1866), the fantastic author of the satirical romances, "Headlong Hall" and "Nightmare Abbey." After a volume of poems, Meredith published "The Shaving of Shagpat" (1855), a burlesque Oriental poem. His first and perhaps his finest novel, "The Ordeal of Richard Feverel" (1859), opens with a beautiful love idyll, exhibits a variety of eccentric characters, and closes with tragic gloom. Most of his books deal with the comedy of life, yet in a highly philosophic, rather than amusing way. The most noted are "The Egoist" (1879), "The Tragic Comedians" (1881), "Diana of the Crossways" (1885), and "The Amazing Marriage." Women are his favorite study, and Diana, the strong and beautiful Irish gentlewoman, is most radiant, while her lovers are satellites to her glory. Meredith's poems are full of the same philosophic spirit as his novels, and his imagination and love of nature carry him to even greater achievement.

STEVENSON

The life of Robert Louis Stevenson was spent in the constant pursuit of health and happiness. Early doomed to death by consumption, that scourge of the Scotch race, he struggled manfully to stave it off by traveling and residing in the most favorable climates. In spite of this incubus, he was diligent in writing and left a large number of delightful volumes in prose and verse. He belonged to a family famous from his great-grandfather down to his father, for the erection of light-houses. He was intended to be an engineer himself, but fate by his physical and mental constitution decided otherwise. He was born at Edinburgh in 1850, studied there at school and university, was called to the bar, but did not practise law. From his boyhood he had been a persistent cultivator of style in writing, not originally for publication, but for its own sake. He imitated various authors, from Sir Thomas Browne to Hawthorne, and then became expert in the choice and collocation of words. For the sake of his health he went to the South of France in 1873, leading a seemingly idle life. He had begun to publish essays in the "Cornhill Magazine," which were afterwards gathered in two volumes. His first books were "An Inland Voyage" (1878) and "Travels with a Donkey in the Cevennes" (1879). He crossed the Atlantic as a steerage passenger in 1879 and went to California, where he married Mrs. Osbourne, whom he had first met in France. She took special care of his health and collaborated with him in some stories. His "Treasure Island" (1883) first gave him wide reputation. It is just such a story as boys delight in, full of adventure, pirates and fights. Quite as entertaining are the short stories of the "New Arabian Nights" and "Prince Otto," which introduces a few fine poems.   Some of his stories were written in collaboration with his stepson.

In 1886 Stevenson created wide sensation by his "Strange Case of Dr. Jekyll and Mr. Hyde," in which the chief personage is transformed at intervals, physically and mentally, so as to appear and act in entirely different ways. The story is told in a restrained, measured way, which helps to retain the reader's belief in the good faith of the narrators.   In the same year came another adventurous story, "Kidnapped," which the author considered his best in fulfilling the purpose intended.   It is a story of the early Eighteenth Century, full of grim and terrible scenes and characters, in dealing with which lay, as he believed, his forte.   "The Black Arrow" is an historical romance of the War of the Roses.   "The Master of Ballantrae" (1889) is another of the powerful stories with terrible scenes.   Before this Stevenson had begun his voyages in the Pacific, which resulted in his making his home in Samoa.   There some measure of health came to him again, and he was able to spend much time out of doors. His "Vailima Letters" (published after his death) and "A Foot-Note to History" show what interest he took in the strange people among whom his lot was cast.   Their fond regard for this new friend was proved by their making, at his suggestion, the Road of the Loving Heart, which was the name they bestowed on him.   One more novel the invalid lived to complete, "David Balfour" (1893); one he left unfinished, "Weir of Hermiston." Both are reckoned among his best achievements.   After the many years of watchful care of a frail, diseased body, he died suddenly December 3, 1894.

Besides his prose writings, Stevenson wrote considerable amount of verse, which is gathered in "Underwoods" (1887), "Ballads" (1891), and the earlier "Child's Garden of Verse" (1885). These are all simple in style and metre, and especially the last has won much favor. They seem to be the spontaneous expression of his thoughts, while his prose is distinctly labored. He has told in full detail how he wrought to obtain a perfect style, and admitted that he had not always succeeded. While most critics award him high praise, a few have alleged against him an occasional strain after effect. It has also been objected that his stories are not brought to a close as carefully as the case demanded. Yet his story-telling faculty remains unimpeached, and the general verdict pronounced him the most delightful of essayists and most fascinating of romance-writers of his time.

While the story of "Dr. Jekyll and Mr. Hyde" was terribly tragical, another story of transformation was entirely comical. This was Frederic Anstey's "Vice Versa," which showed a respectable middle-aged, common-place father metamorphosed into his small son at school, while the boy takes the father's place. The joke was received with loud laughter throughout England.

BARRIE

In the latter part of the eighties a small group of novelists appeared who depicted in a life-like manner the peculiarities of Scotch character. The first was James Matthew Barrie, born in May, 1860, at Kirriemuir, which he has described under the name Thrums. He was the son of a physician, and after graduating at Edinburgh University, went to London to work as a journalist. In the "St. James's Gazette" he began the series of "Auld Licht Idylls," showing the stiff, stubborn character of the members of the smallest body of Scotch Presbyterians, yet awakening sympathy for their kindly nature, hidden deep under the forbidding surface. In "A Window in Thrums" the sketches of life in the little village are continued, from the point of view of a crippled woman, Jess, and her daughter Leeby. But Barrie's real success came with "The Little Minister" (1891), a romantic story in which a Scotch minister who undertakes to reprove and rebuke a half-gipsy girl ends by being married to her with gipsy rites. In spite of the improbability of the plot, the whirl of the incidents, the gay humor of the writer, and the variety of strange characters, enlist the reader's favor. "Sentimental Tommy" (1895) is a grim revelation of the miseries of child life in London, mitigated by the fancies and posings of the hero.

IAN MACLAREN

The second of the "Kail-yard Group," as these Scotch novelists have been somewhat contemptuously called, is the Rev. John Watson, who writes under the pen-name Ian Maclaren. Though of Highland Scotch descent, he was born in 1850 in Manningtree, Essex, England, but was taken to Scotland in childhood. He was educated at Edinburgh University in the class with Robert Louis Stevenson. Watson was ordained to the ministry in the Free Church of Scotland, and became pastor at Harvestfield, in Perthshire, a village which he has described as Drumtochty. Hence he was called to be assistant pastor in Glasgow, and thence in 1880 to take charge of a Presbyterian Church in Liverpool. His sermons exhibit his culture as well as the liberality of his views and deep spirituality. In 1896 he delivered the Lyman Beecher lectures at the Theological Seminary of Yale University, which were published as "The Mind of the Master." In his profoundly pathetic story, "Beside the Bonnie Brier Bush" (1894), the characters of the ambitious scholar, of his loving mother, and above all of Doctor William Maclure, strongly touched the hearts of the people. In "The Days of Auld Lang Syne" other sketches of Drumtochty were presented. In "Kate Carnegie" (1896) the theological disputes which make so much of Scotch Church history, are so treated as to impress the truly religious feeling which underlies them. Dr. Watson's combination of droll humor, with genuine religious sentiment, has given him his deserved popularity. It has frequently been urged that his characters were a trifle too good to be quite true.

MRS. HUMPHRY WARD

No novel of recent years has excited wider discussion than "Robert Elsmere" (1888). Mr. Gladstone honored it with a long article in the "Contemporary Review," and at once it secured an enormous sale. It boldly presented an existing phase of the moral and intellectual world, portraying the gradual loss of faith in a cultivated religious mind through the sceptical tendency of the times. The novel thus became the vehicle of fundamental religious controversy. This startling innovation was made by Mrs. Humphry Ward, a granddaughter of Dr. Arnold, of Rugby. Her maiden name was Mary Arnold. Her father, Thomas Arnold, had become a Roman Catholic, and after doing considerable literary work in England, had gone to Tasmania to teach. Mary was born at Hobart Town in that island in 1851. The family afterwards removed to Oxford, England, and Mary was thoroughly educated. She was married to Humphry Ward, editor of various works. Her scholarship was shown in reviews and translations, including "Amiel's Journal." Her first novel, "Miss Bretherton" (1884), told the growth of love between a young actress and a middle-aged man of letters. "Robert Elsmere," depicting a tragedy of

the soul, was the next. It was criticized as being too
didactic, but its vitality was seen in other characters as well
as the central figure. "The History of David Grieve"
(1892) is a contrast as well as a companion to its predecessor. It showed the growth of faith in persons of
humbler class than Elsmere, but brought them through
severe straits. The earnest David, who had spent his boyhood with his more spirited sister Louie, in a quiet nook
of England, is transported to the bustling streets of London and the gay scenes of Paris before his moral development is completed.

Mrs. Ward turned next to the training of a noble
woman, and did it through social and political rather than
religious influences. In "Marcella" (1894), a crudely
romantic English girl becomes finally a worthy leader of
society. The English world, London and Parliament, the
rich and the poor, politics and socialism, are all described
with minute fidelity. In "Sir George Tressady" (1896)
Marcella appears again as Lady Maxwell and passes un-
scathed through a perilous temptation. Tressady, married
hastily to a pretty wife, finds her unfit intellectually for his
companionship. In a later novel, "Helbeck of Bannis-
dale" (1898), Mrs. Ward took up again the subject of
religion. Helbeck is a Catholic bachelor, who, in his zeal
for the faith, is consuming his estate to build chapels. To
his house comes an invalid relative, whose daughter Laura
has been trained by an agnostic father. They fall in love
with each other, and Laura strives to overcome her repugnance to her lover's religious zeal, but fails and drowns
herself. Though the characters are finely portrayed, they
become to the thoughtful reader mere pawns in the great
game between Roman Catholicism and Agnosticism.

DU MAURIER

The most suddenly successful novel of recent times was "Trilby," first published in "Harper's Monthly" in 1894. It was written by George du Maurier (1834-1896), who had long been a special artist of "Punch," and had published "Peter Ibbetson" in 1891. His father was a Frenchman, who wished his son to be a chemist, while the latter had stronger propensity for art. Severe study so injured his sight that he had to give up painting. After two years of idleness he began to draw for periodicals, and soon had permanent engagement on "Punch." No attempt was made at broad fun or political satire. Certain phases of London society occupied his attention, and he was especially successful in the delineation of women. Much care was given to the brief dialogues below the drawings, and in this way Du Maurier was trained to write. The story of "Peter Ibbetson" had often been told to his friends before it was written. When given to the public, its quotations from American poets helped to commend it. "Trilby" was founded partly on the author's experience in Paris studios, while the hypnotism was a recognition of a fashionable fad. The immense popularity of the story was due to its revelation of life-like characters in a singular society. Du Maurier, who had long suffered from ill health, did not live long to enjoy his success. He died before his next novel, "The Martian" (1897), appeared.

KIPLING

The Nineteenth Century was drawing to a close; students of literature lamented the passing of the great masters of song and story; watchful critics noted with sorrow the signs of decadence; careful judges pronounced that henceforth in this age of science and materialism the spirit of poetry and imagination was extinct, nor could it possibly be revived; when lo! from the far East was heard a voice like a trumpet, waxing louder and stronger and sweeter, and the cry arose, "The new genius has arrived; Kipling is here." "Plain Tales from the Hills" (1888) was the unexpected herald of a new era. The stories were realistic in a new style, of new characters, new scenes, new life. Other tales quickly followed, treating of English private soldiers and native Hindoos and Mohammedans, sometimes pathetic, sometimes tragic, always startlingly real, and strongly masculine. In the humorous group of "Soldiers Three" came a revelation of the inner and outer man of the British private, previously unknown even to those most concerned. Again came touching stories of children in "Wee Willie Winkie" (1888). After some preliminary tuning there arose in the air also a burst of soldiers' songs, gay, reckless, warlike, irresistible, in "Departmental Ditties" (1891) and "Barrack-Room Ballads" (1892).

Rudyard Kipling is the son of John Lockwood Kipling, principal of the school of industrial art at Lahore, and was born at Bombay in December, 1865. He was sent to school in England, but returned to India in 1882, and became sub-editor of a newspaper at Lahore. Here he learned to write swiftly and effectively, and soon produced stories and verses that were circulated through India. From these a selection was made in the "Plain Tales from the Hills," his first challenge to the outer world. The response of welcome was clear and unmistakable. In 1889 Kipling went to England and soon afterwards made a tour across the United States, writing descriptive letters as he journeyed. Then he married Miss Balestier, the sister of Wolcott Balestier, with whom he had collaborated in a novel, "The Naulahka" (1892). He built a house at Brattleboro, Vermont, and settled there for a few years, but went back to England in 1897.

Besides his Anglo-Indian stories, Kipling in 1894 produced an entirely unique kind of fables in "The Jungle Book." These are dialogues and stories of the life of the wild beasts of India from their own point of view. For these almost a special dialect was invented, marvelously appropriate and suggestive. Compared with Æsop's simple moralizings and the grotesque German stories of "Reineke Fuchs," these jungle stories are intensely realistic, yet are not lacking in ethical suggestions. "The Light that Failed" (1890), Kipling's first novel, included a graphic account of an Egyptian campaign, with a sketch of studio life in London. "Captains Courageous" (1897) is a breezy narrative of the perilous adventures of the fishermen of Gloucester, Massachusets. In some short stories Kipling has availed himself of his observations in America. His quickness in perceiving and accuracy in reproducing details of new subjects are equally astonishing. Yet he leaves the impression of being able to tell more if it were necessary. His poems, even the coarse soldiers' ballads, are full of imagination and patriotism. He has proved himself, without appointment, the inspired poet laureate of England. His "Seven Seas" is a glorification of the British imperial policy; his "Recessional" was an appropriate hymn of humble praise for the celebration of the sixtieth anniversary of Queen Victoria's accession; the "Truce of the Bear" was a startling yet genuine British response to Czar Nicholas' suggestion of the disarmament of nations; "The White Man's Burden" is a thrilling presentation of the unavoidable duty of the capable white race to the incapable, unreliable colored races of the world, in spite of all the inherent difficulties of the glorious task.   With this royal leader in prose and verse, England grandly enters a new literary era.

FRENCH LITERATURE

Literature of a high order was virtually extinguished in France during the terrors of the Revolution. The public mind was too excited by grim realities for the necessary calm to consider works of the imagination or reason. Yet the mind must still be supplied with intellectual food, and found it in parliamentary eloquence and journalism. The latter, indeed, may be said to have been created for France at this time. There was also, strange to say, considerable scientific writing; chemistry and natural philosophy were cultivated throughout the stormiest period. But literature proper had to await a breathing time, when public thought could regain its balance and recover from the shock of the explosion. The national ideal had been cast from its throne at the very time and by the very means which were expected to extend its sway over the earth.

Before the Revolution, while France in general was still professedly and really Catholic, the skepticism of the English deists of the Eighteenth Century had permeated its higher literature. Voltaire had early and prophetically declared, in view of the general borrowing from the English, "we shall imperceptibly acquire from them their noble freedom of thought and their profound contempt for the petty trifling of the schools." The French wits and thinkers went far beyond their English teachers. Nothing was free from their mockery, which was open and undisguised. The church, the government, the throne, did not escape. The Classicism, which had prevailed in literature for nearly

197

two centuries and formed its finest models, was contrasted
with the Gothic freedom of Shakespeare and Milton.   But
in pure literature the classic spirit was not lightly to be
extinguished.   The Encyclopædists, D'Alembert and
Diderot, with their destructive criticism, did not in their
great work undertake to dispel all illusions.   They
restricted themselves to statement of facts.   But in the
salons profound human problems were discussed and
solved by means of epigrams.   Faith was undermined
and when the fearful time of trial came, it fell, and great
was the fall thereof.   Church, state, religion, literature,
went down—in one vast ruin blent.   At the close of the
Century France, so far as literature is concerned, was
living on husks.   The soul seemed to have left the body of
her poetry; the outward form of the drama was devoid of
substance; philosophers discoursed in lifeless platitudes.
Brunetière, the greatest living French critic, declares that
the decay of classicism in his country's literature was due
to its rule of preserving the impersonal.   In literature
abstractions were sought for, the presentation of real character was excluded.   The decadence of the later Eighteenth Century literature was derived from these two
causes, the growth of philosophic materialism on the one
hand, and a sham idealism on the other.

The powerful Voltaire, the crowned laureate of the
nation, the perfect embodiment of the Gallic mocking
spirit, never disturbed the prescribed rules of literature in
poetry or prose.   However revolutionary in actual effect
were his utterances, in form they were of perfect propriety
according to the canons of the time.   He therefore remains distinctly the national classic, whose precise work
is imperfectly comprehended outside of France.   But
Rousseau, his younger contemporary, the gloomy, dreary
Swiss republican, was more than a Frenchman—he be-

longed to all Europe. He was the inventor of new modes
of thought and writing, the apostle of sentimentalism, the
teacher of love of nature, the reformer of education, the
reconstructor of human society. In due time his ideas
germinated. All Europe heeded his voice and gave reality
to his dreams. Literature, education, government, society, took on new forms according to his bidding. One
man, of little account in literature, Rouget de Lisle, was
inspired at the opening of the Revolution to give voice
to the impassioned feelings of his countrymen in the spirit-
stirring "Marseillaise," still the national song of France.

Three other men of moderate power have had a lasting
influence on French literature. Beaumarchais, in his
Figaro comedies, taught the Nineteenth Century how the
drama can sparkle with wit, satire, wholesome merriment,
but, like too many others, tainted it with indelicacy. Ber-
nardin de Saint-Pierre was the successor of Rousseau in
propagating love of nature and made the world his debtor
by the romantic story of "Paul and Virginia." The third
figure is André Chenier, guillotined at thirty-two, who
combined the sensuous feeling of modern verse with a
marked classic simplicity. These three, so different in
life and work, were yet, each in his own peculiar way,
harbingers of the coming Romanticism. They agreed in
proclaiming individualism as a protest against the impersonal ideals of the later decaying classicism.

Even the pioneer scientists, like Buffon, and philosophers, like Condorcet, showed regard for this individualism. Man in himself was to be regarded as greater than
mathematical and political and theological systems.
Henceforth the human heart was to be the theme and realm
of an awakened literature. None of these forerunners
saw the tendency of their own work, but in retrospect it is
possible to trace a sure movement toward the old faiths

that had been so violently flung off.   The transition from lifeless classicism and materialistic philosophy to sunny Romanticism and renewed Christianity may be dated from the very opening of the Nineteenth Century.

By the Revolution of the 18th Brumaire (9th of November, 1799), Napoleon Bonaparte was made First Consul and became virtually supreme dictator of France. His unparalleled military and unscrupulous political glories had raised him to that proud eminence.   Fully aware of the unstable foundation of his suddenly acquired power, he was desirous to cement it with the potent traditions of the past.   Utterly indifferent as he was personally to spiritual considerations, he was well aware of their incalculable influence on the mass of mankind, and he saw clearly the growing desire of the people for much that they had lost.   The failure of the vaunted Revolution to realize the sublime dreams of its self-deceived promoters was palpable to all.   For liberty, equality, fraternity, they had received slavery, anarchy, bloodshed.   They longed for the restoration of order, for a government which should possess the ability and will to maintain itself unmoved against foreign enemies and domestic factions, for the restoration of the Christian worship.   Napoleon declared that his object in the permission of public worship was to gain the hearts of the people.   In return for the contemplated ridicule of the skeptics he won the gratitude of millions throughout the Empire.   But further he made way for an unexpected triumph of Catholicism which not only greatly assisted him at the time, but eventually revolutionized the literature of France.

THE RISE OF ROMANTICISM, 1800-1830

CHATEAUBRIAND

If one man and one book can fairly be fixed as marking the entrance of the new order of French literature, that honor belongs to François Auguste, Vicomte de Chateaubriand and his work, "Le Génie du Christianisme" (The Genius of Christianity), published in 1802. In that work was included "René," a somewhat gloomy youthful romance of the "sensibility" type, afterwards issued separately. Though not strictly great as a writer, and certainly not great as a man, Chateaubriand fancied himself to be Napoleon's literary counterpart. He really had an immense influence not only on literature, but on popular thought. He was born of a noble Breton family in 1768, and was intended for the church, but entered the army at sixteen, and was presented at the court of Louis XVI. On the outbreak of the Revolution, having neither accepted nor rejected the new opinions, he voyaged to America in a fruitless attempt to discover the northwest passage, still dreamed of by geographers. He journeyed from Niagara to New Orleans, and this visit gave him direct knowledge of American scenery, which he utilized later. He dined with Washington in Philadelphia, and said with reference to him, "There is virtue in the look of a great man. I felt myself warmed and refreshed by it during the rest of my life." On hearing of the execution of the King, Chateaubriand returned to France, and as a royalist joined the "emigrants." He also, at his sister's suggestion, married a lady from whom he soon parted, though he continued to show her respect. After being wounded in

Condé's army, he took refuge in London, where he remained until 1800, in honorable poverty. Here he wrote an essay on the Revolution, showing the bitterness of his spirit. He also began his work on Christianity, which occupied altogether four years. In 1801 he published the romance "Atala," portraying the loves of idealized American Indians, and depicting the primeval forest scenery of the New World. Amid the plaudits awarded to this picturesque romance of natural emotions and primitive society Chateaubriand issued the "Génie du Christianisme" (1802). It was likewise an innovation, both as a literary and a philosophical performance. After the multitude of books and discourses which had dismissed Christianity as vulgar and obsolete, here was a champion who exalted it above Paganism and skepticism, who did not dwell on its truth, but on its artistic superiority. The new work showed religion possessed of all the arts of refinement and the dignity of a royal career. In it were displayed Chateaubriand's poetical gifts of interpretation and expression. His readers enjoyed his delineation of historic events, of the experiences, emotions and outpourings of Christian life. Compared with these the pretentious fictions and stilted poems of the Century just past seemed hollow and worthless. The terrible realities of social convulsion made these pictures of a better life strongly captivating to wearied and anxious minds. The author had struck the right chord for the times and the public mood, by lifting poetical romance into the region of religious feeling. He revealed the beauties and elevation of religion. Subsequent historians and philosophers, as well as poets and romancists, confess their indebtedness to Chateaubriand for splendor of style.

Napoleon recognized the author, now famous, by appointing him secretary to the embassy at Rome. But

Chateaubriand was estranged from the Emperor by the murder of the Duc d'Enghien, and he later pronounced the condition of France under Napoleon "slavery without shame." In 1806 he made a tour to Greece and Palestine to familiarize himself with regions in which he proposed to lay the scene of a new romance. This was a prose epic, entitled "The Martyrs; or, the Triumphs of the Christian Religion" (1809). It treated of the persecution of Diocletian, and wanders from the Holy Land to Gaul and mythical Frankish Kings. It presents the argument of his greater work in a more popular form. The "Itinerary from Paris to Jerusalem" (1811) is a picturesque record of the author's travels. His implacable enmity to Napoleon was shown in his eloquent pamphlet "Bonaparte and the Bourbons" (1814), which Louis XVIII afterward declared had been worth to him a thousand men.

Under the Restoration the renowned Chateaubriand showed himself an ultra-royalist. He held embassies to Berlin, London, and Rome, and was for some months minister of foreign affairs. After the Revolution of 1830 he refused to take the oath of allegiance to Louis Philippe. His waywardness in politics is indicated in his own words: "I am a Bourbonist by honor, a royalist by reason and conviction, and a republican by taste and character." His writings after the Restoration added nothing to his reputation or influence. His brilliant imagination and eloquent style enabled him to endow his books with vital force. He died in July, 1848, having witnessed the advent of the second Republic. His posthumous memoirs, "Mémoires d'Outre-Tombe" (1849), displayed his genius and egotism. He had filled a large space as author, traveler and politician, but his chief distinction is in having inaugurated the return of French literature from artificialness and negation to the natural and supernatural in art.

MADAME DE STAEL

From a different starting-point and in a different way Madame de Staël contributed to infuse new ideals and methods into French literature. It is impossible here to give full consideration to the genius and unique personality of this extraordinary woman. She was born at Paris in 1766, Anne Louise Germaine Necker, daughter of the famous Swiss banker and financier, Jacques Necker, who had been made a baron and minister of France. Her mother was Suzanne Curchod, with whom the historian Gibbon had once been in love. As a child the daughter was trained by her mother in rather a rigid way, but at her more liberal father's instance she was early permitted to converse with the distinguished men of the time. Her precocity was extraordinary and her vivacity baffled her mother's efforts to control it. At the age of twenty she was married to Eric Magnus, Baron of Staël-Holstein, who was preferred by her father to other suitors, but for whom she had no real affection. She obtained by this marriage a privileged place at court, as her husband was the Swedish Ambassador. After his death in 1802, if not even before, she professed enthusiastic attachments to various distinguished public characters, not excepting Napoleon himself, who hated her as a woman that had departed from her sphere and as a political idealist. Her mental development, social experiences and philosophical aims must be rehearsed.

In 1788 she published "Letters on Rousseau" and other short papers on literary topics, in which her coming powers are discernible. During the Reign of Terror she made courageous and successful efforts to save the lives of some proscribed persons. In 1793 she withdrew to England, where she lived with Talleyrand and other exiles. But in

1795 she returned to Paris to wield considerable influence under the Directory. In 1800 was published her important treatise *"De la Littérature considérée dans ses Rapports avec les Institutions Sociales"* (On Literature Considered in its Relations with Social Institutions). Here she contended nobly for the greater liberty asserted, claimed, and ultimately won by the patriots of the American Revolution. She declared her faith in human nature, in progress, and in republican principles, which would inspire a grand world-literature, uniting the practical and the ideal. So far she still adhered to the philosophical style then in vogue. In her first novel "Delphine" (1802) she bewailed the lot of gifted women with ambitions. The heroine's free will, free speech and free acts are all misinterpreted by a stupid community so that despairing of liberty with a good name, she flies to the wilds of America.

Madame de Staël was herself banished by Napoleon's order from Paris and forbidden to reside within forty leagues of that capital. She went to Germany and sought the society of Goethe, Schiller and Schlegel at Weimar. The great German poet listened to her brilliant conversation "with vast admiration and not a little fatigue." She insisted on philosophizing in society, and gave her hearers, who were expected to reply, not a moment for reflection on the most important topics. They must dispatch the deepest concerns as lightly as in a game of shuttlecock. After a tour in Italy, this swift-witted woman produced, in 1807, her best-known novel, "Corinne," in which she herself, somewhat idealized, is the heroine, a woman of genius hemmed in by conventional restrictions. She has a faithless lover, and dies of a broken heart. The author had returned to France to attend to the publication of this work, but its success drew from Napoleon an order

banishing her from France. She had incurred his enmity
persisting in severe criticisms of his actions in spite of
warning. After traveling in Germany, she settled at
Coppet, in Switzerland, where several of her friends went
to console her. Her book on Germany *"De l'Allemagne"*
was printed at Paris in 1810, but seized by the police, and
not reprinted until 1813 in London. In it she portrayed
intellectual and political Germany with keen feminine
intuition. Contrasting the literatures of France and
Germany she showed that the former concerned itself
mainly with a limited society and consequently lacked the
element of growth and elevation traceable in the literature
of the Northern races, marked by imagination, introspec-
tion, and religious sentiment. Goethe declared the work
ought to be "a powerful battery making a wide breach in
the wall of superannuated prejudices between the two
nations." By this tribute to the rising German literature
and by example in her mature writings, Madame de Staël
gave a strong impulse to the Romantic movement.
Though aristocratic in sentiment, she was not hostile to
the Revolution. She admired the German temperament
and believed that reason and philosophy made steady
progress despite the innumerable misfortunes of the
human race. She inveighed against social restrictions
which prevented her from living in freedom from conventional rules. Her timely exposition of German intellectual
power had considerable effect on French thought. Among
her other works are autobiographic memoirs, entitled "Ten
Years of Exile," and "Considerations on the French Revolution," which was published after her decease in July,
1817. She had returned to Paris after Napoleon's abdica-
tion. Her daughter became the Duchess de Broglie.
Madame de Staël was formerly considered the greatest
authoress of modern times, but her fame has declined in

recent years. Critics now maintain that in style she is too diffuse, and in matter she had little originality, but great power of absorption of the best ideas of others, which she then expressed with admirable vigor and clearness.

THE IDEOLOGISTS

The new literature which was to signalize the new Century found its most telling expression in imaginative writings, that class of work which most directly touches the heart. But this spirit also animated the works of philosophers and religionists, whose conflicting contributions to the thought of the day, though sometimes resisting the rising tide, yet in the main added to its momentum. A certain class, who were known as Ideologists, bold propounders of advanced ideas, argued in other literary forms than poetry and fiction. The most accessible and perhaps the most representative book of this class is Volney's "Ruins of Empires," as it has been called in English. Its dreamy meditations are nót without lofty eloquence and poetical charm. The author, Constantin François Chasse-bœuf, Comte de Volney (1757-1820), was a traveler and moderate statesman, who was raised to the peerage and Senate by Napoleon, though he was not a servile partisan. The name of his chief work is in French, *"Les Ruines, ou Meditation sur les Revolutions des Empires."* It was published in 1791, but is mentioned here as being the representative of a class which continued into the present Century. He visited the United States, and wrote a book on its climate and soil. His last work was "Researches on Ancient History" (1814).

Among the general writers a notable figure is Hugues Félicité Robert de Lamennais (1782-1854). As a priest and ardent champion of the church he was deeply distressed by the widening of the gulf between it and the people. With his poetical temperament he set himself to bridge that gulf with mutual concessions and thus unite theocracy and democracy in happy content. This ideal he sought to make practical. After a sojourn in England he published a work that made a startling and deep impression, *"Essai sur l'Indifférence en Matiére de Religion"* (Essay on Indifference in Regard to Religion). The conservative party in the church sharply criticized the work, but this opposition moved him to more aggressive polemics, resulting in more ecclesiastical trouble. His paper *L'Avenir* (The Dawn) had for its flamboyant motto "God and Liberty; the Pope and the People," and called upon the clergy to separate themselves from Kings and join with the working classes. But this programme was too radical and the paper was suppressed. Failing to broaden the church, Lamennais changed his tack and sought to spiritualize democracy. His *"Paroles d'un Croyant"* (Words of a Believer) is a singular but fascinating prose poem. He was derisively charged with flaunting the cross crowned with the red cap of Liberty, like Père Hyacinthe of the present day. Lamennais did valiant service in behalf of intellectual progress, mellowed by religious faith, but his church frowned him down, defied his not unfriendly attacks, and let him die outside its pale. In the history of literature he must be reckoned as one of the forces in the widespread Romantic movement.

BERANGER

We pass to the creative writers whose works appeal to the sense of pleasure first and to the reasoning faculty only secondarily. The first and greatest of these is certainly Victor Hugo, preëminent in both prose and poetry, but on account of the length of his career, treatment of him is postponed. The next greatest is Lamartine, who likewise distinguished himself in the two grand divisions; a third, Béranger, wrote only songs for the people. Treating them in chronological order, the last is first to be considered. Jean Pierre de Béranger, born in 1780, has been denied by some critics a place among the poets, but he was certainly a song-maker, and the dividing line has yet to be discovered which shall exclude the songs of Burns and Béranger from the garden of poetry. If the question were to be decided by the sovereign people, who would be more likely to gain their suffrages than the candidate who could set them singing his ideas in their own simple language? It was because the appeal was to the people that Béranger, to his own amused astonishment, found himself a power in the land. For he did not possess the recognized elements of greatness, either as man or poet. Born of the humblest class, he was apprenticed to a printer, and began to write songs at the age of sixteen. Some of these he sent to Lucien Bonaparte, who rewarded him handsomely and procured for him a clerkship under the Empire. Thenceforth he was equally devoted to Napoleon and the Republic, and despised the emigrant nobles. After the Restoration he lost his place and was fined and imprisoned for his biting satires. His songs helped to bring about the Revolution of 1830, but he refused to accept any office from the new government, nor would he serve when elected to the Constituent Assembly of 1848. Though he lived in a garret, he had long been allowed to sing as he pleased, and this was his only desire. As he says in one of his songs, "God in His grace bade me sing, Sing, poor little one." When he died, in 1854, the Government of Napoleon III accorded this people's poet a grand funeral.

Béranger sent his artless songs straight into the hearts of the people, and set them singing grander sentiments than they could even have comprehended in eloquent prose. A loftier and purer inspiration would have limited his usefulness or have brought it to an untimely end. Of an easy temperament, with a love of simple comfort in perilous times, he gave the people chorus-songs of love and jollity, while waiting for the good time coming, and in each sprinkled some political spice. For more than thirty years he reigned as king of the light-hearted whistling multitude. He was the poet, he felt himself the prophet, of old and young folks, at home and out of doors, and varied his song to suit each class, yet without yielding his own clear view of what was right. Those qualities ensured popularity, which Béranger estimated and utilized to the full. The politics may be obsolete, but other elements of his songs remain, of which many a greater poet would be proud. He was despised by both classicists and Romanticists, in his day as vulgar, but the best critics of to-day recognize his lively wit, his touching pathos, his hearty patriotism, his thorough humanity. His power is still felt in the later popular lyrics.

LAMARTINE

Lamartine, compared with Béranger, fills a nobler space in a loftier realm. Whatever Béranger lacked to make his songs undeniably true poems—depth, dignity, sublimity—Lamartine possessed. His grandeur of soul lifted him beyond the reach of his early comrades. In that age of sentiment even the affectation of it gave some writers reputation. But with Lamartine all was genuine. It was the free spirit rather than his highly finished verses that gave him lasting fame. Alphonse Marie Louis Prat de Lamartine was born at Mâcon in Southern France in 1790. From his infancy, he revelled in the beautiful, as his expanding mind perceived it in his mother's readings, in the dawn of love with sorrow in its train and in Italian travel. He entered the life-guards of Louis XVIII in 1814, but retired to Switzerland during the Hundred Days. In 1820 he published his *"Méditations Poétiques,"* the masterpiece of which is the elegy *"Le Lac"* (The Lake), expressing the contrast between the instability of human affairs and the perseverance of nature. The appearance of this book has been likened to that of a new planet in the firmament, brilliant and abiding. Here was a singer who, discarding artifice, struck the new, true note. His beloved one had passed away, but the love survived. In these meditations on the mysteries of life, love, and death Lamartine gave play to the elemental emotions common to all men. The book gave a new trend to poetry.

After serving as *chargé d'affaires* at Florence, Lamartine returned to Paris and in 1830, published a new volume, *"Harmonies Poétiques et Religieuses"* (Poetical and Religious Harmonies), declaring his devotion to the church and throne. After the Revolution of that year he gave up his official position. With his wife, an English woman, and his daughter, he made a tour in the East, and returning published, in 1833, what is called in the English version "A Pilgrimage to the Holy Land." He had meantime been elected to the Chamber of Deputies, and in the course of a few years passed from conservative to republican principles. In 1836 "Jocelyn" was published, an ambitious attempt at poetizing an incident of the Revolution. Jocelyn, a peasant child, had taken refuge in the mountains from the perils of the time, and there found a companion, who, after their friendship is established, is discovered to be a girl. "Jocelyn" is an essentially noble poem, soaring to the heights, exquisite in description, and chaste in conception, but its length and monotony of melancholy prevent it from reaching the standard of its predecessors. Lamartine's last great poem, *"La Chute d'un Ange"* (The Fall of an Angel), was still more a failure. It is an unwieldly composition, too flighty for a treatise on human ideals, too sentimental for an epic like "Paradise Lost."

Lamartine had now evidently exhausted his stock of poetic inspiration. He may then have deliberately given to statecraft a genius better fitted for poetry, as Milton had done in the middle of his career, or his ambition may have spurred him to attempt other conquests in the arena of public life. If eloquence and other oratorical gifts had sufficed to sustain a great statesman's reputation, Lamartine might have had that fame. But there seems to have been a glittering insincerity in the poet, and the same quality made him in his political career a skilful time-server. His eloquent "History of the Girondists" (1847), in which he first avowed democratic principles, had an important political influence in bringing about a new Revolution. For a few glorious months in 1848 Lamartine seemed the master of his country's destinies, and then fell to an inglorious obscurity. He labored diligently with the pen, pouring out a vast quantity of his historical, biographical and autobiographical works, which are useful but not inspiring. His last purely literary work was the pretty romance of "Graziella" (1852). He lingered under the imperialism which he had anathematized and even became a pensioner of Napoleon III before he died in 1869.

The immortal part of a man's work must be viewed in the light of the times and conditions in which it was done. Lamartine came when poetry was limping, unbound its

wings and set it free to soar. For this his fame may
rightly be judged to transcend that of greater poets who
followed where he had led. His after decline may perhaps be traced to the enervating affectation of sentiment
which brought to light the defects of its noble quality.
Chateaubriand and Lamartine are conspicuous examples
of true genius crippled and finally smothered with insincerity of thought and over-refinement of diction.

The lasting popularity of the affecting story of "Pic-
ciola; or, the Prison Flower" (1825) entitles its author
to mention. Xavier Boniface Saintine (1790-1845) left
nothing of merit besides this brief story.

BEYLE (STENDHAL)

Henri Beyle (1783-1842), who used the pen-name
Stendhal, was a prolific writer of novels, remarkable for
depth and a peculiar power of analysis. Though not
widely known, he is considered by the foremost French
critics to be not simply an able delineator of human passions, but to be the precursor of the psychological novelists of recent times. He practically anticipated both the
coming Romanticism and the later realism. He told
Balzac, in 1840, that he fancied he "might meet with some
success toward 1880." Born in 1783, he served under
Napoleon, and in his hatred of the Restoration, betook
himself to more congenial Italy. Its music, pictures and
sculptures are worked into his early romances. Afterward a bitter philosophy is infused into his profoundly
intellectual stories, and spoils their effect. Beyle wrote
much miscellaneous biography and criticism. His aim
in all his writings was to acquaint the nations with those
literary works which yield the highest degree of pleasure.
He had written first as an artist, but he afterward became a

psychologist. His best novels are *"Le Rouge et Noir"* (The Red and Black) (1830) and *"La Chartreuse de Parme"* (The Carthusian Nun of Parma) (1839), but much of his influential work is of earlier date.

In an essay, which was translated into English in 1823, Beyle contrasts the style of Racine with that of Shakespeare, to the glory of the latter. Voltaire's tribute to the effect of the free note in English literature applies with renewed force to the years when the Waverley novels began to fill his countrymen with enthusiasm for romance. Beyle's efforts to enlarge and enrich the national literature by introducing foreign theories and treatment were being put in execution. French dramatists and poets were busy transferring Othello and Shylock, Cromwell and Chatterton to their stage. The old national romances of Spain, Germany and other lands were also pressed into the new movement. Not only the poetical renaissance, but also the monarchial Restoration, had marked effect on the young writers of the time. The temporary result was a curious blending of effete conservatism with a sham liberty, but this could not last. If the Romantic spirit meant anything, it meant absolute freedom of range. It would discern and employ whatever of beauty the church and the throne had to boast, but it would enslave itself to neither. A small group, known as the Cénacle, withdrew from court service, and became the apostles of Romanticism, liberated from every species of fashionable patronage.

DE VIGNY

The work of another writer belonging in part to this period has provoked considerable criticism. Some complain that he has not received full appreciation. Alfred de Vigny (1797-1863) was one of those men of gloomy genius who prefer the proud isolation of their souls to the applause of crowds. He was a young soldier when the Empire fell, and composed poems in the somber year of Waterloo. His first book was published in 1822, and was followed by another in 1826. These poems are thought by some to have had influence on the works of Hugo and other Romanticists, while others regard de Vigny himself as an imitator. He certainly ceased writing poetry for many years, but he published in 1826 the novel "Cinq-Mars." Here, again, critics differ; some pronounce it one of the finest, as well as earliest, historical romances in the style of Sir Walter Scott. But other critics declare it deficient in dramatic quality and even void of interest. It had an excellent style, and received the favor of the Royalist party. De Vigny married an English lady, but the union proved unhappy, and he took refuge in gloomy philosophy. His knowledge of English served him in paraphrazing "Othello" and adapting "Shylock" from Shakespeare. His own drama, "Chatterton," when presented on the stage, shocked the audience by showing the hero's suicide. His strange book, "Stello," represents an invalid as relating to his physician the sad fate of three unfortunate poets—Gilbert, Chatterton, and André Chénier. His last work, *"Poëmes Philosophiques"* was only partly published before his death. The poems abound in expressions of despondency, mingled with exhortations to stoical resignation.

CLASSICISM AND ROMANTICISM

The radical difference between Classicism and Romanticism, so prominent in French literary history, may be broadly stated to be that between artificialism and naturalism. The former insisted on strict observance of certain rules and principles derived by rhetoricians from the study of the ancient classics, the masterpieces of Greek and Roman literature. These rules were particularly strict in regard to the drama, and in France that form of literature has always had a dominant effect on the rest. The three unities—of time, place, and action—must be strictly observed in every tragedy. The plays are in rhymed couplets, and each couplet must be complete in sense, as in Pope's poetry in English. The diction was strictly limited to dignified expressions, and certain words of constant use in prose were positively prohibited. The dramatist who dared on one occasion to introduce in the most carefully guarded way the word *"mouchoir"* (handkerchief) was compelled to cancel it before the play could be repeated. Other artifices of refinement cramped the genius of French writers, and while many of their productions are truly grand, the wonder to those accustomed to English freedom is not merely that under the stifling panoply genius could achieve so much, but that it could exist at all. Even the great Corneille was censured for his violation of rules in his masterpiece, "The Cid," but the unstinted applause of Paris supported him against the decision of the Academy. The rules of all poetry, whether lyrical, satirical, didactic, or epic, were equally strict and cramping in regard to subject, treatment, diction, and metre.

But from England, just when it was adopting many of these artificial regulations for its own poetry, came the knowledge of what had been achieved by the so-called Gothic genius of Shakespeare and his successors. Both Voltaire and Rousseau resided for a time in England, and both were more affected by their novel surroundings than they were fully aware. Though Voltaire censured Shakespeare as barbarian, he was compelled to admit his power. Bolingbroke, Hume and others from Britain resided in France and diffused acquaintance with English literature. At the same time, Germany, casting off the bondage of French fashion, welcomed the English freedom and helped to transmit it to France. Later the emigrant nobles learned much in their exile, and did not altogether forget it on their return. Still more, the grand wars of Napoleon caused an unprecedented mingling of races, and a breaking down of the barriers between them. Madame de Staël revealed to France the intellectual movement in Germany and called for a European bent of mind. When the French were thus made ready for the acceptance of new ideas, the Romantic movement began, not in one country, but almost simultaneously in all the leading nations of Europe. In Great Britain it was manifest in the genius of Scott and Byron; in Germany in that of Goethe and Schiller.

The open controversy between the Classicists and the Romanticists was started by Lamartine in his *"Méditations"* in 1820, assisted by Victor Hugo's first book in 1822, *"Odes et Ballades."* In the preface to the second edition Hugo roundly declared that he was "absolutely ignorant of what was meant by the Classic School and the Romantic School." But he certainly altered his views within a few years. Romanticism was opposed to artificialism, conventionalism, and formalism in literature. It sought for freedom in choice of subjects and for natural expression of primal feelings. Some of the earliest, like Chateaubriand, to find scope for their feelings, went back to the religious fervor of olden times, or abroad to the simple nature of savage tribes. Later Romanticists, like Hugo, full of self-consciousness, sought to express directly their own emotions or passions.   The impulse of every passing experience was to take the place of the studied phrases of classicism.   Individual aspiration, hope, and despair were to be the body and soul of the new literature. To its exponents and enthusiasts the rules and traditions of poetry were of no value or use, but rather fetters and shackles.   The heart alone must direct the voice or pen.

THE REIGN OF ROMANTICISM, 1830-1870

HUGO

In the land of Romance there are three Kingdoms—that of Poetry, of the Drama, of the Novel. Only once has one strong conqueror worn the triple crown, and that was when Victor Hugo was hailed as first in song, first in stagecraft, and first in prose fiction. Time has corrected not a few of the estimates formed by his contemporaries, nevertheless, it cannot be disputed that he had a truly imperial genius, a mind that spanned the wide earth, and touched the heavens above and the depths of misery below. Hugo was the most romantic of poets and the most realistic of romancers.

Victor Marie Hugo, born at Besançon in 1802, passed as a child under powerful influences, traceable in his mature work. His father was an army officer, who flourished and declined with the Bonapartes; his mother was a Catholic and a royalist. With her children she followed her husband to Spain and Italy, when Victor was but five years old. The characters, Hernani, Quasimodo, and Triboulet, are taken from incidents of that time. At fifteen he won the prize offered by the Academy for a poem on "The Advantages of Study," though there was at first some doubt whether this attempt of 320 lines could be original. Hugo had already written in his diary: "I wish to be Chateaubriand or nothing," and that great writer, then at the height of his renown, pronounced the boy poet "a sublime child." Other prizes were awarded to the youth at the Floral Games of Toulouse. He lived in Paris with his mother and remained in her faith until her death in 1820.   His father, who had been obliged to dwell in seclusion at Blois, on account of his former connection with Joseph Bonaparte, King of Spain, survived her eight years.   In 1822 Hugo published his first book, *"Odes et Ballades."*   The poems were highly finished, but not according to classical rules; they were in wrong metres, and extravagant in style.   Hugo was still a Royalist and had not openly withdrawn from the Classicists.   King Louis XVIII, hoping to encourage a new genius in aid of the Bourbons, bestowed on him a pension of 1,500 francs. This was welcome, for Hugo had married his youthful love, Adèle Foucher.   In 1823 came his first novel, *"Hans d'Islande"* (Hans of Iceland), which shows the fondness for the extravagant and grotesque, found in his later works.   *"Bug Jargal"* (1826), the next tale, was praised in the organ of the "Romantics," who were then beginning their war on the Classicists.

The French Academy, always so potent in literature, was at this time decidedly opposed to innovations, and upheld the principles which had dominated the Eighteenth Century.   The young writers who had grown up amid the storms of the Revolution and Empire, rebelled against its dictation.   Hugo, though deeply filled with the spirit of Romanticism, held aloof for a time, and then entering the new school, passed at once to its head.   In the preface to his drama, "Cromwell" (1827), which was not allowed to be acted, he preached the new doctrine.   "Amy Robsart," which was based on Scott's "Kenilworth," was not successful.   These dramas from English sources showed the direction of the author's thoughts.   When "Marion Delorme," which had been approved by the poet's friends, was offered for presentation on the stage, the censor found disloyal allusions in it and prohibited its produc-

tion.   King Charles X, whom Hugo had eulogized in an
ode, offered to quadruple his pension if he would withdraw
the play, but the poet, who declared that it was not meant
to have any political significance, refused to accept the
bribe, and wrote at once another drama, "Hernani."   The
first performance of the new play on Saturday, February
25, 1830, was made a battle between the old and the new,
the Classicists, and the "Romantics." The former gathered to hiss, the latter, comprising several who were afterward notable in literature, decked themselves with red
badges and gay apparel, and came to applaud.   Young
France was victorious in spite of brawls.   Though the
press, with but one exception, condemned the play, it was
repeated for two months.   The King had aided the Classicists in the attempts to crush the play and in July he had
to fly from Paris.   Hugo had been made a power in the
state in spite of himself.

The victorious dramatist published a volume of poems,
"Les Feuilles d'Automne" (Autumn Leaves), which
added to his fame.   This was still further increased by his
great historical novel, *"Notre Dame de Paris"* (1831),
which fairly presents both his strength and his weakness.
It is full of contrasts, guilt and innocence, beauty and
deformity, intrigue and simplicity, ferocity and love.   The
work itself, in spite of its grandeur, is an ill constructed
conglomeration.   The author was entirely destitute of
humor, and therefore liable to pass unconsciously from
eloquence to bombast, from the sublime to the ridiculous.
And yet this great work has not inaptly been compared to
the great cathedral which gives it name—an architectural
wonder, full of splendid sculpture and ornament, brilliant
shows and gloomy recesses, glorious works of religious art
and frightful or burlesque gargoyles.   The censorship of
the stage was relaxed under the new citizen King, Louis

Philippe, and when *"Marion Delorme"* was allowed to appear, it ran for more than two months. The contest between the Classicists and "Romantics" continued at its representation. Then Hugo wrote a new drama, *"Le Roi S'amuse"* (The King's diversion), a play of the time of Francis I, which was performed amid a tumult. The censor had condemned some passages, and the press pronounced against the whole play as indecent. King Louis Philippe was induced by the Conservatives to forbid its repetition. Hugo defended his play against the charge of immorality and sued in the courts for compensation, but was defeated. Still undaunted, he produced another drama, perhaps still more offensive, *"Lucrece Borgia,"* which was presented at a different theater. So he went on, year after year, writing plays, sometimes in verse, as the foregoing were, according to the old rules, and sometimes in prose, according to the new license. His last successful play was *"Ruy Blas,"* in 1838. Then his popularity as a dramatist passed to younger men, who had been trained by his example. In 1843 he tried to regain favor by *"Les Burgraves,"* but it failed and was withdrawn after a month's presentation. Yet Hugo did not altogether relinquish dramatic writing, as some half dozen examples remain to prove.

In the meantime his poetical activity had continued unabated. In *"Les Orientals"* (Songs of the Orient) his lyrical power is displayed in richness befitting its title. In *"Les Chants du Crépuscule"* (Chants of the Twilight) he deals with the realities of modern life, divided between hope and despondency. *"Les Voix Intérieures"* (The Inner Voices), dedicated to his father, and *"Les Rayons et les Ombres"* (The Rays and the Shadows), repeat this mingled strain. On these volumes Hugo's fame as a lyrical poet firmly rests; other French poets have equaled him in power or delicacy; he alone combines both in an eminent degree.

Hugo was defeated more than once in seeking a place in the French Academy, but succeeded in 1841, thanks to the goodwill of Balzac, who retired from the competition, and never became an Academician. Four years later Hugo was made a peer. When Louis Philippe was driven into exile by the Revolution of 1848, Hugo supported the Republic, and in the new Assembly he showed his democratic and socialist tendencies. Though taunted with his political changes, he remained firm in his new principles. He so strenuously opposed Louis Napoleon, that when the *coup d'état* was effected in December, 1851, Hugo's name was put at the head of the proscribed, and a large reward offered for his capture. He was concealed by a Royalist nobleman, escaped to Brussels, and afterward fixed his residence in Guernsey in the English Channel. His exile continued until the fall of the Empire in 1870, and was rich in literary production. In ceaseless diatribes in prose and verse, he continued his war on Napoleon the Little. Among other publications were *"Les Contemplations,"* a poetical record of his own early life; and the first part of a projected epic, *"La Légende des Siècles"* (Legend of the Ages), which was to embody the history of the human race in pictures of successive epochs. But a grander prose work was to extend his fame over the world. In 1862 appeared *"Les Misérables,"* in which he put forth all his powers as if to eclipse the generation of popular novelists by one mighty effort. It consists of five volumes, and reveals to the gaze of the world the life of the wretched and outcast. The author himself with his love for grand phrases, called it "a sort of planetary system, making the circuit about one giant mind that is the personification of all social evil." It was followed in 1866 by *"Les Travail-*

leurs de la Mer" (The Toilers of the Sea), founded on his observation of the fisher-folk of Guernsey. Still another of the same kind was "*L'Homme qui Rit*" (The Man Who Laughs) (1869), which was less popular. Hugo, though a monarch in literature, was a preacher as well as a poet, and though a peer of France, desired to win the hearts and suffrages of the uncultured multitude. From his island retreat he often put forth appeals in behalf of those oppressed or in danger of condemnation to death, and called for the abolition of capital punishment, as he had already done when in the Assembly. On the surrender of Napoleon III at Sedan in September, 1870, Hugo returned to Paris, and at once took an active part in public affairs. He was now an extreme Radical, and as such was elected in 1876 a Senator for life. During the last years of his life he was regarded by the people as a national hero. Yet he did not rest from literary labor, but sent forth pamphlets, poems, autobiographic sketches, a drama, and one more powerful novel, "*Quatre-vingt-treize*," treating of insurrection in Brittany in behalf of the King in 1793. One of his most charming productions is the volume of verse, "*L'Art d'être Grand-père*" (The Art of Being a Grandfather). He died after a brief illness on the 22d of May, 1885. His state burial at the Pantheon was a memorable spectacle.

Hugo's national popularity may be attributed partly to his longevity. He became the Grand Old Man of France. But his fame was founded on the most substantial work. In lyrical poetry he excelled Lamartine and Alfred de Musset in the amount, the variety, the power, and the delicacy of his odes. In the drama he had no close competitor. In fiction he surpassed Balzac, who, though a most laborious workman, never became a real artist. He rivals Dumas in his depiction of adventure, and George Sand in delineation of emotion and idyllic life. Other poets, dramatists, and novelists in various degrees claimed popular attention, but Hugo rose above them in his splendid enthusiasm for humanity and marvelous versatility. He was the typical representative of the Gallic spirit at its best enthusiastic and rhetorical, eloquent in behalf of the oppressed and in denunciation of tyranny, abounding in epigram and prone to exaggeration. No other man of the Century lorded it so superbly over so vast and brilliant a realm as did Hugo, governing with the glad consent of the governed. More than graceful courtesy moved the Laureate of England to lay his wreath on Hugo's coffin, bearing the inscription, "To the World's Greatest Poet."

DE MUSSET

After Hugo there followed a brilliant crowd of writers, who adorn the new reign of Romance. In the Cénacle one of the youngest was Alfred de Musset (1810-1857), a typical Parisian, regarding pleasure as the chief end of life. He was a disciple of Hugo, and still more of Byron, and published at nineteen, *"Contes d'Espagne et d'Italie"* (Stories of Spain and Italy), which had an immediate success. The stories are in verse and are ideals of love-poetry. His first drama, *"Une Nuit Vénitienne"* (A Venetian Night), failed on the stage in 1830, and the author was seriously hurt. After some further poems, Musset returned to the drama, producing *"Les Caprices de Marianne"* (Marianne's Caprices), in which he sought to present a compromise which should combine the merits of the Classical and the Romantic schools. Through adhering pretty closely to the unities, it is fully imbued with the Romantic spirit. It is called a comedy from its fresh dialogue and swift action, but it has also tragical elements in plot and character. The chief event of Musset's career is his unfortunate *liaison* with George Sand, which has given rise to much controversy. The two authors went to Italy in 1833, and after a short period of passionate devotion, separated. George Sand published her version of the story in *"Elle et Lui"* (She and He), charging him with mad jealousy. After Alfred's death, his brother Paul replied in *"Lui et Elle"* (He and She), charging her with infidelity. When Alfred recovered from the shock, he produced his most notable poems, *"Les Nuits"* (The Nights), describing the seasons of love in four parts, May, August, October, December. His prose *"Confession d'un Enfant du Siècle"* (Confession of a Child of the Age), is a wild protest against his surroundings, throwing all the blame of the moral evil of the time on the despotism of Napoleon. The fault of the poet's life lay in the moral weakness of the man himself. His genius enabled him to give expression to the ardor of his youth and to the mental conflict of his later dissipated life. He was admitted to the Academy in 1852, being then regarded as a poet of the highest rank.

Other poets and dramatists of the Romantic school who became also novelists, will be treated later. The most notable were Théophile Gautier and Alexandre Dumas. Petrus Borel and Gerard de Nerval affected wierd poetry with a certain success. Later came Charles Baudelaire (1821-1867), who translated Poe's short stories. He copied and exaggerated the morbid features of his master's imaginative writings. He had, however, original genius which he unfortunately put to vile uses, making the evil of human nature the theme for his artistic skill in language. His excellent critical instinct is seen in some admirable studies of poets.

THE ROMANTIC NOVELISTS

The novel, now all but supreme in the literature of the world, is traced by literary historians to the prose romance which originated, with little, if any foreign impulse, in France in the Twelfth Century. It was at first the telling in simpler form for a ruder audience of the poetical romances of chivalry, as in "Amadis of Gaul." In the Seventeenth Century there arose pastoral romances which described the characters and doings of the French court under a disguise borrowed from ancient history. Then there came tales of the adventures of rogues and vagabonds. But the name Novel was applied to the long drawn out tales which depended for their interest on their "sensibility," or proper regulation of the tender feelings of the human heart. With the opening of the Nineteenth Century some of these forms were partly revived. But the French novel, as commonly accepted, came in with the Romanticism, which has been viewed in its poetical and dramatic aspects. Previous stories had no marked power or length and no special design. The invention of the French novel destined to live and exert influence is ascribed to George Sand, Hugo, Dumas, and Balzac. Their methods and ideals differed materially, but together their efforts made a new species of literature.

GEORGE SAND

George Sand is the literary pseudonym of a woman, who was by birth Armantine Lucile Aurore Dupin, and became by marriage Baroness Dudevant. Born in 1804, her life is as fantastic as her fictions. She inherited an untamable gypsy temperament. Her childhood was a breezy idyll; then she spent two years in the seclusion of a convent. At eighteen she was married to a country squire, and nine years later, with her two children, she left her husband to live by her pen in Paris. Jules Sandeau was one of the new novelists who sought to unfold character and picture the actual life of the time. He was her lover and assisted her in writing a story of this sort, *"Rose et Blanche"* (1831). Though she appropriated a syllable of his name as her pseudonym, their literary union did not continue. She had found her vocation and could go alone. Within a year she wrote "Indiana," the first unrestrained protest against what she felt to be the subjection of woman, and a plea for freedom in love. The book brimmed over with high-flown sentiment expressed in the music of words. The same plea was repeated with variations in a long series of romances which flowed rapidly from her pen. The liberty which she claimed in her books she practiced without concealment in her long, varied, and by no means happy life. She was a child of nature, shrewd enough to utilize her mastery of literary art in adapting her ideas for the market, in which her first book had made her a favorite purveyor. Having shown the evils flowing from unhappy marriages, she next depicted those due to unhappy *liaisons,* and labored to prove that no unions are binding beyond the mutual passion of the hour. Her personal influence upon such weak men of genius as Musset and Chopin was sadly in contrast with the happy results alleged to flow from her theory of freedom. Experience seems to have brought disillusion. Her earlier books expressed the universal unrest in impracticable and passionate ways. In her later books she left off her rhapsodies for abstractions and unreal liberty, and turned back to enjoy the sweet simplicity of her early years in the country. "Consuelo" (1843), which is partly based on her acquaintance with Chopin and her experience in Venice, marks the turning point in her literary career. Among her later books, *"La petite Fadette"* (Little Fadette), *"L'Homme de Neige"* (The Snow Man), and *"La Mare au Diable"* (The Devil's Pool), are the best liked. The *"Histoire de ma Vie"* (Story of My Life), is a romance of reality, but leaves much untold. For her pastorals she invented a style of her own, using words so simple that peasants could understand them, and so pure that the Academy would approve them. In her peaceful old age she wrote fairy stories for her grandchildren. She died in June, 1876, having witnessed many revolutions, political and literary.

BALZAC

As George Sand is the typical emotionalist in romance, Honoré de Balzac is the accepted type of the realists. She was a prose poet, revealing the joys and sorrows, the revolts and aspirations of individuals. He was the mechanical recorder of the people's daily life, yet was able to penetrate into the average man's personality. Honoré de Balzac was born in moderate circumstances in Touraine in 1799. His father wished him to study law, but a sister, who understood his character, helped him to devote himself to literature. His early novels were not read, but he persevered in writing. A few years before Victor Hugo published his "Cromwell," Balzac had tried the same theme for a tragedy, but could not get it printed. At last, when he was thirty, his "Chouans," an historical romance after Scott's style, gained some favor. Then he published a rapid succession of stories, striking while the iron was hot. He was always fond of speculation, and made several ventures in trade, especially seeking to establish a large printing and publishing house, which loaded him with debt. In literature he undertook to make a modern "Human Comedy" to display all the types and varieties of human life and character. And so far as French character represents humanity in general he succeeded in depicting it with marvelous truth. Intense love of money was a part of his own character, and he makes it a universal ruling principle in his work. This binds him to a sordid view of life, and makes his stories less elevated in tone than a cheap daily newspaper. Balzac called himself the secretary of society and was indeed, by choice, a matter-of-fact reporter, and had scant regard for any higher life than the streets of Paris afforded. But his indomitable will and perseverance in his self-appointed task are beyond all praise. Twelve hours from midnight to noon he toiled at his desk, stimulating himself with strong coffee. He sacrificed himself to his ambition. He was engaged to a Polish Countess for sixteen years, and at last, when fifty-one, was married to her in March, 1850. He had looked forward to a happy old age as compensation for years of toil, but was disappointed, dying in the August after his marriage.

In the work which he had planned and systematically arranged, he claimed to have portrayed over two thousand distinct types of character. The idea of the vast comedy was not announced by him until 1842, when he had already been at work twelve years. He undertook to analyze and classify human life as the naturalist Buffon had done with the animal kingdom. The characters of his previous novels were arranged to suit his plan, and he set out to supply all missing parts. But being of plebeian birth, he could not study the patrician aright. He did not disguise his preference for the baser sort and baser side of life. Intellectually he was intense rather than comprehensive. Poetry and refined sensibility were alien to his habit and work. He was deficient in style, and this defect kept him from being recognized early. He had power but not grace, point without polish, and verbosity without fluency. Yet French critics, admirers and lovers of perfect style, have pronounced him the greatest novelist of the world. Taine has declared his works "the greatest storehouse of documents of human nature." If other students may not be able to accept this view and regard Balzac as the supreme master in modern fiction, they can still award him the full honor of being a founder of a grand school of novelists. They may admit that he has done more than any other single writer to intensify the study of human nature in the realistic way.

His *"Comédie Humaine"* was divided into three main sections—Studies of Manners, Philosophic Studies, Analytic Studies. The studies of Manners comprise twenty-four stories grouped as Scenes of Private Life, ten stories of Provincial Life, three stories of Country Life, twenty stories of Parisian Life, and seven stories of Political and Military life. The Philosophical Studies comprise twenty stories and the Analytic Studies only two. The catalogue of these works is immense, and it is difficult to select those which far surpass others. Balzac has several portraits of misers; one of these is the father in "Eugenie Grandet," of whose greed the wife and daughter are victims. In "Cousin Pons," an old musician is preyed upon by rogues. In "Le Père Goriot," the father lives in a shabby boarding house, while his married daughters revel in luxury. In "The Greatness and Decline of César Birotteau" a perfumer who has worked his way to wealth, is made the victim of bankers. In the *"Peau de Chagrin"* (The Magic Skin) Raphael, the hero, has the skin of a wild ass as a talisman, by means of which his wishes can be readily obtained. But a serious condition is attached, that as the skin is diminished his life is shortened, and that every desire gratified takes a certain portion from the skin. It has been truly said that Balzac's own life is symbolized in this story.

DUMAS

Alexandre Dumas shares with Hugo the glory of the revival of the romance of adventure. He was the son of General Alexandre Dumas, who was a Creole, the illegitimate son of a French Marquis and a negro girl. General Dumas was a man of remarkable gallantry, but so little inclined to submit to control that Napoleon dismissed him from the army. His wife was an innkeeper's daughter, who proved an affectionate mother. The great Alexandre was born at Villers-Cotterets on July 4, 1802. He was boisterous and troublesome in youth and at the age of twenty-one went to Paris to seek his fortune. He entered the employ of the Duke of Orleans, and two years later began to write small pieces for the theater. He took quite naturally to the Romantic movement, being influenced by the visit of some English actors to Paris, who introduced him to Shakespeare. The performance of his drama of "Henri III" on February 11, 1829, was the first success of the Romantic school. In the Revolution of July, 1830, Dumas took an active part. But he soon returned to the theater and wrote "Antony," a powerful but immoral play. When his *"Tour de Nesle"* (1832) led to a charge of plagiarism, critics discovered that in his earlier plays also he had appropriated whole scenes from foreign plays, fitting them ingeniously to his plot. Dumas not only continued this practice afterward in his novels, but employed various collaborators, none of whom, however, could ob-

tain the same success, when working independently. On
account of a duel, he was ordered to leave France, and
went to Switzerland. In 1842 he married an actress, who
three years later separated from him and went to Italy.

At last, in 1844, appeared the first of his great novels,
which gave Dumas at once a European reputation. No
romance since "Waverley" had excited such universal
interest as "The Count of Monte Cristo." The brilliance
of its coloring, the unflagging rush of the narrative, the
frequent surprises and the air of probability given to the
most improbable circumstances filled the world with astonishment. Scarcely was this story finished when "The
Three Musketeers" followed, characterized by the same
qualities. The immediate demand for Dumas' services as
a story writer for the daily journals led him to put in
practice the plan already mentioned of employing skilled
assistants. In one year he is said to have issued forty
volumes and still the demand grew for more. Whatever
the amount of help from others, or of direct plagiarism,
which he called "conquest," Dumas had the gift and the
ambition of story-telling. He saw life in fascinating
motion, a series of adventures dazzling and exciting. He
loved the elemental, and believed in it as an artist. The
secret of all genuinely great art is to appeal to the senses
and not in vain. Dumas had this gift in perfection.
Thackeray wrote to Dumas: "Of your heroic heroes I
think our friend Monseigneur Athos is my favorite. I
have read about him from sunrise to sunset, with the utmost contentment of mind. He has passed through how
many volumes, forty, fifty? I wish there were a hundred
more."

Dumas made money by his manufacture of novels, but
squandered it faster than it came. Among his most celebrated works, besides those already mentioned, were

"Twenty Years After," a continuation of "The Three
Musketeers," "The Vicomte de Bragelonne," "Margaret
of Anjou," and "The Memoirs of a Physician." Novel
writing did not withdraw him from the drama. He
adapted some of his best romances for the stage and wrote
original pieces, such as "The Youth of Louis XIV," "A
Marriage Under Louis XV." He also published several
historical works, chiefly relating to France. In 1852 he
began the publication of his "Memoirs," which gives beautiful pictures of his early life. The Revolution of 1848
had cut off much of his income, and his splendid but
unfinished palace of Monte Cristo was sold in 1854 for a
tenth of its cost. Dumas lived to witness the Prussian
invasion, and died at Dieppe in December, 1870.

AUGIER

In the fifth decade of the Century there was somewhat
of a reaction against the Romanticists, which was called
the School of Common Sense. Its nominal leader was
François Ponsard, but Emile Augier (1820-1889) deserves, perhaps, the chief place. He was born at Valence
and was intended for the bar, but became a dramatic
writer. His first play, *"Cigue"* (Hemlock), was a sentimental picture of old Greek life. It was first acted in
1844, and is still occasionally produced. In 1849 Augier
departed from the practice of the Romanticists in his
"Gabrielle." Here, in the usual complication of husband,
wife, and lover, he was bold enough to make the husband
the hero. It won for the author a prize from the Academy. Several other plays of unimpeachable morality followed, and in 1855 as a protest against the younger
Dumas' famous play, *"La Dame aux Camelias,"* known
in English as "Camille," Augier brought out the

"Mariage d'Olympe." A comedy written in collaboration with Jules Sandeau, *"Le Gendre de M. Poirier"* (M. Poirier's Son-in-Law), has been pronounced, perhaps, the best French comedy of the Century. Other comedies, clean and wholesome, helped to make Augier the foremost of French dramatists, and warranted his election to the Academy. After the German war he endeavored to stir the patriotism of his countrymen, and then returned to his usual style.

PHILOSOPHERS AND HISTORIANS

The ideas of England and Germany, introduced by the Romanticists, affected philosophic thought and historical writing as well as poetry and fiction. Their effect in these regions became apparent in the second quarter of the Century. The great philosophers of Germany—Kant, Fichte, Schelling and Hegel—had propounded their systems, and had endeavored to give a rational view of the universe. The French, who have been diffusers rather than creators of philosophy, took up the discussion of these new views and modified them according to their own apprehension. Victor Cousin (1792-1867) was the leader in appreciation and exposition of the new ideas. He was professor at the Sorbonne and after the Revolution of 1830 his services were enlisted in the service of the government and for a time he was Minister of Public Instruction. The English system of philosophy, founded by Locke, and extended by the Scotch philosophers, Reid and Stewart, considered that all human knowledge is derived through the senses. The German philosophers insisted that certain higher ideas are intuitive and are ascertained by pure reason, while the knowledge obtained through the senses belongs to practical reason or understanding. Cousin endeavored to effect a compromise, and formulated the Eclectic system, derived from many sources. He gave much attention to Plato, and translated his works into French. Under his management national education was improved. His colleague, Abel Villemain (1790-1870), held similar positions and in his discourses on Eighteenth Century literature directed attention to the pre-eminence

236

of English literature and oratory. The work of both was direct and fruitful.

There were other thinkers who are generally regarded as philosophical only and yet had considerable influence on literature and the general course of events in French history. They were Eclectics at the outset, but they insisted on carrying their convictions to practical results. Their ideas have become foundation-stones for many latter-day edifices. Claude Henri de Saint-Simon (1760-1825) is interesting as the father of Socialism, a theory which has spread over the world and entered into the life of the present day. He was the seer, the pioneer who blazed the way through the forest, but was not qualified for constructive work. François Charles Fourier (1772-1837) worked out a definite social scheme, which is called by his name. While this system of organized communism failed to take root except in a few places, it contributed to the rapid development of its basic idea, the perfecting of fraternalism. Pierre Joseph Proudhon (1809-1865) went so far in his radicalism as to pronounce that property is theft. He gave the force of literary expression to communistic doctrines.

The founder of the Positive philosophy, belongs to a superior class of world reformers, considered as systematic thinkers. Auguste Comte (1798-1857) is the most original of French philosophers since Descartes. His system is not only philosophic and social, but religious, having Humanity as its Divinity, good people as its Saints, and a new social order made by rule on a vast and complex plan. The Comtist school has had some distinguished men in science and literature among its disciples.

THIERRY

On turning now to the French historians, the work of
Thierry firsts enlists the attention.   History had been
written by Dryasdusts in chronological style for generations.   At best it gathered crude facts, made loose deduc-
tions, and wound up with moral comment.   But what had
been a wilderness Thierry's art turned into a garden.
Stirred by the imaginative writings of Scott and other
Romanticists, he was endowed with sufficient poetic gift
to grace his own substantial work.   He perceived that
history is, if rightly seen, a splendid epic.   Jacques Nicolas
Augustin Thierry was born at Blois in 1795, went to
Paris and passed under the influence of Saint-Simon, to
whom he was secretary.   He dreamt of international
solidarity with national individuality, a view which gave
tone to much of his subsequent work.   But his chief service to progress consisted in his proving by research that
the past cannot be understood without intimate acquaintance with ancient traditions and records, showing the
racial character of the people.   His *"Lettres sur l'Histoire
de France,"* published in 1820 and revised in 1827, marks
the new departure in the interpretation of history.   His
"History of the Norman Conquest of England" first appeared in 1825, and was much improved in the edition of
1840.   Picturesque, brilliant and accurate, it was hailed
with acclamation in England and Germany, as well as in
France.   But the dread calamity of blindness overtook
him in 1830.   Yet, aided by his wife, he persevered in his
labors, publishing *"Dix Ans d'Etudes Historiques"* (Ten
Years of Historic Studies) in 1834, and *"Récits
Merovingiens"* (Merovingian Narratives) in 1840.   He
died in 1856.   His younger brother, Amédée (1797-
1873) was also an able historian, treating chiefly of

Roman Gaul, but did not attain the same success. His most popular work is the "History of Attila" (1856). Under the Empire he was made a Senator.

MICHELET

In Jules Michelet (1798-1874) literature recognizes a brilliant compound of historian, poet, philosopher, naturalist and reformer. The poetic faculty lent his work in the other capacities a characteristic glamour. He was the son of a Parisian printer and having received a good education was made professor of history in the Collège Rollin. His early works were school books, good of their kind, the *"Précis de l'Histoire Moderne"* (Summary of Modern History) (1827) being the best. The "Introduction to Universal History" (1831) first showed his peculiar power of poetizing facts. His great "History of France" occupied him for thirty-seven years, and was completed in nineteen volumes, yet it comes down only to the Revolution, which was treated in a separate work (1852). The history was based on a thorough examination of all the authorities accessible, but the writer's strong religious and political prejudices, as well as his picturesque style, render it often untrustworthy on account of its suggestions, though it never falsifies facts. The part relating to the Middle Ages is the most interesting account of that period. Michelet was a believer in progress, and found in the records of the past support for his visions of the future. While his main work was under way, he sent out a swarm of other books, more or less related to it. His "History of the Revolution" is not equal to Carlyle's though full of enthusiasm for the cause of liberty. When Louis Napoleon became Emperor, Michelet would not take the

oath of allegiance, and therefore lost his place in the
Record office. He began a new series of books on natural
history, probably suggested by his second wife. These
books, "The Bird," "The Insect," "The Sea," "The Mountain," "Woman," "Love," were filled with a fervent pantheism; they showed all nature as divine. In them the
author's peculiar poetic prose was carried to its furthest
limits, and became declamatory. His *"Bible de l'Human-
ité"* (1864) is a similar poetizing of the history of all
religions. After the downfall of the Empire, Michelet,
then seventy-two, began a "History of the Nineteenth
Century," but carried it only to Waterloo. He died in
1874.

GUIZOT

François Pierre Guillaume Guizot (1787-1874),
eminent as a statesman and historian, was born at Nimes,
where his father, a Liberal and Protestant, was guillotined in the Revolution. The son was educated under
his mother's care at Geneva, and studied law at Paris.
There he began to write for the press, and in 1812 was
made professor of modern history. He was a firm believer in constitutional monarchy and upheld that system
against the democratic spirit of the age and the absolutism
of the court. His important political services to his country must be passed by in this notice of his literary career.
Besides editing many historical works, among which was
Gibbon's "Rome," and translating Shakespeare, he published an impartial "History of the English Revolution,
1625-60." His greatest work is the "History of Civilization in Europe," which was only the introduction to his
"History of Civilization in France." They are both reckoned among the classics of modern history. The author's
profound study of the history of France from the Tenth

to the Fourteenth Century gave prominence to the growth
of solidarity in the nation. The chief deficiency in the
work is the author's prosaic plainness of thought and
speech; he rejects enthusiasm and ornament and contents
himself with arguments, dry in presentation, however
cogent in force. Guizot rose to be prime minister under
Louis Philippe, and fell with him in the Revolution of
1848. During the last twenty-six years of his life he
was a philosophical spectator of human affairs. In his
old age he wrote for his grandchildren a "History of
France," which is thorough and attractive, and has proved
immensely popular.

THIERS

Another great historian, who was also a statesman,
was Louis Adolphe Thiers (1797-1877). His difficut
rôle during and after the Franco-German war displayed his
quality as statesman, and has given him a prominent place
in the world's history. He was born in Marseilles, was
educated for the bar, but turned to journalism and became
a noted political writer. His literary fame rests on two
works, "The History of the French Revolution"
(1823-32) and "The History of the Consulate and
Empire" (1840-62). Their chief fault is excess both in
matter and manner of relation. They have also been
charged with unfairness, but this probably arose from
the author's being obliged to decide between witnesses
who contradict each other, and following the one whose
testimony suited his own views. Still another fault is the
glorification of Napoleon, which was due in part to the
writer's patriotism.

DE TOCQUEVILLE

Americans should feel special interest in the French historian who revealed to Europe, and even to America itself, the real meaning and tendency of the institutions established here. Alexis Charles Henri Clérel de Tocqueville, to give him his full due, was a philosopher rather than an historian. His study was of the democratic principle rather than the democracy then entering upon the second experimental stage of it. He was born in Paris in 1805, studied law and was made a judge. In 1831 he visited the United States, being sent with G. de Beaumont to examine the penitentiaries. After his return he published *"La Démocratic en Amérique"* (4 vols., 1835-40), in which he predicted the progress and predominance of democracy in the world. He had a gift for true perception and his work has not receded from the place originally accorded to it by common consent. He believed in the principles of enlightened Liberalism and he anticipated their ultimate triumph, but frankly exposed the errors, observable in this country and his own. He himself became minister of foreign affairs under the French Republic of 1848 and was driven from the public service by the *coup d'état* of 1851. Five years later he published *"L'Ancien Régime et la Révolution,"* a further testimony to his abiding interest in political philosophy. His searching analysis and forecast of popular destiny deserve honorable mention in literature.

LITERATURE UNDER THE EMPIRE, 1852-1870

In the reign of Louis Philippe serious literature had been cultivated. Several of the leading statesmen, as Guizot and Thiers, had already won fame as historians, and political writers. But the overthrow of the Republic drove such men from power. The Empire, founded by violence, was opposed to serious discussion. Its aim was to amuse and entertain the people. Great writers like Hugo were banished. Some of less force of character were bribed by sinecures or lucrative places. Some, indifferent to political considerations, continued to devote themselves to their chosen field of literature. In Paris the condition of affairs under the Empire was favorable to the development of light literature. It was an era of outward prosperity and pleasure. Novel-reading, and theater-going occupied the time of the populace. The dominant note was that of enjoyment, and everything was shaped and directed toward that. Familiar ideas were retold with new readings in plays and stories. Impressionism was cultivated; ingenious subtleties were discovered by those who catered for popular taste. Playwrights began to introduce moral problems or riddles into the drama. Song-writers expanded their light verses into treatises on society and conduct, the art of the singers adding zest to the effect. Music and the graphic arts used the same devices to catch public attention by infusing a more intellectual quality into the lightest performance. Naturally the minor novel multiplied a hundred-fold in such favoring soil.

GAUTIER

Among those who were conspicuous in the contest over the memorable first performance of Victor Hugo's "Hernani" in 1830 none was more so than Théophile Gautier (1811-1872) who had arrayed himself for the occasion in a crimson vest. Born at Tarbes in Gascony, he went to school in Paris, and studied art. But his real bent was toward literature, and he gave much attention to the writers of the Sixteenth Century. He astonished the critic Sainte-Beuve with some poems written when he was but eighteen. The aggressive young "Romantics" who were ready to strike a blow, as well as argue and applaud, for their side, found in him a spirited leader. He had no dramatic faculty and prepared nothing for the theater, except a few masques and ballets. His first long poem "Albertus" (1830) and others of his early career showed great command of language, but were marred by extravagance. For a while he was an assistant to Balzac, but hated the drudgery. His own first novel, "Mademoiselle de Maupin" (1835), was a tale of a girl who sought adventures while dressed in man's attire. The licentiousness of the story offended even French readers and hurt the author's reputation. But Gautier persevered and cultivated his style so that his prose has become a model for his successors. Of his short tales the masterpiece is the highly artistic but ghastly story, *La Morte Amoureuse* (The Dead Leman). It is founded on the mediæval superstition of the incubus, and tells how a devout young priest is ensnared by the beauty of a girl, who transports him in sleep to a distant castle. Finally she is discovered to be but a corpse who receives animation for a while from the blood of her victims. That such an unnatural subject should be so treated as to win the verdict of critics is a testimony to the power of Gautier's perfection of handling. Other weird and fantastic stories are his "Arria Marcella," a revival of the life of Pompeii; "Omphale," in which a gay lady of olden times emerges from a tapestry; *"Roman de la Momie"* (Romance of the Mummy), which reproduces the life of ancient Egypt. *"Le Capitaine Fracasse"* (Captain Fracasse) (1863) is a novel of stirring adventures in the fashion made popular by Dumas, and is considered by many Gautier's best work.

To the last Gautier remained the master of pictorial prose and poetry. His elaborately finished poems were collected in *"Emaux et Camées"* (Enamels and Cameos), first published in 1856. They are polished gems and show his love for beauty in art and nature. To search for beauty he gave all his powers with an absolute indifference to any other consideration. He cared nothing for religion or science, but was acknowledged as supreme in criticism of art and the drama. He formulated the principle of art for art's sake and lived up to it. In his later career he traveled much and wrote brilliant descriptions of various countries and places. Most of his writing was done for newspapers, but he never lowered his style nor took sides in politics. He died in October, 1872.

SAINTE-BEUVE

Charles Augustin Sainte-Beuve might have been included among the early Romanticists, but his valuable work was as a critic. He was one of the staff that made the "Globe" an engine of war against the classical. In its columns he wrote his first work (1827-28) the *"Tableau de la Poésie Française au XVI Siècle."* It is to be noted that the rise of journalism gave criticism its opportunity, may almost be said to have created it. This

half-literary, half-historic sketch was designed to back up
the Romantic revival with proofs that his comrades were
worthy followers of the great poets of old.   He linked
their work with that of Ronsard, whom he pronounced
king of all wielders of the French language, and with the
other famous poets of that age.   In this Sainte-Beuve displeased the Classics, whose national models were of later
date.   He also published a selection of Ronsard's poems in
support of his contention.   Then he ventured a book of
his own poems, the *"Vie, Poésies, et Pensées de Joseph
Delorme"* (Life, Poems and Thoughts of Joseph
Delorme) in the introspective fashion of the hour.   A year
later saw his second venture *"Consolations"* (1830),
pitched in the same key.   In 1834 he issued his solitary
novel, *"Volupte"* (Pleasure) ; and in 1837 his last poetry
book *"Pensées d'Août"* (Thoughts of August).   He was
not a success as poet.   His vein of romance was drying up.
Journalism with free play for his critical pen attracted him.
He considered that French poetry, his own included, lacked
body and soul as compared with that of the English singers, and his constant advice to his verse-making friends
was to study English.   He next undertook the first stages
of a work on Port Royal.   It was not finished for twenty
years.   This work, five volumes, was in part delivered as
lectures before the Academy of Lausanne in 1837.   As
Brunetière pronounces this "beyond question one of the
great books of the Century," it is well to cite his reasons.
Its author, he says, displays in it these master qualities,
examination of works, analysis of sentiments, appreciation of ideas.   In the chapters on Pascal, Montaigne, St.
Francis de Sales, Corneille and Boileau are seen the precision of the historian, the subtlety of the psychologist, and
judicial firmness.   Here, then, we get a first glimpse at
the making of a critic.

Sainte-Beuve was appointed to the Mazarin Library in 1840, a comfortable post which allowed him time to master the Greek poets in the original, and earn an income by his pen. Between 1832 and 1848 he published seven volumes of his *"Portraits Littéraires"* and *"Portraits Contemporains,"* afterward pronounced by himself youthful gush. In 1832 he had written of Hugo in these make-believe criticisms that the poet was "sublime," "adorable," but within four years the idol was pronounced "artificial," "theatrical" and "violent." The critical faculty was asserting itself. Steadily the depth and keenness of the work increased. The Revolution of 1848 indirectly caused his acceptance of the chair of French literature in the University of Liége, his lectures afterward forming two volumes on Chateaubriand and his group. When Napoleon III brought twenty years of stability to the country Sainte-Beuve began his famous series of *"Causeries du Lundi,"* familiar talks on literary men and topics, appearing every Monday in the *"Constitutionnel."* These continued in the *"Moniteur"* until his death, and afterward were published in twenty-eight volumes. His allegiance to the Empire cost him friends and influence. He accepted offices of emolument from it and the cross of the Legion of Honor. In 1865 he was made a Senator, but his health was broken.

As a richly qualified and mellowed master in criticism, Sainte Beuve pronounced himself to be simply a searcher for truth. Having started on the track of the merely beautiful he wisely refused to be longer identified with a cult which he had become convinced was erroneous. "I hold very little to literary opinions; they occupy very little place in my life and thoughts. What does occupy me seriously is life itself and the object of it. I am accustomed to call my judgments in question anew, and to re-cast my

opinions the moment I suspect them to be without
validity." A man brave enough to follow this principle
up is sure of enemies. Sainte-Beuve had plenty. His
method created them, his courage embittered them. From
Romanticism to Naturalism is a clean sweep to the opposite pole. His mode of work was first to ascertain the
interesting thing about the book before him. This found,
described, and explained, he then took its author in hand,
seeking to know all about him and his environment that
could illuminate his work, account for its quality and
mainspring. Thus he would aim to enlarge the man and
his book into the history, or an epitome and reflection of it,
of a period or a movement. The method has its drawbacks even in the hands of so great and clearheaded a
writer as Taine, who owned Sainte-Beuve as his master.
Except the *"Port Royal"* and the early efforts, this great
critic's works are monographs, "infinite riches in little
room." Perhaps he was not always quite fair to some of
his neighbors—Balzac, for example. But he was a noble
spirit, a finely equipped guide, philosopher and friend for
the student of French literature and the literary genius at
large. Not strictly the founder of a system or a school
of his own choice, he was a leader whom the best are
proud to follow.

MERIMEE

The popularity of the opera "Carmen" directs attention to Prosper Mérimée (1803-70), on whose story it is
founded. Born in Paris, he studied law, but entered the
civil service, was expert as a linguist and archæologist,
gradually rose to important positions, and became a personal friend of the Emperor Napoleon III. As a young
man he was affected by the Romantic movement, but his
cynical temper kept him from becoming a partisan. His

entrance into literature was with some pretended translations of dramas by a Spanish lady, Clara Gazul. These
were followed by a book called *"La Guzla,"* which professed to be translated from the Illyrian language. Good
scholars were hoaxed by these tricks. After some smaller
pieces Mérimée published, in 1830, the Corsican story,
"Colomba," and in 1845 the Spanish gipsy story of "Carmen." These and his other short stories are especially
distinguished by their local color, thrilling tragedy and
artistic finish. Mérimée is one of the greatest masters of
French prose style. Besides his stories he published historical works, some translations from the Russian, and
official reports which display his accurate scholarship. He
died in September, 1870. After his death appeared his
interesting *"Lettres à une Inconnue"* (Letters to an
Unknown Lady) which display the same beautiful style
and vary in manner from friendship to love. Other series
of his letters have also been published, and all tend to increase the regard for him as a man and writer.

THE RISE OF REALISM

The transformation of the novel became complete when Gustave Flaubert (1821-1880) startled even Paris with his realistic creation, "Madame Bovary," in 1856. What Balzac had roughly though minutely begun, his pupil worked up to the finest finish. Flaubert had the enormous advantage to a novelist of refined instincts, high culture, and a facility in the strictly artistic use of language. He naturally began life under the banner of Romanticism. A period of travel gave a different bent to his earlier tastes. He took the pessimist's ungenial view of the world. Balzac had portrayed the dismal side of life with a realism that enchained the interest without exhilarating either the sense of pleasure or the better emotions. Flaubert thought he could paint a picture of an unattractive subject, yet which should kindle admiration by the skill and beauty of the workmanship.

Flaubert succeeded so well in this pen-picture that even the police were moved by it. His trial was the grand tournament of literary champions; the romanticists, realists, and rational respectabilities waged a three-cornered duel, with the law as umpire. Flaubert made his own defense, the artist must not be punished for holding the mirror to the mob in the streets. He won the fight, because the game of suppression is liable to turn into the business of oppression. Flaubert took higher artistic ground in his powerful study of ancient Carthage, named "Salammbô," from its heroine (1862). The charm of this is in its ultra-realistic picture of the time and people. Here his years of special study and travel for this result

repay the effort. Great as it is, the average novel-reader
will find it dry. The author carefully suppresses himself
in his books; he refuses to point a moral or make an excursion into happier regions. His *"Tentation de Saint
Antoine"* (1874) is an equally appalling picture of a holy
man of old in the Egyptian desert, before whose vision
passes the nightmare of humanity's evils, incurable woes
intensified by futile efforts to ameliorate them. Flaubert's
best novel of modern life is *"L'Education Sentimentale"*
(1870). He again depicts a phase of sordid life in all
its ugliness. By causing the hero to lose in the long run
by rascality, the author may for once have posed as
moralist to that extent. Flaubert's style may captivate
the stylists. Those who want heart-throbs or romance
will find him cold and repellent. Partly by heredity and
partly by choice, he made himself one of the conspicuously
able school of naturalists, some of whose later disciples
have carried its methods several degrees farther in the
direction of animalism.

That all its followers denied themselves the right to
sunshine is disproved in the case of Octave Feuillet (1821-
1890). A realist he was, but he did not disdain all romanticism. He began his career as one of Alexandre Dumas'
clever young men, who worked up his plots in that merchant's back office. He collaborated with another in two
romantic dramas, produced in 1845, and brought out his
first original novel, *"Bellah,"* in 1850. In this his leanings to realism were marked, though it preserved the
romantic spirit. So in the succession of novels written
during the next few years, *"La Petite Comtesse"* (1856),
and his most popular and durable story, the *"Roman d'un
Jeune Homme Pauvre,"* (Story of a Poor Young Man)
(1858). These have characteristics of importance as
viewed in connection with their date and the author's posi-

tion. The last named has a distinct value as a picture
of rural life in Normandy. Though written on the lines
of simple realism, it is imbued with a softened poetical
influence, possibly suggested by the "Vicar of Wakefield,"
which rises into idealism. There is moral force, if not
purpose, in the story, and the most confirmed naturalistic devotee would not venture to deny that its literary art
gained by this gentle trait. In 1862 he ventured to break
a lance with George Sand in the work, *"Histoire de
Sibylle."* She replied a year later in her romance, *"Mademoiselle de la Quintinie."* It doubtless influenced her in
the departure she was taking from the individualistic
story. Both of them were tired of the selfish claim for
personal gratification at any cost. To this extent Feuillet
was distinctly a reformer of fiction, while continuing to
picture the shadows of life. He contended for legitimate
liberty for women, as for men, but always upheld pure love
and honorable marriage as the ideal happiness and the
only sure path to it. His greater novels are *"M. de
Camoes"* (1867), *"Julie de Trécoeur"* (1872), *"Le Journal d'une Femme"* (1878), and *"La Morte"* (1886).
There are several others, besides five volumes of plays.
One advantage he had in sustaining the tone he adopted,
his novels mostly portray the lives of well-to-do people.
Feuillet was a gentleman, and wrote as one. A high
standard of honor is upheld generally. As a whole, his
work may be pronounced clean, artistic, and with a tendency to the good.

Though Alexandre Dumas, the younger, who was
born in 1824, died in 1895, his fame as a dramatist was
won under the Empire. It is likely to endure, though
disproportioned to the intrinsic worth of his literary influence. His father's wild nature was largely repeated in
the romantic youth. Not until 1852 did he perceive that

he must offer original work, the outcome of hard thinking, if any such celebrity as his father's was to be his. He produced the novel, afterward turned into the better known play, *"Dame aux Camélias"* (1848). As a study of the phase of Paris life with which he was most familiar, it was recognized as faithful and strong. There was some difficulty in getting permission to have it played, but it is a stock piece to this day. The next dramatized novel was *"Diane de Lys,"* which failed, and then came the *"Demi-Monde"* in 1855, which is regarded as a masterpiece. The atmosphere of these plays cannot be breathed for any length of time with pleasure. Following up the lead thus secured, Dumas availed himself of the notoriety of his origin by using it as material for two unabashed character plays, the *"Fils Naturel"* (1858) and the *"Père Prodigue"* (1859). One of these, the *"Idées de Madame Aubray"* (1867), pleaded for sympathetic judgment for those who fall through weakness. Dumas took his success very seriously, favoring the world with several volumes of his plays, prefaced with eloquent arguments in proof of their moral value. From this time he regarded himself as a public oracle. No national event, such as the war of 1870, or scandal, or law suit involving large issues, was allowed to pass without its Dumas play or pamphlet to settle the principle at issue. His dramas, *"La Visite de Noces"* (1871), and *"La Femme de Claude"* (1873), showed that henceforth the stage was to be his pulpit. The point to be remarked here is that in this new departure from stage tradition Dumas was undoubtedly doing his best to widen and deepen its influence. His success was not continuous, but it was something that a mercurial people could be induced to ponder grave problems in the place where hitherto they had sought only merriment. It shows that, irrespective of his fitness for the office of moralist,

Dumas possessed artistic power in no ordinary degree. He had the rare distinction of being admitted to the Academy in 1874 by a large majority, with Victor Hugo among them.

A poet of note in the naturalistic school, Charles Marie René Leconte de Lisle, (1818-1894) may be included here. His work has come to the front again, owing to a new development of the literary principles he formulated for himself and adhered to. De Lisle wrote *"Poèmes Antique"* (1852), *"Poèmes et Poésies"* (1853), and *"Poèmes Barbares"* (1862) and *"Poèmes Tragique"* (1884). The severest canons of art are observed in these poems, which are gaining a new repute among the select. They betray a vein of pessimism, but are instinct with a beauty akin to the classical, and the polish which art gives to ideas, themselves coldly rough.

A set of popular works in fiction involved also political motives. They are sufficiently described as the Erckmann-Chatrian novels, being written in partnership by Emile Erckmann (1822-1899), a Lorrainer, with a taste for literature, and Alexandre Chatrian (1826-1890), an instructor in law. In 1859 their joint work, *"L'Illustre Docteur Mathéus,"* gained a fair success. Thereafter they managed to glorify and keep alive the principles of the Revolution in a long series of stories, most craftily contrived to escape imperial censure. Under the guise of peasant stories of their native region, they depicted the seamy side of Napoleonism, its crushing influence on the poor people, and, by suggestion, the mischievous influence of the Second Empire. This subtle but telling propagandism was veiled in romances, of which the most popular were *"Madame Therèse, ou les Volontaires de '92"* (1863), *"L'Ami Fritz"* (1864), *"Histoire d'un Conscrit de 1813"* (1864), *"Waterloo"* (1865), *"Histoire d'un Homme du Peuple"* (1865), *"La Guerre"* (1866), *"Histoire d'un Paysan"* (1868). The influence exercised by these stories had no little share in ripening the country for the downfall of imperialism. When the Second Empire fell the clever collaborators reaped a golden harvest by their realistic, though also romantic, disclosure of the methods by which the royal adventurer had coerced the nation. This they did in the *"Histoire du Plébiscite, recontée par un des 7,500,000 Oui"* (1872). From then until Chatrian's overstrained mind gave way, they produced a second string of novels, some almost idyllic, others strongly naturalistic, which always appealed to the sympathies of the people.

Not every novelist of philosophical radical leanings indulged in this latent hostility to the Empire. Jules Sandeau (1811-1882), already referred to as collaborator with George Sand in her first romantic novel in 1831, continued to produce his own romances for nearly fifty years. His work was maintained on a higher level than that of the popular novel, the characterization was strong, and his style pure. He did not care to pander to lovers of questionable sensation. He made no sign against the new régime. It gave him two lucrative librarianships, and when the Empire collapsed the republic pensioned him for the loss of his office in the library of St. Cloud. Among his best novels are "Marianna" (1839), *"Le Docteur Herbeau"* (1841), *"La Chasse au Roman"* (1849), and *"La Roche aux Mouettes"* (1871). He was better known as a playwright in conjunction with Emile Angier. The most popular piece, *"Le Gendre de M. Poirier,"* is still a favorite in its English version by Robertson.

Victor Cherbuliez, born in 1829, and elected an Academician in 1882, wrote one of the strongest romances of realism in 1873, "Meta Holdenis," the heroine being a charming deceiver. His fame had been won by the *"Roman d'une Honnête Femme"* (Story of an Honest Woman) (1866), a piece of character portraiture of rare artistic excellence. Cherbuliez did equally striking work as a critic in art and letters, as may be seen in his *"Etudes de Littérature et d'Art"* (1873). He also published works showing deep research and philosophical thought on the political systems of Germany, 1870, and Spain, 1874. Among his popular novels are *"Le Fiancé de Mdlle. Saint-Maur,"* *"Samuel Brohl et Cie,"* and *"L'Idée de Jean Teterol."*

Another brilliant miscellaneous writer who made the best of Napoleonism was Edmond About (1828-1885). His literary career was stormy. He earned his first celebrity by the record of his observations during a sojourn in Greece, *"La Grèce Contemporaine"* (1855). His denunciatory criticisms led to the translation of his book into several languages. This was followed by an autobiographical romance, "Tolla," which he had to defend against a cry of plagiary. Then came a play, *"Guilléry,"* which was hissed off the stage on the second night. His novels, which ran through the *Moniteur,* had better luck, *"Le Roi des Montagues,"* *"Trente et Quarante,"* and others. Then he left for Rome, returning with a book on a political problem of the time, *"La Question Romaine."* Between 1860 and 1869 About published political pamphlets, witty short stories, such as "The Man with the Broken Ear" and "The Notary's Nose," and a quick succession of stories, including *"L'Infame,"* and *"Les Mariages de Province,"* besides a manual of political economy and souvenirs of Egypt. As a friend of the Empire, in the Paris journals, he went into the field as correspondent, when the war broke out. In due course he became a loyal republican and had the honor of being arrested for treason to the German emperor when in Alsace in 1872, but was released without trial. To this indignity he responded by issuing "Alsace," in which his patriotic feelings had full play. He collaborated in several dramas, but without special success. His entire work is marked rather by versatility than special ability.

A new form of novel which arose under the empire was that familiarly known as the detective story. It was probably due to a hint from some of Poe's work. Emile Gaboriau (1835-1873) constructed several of these ingenious novels in which the reader is started on the hunt after the perpetrator of a crime or some other mystery, and for him there is no rest until it is cleared up. Among his best are "M. le Coq," *"Le Crime d'Orcival"* and *"La Degringolade."* He has imitators in abundance to-day. Zola was at first one of the purveyors of this type of novel. Henry Murger had shown a strain of the old romantic feeling in his realistic portrayal of happy-go-lucky student life in the Latin quarter, *"Vie de Boh me."* Of the throng who courted fame and ill-fame by their extravagant fiction during the closing years of the Empire, only a few survivals of merit can be found. The short story established itself on a broader foundation, and the typical decadent naturalistic novel entered upon its questionable career.

Perhaps the downfall of the Empire was a more direct incentive to the typical novel of the Republic than is supposed. By this is meant the excessively materialistic novel, which by glaring portrayal of the gross, pretends to be enhancing the charm of the pure. Once the gayety of imperialism was extinguished, a field was discovered for novels which should unveil its wickedness. It was a neat tribute to stern republican morality. Lest this virtuous motive should not discover itself in the high-colored pictures, the authors prudently avowed their purpose in impressive prefaces. Thus grew the rage for satirizing the frailities of the rich, which has not lessened with the rise of scathing exposures of low life. The popular novel had gradually to tell a more knowing tale, the popular play had to turn upon a still stronger situation involving conjugal honor. Playwright and novelist competed in the skill with which they could dress foul skeletons to simulate ordinary men and women. City life was their study, and of all cities none met the conditions so well as Paris. Once this rivalry commenced, it had to run its course. The pace steadily increased. Plays that were prohibited and novels that were prosecuted under the old régime had now a free course. Here and there a venture would be made into the realm of romance, and there are still attempts at a revival of the idyllic story.

LITERATURE UNDER THE REPUBLIC—1870-1899.

Giving precedence to fiction over serious literature, the extraordinary work done by Jules Verne is entitled to first notice. Beginning as a writer of comedies, he turned in 1863 to a Poe-like romance, *"Cinq Semaines en Ballon"* (Five Weeks in a Balloon), the start on a trail peculiarly his own. He can now point to books that average nearly one for each year of his life. This is the more wonderful because they have demanded harder and drier study in their composition than the average novel. Verne had an aptitude for the learning necessary to successful exploration, as his books on travel bear witness. Having hit on the notion of substituting achievements and possibilities of science for magical absurdities, he set to work and devised a series of modern Arabian Nights Entertainments which are worthy to rank alongside those masterworks of Eastern genius. His books need not be named, they are well known to old and young, and are in no danger of being forgotten or surpassed. By the exercise of a strictly matter-of-fact wizardry, prosaic to the last degree, he compels a not unwilling credence to the wildly impossible, trading on popular faith in the potential omnipotence of science to-morrow. In a way this trick borders on the poetical without touching it, though the reader may find himself projected far into the domain of fantasy when he has closed the book. If novels of life and manners played no worse pranks with our imagination than these of Verne, there would have been much less mischief and more happiness to lay to the account of fiction.

ZOLA

Two novelists of equal talent and fame were born in 1840, Zola and Daudet. Both claim to be of the Naturalistic school. Both have sought to present life as they saw it, in all verity, and they are allowed to have succeeded to unusual perfection. Zola came first into a notoriety which was not then fame. He began as a journalist, then turned to novel writing for years on starvation wages. Experience of this kind is not a sweetener of disposition, especially of naturally gloomy temperaments. Zola might have been inspired by the spirit of revenge against his fellows high and low alike, so ruthlessly does he pillory them all.. The power of works such as *"L'Assommoir," "Germinal," "La Terre," "Nana," "La Débacle,"* is extraordinary. The degrees in which they are edifying, amusing, comforting, which are the three main ends of fiction, is to be determined by the reader and not for him. The courage behind the perseverance which created this burden of nominally light literature is not less extraordinary, and it is due to Zola to recognize that he insists on the worthiness of his intention. He declares he is not of the licentious school. The shoveling of filth in broad daylight before the public eye is not his chosen delight, yet he persists in it.

After a time Zola, having finished the long family history of the Rougon-Macquart tribe, turned to the subject of religion of the present day, as he views it. He prepared after his usual close studies a set of three books, "Lourdes," "Rome," and "Paris." A priest, named Froment, but practically Zola himself, finding his mind troubled, goes on a pilgrimage to Lourdes, but is disgusted with the worldly aspect of religion there. Then he goes to Rome to see the Pope and get his faith renewed. Again he is disappointed, and returns to Paris, where he devotes himself to self-sacrificing work in behalf of the afflicted and distressed. Zola, not content with his fame as an author, has drawn the attention of the world upon himself by his interference in behalf of Captain Dreyfus, who has been unjustly condemned, as he alleges. Zola and his works, the degradation of naturalism, are phenomena of a curious transition period, to be studied scientifically, not to be enjoyed.

DAUDET

In sharp contrast with Zola stands his contemporary, Alphonse Daudet (1840-1898). Born at Nîmes of Gascon blood, his first utterance was a book of verse, *"Les Amoureuses."* To this succeeded plays and novelettes, in which he introduced public men and topics with playful satiric touches. The story, afterward dramatized, which gained his popularity was *"Fromont Jeune et Risler Aîné"* (1874). This became fame after *"Le Nabab"* (The Nabob) appeared in 1878. It was an undisguisedly scattering satire of public characters under the Empire, much of it gratuitous and cruel slander. In better vein are his delightful short stories in "Letters from My Mill," and his entertaining books, the lively adventures of "Tartarin de Tarascon," of which there are three. They may take a permanent place alongside the D'Artagnan and Mousquetaire romances, and perhaps Don Quixote. *"L'Evangeliste"* (1883) satirizes the Salvation Army, and *"L'Immortel"* (1888) the Academy, on which he vents considerable personal spleen. With all his satirical power Daudet preserved a charming gentleness, a grace of blended poetry and humor, which beautifies his work as a whole. He shows nature, Zola shows it up. For this reason Daudet is and will be read with a slightly alloyed delight, where Zola is tolerated for the fascination of his experiments in social vivisection.

DE MAUPASSANT

Though only a writer of short stories, Guy De Maupassant (1850-1893) won a reputation equal to the best as an artist. He had the advantage, for such it was to one who aspired to literature in writing, of knowing Flaubert. It is told that the elder insisted on his docile pupil practicing at descriptive writing for years, giving him the most trivial objects on which to exercise his powers. At last he attained the Flaubert standard of proficiency, and his schooling gained instant attention to his work. The French short story is now thoroughly acclimated here and need not be analyzed. Maupassant followed his master's method, devoting his days and nights to intimate exploration of the life he sought to paint. His fatal enthusiasm landed him in a madhouse and a suicide's grave, perhaps the strongest testimony to the realism of his work. The stories show all the qualities held supreme in this kind of art work, graphic power, microscopic observation, knowledge of the morbid mind, quick changes of scene and impression. If most of them leave a nasty taste in the mouth, the more enjoyable to those on whose palate the pleasing is sickly flat.

The brothers Goncourt added notably to the literature of their day. Edmond, born in 1822, died in 1896; Jules, 1830-1869. Their first joint novel, *"En* 18—," failed on its first appearance in 1852, owing to the excitement of the time. They also failed in journalism before they took to history as material for romance. They made fanciful pictures of Eighteenth Century personages, royal and other. The *"Soeur Philomène"* (1861) was a success. Four years later came *"Germinie Lacerteux,"* a study in morbid psychology, which caused a sensation. Their productions have influenced recent writers ambitious to succeed in this school. They formed a new Academy de Goncourt, and Edmond left a large estate for its support.

Anatole France is known by his novel, *"Le Crime de Sylvestre Bonnard,"* a striking production. In *"Thais"* and other stories he goes back to early Christian times without intent to create sympathy for Christianity. *"La Fille de Lilith," "Le Livre de Mon Ami,"* and the collection of stories *"Balthasar,"* display a remarkable versatility, with a subtle vein of irony which somewhat shakes one's faith in the writer's general seriousness. He is equally clever as a miscellaneous writer and critic, and may yet do a strong piece of work.

Jules Viaud, known in literature as Pierre Loti, was received into the Academy while quite a young man, the more interesting, seeing he was a lieutenant in the navy. His claim to remembrance will rest upon his style rather than his strength. His first books were the outcome of voyaging round the world. The *"Mariage de Loti"* is a story of Tahiti, with natives for its heroines, affording opportunities for the study of love in its primitive manifestations, and for sentimental reflections in the vein of the early romanticists, who pitched their stories among half- savage people. *"Les Pêcheurs d'Islande"* (The Fishers of Iceland) ventures into a quasi-philosophical analysis of motives in love and duty. The general tone of his writings, beneath their fantastic peculiarities, is that of a deep-rooted pessimism, all the gloomier for the half-poetic flights into introspective wonderland, seeking happiness and finding none.

As author of *"Cosmopolis"* Paul Bourget gained his footing among novelists who introduce their readers to fashionable and brilliant metropolitan circles. He dwells among the sons and daughters of wealth, gathered for its most effective display in the gayest of cities. These mixed people he pictures with no marked power, and with no particular moral, unless to inspire contempt. A criminal trial suggested the psychological novel, *"Le Disciple,"* as morbid and artificial a story as need be read. *"Un Crime d'Amour,"* and other books of his confessedly excel in the presentation of figures which are not men and women. His fluent style and superficial penetration commend his books to certain readers, but his better work is seen in essays and critical studies. His last novel, *"La Duchesse Blue,"* is an argument for the impersonality of the novelist.

These are the popular men of the hour, whose slightest productions are sure of a ready sale. They indicate the parting of the ways, on the one hand toward rigid realism, on the other bearing toward a mystical region not far from the old personal romanticism. In both there is a strange lack of the rational romantic spirit which lifts the mind above the oppressive materialism of existence without losing it in pure moonshine. For the present the French novelist holds aloof from the old, old story of honest love, beset with ills from without and frets within, tested by troubles, strengthened by patient struggle, triumphing over all in the long run with a happiness all the richer for their buffetings. The passing appetite is for seasoned and overseasoned meats. The novelist by profession takes note of public taste. Much excellent naturalistic work has been done by Hector Malot, René Bazin, du Boisgobey, and a few others.

POETRY AND THE DRAMA

Much of the foregoing applies to the dramatic output of the last quarter-century. Indeed, it is more true of the playwright than the novelist that he is fettered by the fickle taste of the hour. On the stage, aided by its well-skilled interpreters, a glittering picture of some phase of social life catches the public attention quickly and holds it as tenaciously as the national temperament allows. For pecuniary reasons the literary men of France court the theater. Success is more rapidly won by a play than a book. Scarcely a writer of note but has tried his hand at the drama. Novels have been turned into plays and vice versa, with considerable gain to the authors, and occasionally to literary reputations. Victorien Sardou (1831) is the ablest as well as the most successful dramatist of the period. From *"Candide,"* produced in 1860, to *"Diplomacy,"* *"Fedora"* and the later plays, he has achieved a succession of literary triumphs not less than theatrical. Of these, many hold our own stage under other names, not always translations. His comedies have been political, as when *"Rabagas"* satirized Gambetta, and have freely treated passing questions, sometimes polemically. They are invariably brilliant, and well-earned his elevation to the Academy in 1877.

François Edouard Joachim Coppée (1842-1897) issued poems in his youth. His first drama, *"Le Passant,"* was acted in 1869, with success. Among later poems were *"Les Humbles,"* *"Exilée,"* and a romance, *"Une Idylle Pendant le Siège."* Napoleon III made him librarian of the Senate at Luxembourg, and afterward he was

appointed keeper of the archives of the Comédie Française.   Coppée was not only a true, but an exceptionally
gifted poet.   Five volumes contain his poetical and dramatic work.   He has maintained a pure and noble tone
throughout.   His verse interprets the thought and aspirations of the genuinely patriotic of his countrymen.   He
has abundant wit, and the charm of native geniality per-
vades all his work.

A number of the prose writers named have been mak-
ers of verse also.   Among the aspirants for the laurel
wreath have been a few whom posterity may class outside
the pale of mediocrities.   The characteristics of modern
French poetry resemble those of the typical novel and play
in the main. ˙Impressionism has marked it for its own.
There is little to call for remark outside the lyric, and of
its innumerable devotees the one who claims consideration
above the rest is Paul Verlaine (1844-1896).   What
Francis Villon was in the Fifteenth Century, Verlaine has
realistically been in ours, to this extent—a voluntary outcast if not outlaw, a poet in spite of his rags and tatters,
a pariah despite a wealth of genius.   Married and always
in love with his wife, he poetically expended her small
dowry in a merry-go-round with which he haunted village
fairs.   Practically it did not pay.   The lady upbraided,
and when an onlooker enjoyed the sport Verlaine flew at
him with a knife.   In his Belgian prison the poet found
his better self.   But the pretty verses, which are pure
poems, he composed for his wife did not bring him good
fortune all at once.   He was two years in the cells and the
infirmary.   When he came out he was very good, thanks
to the chaplain and nuns.   He sang fine hymns of bitter
repentance, then, and on many similar occasions afterward.   It is told of his artless conception of life that once,
when in trouble, friends collected 300 francs and gave

them to him. That night he drove his boon companions
in a hired carriage the whole round of the drinking places,
until there was no more money, drink, or sense. Verlaine
was always pouring out rich devotional verse on these
morrows. His poems commanded cash on the instant,
yet his friends had to fine their slim pocketbooks by making constant contributions for his recovery rather than
maintenance, for he managed to exist between whiles.
With body and brain damaged by long neglect, and
toward the last avoided by those who still felt pity for the
hopeless, the poet took to bed for the last time and expired
while imploring his wife to come. Coppée, Zola, and
others who knew the man, declare that Verlaine's poetry
will survive. It meets the requirements of true lyric verse
in being artless, spontaneous, touching, and musical. He
had a perfect ear and taste, and gave polish without hard-
ness to every expression.

HISTORY, PHILOSOPHY, CRITICISM

The French Academy has no brighter names on its roll than those of Renan and Taine. Each in his department and degree shed bright luster on the literature of the half-century. If style can be regarded, as some claim, apart from the subject matter it illuminates as in itself a source of intellectual good, then French literature may be proud of its two glorifiers of the themes usually dulled by the absence of their art. With the advent of these great writers it was perceived that the gravest subjects and solid scholarship could be endowed with high literary charm, giving a glow as of romance to the hitherto cold records of special fields of research. In this aspect the service these men rendered to their country is greater than that of their several contributions to knowledge. They disclosed the secrets which had been supposed the peculiar property of *belles-lettres,* and demonstrated that they belonged in common to all craftsmen who knew how to use them in the fashioning of learned works. Their example told with varied effect on many disciples in their country and out of it, on the whole with undoubted benefit to literature generally, and to the special gain of all who study in their departments.

RENAN

Ernest Renan rose from a Breton peasant's cottage to be perhaps the first of those who added the distinct attraction of literary style to studies in history and allied subjects. He was born in 1823, was brought up religiously, and trained for the priesthood. In his study of Semitic

languages he encountered difficulties in his religious belief
which he afterward ascribed to philological causes,
though this was probably a minor reason. In 1845 he left
the Seminary, and was assisted by his sister until he
could gain a living by teaching. He won a public
prize for an essay on the Semitic languages, whereupon
he was commissioned to make researches in Italy, the
outcome of which was the important work on Arabic philosophy, "Averroès et l'Averroïsme" (1852). Various
flattering promotions came within the next few years, during which he published *"Etudes d'Histoire Religieuses,"*
and an *"Essai sur l'Origine du Language"* (1858). When
the army went to Syria, 1860, Renan was appointed scientific commissioner, which enabled him to explore the
Holy Land. His first lecture, as professor of Hebrew in
the Collége de France, caused a disturbance, of which the
result was the withdrawal of the course. Now appeared
the book with which his popular fame is most identified,
the *"Vie de Jésus"* (Life of Jesus) (1864). It marks an
epoch in modern religious literature, theological, historical and critical. The title indicated its humanistic bias,
which aroused hostility so strong that the author was dismissed, and he refused to accept a proffered appointment
in the Imperial Library as a consolation. The character of his book gave it notoriety, but its captivating style
won the place it still holds in the literature of the world.
Strauss's *"Leben Jesu"* had presented a mythical being
instead of the Christ of loving tradition. Renan portrayed an ideal human character, full of beauty and the
genius which touches the divine, yet shorn of the supreme
qualities cherished by and essential to the Christian faith.
The exquisite charm of the book did not conceal its radical weakness as offering a substitute for the Jesus of the
Gospels. It was the first installment of an elaborate work,

"Origines du Christianisme," of which there followed these volumes, *"Les Apôtres"* (1866), *"Saint Paul et sa Mission"* (1867), *"L'Antechrist"* (1873), *"L'Eglise Chrétienne"* (1879). The same graceful lucidity characterized these studies, which did not wholly escape damage from more drastic criticisms than Renan favored. His subsequent work included *"Marcus Aurelius"* (1881), "History of the People of Israel" (1887-1892). In his earlier years he issued translations of the Book of Job and Ecclesiastes. Besides these Renan wrote several philosophical essays and miscellaneous pieces in lighter vein. He was elected to the Academy in 1878, and delivered the Hibbert course of lectures in London, in 1880, on the "Influence of Pagan Rome on Christianity." So great and diversified a body of literary work of such high character gives its author enviable distinction among the best writers of his age. His immense learning, patient research, and his gift of utterance, while they placed him high among the scholars of the century, and the favorites of the public, seem nevertheless to have crowned him with the laurel of a graceful rather than a powerful intellectual athlete. He wrote *"Recollections of Youth"* in 1890. Having found after a long life of study that, as he expressed it, he really knew little more of the truth than a street boy gets at a first guess, his future influence may be gauged as that of a literary stylist first, scholar next, and a teacher last. Considerable egotism of a weak kind detracts from the value of his later and more personal writings.

TAINE

Hippolyte Adolphe Taine, born in 1828, had at twenty-five earned the degree of Doctor in Letters; in the year following the Academy crowned his essay on the

historian Livy, and the public applauded his next effort,
"Voyage aux Eaux des Pyrénées" (Travels in the Pyre-
nees). In 1857 he showed a stronger hand in his *"Phil-
osophes Français du XIX me Siecle,"* and in the *"Essais
de Critique et d'Histoire"* (1858). He had formed a system of criticism for himself, influenced by the Positive
philosophy, which suited his somewhat dry temperament.
As the realistic school in poetry and romance eliminated
considerations of sweetness and light, moral purpose or
tendency, so his method should content itself with simple
description of what it might find as a fact. Certain influences from the past operate to shape present conditions;
men born under those conditions do but reflect them in
their views and acts; writers only voice the average sentiments of their day, and it is waste of brain to try and
elevate them to the level of creators. Under these controlling convictions Taine produced his justly famous
work, *"History of English Literature,"* in 1863. What
Renan was at the same instant doing for the author of
Christianity Taine was doing for the kings of English literature, deposing them from the throne, supposed to be
hedged round with divinity. It was a splendid attempt,
to demonstrate that the great were only the small creatures of circumstance, but it was working a theory to
death. The literary criticism was of itself masterly and,
from a Frenchman's point of view, admirably conceived,
but the backbone of logic seemed to have got a twist.
Taine found it impossible to cover up every trace of originality in the great poets with his theory of environment.
Within two years, when he was appointed professor of
æsthetics and the history of art in 1865, he had developed
broader views. Gradually he let it be seen that this hard
and rigid naturalistic method was not working well. In his
"Philosophie de l'Art" and *"Voyage en Italie"* (1865-66)

he takes account of things below the surface. In his *"Ideal dans l'Art"* (1869) he admits not only the wisdom, but the duty of judging men and their works, not simply in themselves, but as influences. This was a departure from the doctrine of art for art's sake. He visited England in 1871, receiving honors from Oxford, and next year published his *"Notes sur l'Angleterre,"* which testify to the enlarging of his perceptions. The result was a determination to write a history of Contemporary France and its beginning. The first volume appeared in 1876, *"L'Ancien Régime;"* then *"La Revolution"* (1878), and *"La Conquêste Jacobine"* (1881), with other volumes down to 1890. He died in 1893, not having completed his work.

When well-matured in years and thought Taine laid aside the machine standard of criticism in favor of one which should judge men according to their good or bad aims or tendencies. Hence his impartial distribution of praise and blame among royalists, republicans and revolutionists alike. It is not so important to fix on the precise technical classification of this method of criticism, whether and how far realistic or romantic. The grand mission of sound criticism is to discover all essentials to fair judgment, and having displayed them, assist the reader to discriminate wisely. Taine started out with the opposite theory, but came back to a more free method of rational adjudication. His impartiality struck the Academicians as a welcome progress in conservatism, whereupon he, with Renan, was admitted in 1878, after having suffered two rejections. Compared with Renan's the style of Taine, fine as it is, seems artificial. It has great force, surprising effectiveness, is occasionally eloquent by simplicity and more often by careful rhetoric. His work as an historian is probably superior in the higher qualities to his more strictly critical work, though the two are really one. As a philosophical thinker he must always rank among the most influential by virtue of his power in setting his readers to work out his conclusions for themselves. His "English Literature" is one of the greatest, most instructive, and delightful reading books on that subject despite all drawbacks.

<h2 style="text-align:center">RECENT CRITICS</h2>

The name of Edmond Henri Adolphe Schérer (1815-1896) commands exceptional respect. Trained as a theologian he parted company with orthodoxy in a thoughtful work, *"La Critique et la Foi"* (1850). He became a Liberal leader of moderate views, and a moderator of factionism in his capacity as member of the National Assembly in 1871. Journalism occupied his pen for a few years, but his standard works on theological and especially literary subjects have placed him among the soundest of philosophical writers.

Jules Lemaitre, born in 1853, is one of the foremost journalists of the younger school. His reviews, especially of the drama, ancient and modern, have high authority and make brilliant reading. He was elected an Academician in 1896. As usual with his fraternity Lemaitre has attempted play-writing, and since 1891 with success. Politics, Platonic affection, and less attractive topics he treats with a light vein of humor, pointed with sharp satire, the end in view being an evening's entertainment.

Eugène Melchior de Vogüé was born in 1848 and was made an Academician at forty. His mental endowment and general career have been likened to those of Lamartine. First appeared, in the *"Revue des Deux Mondes,"* his *"Voyage en Syrie et en Palestine"* (1873). That so young a writer should make a striking success of a well-worn theme denotes more than ordinary powers. The book displays some of the features of the Chateaubriand style, prose poetry, fine sentiment, put into exquisite French. The dreamy tone befits wanderings in the Holy Land. An official sojourn in Russia, where he married a native lady, brought him into sympathetic contact with Tolstoi and his school, whose ideals and crusade Vogüé eloquently commends to his own people. He has written largely on Russia, its people, history, and outlook. He has served on several diplomatic missions to foreign courts. Of their order his writings have most of the qualities prized by lovers of refined language expressing lofty sentiment. He does not write for art's sake alone. He stands for the new idealism, a religion of heart freed from ecclesiastical trammels, a standard of personal and national honor that shall lift men up out of the slough of materialism in which they have so long been dragged by the ultra-naturalistic blind guides, as he conceives them. It is claimed that he has an enthusiastic following in the young men of the land, and it is assured that his influence will spread and prove a power for good.

The latest critic of eminence is Ferdinand Brunetière, who was made known to Americans by his visit in 1897 when several universities listened to his lectures on modern French literature and its tendencies. He was born in 1849 and was elected to the Academy in 1894. He is a pronounced Catholic and upholds his religious convictions with courage. His journalistic career was signalized by the bold onslaught he made against the Naturalistic school. Recognizing its ability he denounces what amounts to the prostitution of it. He went so far in one of his lectures as to honor George Eliot above Gustave Flaubert, her superior in point of art, because "she has the advantage of not resorting to adultery. The observation of simple facts suffices her without crime." He was invited to give a course of lectures in the Odéon Theater in 1891, on the Classic Drama. Since then he is the favorite lecturer in the Sorbonne and elsewhere. He has published several volumes, and though he is trenchantly criticized by his contemporaries and has been honored with the hostility of the extreme naturalists, his broad championship of the pure and uplifting as the criterion of all good literature has made him a power. His last utterance on the present phase of French literature is hopeful. He shows that individualism was the note of the Romantic movement, which the naturalistic school has changed to the impersonal. Now there is in progress a movement toward the social, in the sense that literature now aims at the good of all as contrasted with the interests of the individual. If this is correct, and it is to a large extent, the new Century will probably bring with it a national literature purified of its adulterants. When the transparency of its moral tone shall match the clearness of its expressive language, French literature may claim the crown and wear it with the approval of all nations.

GERMAN LITERATURE

LITERATURE AT THE END OF THE EIGHTEENTH CENTURY

The literature of Germany in the middle of the Eighteenth Century had shown many signs of social unrest and impending political revolution. This was especially evident in the drama. One of Klinger's plays *"Sturm und Drang"* (Storm and Stress), first acted in 1775, has given an appropriate name to the whole period. Many of these dramas, written by noblemen, revealed the deplorable condition of the down-trodden masses. They extolled liberty in hysterical speeches and urged revolt against tyranny and superstition. Yet while the feelings of the intellectual classes were deeply stirred, the people did not respond to the alarm. The threatening political storm seemed to pass over the land to take effect in France, from which much of the original impulse had come. The reason for this failure of political action undoubtedly lay in the divided condition of the Fatherland. Germany was broken up into some forty different States, varying in size and importance from the extensive territories of Austria and Prussia to petty principalities, the boundaries of which the ruler could traverse in a day's ride. The jealousies and absurd quarrels of these petty sovereigns and the rivalry of their subjects attracted and carried off the lightning which seemed about to dart from the lowering clouds.

Yet the great epic and lyrical poet, Klopstock, who survived a few years beyond the Century, had already roused a general enthusiasm for religion and the Father-

land. He was the first to direct the attention of modern
Germans to the ancient hero Hermann or Arminius, who
defeated the Roman legions in the Teutoburger forest.
Hermann has now become the symbol of united Germany,
but a full century was required to raise him to his destined
elevation. The popular desire for unity steadily grew,
but the people must pass through terrible trials, bloody
wars and destructive commotions before a real union could
be accomplished. The first of these afflictions was
brought about by the agreement of the Emperor Leopold
II and the King of Prussia to support the cause of Louis
XVI against the revolutionary movement in France.
This unfortunate coalition plunged all Europe into a conflict which destroyed the entire State system of the Continent. The Holy Roman Empire, which had prolonged
into modern times the name, though not the glory, of the
grandest political structure ever erected, was brought to
an ignominious end when Francis II resigned the imperial crown at the bidding of Napoleon in 1806. During the struggle between France and Austria Frederick
William III, King of Prussia, had selfishly held aloof,
but he was destined to suffer in turn. When the Confederation of the Rhine, composed of the chief central and
southern States of Germany, was formed under the pro-
tectorate of France, Frederick William, hoping for aid
from England and Russia, declared war for which he was
ill prepared. The first battle at Jena in October, 1806,
laid Prussia prostrate at Napoleon's feet, and after a
second battle at Friedland, the King was compelled to sign
a treaty giving up the best part of his Kingdom and more
than half his subjects. This national humiliation sank
deeply into the hearts of the German people. The national spirit had already been roused by the lyrics of Klopstock and of his followers known as the Hainbund (Grove-

alliance) ; they were students of Göttingen and had obtained this name by their dancing one night by moonlight around an oak tree and swearing to devote themselves to their native land.   Under the wise and vigorous statesmanship of Stein and Hardenberg the Prussian system of education was remodeled, her people trained to be intelligent soldiers, and the whole country was regenerated. In a few years the War of Liberation, by which the French were driven out, called forth a grand outburst of patriotic song.

At the opening of the Century Goethe reigned supreme in the literary world.   In his youth he had been deeply moved by the influences around him, but now he seemed to withdraw from the external world and find peace and comfort in the lofty regions of art.   Yet in his heart he believed in a grand future for Germany and felt his duty to increase and promote the national culture.   Before considering his career in detail, it is necessary to look at some of his predecessors.   Johann Gottfried Herder (1744-1803) does not rank high as an original poet.   Animated by a real enthusiasm for human happiness he was unable to give proper poetic expression to the deep feelings of his soul.   But in his *"Stimmen der Völker"* (Voices of the Peoples) he brought together a splendid collection of the lyrics of many races, and thus prepared the way for the lyrical revival among his own countrymen.   In his *"Ideen zur Philosophie der Geschichte der Menschheit,"* (Ideas on the Philosophy of the History of Humanity), he developed the idea of progress in the history of the world, and thus enlarged the scope of historical inquiry.   He had the high honor of directing and stimulating the genius of Goethe at a critical stage, and had powerful influence on other leading writers.   Friedrich Gottlieb Klopstock (1724-1803) is best known as the author of "The Mes-

siah," an epic poem on the sufferings of Christ, in which
he sought to surpass Milton, but failed to give the central
figure distinct outlines. It has been pronounced an oratorio rather than an epic. His dramas are also failures
from his want of sufficient knowledge of real life and
stage craft. But in his lyrics his genius was shown in
fiery patriotism, enthusiasm for humanity, and strong love
for the grand phenomena of nature. Christoph Martin
Wieland (1733-1813) at the outset of his career was as
religious and patriotic as Klopstock, but he passed into
an Epicurean indifference. Of his numerous works the
most pleasing is the romantic narrative poem "Oberon"
which transports the hero on a fantastic errand to the
court of the Caliph of Bagdad. In his later prose romances he discouraged enthusiasm and ridiculed the aspirations of his youth. Some of his stories treated themes
of ancient Greek life in a thoroughly modern spirit. Gott-
hold Ephraim Lessing (1729-1781) had more influence
on the course of German literature. He produced dramas
which still hold the stage, and wrote criticisms which
have borne fruit in successive generations. In his "Laokoon" he defined the domains of art and poetry; by his
work on the drama he abolished slavery to the French
classical rules; and by his "Wolfenbüttel Fragments" he
started the movement for higher criticism of the Bible.
In his "Education of the Human Race" he showed that
religions which may not be absolutely true may yet have
value in leading toward higher moral ideals. The same
idea is presented artistically in his finest work, the drama
of "Nathan the Wise," the hero of which is an idealization of his friend, Moses Mendelssohn. It inculcates the
duty of religious toleration.

GOETHE

Born in 1749 and dying in 1832, Johann Wolfgang Goethe belongs to two Centuries and in his active and varied intellectual career expressed the spirit of both. He is not only supreme in German literature, but in the European literature of his time. In modern times only Dante and Shakespeare hold similar places. Goethe was born and spent his boyhood in Frankfort, then still the capital of the Empire, though not the residence of the Emperor. His father, descended from a family which had steadily risen in wealth and importance for some generations, was the Emperor's representative in the town council. He was formal and pedantic and exercised his talents in the strict education of his son and daughter. Their mother was a lovely, bright-witted woman, who cultivated their affections. While French garrisons occupied the city during the Seven Years' War, young Goethe learned their language and found pleasure in their theater. He went to the University of Leipsic, and in 1770 to Strasburg to obtain his degree in law. Here two important influences came upon him. First, he met with Herder, poet and theologian, who taught him that poetry is the expression of national life, and introduced him to the beauties of English literature. Secondly, he, then handsome as Apollo, met with the fair Friederike Brion, whose presence gives charm to his "Autobiography." On his love affair with her was founded the story of Gretchen in "Faust."

After taking his degree in law, the young man went home and began to write lyrical poems, but he soon attempted a drama after the boisterous style then prevalent. "Götz von Berlichingen," though written without a plan, displayed his genius in vivid representation of a powerful character of the Sixteenth Century. Still another manifestation of his literary ability was seen in his "Sorrows of Werther," a story told in letters in the sentimental style of Rousseau. It was really founded on his own hopeless love for Charlotte Buff. It exhibits the force of unrestrained youthful passion and expresses with deep pathos that weariness of life that overtakes imperfect natures. Werther, a well-educated young man, falls in love with a friend's wife, but shrinks from temptation and at last in fond despair, commits suicide. But Goethe was too strong intellectually and morally to yield thus. In his many lyrics the emotions of his soul found vent. In 1775, at the invitation of the Duke of Saxe Weimar, Goethe removed to his capital where Wieland already was, and whither Herder and Schiller came later. The little Saxon town of Weimar became the intellectual and literary center of Germany. "Here," says a biographer, "everybody worshiped him, especially the women." For ten years Goethe was busy in official duties and published little except some dramas. Then he visited Italy to complete his study of art and arouse his slumbering genius. He traveled incognito, that his studies might not be disturbed, and spent two years in the land.

On his return he produced his beautiful drama of "Iphigenia," a masterly imitation of ancient Greek tragedy, yet with Christian sentiment interfused. In "Tasso" are exhibited the woes of a poetic nature which cannot fairly discriminate between the real and the ideal world. In "Egmont" there is some splendid historical portraiture, but the hero is not the real Egmont of the great struggle of the Netherlands for liberty. He is a young high-minded patriot resisting the relentless bigotry and despotism of Alva. His love-romance with Clärchen is especially admirable. To this period also belongs the first chapter of "Faust" (1790) whose romantic exuberance combines wild outbursts of passion with touching innocence, coarse exhibitions of folly with the highest aspirations of the soul.   The old folk-story of "Reineke Fuchs" was retold in flowing hexameters.

In 1794 began the intimacy of Goethe with Schiller, which was fruitful in effects upon both.   As the younger poet had won fame by his ballads, Goethe entered into friendly competition with him and generously acknowledged that his rival's were superior.   To this period belongs the pastoral epic, "Hermann and Dorothea," written in hexameters.   According to the story the son of the landlord of the Golden Lion is attracted by a girl in a group of German emigrants who have been driven from their homes by French pillagers and encamp in the fields. After suitable explanations and introductions Hermann leads her to his home as a bride.   This pure domestic poem has been called a "hymn to the family."   In 1796 "Wilhelm's Meister's Apprenticeship" was given to the world.   In this prose romance are related a young man's adventures with a band of strolling players, who include a variety of characters—the worldly Philina, the romantic Mariana, and the mysterious fascinating waif, Mignon. The story contains much of Goethe's mature thought on human life.

In the new Century Goethe continued to make valuable additions to his output.   In 1805 the greatest work of his life appeared.   The legend of Faust which had occupied his mind from his childhood, had now taken its final shape.   "It appeals to all minds with the irresistible fascination of an eternal problem, and with the charm of endless variety.   It has every element—wit, pathos, wisdom, buffoonery, mystery, melody, reverence, doubt, magic, and irony; not a chord of the lyre is unstrung, not a fiber of the heart untouched."   In most of the succeeding twen-

ty-six years of his life Goethe enjoyed contentment and
honor. He now married Christiane Vulpius, a beautiful
woman, who had lived with him since 1788, and
borne him a son. Though not fitted for intellectual companionship, she was a faithful manager of his home.
When he was disturbed by the French troops, he took
refuge in study and scientific experiments. The new
treasures of Oriental lore which were made accessible
about this time deeply impressed the veteran poet's mind.
In 1813 he published his "West-Easterly Divan," a collection of fine lyrics after the fashion of the Persian Hafiz.
In one of them, "Timur," Napoleon's invasion of Russia
is noticed. In 1818 he published the second part of "Wilhelm Meister."

Goethe's entertaining autobiography is called "Poetry
and Truth; Pages from My Life." The most impression-
able part of his life is told elaborately, and as the title
seems to imply, with a certain amount of idealization.
He had played many parts in his time; as a child, studious
and observant, as a youth somewhat frivolous; on his ar-
rival at Weimar, a man disposed to take his ease; later,
a dignified official; finally, the serene sovereign of the intellectual world, graciously receiving homage from aspiring intellects of every part of the civilized world. He
died at Weimar, March 22, 1832. To the last he retained his sentimentality especially with regard to women.
All his works, he said, constituted a great confession, but
"Faust," more than any other, is the confession of his
life. In the Second Part, published in 1831, was given
his final solution of the deepest problems of human-exist-
ence. Yet it is still disputed whether his answer to the
grand question is correct. The whole work remains the
mightiest achievement of German genius.

There was a grand selfishness in Goethe through most

of his career.   It was fostered by the admiration, and even worship, which he everywhere received.   He came to regard it as his own duty to cultivate himself, and he soon urged it as a duty upon others.   Hence even during that grand struggle for the liberation of the Fatherland in 1813, he kept quiet, except in an occasional outburst in a letter or in conversation with a friend.   When others complained of his indifference, he declared that he was true in heart, but that he was convinced the struggle would then be ineffectual.   He went further, and said, "As a man and citizen, the poet will love his fatherland, but the fatherland of his poetic strength and his poetic activity is the good, the noble, the beautiful, which is confined to no special province or land, which he seizes wherever he finds it."

Goethe was unexcelled as a lyrical poet, and retained his power in this respect to the end.   In his lyrics as Heine finely says, "the word embraces you, while the thought kisses you."   But his fame rests upon "Faust," the greatest drama of the world, yet with a simple well-known plot. Faust, the most learned scholar, finding at last that human knowledge is vain, is in despair, when Mephistopheles in the disguise of a black dog, follows him to his study. He reveals himself as the spirit of negation, and by echoing Faust's notions, persuades him to sign a compact in his own blood that when his desires had been fully gratified his life should end.   The spirit then transports him to a students' revel, which only disgusts him; then to the horrors of the Witches' Kitchen.   Faust drinks a magic potion which renews his youth.   He beholds Helena, the most beautiful of women, and is told that this drink shall cause him to see Helena on earth.   When he returns to earth, he meets Margaret (or Gretchen, in familiar German), a pretty maiden who is afraid of him as so much above her. By the aid of Martha he conveys a casket of jewels to her room. These awaken a desire for finery which leads to her ruin. Her mother is removed by a poisonous sleep-potion. Her soldier brother Valentin, discovering her shame, fights a duel with Faust and is slain. To the cathedral the betrayed woman goes as a penitent, but an evil spirit mocks and taunts her till she faints. Faust seeks relief from his sense of guilt and Mephistopheles takes him to the witches' festival on Walpurgis night (May 1) on the Brocken. When Gretchen is imprisoned, having been convicted of slaying her child, Faust returns. Her mind wanders, and she dies assured of pardon by angel voices. Thus the First Part ends. The story of the Second Part is so intricate that it is impossible to relate it briefly. Faust continues to work out his problems and is bidden to follow Gretchen's spirit in a new life. He tries in various ways to benefit his fellow-men. At the last Mephistopheles is baffled, and angels, among whom is the spirit of Gretchen, escort his soul to Heaven. It may be added that in the prologue to Part First there is some indication that Goethe intended from the start, to end with Faust's redemption, in spite of his sins.

SCHILLER

The name of Friedrich von Schiller is inseparably associated with that of his great friend. While the strong and healthy Goethe lived to his eighty-fourth year, the frail Schiller passed away in his forty-sixth. Yet he had accomplished a vast amount of work in both poetry and prose which the world will not willingly let die. He was pure and noble in heart and won the affectionate regard of his countrymen. He was born at Marbach in the Duchy of Würtemberg in November, 1759. His father

was a Major and overseer of the Duke's gardens. The
son was trained to be a military surgeon, but early showed
his dislike for the army and his predilection for literature.
Under the influence of the "Storm and Stress" period he
composed at nineteen his first drama, "The Robbers," full
of faults yet showing unregulated genius. The hero, Karl
Moor, had been defrauded by his brother and ill-treated
by the world. Therefore he became the chief of a band
of robbers who revenge themselves on society. They
commit many crimes, but at last Moor, on whose head a
price is set, surrenders to a poor workman. Schiller was
still a pupil in the medical school, and the Duke, learning
that he was the author, forbade him to write except on
medicine. When the dramatist slipped off to see his play
he was imprisoned for two weeks. On his release he left
the duchy altogether. But the popularity of the play
went on. Schiller wrote more, attacking in the same
revolutionary style the despotism and vices of the petty
German courts. In "Love and Intrigue" he rebukes the
sale of Hessian soldiers by their rulers. His tragedy,
"Don Carlos," founded on the gloomy story of the son
of Philip II of Spain, showed change in dramatic method.
There is less extravagant declamation. The wayward
Don Carlos falls a victim to the Inquisition and a court
intrigue, while his magnanimous friend, Marquis Posa,
dies for him in vain.

In 1789 Schiller was called to Jena to be professor of
history. He wrote his "Rise of the Netherlands," and
"History of the Thirty Years' War." After a few years
he became acquainted with Goethe and in 1794 they
became fast friends. The older poet declared that Schiller
"created for him a second youth and made him again a
poet, which he had almost ceased to be." The loving intercourse was equally beneficial for the younger; it made

him more artistic, so that his poems became perfect in
form without losing energy and warmth.   Schiller published a literary journal to which Goethe contributed.
The two friends competed in ballad-making, and Schiller's ballads of this period are his best in strength of conception and dignity of style.   They generally represent the
conflict between the higher and the lower in man, and
call upon the will to assert itself against circumstances.
Such are "The Diver," "The Fight with the Dragon,"
"The Security."   Others are remarkable tales from ancient history, as "The Cranes of Ibycus," "The Ring of
Polycrates," dealing with the moral government of the
world.   His lyrical masterpiece is "The Song of the Bell,"
which describes the course of human life in connection
with the casting and founding of a bell.   The charm is
enhanced by frequently varying the meter to suit the
different aspects of the theme.   This poem is nobly imitated in Longfellow's "Building of the Ship."   Schiller's
exultant "Hymn to Joy" was set to music by Beethoven.

In this period Schiller wrote a noble series of historical plays.   His study of the Thirty Years' War had made
him familiar with the grand figure of Wallenstein, who
was drawn on by belief in his destiny to betray his Emperor.   The trilogy relating to him consists of "Wallenstein's Camp," "The Piccolomoni," and "The Death of
Wallenstein."   In the first the devotion of the disorderly
soldiers to their great leader is realistically shown.   In
the second the interest lies in the struggle in the soul of
Max Piccolomini between his love for the beautiful
Thekla, Wallenstein's noble daughter, and his loyalty to
the Emperor.   To end the struggle he dashes against the
host of Swedes and falls.   In the third Wallenstein is led
by his self-deceiving belief in astrology to trust implicitly
Max's father, Octavio, by whom he is betrayed.   In the

tragedy of "Mary Stuart," as in some others Schiller sacrifices truth of history to dramatic exigencies. The imprisoned Mary Queen of Scots is so carried beyond propriety by her unexpected liberty that on meeting Queen Elizabeth suddenly in the garden of the castle she insults her so as to bring upon herself the death sentence In "The Maid of Orleans," the heroine is not the peasant girl of history, who is burnt at the stake, but an ideal warrior maid who dies on the battle-field, because she has yielded for a moment to love for the English Talbot. His "William Tell" is a dramatic masterpiece, full of local color and noble patriotism. In this final tragedy Schiller renews his youthful energy and love of freedom and combines with them the highest art. It may be regarded as an emphatic protest against the despotism of Napoleon. Yet the author died at Weimar May 9, 1805, before he had seen the lowest degradation of his native land.

RICHTER

Jean Paul Richter is unique among the writers of the world. His works sparkle with gems, but these are thrown together without order or reason, and though delightful at first view, they become tiresome when read continuously. Nevertheless there is strong temptation to go back again for a fresh look at the riches. Richter, or Jean Paul, as he is usually called, was born at Wonsiedel in Bavaria in 1763, the son of a poor country pastor who died in debt. While he studied at the University of Leipsic he suffered from pinching poverty, and finally ran away to escape imprisonment for debt. After a time the poor lad became a private tutor, then a schoolmaster, then an author, and finally a celebrity. His first book was "Lawsuits in Greenland" (1784), a collection of thin satirical sketches. He did not fairly succeed until he published his quaint romance "The Invisible Lodge" in 1793. Then followed, with continued success, "Hesperus" (1794), "The Life of Quintus Fixlein" (1796), "Flower, Fruit and Thorn-Pieces" (1797) and several more. The eccentric Jean Paul became the fashion of the time and giving up his school he visited the literary centers, being everywhere welcomed. After his marriage at Berlin in 1801 he went back to Bavaria and wrote more books, his great romance, "Titan," the novel, "Wild Oats," "Levana" (1807), a treatise on education, and a host more. His collected works comprise sixty-five volumes. They consist of poetical rhapsodies about everything in the universe great and small. He is a splendid landscape-painter, an interpreter of the emotions of the soul, a describer of odd characters and grotesque incidents, a touching painter of domestic life, a scholar of recondite learning. His books abound in strange men and women who move about in a bewitched world, simple dreamers, gay wanderers without care, cynical philosophers, and burnt-out prodigals. Yet his pages reveal the real life, domestic and civil Germany a century ago. He paints the poor with their virtues and joys, rather than their sin and misery. Among the most attractive figures are the schoolmaster Quintus Fixlein and his beloved Thiennette, Dr. Katzenberger, Wuz, and Lawyer Siebenkaes. His language and style are as queer as his characters. He enlarged the German dictionary and tore pages out of the grammar. His abounding quality, for which many sins of writing are forgiven, is his humor. While he heaped scorn upon everything that smacked of vulgarity and pretence, he was tender in sympathy for the weakness and failings of others and earnestly desirous to promote their spiritual and intellectual enlightenment. Carlyle, who borrowed some pe-

culiarities of style from the German, says of him: "In
the whole circle of literature we look in vain for his parallel. Unite the sportfulness of Rabelais and the best
sensibility of Sterne, with the earnestness, and even in
slight portions, the sublimity of Milton; and let the mosaic
brain of old Burton give forth the workings of this strange
union with the pen of Jeremy Bentham."

THE ROMANTICISTS

The Romantic school in Germany had much in common with the Romanticists of France, whose views and
practices, aims and doctrines have already been described.
Yet they had peculiar features, due to nationality, circumstances, and above all philosophy, which had been so popularized by the labors of Kant, Fichte and Schelling, that
it had become a fashion and indeed a craze. J. G. Fichte
(1762-1814) who was professor at Jena, then the focus of
philosophy for Germany, regarded the external world as
the projected creation of the *Ego* or individual. Each
man has or makes his own world. There is therefore an
infinite variety of worlds and no uniform principle per-
vades them. This Transcendentalism, or rather wild idealism, had important moral and social consequences. It
abolished at once the moral law, for no law could be made
to bind the differing and opposing worlds. It made the
individual superior to society, and his will superior to any
agreements of others, for after all, what were they but creations of his mind? F. W. J. Schelling (1775-1854), who
also lectured at Jena, gave a poetical turn to the new doctrine by dwelling on the relations between mind and nature. He called his system Nature-philosophy; it was
really an idealistic pantheism, such as may be seen in the
philosophic poetry of Wordsworth. Some of his disciples

insisted on the mystery of human life and the world, and thus assisted the movement toward the introduction of supernatural in literature.

The students trained under these philosophers found different modes of expression for their intellectual activity. Some in wild dramas and romances gave examples of the individual will opposed to the laws and conventions of society in whatever shape. From this substitution of individual caprice for moral law of any kind, others went on to declare opposition to spiritual progress and to glorify the flesh. Instances of this reversion to barbarism are not wanting in the Romantic literature of any country. Byron and Shelley furnish examples in some of their works. Friedrich Schlegel is a German example of the same, and in one of his works has set forth his idea of "charming lawlessness," which is really moral dissoluteness. He insists upon being allowed this freedom in writing as in practice. On the other hand, there were refined, spiritual natures who sought for separation from the sin-stained world, and longed for a perfect transfiguration. Such a person was the saintly Hardenberg, known by his assumed name Novalis (1772-1801). He concluded that the highest attainment of the human spirit is rest and that conscious activity is sin. The visible world is a chaotic dream, and actual life which calls constantly for exertion of the will is a disease of the spirit. He went on to hold that the true object of poetry is to represent the supernatural, miraculous and irrational. His poems and mystical prose writings still find admirers.

But there were other professors at Jena who were directly concerned with literature. The chief was August W. von Schlegel (1767-1845) who made the admirable poetic translation of Shakespeare, which has rendered the great English dramatist a German classic. Schlegel founded the "Athenæum," a literary journal to propagate his views. He accompanied Madame de Staël in her tour in Germany. With his brother, Friedrich, he promoted the study of foreign literatures, including the Sanskrit. Heine, however, has maliciously caricatured A. W. Schlegel, who was lacking in creative power. Friedrich was the first to attempt a complete history of the literature of the world.

The early Romanticists were not in sympathy with the world around them. They found it dull and formal and without the proper elements for the nourishment of the mind and spirit. Some of them in their search for what they missed went back to the Middle Ages, when chivalry and faith prevailed. They drew splendid pictures of the devout piety which was supposed to regulate all the affairs of life and produced the grand cathedrals with their splendid architecture, painting and sculpture, and their elaborate ritual. Others were attracted by the recent discoveries of the wealth of Oriental literature— Arabic, Persian, and Sanskrit. Others found satisfaction in English literature, making Shakespeare the god of their idolatry. Still another group were content with the early writers of their own land. Many mediæval authors, who had been neglected, were now brought to light. In this search for the new and strange, or for the old and forgotten, some called attention to the folk-lore and folk-songs which had previously been considered outside of the pale of literature. The noble-hearted brothers Jacob and William Grimm, in addition to their scholastic labors, gathered the simple nursery tales which have since become household favorites in all lands. The merit of these simple stories once revealed, some writers, as Tieck, set to work to enlarge the stock. But there is generally an extravagance and pretentiousness in the modern inventions which distinguishes them from the simplicity and playfulness of the genuine antiques.

The Romanticists at first regarded themselves as disciples of Goethe in literature, for there was much in his writings that seemed to favor the new tendency, but they gradually separated themselves from his dominion. Where Goethe urged self-restraint, they clamored for freewill. They rejected the sense of order in literary form, and indulged in all manner of extravagant freaks. In this respect Jean Paul Richter, who preceded the Romanticists, was the chief offender.

The influence of the Romanticists was not confined to literature. It entered into practical life. Many of its adherents became so filled with enthusiasm for the Middle Ages, as reconstructed by their fancy, that they sought to revive mediævalism in every direction. On art it had profound influence, which still remains. It deepened the sense of mystery in religion, and led many into the Catholic Church. It restored general appreciation of the life of the Middle Ages, and led to closer and fuller examination of its history with many marvelous results. It led to a universal recognition that there are elements in man and the world which cannot be definitely stated but can only be felt in their manifestations.

The most prominent and most prolific of the German Romantic novelists is Ludwig Tieck (1773-1853). He was born in Berlin and from boyhood showed passionate fondness for Shakespeare and the theater. On graduating from the University of Halle, he devoted himself to literature, his earliest work being melodramatic tales. His "William Lovell" (1775), is a wild story of seduction, murder and robbery. Next he made satirical farces out of "Puss in Boots" and "Blue Beard." Then coming

under the influence of the Schlegels, he translated dramas
from the Spanish and from Ben Jonson.   In original work
he was an interpreter of mediæval life in the curiously
constructed dramas "Genoveva" (1800), and "Emperor
Octavian" (1804).   For the sake of his health he went to
Italy in 1805, and made a long stay during which a change
came over his spirit and manner of writing.   He dropped
his mediævalism and gave attention to artistic construction.   Henceforth there is in his tales considerable resemblance to some of Hawthorne's weird short stories.
It is probable that the American learned from the German
something of his art of making nature exercise direct and
conscious influence on the human spirit.   Tieck's new
manner was first shown in the collection called "Phanta-
sus" (1812), in which plays and stories are brought together in a framework of æsthetic conversation.   In later
works with great ingenuity he blended with the story
his comment, which is often ironical, here again resembling Hawthorne.   In "The Pictures" there is a dissipated
painter Eulenböck, who gets a beggarly living by forging
old masters when he might have acquired fame and fortune by original work.   On the other hand in "Luck
Brings Brains" a man of weak character is roused to
proper exertion and realization of his powers by having
responsibility thrust upon him.   Two contrasted historical
pieces are "A Poet's Life," referring to Shakespeare, and
"A Poet's Death," to Camoens.   More than once Tieck
seems to have tried to make a story counterpart to "Wilhelm Meister."   This may have been the case with "William Lovell," written in his youth, and more probably with
"Sternbald's Travel" and "The Young Carpenter."   In
"Vittoria Accorambona" (1840), Tieck approaches the
modern French school of fiction.   Since 1819 he had been
a resident of Dresden, where he was active in directing the

royal theater and gave dramatic readings in the court circle. He translated the English dramatists before Shakespeare, and lent his name to the completion of Schlegel's poetic translation of Shakespeare. At the age of seventy he returned to his native city by invitation of the King of Prussia. He died in 1853.

Tieck's original powers seem to have been held in check by self-criticism, which produced self-distrust. He was never able to do any large work, but his small pieces often exhibit unmistakable genius. His want of self-confidence is shown in his ready submission to successive influences, while his genius enabled him to produce excellent work in each new style. His natural inclination was most in accord with a moderate Romantic tendency.

The weirdly beautiful tale of "Undine" is the immortal classic of the Romantic era. Its author, Baron Friedrich de la Motte Fouqué (1777-1843), was a valiant warrior as well as an industrious writer. His family name shows his French descent, and his Christian name was taken from the great Friedrich, of Prussia, whose godson he was, and in whose army his father and grandfather were officers. At the age of seventeen he himself commenced his military service, and ten years later he became an author. With the encouragement of the Schlegels he published various dramas under the name Pellegrin, then poems and a romance. By 1808 public favor shown to these warranted his putting his own name to his story of "Sigurd the Dragon-Slayer," the first of a series taken from the old Norse legends. Then came the chivalric romance of "The Magic Ring" (1811), and other tales and plays. The year 1814 was signalized by a story for each season, the spring number being "Undine," the autumn number "Aslauga's Knight," which Carlyle translated in his "German Romances," and the winter num-

ber "Sintram and His Companions." In 1813 the baron
had buckled on his sword again, but after the battle of
Lützen was disabled by illness and honorably discharged.
Again he took up the pen and nearly every year till his
death in 1843 issued a volume. For some years the German people eagerly waited for each new romance, then the
fashion changed. The popular writer outlived his vogue.
But "Undine" has never lost its charm, and the other re-
mances of the year 1814 are often bound with it.

"Undine" tells how a water-nymph, of beautiful
human form, desired to obtain a human soul. This could
only be done by winning and retaining the love of a human
being. She frequented the hut of two old fisher-folk on
an island, and was treated as their daughter. By rendering help to a wandering knight she won his regard and
was married to him. For a time their lives were happy,
but his cousin, who had hoped to marry him, excited dis-
trust of the gentle nymph, and when she is called by her
former companions to rejoin them in the Danube, she
plunges in the stream. Throughout the story there is an
ethereal beauty, enhanced by the simple style. The supernatural is so exquisitely blended with the natural that the
reader gladly accepts the whole as poetically true.

Far different in effect, and more widely improbable,
are the gruesome tales of horrors presented by Ernst
Theodor Amadeus Hoffmann (1776-1822). The man
himself was as different as possible from the moral, ami-
able Fouqué. Though clever in music and painting, and
learned as a jurist, he was dissipated and reckless, mali-
cious and sarcastic, and frequently brought disgrace on
himself, and trouble on his friends. Yet he was powerful
as a writer, and used his imaginative talent on frightful
superstitions and myths. But these are so accompanied
by brilliant descriptions, and stirring dialogue, that they

allure even while they repel. *"Der Elixire des Teufels"* (The Devil's Elixir), shows revolting delusions; but among his smaller pieces "The Golden Top," and "Master Martin and His Comrades" are the most pleasing.

Among the Romantics whose fame has passed away was Clemens Brentano (1777-1842), who had some originality of thought and fancy, and with the aid of his brother-in-law, Achim von Arnim (1781-1831), made a collection of popular lyrics, *"Des Knaben Wunderhorn"* (The Boy's Wonder Horn). Adelbert von Chamisso (1781-1838) was by birth and training a Frenchman, but in his literary activity, a German. In 1815 he was appointed the botanist of a Russian expedition which circumnavigated the globe, and after his return he had charge of the botanical gardens at Berlin. He wrote some tales after the romantic fashion and lyrics in which there is often true pathos. But he is best known by the story of "Peter Schlemihl" (1814), the man who lost his shadow. It was written for a friend's children, and has proved popular with children of all nations by its fun and lively incidents, while to older readers it may seem an allegory of the author's life. With the Romanticists may be associated Johann Heinrich Daniel Zschokke (1771-1848), who, though born in Prussia, lived most of his life in Switzerland, and devoted his historical labors to his adopted country. His "Pictures of the Swiss" and his romantic tales, "The Creole," "The Goldmakers' Village," "Jonathan Frock," had wide circulation. But his most celebrated work is *"Stunden der Andacht"* (1806). (Hours of Devotion), which consists of meditations on death and eternity.

The lovely collection of "Household Fairy Tales" has rendered the names of the brothers Grimm familiar in all parts of the world. Yet it was only an episode of their life-work. The elder, Jacob L. C. Grimm, was born at Hanan, in Hesse Cassel, in 1785, and William a year later. Jacob, at the University of Marburg, came under the influence of Savigny, the celebrated investigator of Roman law, and followed that scholar to Paris as his assistant for a year. He returned to become a librarian at Cassel, yet was employed occasionally in diplomatic duties at Paris and Vienna. The two brothers henceforth worked together in more than one library. They, with others, were dismissed from Göttingen in 1837 for signing a protest against the King's abrogation of the State Constitution, but in 1840 they were called to Berlin. Jacob was stout and robust, and worked without pause at his great "German Dictionary and Grammar." William, who had been equally robust in boyhood, lost his health in youth, and remained weak the rest of his life. When he married, his elder brother continued to live with him. William had greater love of poetry, and was fond of storytelling. The two brothers had begun to collect the old epics, ballads, and tales, when the younger suggested a collection of popular stories from books and from mouths of the people. The first edition of the *"Kinder und Haus-Märchen"* (Children's and House Stories) came out in 1812-15. Then they went on to a critical sifting of the oldest epic traditions of the Germanic races in their *"Deutsche Sagen"* (German Stories). This prepared the way for Jacob's great work on "German Mythology" (1835), which traced the Teutonic myths and superstitions as far back as evidence would allow. It also treated of the decay of these myths under change of religion and showed their fragmentary survival in traditions, stories, and proverbial expressions. William died in 1859, while the elder Jacob survived till 1863. Out of their lighter labors, so apparently trivial in their origin has grown, not

only the vast literature of folk-lore, but the important
science of comparative mythology. But the literary value
of these stories really lies in their delightfully naïve style,
which has captivated all readers. The tender-hearted
brothers, whose affection and kindred tastes bound their
lives so closely together, opened the doors of fairyland
to the whole world.

William Grimm, in his preface to the Tales describes
their character: "The sphere of this world is limited.
Kings, princes, faithful servants, honest craftsmen, fishermen, millers, charcoal-burners, and shepherds, all the
folk who live nearest to nature, appear in it; what lies
beyond is strange and unknown. As in myths that tell
of the Golden Age, all nature is alive; sun, moon, and stars
are accessible, bestow gifts, or may, perhaps, be woven in
garments; in the mountains dwarfs are digging for
precious metals, in the sea the water spirits rest; birds,
plants, and stones talk and express their sympathy; even
blood speaks and cries out. This innocent familiarity of
the greatest and the smallest has an inexpressible charm,
and we could rather listen to the conversation between the
stars and a poor child lost in the forest than to the music
of the spheres."

Somewhat allied with the Romantic movement, was a
class of plays known as Destiny dramas. The chief
author of these was the eccentric poet, Friedrich Ludwig
Zacharias Werner (1768-1823). It is said that his
mother, at the time of his birth, was insane, and believed
herself the Virgin Mary. Leaving the Prussian civil
service, in 1806, Werner traveled through Germany and
Switzerland, visiting Goethe and Madame de Staël, who
sent him on to Italy. At Rome he was converted to
Catholicism, and in 1814 was ordained a priest, and became noted for half-mad pulpit eloquence. In his Destiny

dramas, the heroes are shown to be guided by fate, either to the realms of light, or the abode of night and flames. Those who are born angels pass through some trials and are duly admitted to the destined heaven. Destined lovers find each other, no matter how widely separated. In most of these dramas Werner took the cheerful view of fatalism, but in the "Twenty-fourth of February" he shows a person destined to a succession of misfortunes on that day on account of a curse pronounced upon him by one whom he had offended.

PHILOSOPHERS

KANT

Speculative philosophy had direct as well as indirect effect upon German literature, but it is impossible here to do more than glance at this vast and profound subject. Immanuel Kant (1724-1804), the son of a saddler, rose to be a great metaphysician at Königsberg, his native city. He set himself in opposition to John Locke, who had maintained that the mind has no ideas except what it gains, through sensation and reflection, from the external world. Kant, on the other hand, asserted that besides the ideas thus obtained, the soul has certain ideas which it perceives by intuition. His system was set forth in his "Critique of Pure Reason" (1781), and later works. By determining the laws and limits of reason he sought to guard against the dogmatism which overestimates the power of the human intellect and against the skepticism which underestimates the same. Johann G. Fichte (1762-1814) was the second great metaphysician of Germany, but he was also an orator and public agitator. He began his career as philosopher by an "Attempt at a Criticism of all Revelation" and developed his system in his "Doctrine of Knowledge." He rejected sensation altogether as a source of knowledge, and held that the only thing of whose existence we are sure is the ego, the thinking soul. The external world has no existence except in the mind perceiving it. Fichte was charged with atheism, and resigned his professorship at Jena, but made an appeal to the public. He really held an idealistic pantheism. In 1810 he was made professor of philosophy in the newly-founded University of Berlin. In the War of Liberation he used all his influence and eloquence to arouse the patriotism of his countrymen and finally entered the ranks himself. He died in January, 1814, at the age of fifty-two. The third great philosopher was Friedrich W. J. Schelling (1775-1854), who was for a time associated with Fichte at Jena. He passed to Munich in 1826, and thence to Berlin in 1841. From the pure idealism of Fichte he developed a new system, according to which the external world is not derived from, or dependent upon, the ego, but exists along with it; and further that the opposition in which they stand to each other is united and reconciled in the Absolute or God. Another great philosophical leader was Georg Wilhelm Friedrich Hegel (1770-1831), who succeeded to the chair of Fichte at Berlin in 1818. His system has been pronounced more logical, complete, and comprehensive than those of his predecessors. But his followers have been divided into several groups, some maintaining that Hegelian philosophy is perfectly harmonious with Christianity, while others deny the personality of God as well as the doctrines of Christianity.

Another philosopher, who seemed to start with the extreme individualism of the Romantic movement, but departed from it later, was Friedrich Ernst Daniel Schleiermacher (1768-1834). An "Essay on the Immorality of All Morals" first attracted attention to him. In his "Discourses on Religion" he placed the true aim of life in becoming filled with the Divinity. This pantheistic religion he presented as the fulfillment of Protestantism. His translation of Plato did much to elucidate the ancient philosopher, and apply his principles to modern thought. Schleiermacher was active in founding the University of

Berlin in 1809, as part of the new national system of education in Prussia. His later work was chiefly theological.

Kant had considerable influence on Schiller, who, in order to represent the working of the passions, made many of his characters untrue to nature, and many scenes untrue to life. The Romantic writers carried this subjective tendency to still greater excess, and some, by utter carelessness for external form, made their works mere dreams. Following Fichte, young men of genius regarded the ideal as all-in-all, and demanded for their own will unlimited freedom. The form is dependent altogether upon the idea, and cannot be regulated. In poetry, fancy is the creative principle and the poet follows wherever it leads. As Schelling had said, "Every phenomenon in nature is the embodiment of an idea," another class of men of genius made it the poet's task to point out the ideas to be thus found in nature. Poetry therefore became symbolical and allegorical. Some early examples of this may be found in Schiller, but it became the moving principle of inferior poets. In their attempts to explain these phenomena, many fell into an abyss of mysticism. Goethe rejected the mysticism and enthusiasm for the Middle Ages, and retained his love for the ancient classics, so that he was reproached as "the great heathen."

SCHOPENHAUER

Still another philosopher long suffered from neglect of his teachings, but has in recent time had powerful influence on thought: Arthur Schopenhauer (1788-1860). He was full of contempt for the superficiality of existence and became the boldest assertor of pessimism. His life corresponded to his doctrine. He was unsociable and dogmatic, in youth immoral, and in age cynical. When his fellow students were filled with enthusiasm against Napoleon, Schopenhauer recognized in the conqueror merely the stronger expression of the selfishness of all men, and instead of taking arms against him, went to the Weimar Library to write a philosophical essay for his degree. His chief treatise is "The World as Will and Idea" (1819), in which he maintained that previous philosophers had erred in making reason the primary object in philosophy; whereas, he argued that in knowing, the ego, or subject perceiving, and the object perceived, are but opposite poles of the same thing; but in willing, there is a revelation of an inner real existence. The identity of the ego in "I will" and "I know" is the mystery which philosophy must ponder. Schopenhauer expressed his admiration for Plato and Kant, his contempt for Fichte, and his hostility to Hegel. There was practically no call for his services at any university. He renounced all superstitions of duty to country, kindred or associates, and found pleasure in reading the ancient and modern classics. He admired asceticism and was attracted to Buddhism, the similarity of which to his own philosophy is generally recognized. While the former philosophers had almost immediate effect upon literature, Schopenhauer did not exert any in his lifetime, but since his death his views have appeared in the literature of many countries.

It may be added to this brief sketch of the philosophers of the earlier part of the Century, that their work has been continued by eminent successors. Hermann Rudolf Lotze (1817-1881) was professor in Göttingen and ranked first among metaphysicians. Among his works are the "Microcosmos of Philosophy" (1856-64), and his valuable "History of Æsthetics in Germany" (1868).

He gave countenance to the later development of physiological psychology.

The successor of Schopenhauer as an exponent of pessimism is Eduard von Hartmann, born in 1842. On retiring from the Prussian military service in 1865, he devoted himself to philosophy. His greatest work is "The Philosophy of the Unconscious" (1868), which was based on physiology. Among his later works are "The Ethical Consciousness," "The Philosophy of Religion," and "Æsthetics" (1886), besides numerous essays on philosophical, religious, and social questions.

POETS OF THE WAR OF LIBERATION

When Prussia was crushed to earth under the iron heel of Napoleon it seemed impossible that she should ever recover her former status. But Baron von Stein (1757-1831), the great forerunner of Bismarck, was able in a few brief terms of office, in spite of the opposition of those with whom he had to work, to set in motion forces which liberated the country and started it on a new and more splendid career. His reputation as a clever financier had caused him to be recalled to the Prussian ministry after the disastrous battle of Jena, and he set about reorganizing all the departments of the government with such energy that Napoleon required his dismissal, but the work he commenced went on. German unity, which had long seemed to be a chimera, was made to appear feasible and the moral forces were roused in its behalf. Feudalism and serfdom were abolished and the people were roused to take an interest in governing themselves. The disastrous retreat of Napoleon from Moscow gave an opportunity for the new German spirit to manifest itself. At once a wave of enthusiasm passed over the land, the universities taking the lead in furnishing volunteers for the War of Liberation. The spirits of the people were cheered by the splendid lyrics of various poets, among whom the youthful martyr, Theodor Körner (1791-1813), takes the foremost place.

Körner, born at Dresden, went to the University of Leipsic, and afterward to Berlin and Vienna, where his dramas and the librettos to operas met such approval that he was appointed poet to the Court Theater. He was just engaged to be married when he heard the call to arms for the liberation of the Fatherland and responded. He was made lieutenant in the Prussian army and his wild war-songs sung to old national melodies round the camp-fires at night, spread such fervor in Lützow's volunteer corps, to which he belonged, that it became especially terrible to the enemy. They were afterward collected under the name "Lyre and Sword." His last poem, the celebrated "Sword Song," a love rhapsody to his sword, was written in a memorandum book at dawn of the 26th of August, 1813. In the pursuit of the French, who had been defeated, Körner was mortally wounded. Of his other pieces the most notable are "Lützow's Wild Chase," "Father, I Call Thee," and "Farewell to Life," written while he lay wounded.

Of much longer life, and equal patriotism, was Ernst Moritz Arndt (1769-1860). He was one of the pupils of Fichte, and became a professor of history at the University of Greifswald. His bold "History of Serfdom in Pomerania and Rügen" (1803), led to the abolition of that relic of barbarism. In *"Geist der Zeit"* (Spirit of the Time), (1807), he denounced the tyranny of Napoleon and called on the German people to unite in throwing off the hateful yoke. Great excitement followed, and the professor had to flee to Sweden. But his indefatigable pen kept up its activity, and numerous pamphlets excited hatred of the French domination. His poems and songs increased the popular enthusiasm, especially that famous one, "What Is the German's Fatherland?" When the liberation was effected, the poet returned and was made professor of history at the newly established University of Bonn, but his demands for constitutional reform offended the authorities and he was deprived of his chair. After twenty years' retirement, he was restored in 1840. He con-

tinued to lecture and write until his ninetieth year. His
patriotic poems were collected in 1860, another of the
famous ones being that "Song of the Fatherland" in which
he thanks God for making iron that there might be
weapons for freemen.

Friedrich Rückert (1788-1866) was another poet of
the struggle against Napoleon, writing then under the
name Freimund Reimar. Later he gave attention to
Oriental studies and was made professor at Erlangen in
1826, and thence called to Berlin in 1841. Eight years
later he retired to his estate at Coburg, where he continued
to write inferior dramas and superior poems, many of
the latter being translated or imitated from Oriental literature. He was master of thirty languages. His love of
splendid imagery made Eastern poetry congenial to him,
and his works exhibit a wonderful variety of lyrical forms
from the most simple to the most complex. His most
elaborate work is *"Die Weisheit des Brahmanen"* (The
Wisdom of the Brahmans), (1836), in six volumes.

August Graf von Platen-Hallemund (1796-1835)
was another poet who was affected by Oriental influences.
He had been educated for a military career and served
against France. He became proficient in many languages
and wrote lyrics and other poems in the Oriental style,
sonnets, and a long narrative poem on "The Abbasides"
(1835). His fierce controversy with Heine afforded
amusement at the time. He is considered the best classical poet of modern Germany, an aristocratic "sculptor of
words and connoisseur of the sublime." He ridiculed the
Romanticists in two comedies.

Wilhelm Müller (1794-1827) was a lyric poet who
won the praise of the caustic Heine. Born at Dessau, he
left his studies at the University of Berlin to take part in
the War of Liberation, but returned in 1814. Later he

traveled in Italy, and then became a teacher and librarian in his native town.   He was cut off at the early age of thirty-three, but had already published several volumes of poems, edited a collection of the poets of the Seventeenth Century and translated "Modern Greek Popular Songs." His son, Friedrich Max Müller, has won fame by his philological labors in England.   Two series of Müller's lyrics have had wide circulation from their having been set to music by Schubert: *"Die Schöne Müllerin"* (The Pretty Maid of the Miller), and *"Die Winterreise"* (The Winter Journey).   In his "Songs of the Greeks" Müller gave voice to the sympathy of the German people for the Greeks in their struggle for independence against the Turks in 1822.   The Greek Parliament afterward voted marble for the monument to Müller, erected at Dessau.

Two Austrian poets deserve mention, Zedlitz and Auersperg.   Baron Joseph von Zedlitz (1790-1862), whose "Wreaths for the Dead" is a series of eulogies on noble men.   His "Dungeon and Crown" treats of the last days of Tasso, who died before the day on which he was to be crowned King of Poets.   Anton, Graf von Auersperg (1806-1876), chose to be known in literature as Anastasius Grün.   His "Walk of a Vienna Poet" is his best work; he also wrote an epic, "Robin Hood."

THE REACTION AGAINST ROMANTICISM

After the downfall of Napoleon there was need for reconstruction of Germany. The people expected that they should receive back all the lands that had ever been taken from them by France, but the Treaty of Paris in 1816 fixed the boundaries as they had been at the outbreak of the French Revolution. As regards the internal arrangements of Germany, bitter experience had taught the need of a real union, and the people would have welcomed the establishment of a vigorous Empire. But Austria and Prussia could not forego their ancient jealousy, and the lesser princes objected to their petty States being wiped out. Instead of an Empire the Congress of Vienna organized merely a Bund or Confederation, leaving each State independent in its internal affairs. A permanent Diet, in which each State should be represented, was to meet at Frankfort and the Austrian representative was to be its presiding officer.

But the German people had been roused to seek not only national unity, but constitutional liberty. In the districts ruled by the French a higher regard for the natural rights of man had been introduced, and the principles of the Revolution had obtained general acquiescence. The selfish policy of the old German princes was detested, and the restoration of the old abuses was resisted. During the struggle with Napoleon the princes had made lavish promises of reform and concessions after peace should be established. In the very Act of Confederation there was a decree that a constitutional system should be established in every State. But the sovereigns of Europe, who had suffered so severely from the wars of Napoleon, and who regarded him as a product of rebellious democracy, determined to prevent the recurrence of such dangers. Alexander of Russia, Francis of Austria, and Frederick William of Prussia, before leaving Paris in 1815, had instituted the Holy Alliance, which was joined by every European sovereign, except the Pope and the King of England. The sovereigns were to be brothers to each other, fathers to their people, and would maintain religion, peace, and justice. This alliance was soon made the instrument of a faithless policy which sought to establish the absolutism of rulers, and suppress the doctrine that the people had any right in the government. The power of religion was invoked to crush the rising democracy and to set at naught the attempts at constitutional government. Eventually the Holy Alliance drew upon itself the reproach of hypocrisy and the hatred of the people. Prince Metternich, the Prime Minister of Austria, governed the diverse nationalities of that Empire without any regard to their separate characters and customs. His system was pure despotism. The King of Prussia repressed the popular aspirations; he refused a general parliament, but allowed provincial councils. Bavaria, Würtemberg, and smaller States, in which constitutions were granted, soon found their rulers endeavoring to annul them in practice. Every opportunity was taken to repress the free movement of ideas. The universities which, in the days of Napoleon, had been filled with crowds of students, enthusiastic for liberty, were put under police supervision. Professors who dared to raise their voices in behalf of constitutional liberty were silenced. Such was the treatment of the patriotic poet Arndt, the inoffensive brothers Grimm, and others. A rigid censorship of the press was established. Secret societies were hunted out. In the Diet the representatives of some small States favored conciliation and concession to the wishes of the people, but the reactionary party was united and determined, and long checked the wheels of progress. During this dismal period literature was repressed. Goethe, who held aloof from politics, busied himself with science, and labored to complete his "Faust."

Great hopes were entertained when Frederick William IV succeeded to the throne of Prussia, in 1840, that a change in the direction of greater liberty would be made. Concessions were made; professors who had been dismissed were restored to their places; the brothers Grimm were welcomed to Berlin. But there was no disposition to allow the people a real share in the government. The new King ruled more wisely than his father, but not less absolutely. The people were disappointed and the King soon lost all the popularity he had at the commencement of his reign.

In the fourth and fifth decades of the Century there arose a group called "Young Germany," different, however, in spirit and aims from the "Young England," to which Disraeli gave countenance. "Young Germany" was inspired by the influences which led to the Revolution of 1830 in France. It rose in opposition to the reactionary tendency in theology as well as politics and proclaimed rationalism as its creed. Among its leaders or supporters were Börne and Gutzkow. Ludwig Börne (1786-1837) was a child of the Ghetto, but in later life professed Christianity. He was chiefly engaged in journalism, and in his "Letters from Paris," where he had gone in 1830, he assailed the leading German orthodox writers with caustic wit. He had been an associate of Heine's, but they quarreled, and Heine wrote a severe criticism of his former friend. Karl Ferdinand Gutzkow (1811-1878) was the acknowledged head of "Young Germany." His novel,

"Wally, die Zweiflerin" (Wally, the Female Skeptic) (1835), was pronounced atheistical and subversive of public order, and he was imprisoned three months. But his drama, "Nero," was not any better. He was an able critic and for a time was an assistant to Menzel, but quarreled with him. Among his later works are "Blasedow" (1839), a satirical tale; *"Der Zauberer von Rom"* (The Magician from Rome) (1859). But his masterpiece is the tragedy of "Uriel Acosta" (1847).

Franz von Dingelstedt (1814-1881) also did his best work in this period, though he lived to become a famous stage director at Munich and Vienna. His "Songs of a Cosmopolitan Night-Watchman" (1841) produced a profound sensation. They gave poetical utterance to the sentiments of the free-thinking class. Among his novels the most admired are "Seven Peaceful Tales" (1844) and "The Amazon" (1868). He wrote also excellent criticism on Goethe and Shakespeare.

HEINE

Heinrich Heine and Goethe are in many respects opposite as the poles, yet the former is also the real successor in literature of the great German. Heine was born at Düsseldorf, of Jewish parentage, on the 13th of December, 1799. While he was a schoolboy, the French troops occupied the town and made deep impression on his mind. Thenceforth he was a worshiper of the great Napoleon. Though Heine had been intended for mercantile pursuits, his evident inclination to literature led his uncle, a Hamburg banker, to assist him generously. He went to the University of Bonn, then to Berlin, where he was admitted to the best literary society, and published his first poems in 1822. Neither this nor the tragedies which followed attracted any attention. Heine obtained his degree in law at Göttingen in 1825, and professed Christianity in order to be allowed to practice. But the change brought him sorrow rather than fortune. Literature claimed him for her own. His *"Reisebilder"* (Pictures of Travel) (1826) caused a great sensation by their bold ridicule of every idea and institution usually treated with reverence. In its method it resembles Sterne's "Sentimental Journey," but the spirit is far different. Its readers were delighted with its wit, elegance, and vivacity, while they were shocked at its blasphemy. The author added three volumes to the first, attacking every literary leader of the day. The audacity with which he voiced the youthful opposition to the official reactionary policy captivated the students of the University. Then in 1827 Heine published his *"Buch der Lieder"* (Book of Songs), comprising most that had been in his first book, and these now found delighted readers throughout Germany. The poems had a new beauty; they treated everything, from the greatest historical themes to the ordinary incidents of life, in a wonderfully fresh and lifelike way. Some were filled with melancholy, some with mockery, some with grief, and some with joy. But they were always original and impressive.

Heine was now called to Munich, where he edited a political periodical, but he also visited Berlin, where he had a quarrel with Count Platen, which produced some witty and scandalous writing. After the Revolution of 1830, which had put him in a frenzy, the Prussian Government so persecuted him that he was obliged to leave Germany. Henceforth Paris was his home. Soon he became intimate with Victor Hugo, Balzac, Dumas, and other leaders of the literary world. His pen was active in journalism, and his contributions to the press are still attractive by their art, elegance, and keenness of judgment of affairs. But he wrote also articles of more substantial and permanent literary value. His discussions of the religion and philosophy of Germany threw new light on a subject only half understood. His history of the German "Romantic School" is a valuable but bitter critical sketch of the period to which it relates. In 1839 he published "Shakespeare's Maidens and Wives," an exquisite guide to the dramatist's portrait gallery. In the preface he has bitter flings at England: "My spirit faints when I consider that Shakespeare was an Englishman, and belongs to the most repulsive people that God in his wrath has created. What a disgusting people! What an unrefreshing country!" In 1843 Heine made a visit to Germany and recorded his impressions in *"Deutschland, ein Wintermärchen"* (Germany, a Winter Tale), treating the country in the same sarcastic, irreverent style.

In 1848, while Heine was in full tide of activity, he was attacked with a spinal disease which inflicted intense suffering and confined him for seven years to a "mattress grave." But his mental faculties were unimpaired, and to the end he continued to write poetry of the finest luster and prose of the keenest satire. He had already formed an attachment for an uneducated grisette, and after some years of cohabitation they were married. Now she proved a faithful, loving wife, assiduous in her attentions to the slowly dying man. He died on the 17th of February, 1856. In his will this strange, witty blasphemer wrote: "I die in the belief of one only God, the Creator of the world, whose pity I implore for my immortal soul. I lament that I have sometimes spoken of sacred things without due reverence, but I was carried away more by the spirit of my time than by my own inclinations. If I have unwittingly violated good manners and morality, I pray both God and man for pardon."

Heine is one of the greatest song writers of the world. Many of his pieces were set to music by Schumann and Mendelssohn. His intense personal feeling was essential to these, to enable them to reach the heart of the people. The sweetest of his early poems were inspired by a strong affection for his cousin, and some critics have asserted that the bitterness of his later years arose from his love not having been requited. His lyrics are usually very short, sudden ejaculations or expressions of a momentary feeling, pain or pleasure, regret or love. The tone of sadness prevails; they never rouse the spirit with words of power. Among the best of his lyric poems are "The Rose, the Lily, the Dove, the Sun," "On the Wings of Song," "Thou Art Like a Flower," "The Sea Hath Its Pearls." Many of his ballads and narrative pieces have great charm, as "The Lorelei," "The Princess Sabbat," "Jehuda ben Halevy," "Wicked Dreams," "The Pilgrimage to Kevlaar," "The Island Bimini." His "North Sea" and "Return to Home" are cycles of song, celebrating the mystery and greatness of the sea. Many of his poems which open sweetly allow a sudden discord to enter and destroy the charm.

In his prose Heine set himself forth as an enemy of Philistinism, that dull, narrow-minded adherence to conventional ideas in literature and art. But he abused his power of ridicule, directing it not merely against pedants and hidebound critics, but against the masters in literature and philosophy. His "Romantic School" was a violent blow against the monstrosities and absurdities into which that school had fallen. His "Pictures of Travel" is his chief prose work, and contains every variety of description, from simple narrative to satirical caricature.

C. VON BODENHAUSEN, PINX.

LORELEI.

THE SUABIAN POETS

As an offshoot from the Romantic School there arose a group which has been called the Suabian School, its modest leader being Ludwig Uhland (1787-1862). He was born at Tübingen, and after studying law, became a professor of literature in the university of his native town. His has been called the Classic of Romanticism, to denote that while affected by the Romantic spirit, he returned to the moderation of the Classic School. No frightful phantasms or shadowy monsters appear in his ballads. His figures are usually simple, poetic types of German nationality, children of the Black Forest, fair shepherds, and mountain boys. To the experiences of common life he imparts a warm imaginative coloring. In his poems of the Middle Ages there is the same natural beauty, far apart from the mystical and supernatural favored by the extreme Romanticists. His heroes of early times possess the genuine German nature, strong, brave, good humored, patient, faithful. Next to Schiller, he is the most popular of all the German poets. Several of his poems have been translated by Longfellow, with whose genius Uhland had much in common. Among these are "The Luck of Edenhall," "The Passage," "The Castle by the Sea," "The Black Knight." Another of Uhland's best poems is "The Minstrel's Curse."

Other poets of this school are Gustav Schwab (1792-1850), inferior to Uhland in feeling; and Justinus Kerner (1786-1862), who was still inclined to the supernatural and morbid. Kerner's best poems are "Kaiser Rudolf's Ride to the Grave" and "The Richest Prince."

Karl Lebrecht Immermann (1796-1840) was one of those poets who started under the influence of the Romanticists and then diverged. Born at Magdeburg, he left

the University of Halle to take part in the war against
Napoleon.   He fought at Waterloo and entered Paris
under Blücher.   Returning to Halle, he opposed political
agitation among the students.   He completed his law
studies and entered the Prussian service, and became a
judge.   In 1826 he settled at Düsseldorf, and here became
a theater director, noted for his perfect taste.   He was
now a follower of Goethe, who had approved his early
poems.   His first romance, "The Epigoni" (The After-
born) (1835), holds the mirror up to his own age as
degenerated from the virtues of its predecessors.   Another
of his dramas had Andrew Hofer, the patriot of the
Tyrol, as its hero.   But his chief work is his romance,
"Münchhausen, a Story in Arabesques" (1839), a love-
story of peasant life, in which are introduced the marvelous tales of the hero's grandfather.   His Platonic literary
affection for the Countess of Ahlfeldt had considerable
influence on his work.   In 1839 he married another lady
and wrote a love epic on "Tristan and Isolde."   A volume
of memoirs was left unfinished.

August Heinrich Hoffmann (1798-1874), called von
Fallersleben, to distinguish him from other literary
Hoffmanns, was professor in the University of Breslau
until 1842, when his *"Unpolitische Lieder"* (Unpolitical
Songs), which were really political, caused his dismissal.
He traveled in various countries until 1848, when he
returned to Prussia and received a pension.   He was librarian to the Duke of Ratibor from 1860 till his death.   His
poems were popular, sometimes describing rural life with
hearty affection, sometimes full of kindly satire, and sometimes representing the political movements of his time.
In his song on "German National Wealth," he shows the
emigrant carrying to the New World the old parchments,
liveries, books of heraldry, tax receipts, and passports, all

of inestimable value in the old life. Without them the German will not feel at home.

Nikolaus Lenau is the pseudonym under which Nikolaus Niembsch von Strehlenau (1802-1850) wrote. He has been styled "the German poet of sorrow." This unhappy Austrian poet was a victim not only of melancholy, but of insanity. Its gloom overshadowed his whole life, even before his madness fully declared itself in 1844, on the eve of his contemplated marriage. His yearnings for the release of death had been breathed forth in his poem, *"Der Seelen Kranke"* (Soul-Sickness). Hoping to find happiness and a brighter inspiration in the New World, he came to Pennsylvania in 1832. But, soon disgusted, he returned to Europe, still under the spell of melancholy, and died in a lunatic asylum. In his "Faust" (1836) he made suicide the goal of free thought; in his "Savonarola" (1837) he denounced modern science; but in "The Albigenses" (1842) he hailed the progress of liberty.

MID-CENTURY POETS

Ferdinand Freiligrath (1810-1876), born at Detmold, was from childhood a scribbler of verse, original and translated. He was engaged in commercial pursuits until the success of his first volume of poems in 1838 induced him to devote his time to literature. He edited various periodicals, and, after 1845, took part in politics, from which he had previously held aloof. Giving up his royal pension, he joined the democratic party and aided it effectively by numerous spirited songs. But he was soon obliged to seek refuge in Switzerland, where he published a collection of poems translated from English. He was about to emigrate to America, when the Revolution of 1848 broke out and allowed him to return to Düsseldorf.

In the political strife of the succeeding years he was active for liberty in spite of trials and imprisonment until 1851, when he went to London. He continued his translations from English into German. In 1868 he was allowed to return to his native land. New songs were composed for the new war with France, among them "Germania" and the *"Trompete von Gravelotte"* (The Trumpet of Gravelotte). Freiligrath was a cosmopolitan poet and cannot be claimed by any poetic school. His poem, "The Lion's Ride," describes grandly a lion's fierce attack on a giraffe, which carried the king of beasts in its flight. Many others of his poems are equally original in subject and treatment. From Iceland to South Africa, he laid the whole world under tribute, and yet he was intensely patriotic. Germans regard him as a political poet-martyr, "the inspired singer of the Revolution." One of his famous Revolutionary poems is the *"Ca ira."* His early poems, by their mastery of rhyme and melody, have attracted most attention, but his love lyrics and his spirited songs of freedom are his noblest monument. He is a splendid colorist, and has been called "the Rubens of German poetry."

Emanuel von Geibel (1815-1884) was a highly cultivated and earnestly religious poet. In 1838 he went to Greece as tutor in the family of the Russian ambassador. With his friend, Ernest Curtius, he traveled over the land and wrote a volume of "Classical Studies." He assisted in editing a large collection of poetry from the French, Spanish, and Portuguese. His original poems were "Voices of the Time" (1841), "King Sigurd's Bridal Journey" (1843), and "Twelve Sonnets" (1846). In 1852 he was made professor of æsthetics in the University of Munich, but resigned in 1857 and returned to his native Lübeck, where he died. Geibel's poetry is characterized

by rich fancy, melodious versification, and beauty of
diction.

Friedrich Martin von Bodenstedt (1819-1892) is best
known by his "Songs of Mirza Schaffy," long supposed
to be really translations from the Persian. He was born
in Hanover and bred to business, but devoted all his leisure
to study, and at the age of twenty-one was able to go to
the University of Göttingen. He studied later at Munich
and Berlin, and, going to Russia as a tutor, plunged into
the Slavonic literature. His excellent translations of Russian poets were considered equal to the originals. While
teaching at Tiflis, he studied Tartar and Persian under a
real Mirza Schaffy, a Tartar philosopher, who had
obtained Persian culture. On his return to Germany
Bodenstedt published a romantic picture of his travels in
"A Thousand and One Days in the East" (1850). Here
Mirza Schaffy, idealized, occupies a prominent place, but
the poetry was Bodenstedt's own, adapted to the character of the Eastern sage. The poems were soon published
separately and were enthusiastically received. They treat
of wine and love, of the pleasures of life and the charms
of maidens, in joyful, melodious verses. In a later volume
called "The Posthumous Works of Mirza Schaffy"
(1874) the poet gave a more serious tone to his philosophy. Bodenstedt was professor in the University of
Munich, and director of a theater in Saxony. After a
visit to the United States in 1879 he wrote an account
of his travels to the Pacific, and an interesting autobiography.

South Germany, although the home of the Minnesingers in the Middle Ages, has been less rich in poets than
North Germany in modern times. Perhaps the most distinguished Austrian poet of recent date is Robert Hamer-

ling (1830-1889). He was born at Kirchberg, became a chorister, and was educated at Vienna. A volume of poems, published in his twenty-first year, gave promise of his ability. He was engaged in teaching at Trieste until 1866, when he retired on account of ill-health, and was allowed a pension. His fame rests chiefly on his epic poem, "Ahasuerus in Rome" (1866), which exhibits the failing power of paganism in the time of Nero. Another work of note is "The King of Lèon" (1868), written in hexameters. "Aspasia" is a graphic picture of Athenian life in the time of Pericles, but the erudition interferes with the poetry. A few dramas, satires, and minor poems flowed from the author's pen. Toward the close of his life he wrote an autobiography.

THE REALISTIC NOVELISTS

As in other literatures, realism came to prevail in Germany after the middle of the Century. Fanciful romanticism could not be content with lower personages than Kings and knights, and sought its subjects in the remote idealized Middle Ages, or in a supernatural world, unvisited except in dreams. But the extravagance of its practitioners caused a reaction which was helped by some of themselves who repented of their early works. Heine confessed that he had once belonged to that school which he mercilessly exposed after he went to France, and declared himself a "disfrocked Romanticist." But there were others who were fortunate enough to be born so late as to escape the epidemic. They were warned in due time and avoided the plague. For them real life has furnished the staple of their works. In the commonplace lives of ordinary people of town and country have been found the possibilities of humor and pathos, and occasionally, as in life itself, grim tragedy may enter.

FREYTAG

Of German novelists Gustav Freytag holds the foremost place. He was born at Kreuzburg, in Silesia, in 1816, and graduated at the University of Berlin in 1838. After lecturing for a few years on the German language and literature he devoted himself to literature at Leipsic, where he edited *"Die Grenzboten."* In 1870 he served in the Franco-Prussian War, on the staff of the Crown Prince. After the war he resumed his newspaper work.

He died at Wiesbaden in 1895. His first publication was
a volume of poems, then a comedy, then a tragedy. His
greatest success was with the comedy "The Journalists"
(1853), which still remains on the stage. His first novel,
"Soll und Haben" (Debit and Credit) (1855), was notably successful. It depicted accurately the social conditions of its time, showing the relation of modern industrialism to the life of the times. A wholesale grocer, prosperous in business, is set in contrast with a nobleman who
represents the effete force of feudalism. The hero, Anton
Wohlfahrt, begins a commercial career in the store, and
becomes a member of the firm, and falls in love with the
baron's daughter, Lenore. Her mother asks Anton to
help her husband out of embarrassments produced by an
attempt to run a mill on his estate. The baron rejects his
aid, and Anton returns to the store. Lenore is engaged
to a young nobleman, Fink, who has served in the store
and has visited America. Fink advances money for the
improvement of the estate and ultimately purchases it.
Fink marries Lenore and Anton marries his partner's sister. Freytag's second story, "The Lost Manuscript"
(1864), tells how Werner, a scholar, seeking for the lost
books of Tacitus, finds his future wife, Ilse, a noble type
of a German woman. But Werner in his devotion to
scholarship, neglects his wife, whose beauty attracts a
Prince. The seducer endeavors to ensnare the innocent
wife until even Werner sees his aim. The covers of the
lost manuscript are at last found, but the precious contents have disappeared. The professorial life is vividly
and humorously described, and the nobleman is contrasted with him to his own discredit.

Freytag next published "Pen Pictures from the German Past" (1859-62), which consisted of studies of German life in various periods since the Fourteenth Century.

The sketch of Doctor Luther in this series has been most popular. Then followed the series of historical novels called "The Ancestors" (1872-80), in which the author traced a typical German family in each successive period with most careful attention to historical accuracy. This ambitious work was intended to be not merely correct in external antiquarianism, but to reveal the true spirit of the actors at each successive stage. In this series "Ingo" and "Ingraban" are the most attractive. Freytag's fault is his tendency to point a moral, and to philosophize too much. Besides his novels he wrote an autobiography and some critical and historical essays. He died at Wiesbaden in 1895.

Diversified experience in mercantile and military life as well as in foreign gave Baron Friedrich Wilhelm von Hackländer (1816-1877) abundant material for authorship. Having served in the Prussian artillery, he wrote sketches of soldier life which attracted the attention of Baron von Taubenheim, who took him on a journey to the East. After his return he became secretary to the Crown Prince of Würtemberg and traveled with him in Italy. He accompanied the Austrian Marshal, Radetzky, in the campaign against Piedmont in 1849. When again in Italy in 1859 he was invited to the headquarters of the Emperor of Austria, who afterward gave him a patent of hereditary nobility. His chief residence was at Stuttgart, where he was director of the royal buildings, but he went on many tours. He was in 1857 one of the founders of the well-known illustrated journal *"Uber Land und Meer"* (Over Land and Sea). For this he wrote many of his stories and sketches of travel. His novels include *"Handel und Wundel"* (1850), translated by Mary Howitt under the title "Behind the Counter"; "The New Don

Quixote" (1858), "Day and Night" (1860), "The Last
Bombardier" (1870), "Forbidden Fruit" (1876). His
faculty of quick observation and humorous sketching
were better adapted to books of travel than to long novels.
Among his comedies the best are *"Geheimer Agent"* (The
Domestic Agent) and the "Magnetic Cures." A number
of one-act pieces proved very popular on the stage. After
his death an incomplete autobiography was published.

Fritz Reuter is a master in German dialect stories. He
describes with genial humor the joys and sorrows of the
humblest class in country and village. The characters are
so carefully and vividly drawn that they are immortal-
ized. Fritz Reuter was born in 1810 at the sleepy old town
of Stavenhagen in Mecklenburg-Schwerin. He was educated at the Universities of Rostock and Jena. It was
a troublous time, and the Government was still alarmed
by the Revolution of 1830. When some students made
a noisy demonstration in 1833, Reuter was arrested, tried
and condemned to death for high treason. But the King
of Prussia commuted the sentence to thirty years' imprisonment, and after Reuter had had experience of several
prisons, he was discharged by the amnesty granted by
Frederick William IV in 1840. He now took to farming, but failed, and became a private tutor. In 1853 he
published his first volume, "Funny Stories and Rhymes."
It was written in Platt Deutsch or Low German, and the
homely mirth of the stories was strengthened by the appropriate dialect. Its success led to the publication of another,
"Wedding Eve Stories," and still another, "The Journey
to Belgium," telling the adventures of some peasants who
traveled to Belgium to find out the secret of industrial
prosperity. "Kein Hüsing" (1858), a poem of village
life, was followed by other poems. "Old Camomile Flowers" (1862) is a series of sketches, chiefly autobiographic.

He tells of the part played by the village of Stavenhagen in the uprising of the German people against Napoleon in 1813, of his own imprisonment, how he courted his wife, and his apprenticeship on the farm. The leading characters are the comical bailiff, Uncle Bräsig, pious Parson Behrens and his bustling wife, and the rascal Pomuchelskopp. The truth of these pictures of village life places Reuter high among the realists of the Century. He died in 1874.

Berthold Auerbach (1812-1882) became widely known by his homely stories of peasants of the Black Forest and afterward published large novels which, though powerful, had only a temporary success. He was born at Nordstetten in Würtemberg and was of Jewish parentage. He studied at the Universities of Tübingen, Munich, and Heidelberg, and for his participation in students' riotous frolics in 1836 he was imprisoned for some months. His first essay in authorship was on "Judaism and the latest Literature;" then came "The Ghetto," a series of Jewish romances, and a translation of the Jewish philosopher Spinoza. But meanwhile he was contributing to periodicals his tales of peasant life, which, when collected as "Black Forest Village Stories" (1843), were enthusiastically received, not in Germany alone, but throughout the civilized world. Their happy mingling of the real and the ideal was helped by their genial humor. Auerbach's tragedies met with little success on the stage, but the story of "Little Barefoot" (1856) renewed his former reputation. His most ambitious work, "On the Heights" (1851), contrasted tiresome court life and its ambitions and intrigues with quiet peasant life, and aimed also to inculcate the philosophy of Spinoza. It belongs to the class of "purpose" novels. The heroine is an admirable character and there are others truly human. "The Villa on the Rhine"

(1868) was another philosophical romance, but treated different problems. "Waldfried" (1874), a patriotic story of a German family from 1848 to 1871, has not the attraction of good literary style. Auerbach afterward returned to sketches of the Black Forest in "After Thirty Years" (1876) and other stories. After 1859 he lived chiefly in Berlin, but he died at Cannes, in France, where he had gone for the sake of his health.

Friedrich Spielhagen's best novel is a worthy successor of Goethe's "Wilhelm Meister," but he has been so busy in production that he has not always kept up to his high standard. He was born at Magdeburg in 1829 and studied in the Universities of Berlin, Bonn, and Greifswald. His literary ambition was aroused but his earliest novels seemed failures. In 1860 he began to publish his "Problematic Natures" showing the struggle between old established feudalism and the rising industrialism of the time, yet showing also the futility of the efforts of a man, richly endowed by nature, to attain high ideals unless he recognizes his own limitations and the conditions of the world around. It was intended partly as a picture of his own mental state, but in the very act of making the picture he was enabled to outgrow it. The work attracted attention and Spielhagen was engaged to furnish novels to a newspaper. He wrote some dramas which were partially successful, and made several translations from French and English, chiefly of important works, as Emerson's "English Traits." But his chief and almost incessant work has been as a novelist. "In Rank and File" was his second strong novel. "Quisisana" (1880) is highly interesting, showing a vigorous man of fifty, who falls in love with a beautiful ward, but overcomes his passion and marries her to the young man of her choice, while her filial affection only distresses him who has made the sacrifice. In 1890 Spielhagen published an autobiographical work called "Finder and Inventor," which treats particularly of his early life and the circumstances under which he produced his typical novel.

Georg Moritz Ebers (1837-1898) won distinction both as an Egyptian archæologist and as historical novelist. Born at Berlin, he studied at the University of Göttingen, and during convalescence from an injury to his feet began to investigate the Egyptian hieroglyphs. Afterward by the instruction of Richard Lepsius he became well versed in that science. His first novel, "An Egyptian Princess" (1864), was written to impress on his own mind the period he was studying. He had already visited the principal museums in Europe and in 1869 went to Egypt, Nubia, and Petra. On his return he was made professor of Egyptian antiquities in the University of Leipsic. A visit to Egypt in 1872 resulted in the discovery of a papyrus which now bears his name. Various treatises on his special subject maintained his reputation as an Egyptologist. He resigned his professorship in 1889, and died after long illness in 1898. In literature Ebers owes his fame to his romances reconstructing the ancient life of the valley of the Nile. The "Egyptian Princess" is a story of the conquest of Egypt by Cambyses, the king of Persia. "Uarda" (1877) belongs to a much more ancient period, when Rameses the Great was ruler. "Homo Sum" (1878) tells of the desert anchorites of the Fourth Century after Christ. "The Sisters" (1880) again takes the reader back to Memphis in the time of the Ptolemies. "The Emperor" (1881) treats of Christianity in the time of Hadrian. In other novels Ebers comes down to modern history, as in "The Burgomaster's Wife" (1882), which shows the struggle of the people of Leyden against Spanish rule in 1547. "Gred" is a story of mediæval

Nuremberg. "A Question" (1881) is a modern idyl, and "A Word" (1883) a psychological study. After these Ebers returned again to his familiar field in "Serapis," "A Bride of the Nile," and "Cleopatra." He wrote also an excellent biography of his instructor, Lepsius.

HISTORIANS

History has been raised to the dignity of an independent science in the Nineteenth Century. It was formerly regarded as the servant of other sciences, the handmaid which supplied to them what was needed in any exigency for argument or illustration. "History," said Bolingbroke, "is philosophy teaching by examples." But it was more commonly regarded as merely gathering and having ready whatever examples the great dame Philosophy might see fit to call for. The art of history was to join these examples in a narrative which should recommend itself to the reader's taste or prejudices. It was to furnish arguments or morals. But the error of this relegation of history to a subordinate position has been rebuked and the practice generally abandoned in the Nineteenth Century. The change was brought about gradually, but credit for the first step toward it may be given to Barthold Georg Niebuhr (1776-1831), who was a Dane, son of a famous traveler, Karsten Niebuhr. This scholar was called to Prussia to assist Stein in the reformation of its government, and was for a time ambassador at Rome. He settled down as a professor at Bonn in 1823, and soon began his "History of Rome." The new departure in his work was his entire discarding of the fables which had previously passed current in regard to the kings and heroes of Rome. The true history begins centuries later than the accepted date of the foundation of the city. To prove this conclusion so clearly that it could not be controverted was the work of Niebuhr. He went on to show how fragments of the truth could be detected in later writers and in various institutions of the historical period.

From new materials, gathered by independent researches, philological and archæological, he reconstructed the true course of the history of Rome. But his labors really went much further and involved the reconstruction of historical study everywhere. He settled the fundamental distinction between history and legend. The method corresponding to this distinction inaugurated a new epoch in the study of history. Niebuhr was cut off before he had fully exhibited the results of his method even in regard to Rome. Some of his hypotheses have been rejected by later investigators. It was left to his successor, Mommsen, to write the "Roman History" which exhibits the truth in regard to the origin of the Eternal City and its mighty power.

RANKE

Of the great historians of Germany Leopold von Ranke is the most distinguished. Born in Saxony in 1795 he began his historical studies under Niebuhr and Savigny. In 1825 he was called to Berlin and nine years later was made full professor. He retired from his professorship in 1871, and undertook the revision of his numerous books. Many honors had been conferred upon him. In 1865 he was raised to knighthood; in 1882 he was made a privy councilor, and in 1895 his ninetieth birthday was celebrated amid general rejoicing. He died in the following year. Ranke's first work was a "History of the Romanic and Germanic Nations," published in 1824. The first volume covered but twenty years, from 1494 to 1514, the beginning of modern history. The author declared his purpose to show the fundamental unity of modern European civilization, and to trace the mingling of the Romanic and Germanic elements. Throughout his long career he remained faithful to his method of thoroughly sifting the primary authorities and carefully examining original documents. The Prussian government aided him in making researches in Rome and other foreign capitals. His second volume (1827) treated of the Turks and Spain in the Sixteenth Century. Then his great work on "The Roman Papacy: Its Church and State" (1834-37) gave the author fame throughout Europe. When translated into English it was reviewed by Macaulay in a memorable article. The reviewer justly characterized the spirit of the history as "admirable . . . equally remote from levity or bigotry; serious and earnest, yet tolerant and impartial." The whole work was a new revelation to Protestant Christendom of the greatness and power of the Roman Catholic Church. Particularly was attention directed to that counter-reformation by which that church recovered one-half of the countries which it had lost in the Sixteenth Century.

In 1841 Ranke was made historiographer of Prussia. The great historian turned from Southern Europe, in which Catholicism remained unshaken, to Northern Europe, where the Reformation had been successful. First the history of Germany in the time of the Reformation was presented; then Prussian history in three volumes (1847-48), which were revised and enlarged after the new German Empire was organized in 1871. Meantime there had been issued histories of France (1852-61), and England (1859-67, afterward enlarged). Altogether nearly fifty volumes of conscientiously elaborated works testified the diligence of the veteran. But amply learned and still vigorous, the old man looked abroad for new oceans to cross, and continents to discover. At the age of eighty he ventured to undertake the history of the world from the dawn of civilization. He lived to complete twelve volumes, bringing his great work down to the Middle Ages. Of course there was not in this universal history the same diligent investigation of original sources, nevertheless in regard to interest of the narrative and correct presentation of facts there was no apparent diminution of the writer's intellectual force. As historiographer of Prussia, it became Ranke's duty to edit several important works. He published treatises on important epochs in German history and a volume of "Biographical Studies" (1877).

Ranke in his first work announced a new method of history and adhered to it during his long career. He declared that the proper aim of history is not to support any preconceived notions, but to relate the facts without regard to moral lessons. History is not to be regarded as the handmaid of any other science, but is mistress in its own domain. The aim therefore of the historian should be to ascertain the exact facts in regard to which he gives evidence. He should discard, as far as possible, his own views and prejudices. The result will be an objective presentation of the truth. As previous writers, even when contemporary, had not followed this plan, but had recorded events as distorted by their own feelings, their histories should not be accepted as authorities. The only safe method of ascertaining the truth is to examine genuine primary sources of information, diplomatic correspondence and State papers. Not only did Ranke carry out this method faithfully, but in the discharge of his duties as professor he trained a number of others in the same patient examination of documentary evidence, so that all recent historical writing has been largely affected by him.

The most popular of his works is generally known in English as the "History of the Popes." It sketches the rise of the Papal power, shows its characteristics in different stages of development, and exhibits the benefits it conferred upon Europe in the Middle Ages.

Theodor Mommsen, the great historian of ancient Rome, was born at Garding in Schleswig, in 1817. He graduated at the University of Kiel in 1844, and spent two years in further study of archæology in France and Italy. In 1848 he was made professor of Roman law in the University of Leipsic, but his political activity as a Liberal caused his dismissal. In 1852 he was made professor of law at Zurich; two years later he was called to Breslau, and in 1858 to Berlin. His careful study of Italian antiquities had borne fruit in several works on the early languages of that peninsula, its coins and inscriptions. He is the chief editor of the great "Corpus" of Latin inscriptions, the greatest memorial of German classical scholarship. But the greatest work of his own labors is his "Roman History," which began to appear in 1854, and has been brought down to the time of the Empire. The Imperial Government of the Provinces has been treated in volumes intended to form part of the completed work. Mommsen's thorough scholarship, the basis of his history, is not displayed in notes, but is shown in many monographs on particular points. He has gathered into one continuous narrative the results of life-long investigations. In regard to the better known portions of his subject he has taken positions at variance with the common judgment. Thus for Cicero, as a politician, he has nothing but censure, and for Cæsar nothing but eulogy. He is ready to cite modern parallels and illustrations for his judgment of these and other public men of ancient times. His history has been well translated into English by W. P. Dickson.

Another distinguished historian of the objective school is Heinrich von Sybel, who was a pupil of Ranke. He was born at Düsseldorf in 1817, and chiefly educated at Bonn. His first work was a "History of the First Crusade" (1841), which exposed various popular errors in regard to that movement. Then came his "Origin of the German Kingdoms." From Marburg, where he was professor of history, he was called in 1856 by Duke Maximilian II of Bavaria to the University of Munich. There he introduced Ranke's method, training his pupils in original research. On the death of his patron he went to Bonn as professor, and was soon active in political affairs. In 1875 he was made director of the State archives at Berlin. His edition of these important historical documents began to be issued in 1878. Von Sybel's great work is a "History of the Revolution Period from 1789 to 1795" (1853-67). Based upon faithful study of State papers in all the capitals of Europe, it is the most accurate account of the French Revolution. Nor is it deficient in graphic presentation of the facts, though it is free from the poetic glamour of Carlyle's prose epic. Von Sybel has published many historical essays and "The Rising of Europe Against Napoleon" (1860).

Heinrich von Treitschke also takes high rank among the German historians. He was born at Dresden in 1834, studied there and at Leipsic, and in 1858 became an assistant in government publications at Berlin. For three years he was professor in the University of Freiburg, and in 1866 passed to Heidelberg, and thence in 1874 to Berlin. He was active in the German Parliament as a National Liberal, and supported Bismarck's efforts for German unity.   Treitschke's early work comprised two volumes of "Patriotic Poems" (1856), but his later work was confined to history and politics.   In *"Der Socialismus und Seine Gönner"* (Socialism and Its Protectors) (1875) he attacked the professors who were giving aid to socialism by their lectures.   In *"Zehn Jahre Deutscher Kämpfe"* (Ten Years of German Conflict) (1875) he rehearsed the movements by which the new German Empire was formed. But his most important work is *"Deutsche Geschichte im 19 Jahrhundert"* (German History in the 19th Century). The value of von Treitschke's labors is admitted by every historical student of the period.   His sagacity and industry are equal to those of Ranke; his style is more sprightly, and his judgment of men and events is impartial.

SOCIALISM IN LITERATURE

Karl Marx (1818-1883), the founder of modern German socialism, deserves mention since his masterpiece "Capital" has become almost the Bible of the Social Democrats. Like Ferdinand Lassalle, Marx was of Jewish descent. He was born at Cologne, and studied jurisprudence at Bonn and Berlin. When the newspaper which he edited at Cologne was suppressed in 1843 for its radical utterances, he went to Paris and studied political economy. But driven from France and Belgium, he found refuge in London. Here he took part in the Workingmen's Congress in 1847, but went to Paris during the Revolution of 1848. Then he was allowed to return to Cologne, where he revived his paper and advocated a Communistic Revolution. Though the paper was suppressed, the juries acquitted him. Again he was banished from Germany, went to Paris, and thence to London. In 1864 he founded the society known as the International, and was thereafter the leader and inspirer of its work. For a time European statesmen were greatly alarmed about its possibilities, but were relieved when the British workmen in 1871 refused his leadership as tending to anarchism, and insisted on confining the work of the society to amelioration of the workingmen's condition.

Marx's book was published in London in 1867. Volume I is on the process of capital production; Volume II on "The Circulation of Capital"; Volume III, which was written by a friend, deals with "Forms of Process and Theory of History." The literary power of this work lies in Marx's consummate skill as a thinker and logician.

Its spirit may be seen in his description of capital as "dead labor, which, vampire-like, becomes animate only by sucking living labor, and the more labor it sucks, the more it lives." His theory of the development of history recognizes four eras: First, the Classic Age, when wealth was represented by slaves; second, the Middle Age, when it lay in serfs, but has been destroyed by the bourgeoisie and the Third Estate; third, the age of modern capitalistic production; fourth, the coming age, when the proletariat, or Fourth Estate, is to rise and overthrow this capitalism. It must be borne in mind that Marx limits the term "capital" to economic goods in the hands of employers. His work is based on the political economy of Ricardo and Rodbertus.

Marx's theories were popularized by Ferdinand Lassalle (1825-1864), the son of a rich Jewish merchant of Dresden. Lassalle had a fiery romantic temperament which led him to champion the cause of the workingmen and to sacrifice his life in a duel about a lady. He was a prodigy of learning, and had published a work on an ancient Greek philosopher, who was surnamed "the obscure." He called himself the "President of Humanity," and the workingmen "the disinherited." His attack was directed against "the iron law of wages" as the keystone of the capitalistic system. Unlike Marx, Lassalle was a monarchist and desired the unity of Germany.

CONTEMPORARY WRITERS

Some of the later German novelists, following the French example, have cultivated the short story. Probably the most successful of these is Paul Heyse, who has, however, also written "purpose" novels, that is, novels intended to present a social problem of the times, or to urge a reform. Heyse is a man of high culture, a poet of considerable ability both in lyrics and in the minor epic, and a dramatist of no mean repute. He was born at Berlin in 1830, the son of an eminent scholar. He studied at the University of that city, and afterward at Bonn, devoting himself chiefly to the Romance languages. His earliest works were poems and dramas, and while he has never abandoned these departments, he has later given more attention to prose fiction. His short stories are picturesque, dreamy and melancholy, sentimental and sometimes dangerously sensuous. His "purpose" novels, "Children of the World" (1870) and "In Paradise" (1875), have given him widest fame. They are strongly individualistic, asserting the right of every person to seek happiness as he pleases in spite of conventional regulations and religious restraints. Self-culture is made the aim of life. The earlier novel, while somewhat philosophical, is more pleasing, involves a charming love experience and has a happy ending. The later is more in the spirit of Omar Khayyam. Both abound in poetical passages. Of Heyse's dramas the best are the "Sabine Women" (1859) and "Hans Lange." His chief epic is "Thekla." Both Italian and French influences are strongly manifest in his work, and yet he remains German in the spirit of Goethe.

In the latter part of the Century there has been a certain revival of the Romantic spirit, free from the wild disregard of the natural seen in the early Romanticists. No better example can be found than the works, both prose and verse, of Count Joseph Victor von Scheffel (1826-1886). He was born at Carlsruhe, Baden, and was educated in law at Heidelberg and Berlin. He was for a time in government employ and afterward lived at Weimar, but spent his last twenty years chiefly in his native city. In 1853 while in Italy he composed his romantic epic "The Trumpeter of Sackingen," which has become a favorite classic. It relates how Werner, who had been a student at Heidelberg, became trumpeter to the Baron von Schönau. Being wounded in a riot, he is tenderly nursed by the Baron's daughter, Margaretha, who is already in love with him. The Baron refuses his consent to their marriage and Werner bids farewell to Sackingen. But his skill in music enables him to become chapel-master to Pope Innocent, and thus finally to obtain the fair Margaretha's hand. The Baron's tobacco-pipe and his cat Hiddigeigei are prominent features of the quaintly humorous poem. The romance "Ekkehard" (1855) is a fine reconstruction of mediæval history. It includes a German version of the Latin poem of "Walter of the Strong Hand," attributed to Ekkehard, a monk of St. Gall in the Tenth Century. Another of Scheffel's novels is "Juniperus, the History of a Crusader" (1883). His collection of poems "Frau Adventiure, Songs of the Time of Heinrich von Ofterdingen" is an echo of the old Minnesingers. His "Gaudeamus, Songs from Far and Near" are marked with genial humor.

In contemporary German poetry the most prominent figure is Baron Detlev von Liliencron, born at Kiel in Holstein in 1844. In spite of his Danish birth he has

been a firm adherent of Prussia, in whose army he fought
through both the Austrian War of 1866 and the French
War of 1870. He was wounded in both campaigns. His
first small volume of poems "The Rides of the Adjutant"
appeared in 1883. He has published a comic epic "Pogg-
fred" and two volumes of poems, *"Kampf und Spiele"*
(Conflict and Play) and *"Kämpfe und Ziele"* (Struggles
and Goals). His North German moorland pictures have
a peculiar charm. He is best as a writer of ballads, and
has shown in striking verse the terrible tragedy of war.
His poems "Who Knows Where?" and "In Remembrance" are full of true pathos.

The work and story of Joanna Ambrosius have called
forth special interest. This daughter of a poor laborer
was born in miserable circumstances in a little village in
East Prussia, and early, while occupied with the drudgery of household toil, had charge of an invalid mother.
At the age of twenty she married a field laborer named
Voigt. Two children increased her cares, but love of
them seems to have awakened the poetry slumbering in
her soul. This humble woman began to compose poems.
Professor Karl Weiss-Schrattenthal, who had discovered
her merits in her obscurity, aroused not only national but
international astonishment by reporting her case in 1894.
She deals with simple peasant life, singing from the heart
songs of consolation. In spite of the weariness of toil
she finds in the love of her children a spiritual happiness.
"Believe in pain and anguish," cries this daughter of the
soil, "thy Father means it well."

DANISH LITERATURE

In the Eighteenth Century, Denmark, like the rest of Continental Europe, was strongly under the influence of French ideas. The tragedies of Voltaire were the most popular dramas and native writers strove to imitate this pseudo-classical style, but one effective parody, in which its rules and meter were applied to a trivial plot, Wessel's "Love Without Stockings," was sufficient to banish all French plays from the Royal Theater. Only Danish plays on national subjects were henceforth allowed. A number of young poets, fellow-students at Copenhagan, celebrated in lyrics the mountains and scenery of their native Norway. But this revival fell off in the next generation, and poetry became mechanical.

At the beginning of the Nineteenth Century the new fight of Romanticism penetrated into Denmark. The chief factor in this was the work and influence of the native Adam Gottlob Oehlenschläger (1779-1850). In youth he aspired to be an actor and had written poems in the French didactic style then prevailing, but in 1802 Henrik Steffens, who had studied at Jena under Fichte and Schelling, converted his friend to the new Romanticism by one memorable interview, which lasted sixteen hours. Oehlenschläger on the next day wrote "The Golden Horns." In this poem two carved and inscribed relics of antiquity recently unearthed are celebrated as the gifts of the gods, reminding men of their divine origin. Casting aside his former work the poet devoted himself ardently to the new impulse and published in 1803 a volume of ballads and lyrics which inaugurated a new era in Danish literature. Oehlenschläger, who had already given some attention to ancient Scandinavia, now reproduced the "First Song of the Edda," and wrote a pantheistic interpretation of nature in "The Life of Jesus Christ Annually Repeated in Nature." In the dramatic fairy tale "Aladdin," dedicated to Goethe as his master, Oehlenschläger sought to illustrate the marvelous power of genius. The Danish poet went to Germany in 1805, visiting Fichte and Goethe, thence to Paris, Switzerland and Rome. During the four years thus spent he wrote the national dramas "Hakon Jarl" relating to the overthrow of Pagan sacrifices in Norway by Christianity; "Palnatoke" describing the same period in Denmark; "Axel and Valborg" a romantic love-tragedy. "Correggio" is a tragedy in German in which that gentle painter is set in contrast with the sublime Michael Angelo. On his return to Copenhagen Oehlenschläger was generally lauded as the greatest Danish poet, but was severely criticised by Grundtvig and others. His most important production in later years was a cycle of splendid poems on "The Gods of the North." Among his dramas are "Charles the Great," and "The Land Found and Vanished," which treats of the discovery of Vinland by the Norwegians. He requested that "Socrates," his only attempt at a Greek play, might be performed as a memorial after his death.

Jens Emmanuel Baggesen (1765-1826), who was born fourteen years before Oehlenschläger, did not come under the Romantic influence. He had risen from poverty and won his first success by "Comical Tales" in verse, but when his opera was ridiculed he left the country for foreign travel. His descriptive poem "The Labyrinth," published on his return in 1790, received applause. Thereafter he roamed over Europe, still publishing in Danish and German. When Oehlenschläger had achieved fame, Baggesen was more determined than ever to prove his own superiority. He remains simply a fine comic writer, but the best of all his pieces is the simple poem "Childhood," translated by Longfellow.

The lyrical dramatist Henrik Hertz (1798-1870) was of Jewish parentage. His satirical "Letters of a Returning One" (1830), professing to be written by Baggesen's ghost, were published anonymously and caused great sensation. After a visit to Italy and France, Hertz showed new power in his romantic dramas "Svend Dyring's House" (1837) and "King René's Daughter" (1845). These two beautiful creations still hold the stage in Denmark and the latter has been produced in every civilized country. Yet the troubadour genius of Hertz shines most in his sweet impassioned lyrics.

Frederik Paludan-Müller (1809-1876) was the best successor of Oehlenschläger. He wrote under the influence of Byron. His dramas "The Death of Abel" (1854), the philosophic "Kalanus," and "Paradise" (1861) raise him to a high rank among European poets. He obtained even greater success in a long humorous epic, "Adam Homo" (1841-48), which proved him to be a keen satirist.

Nikolai Frederik Severin Grundtvig (1783-1872) was more noted as an earnest theologian than as a poet, and after long service in the Church was made a bishop. His study of Scandinavian antiquities resulted in his publishing "Northern Mythology" and "Decline of the Heroic Life in the North" (1809). In lyrical and historical poetry he rivaled Oehlenschläger, as in "King Harald and Ansgar." From the vehemence of the writings which gave him influence over his countrymen he has been compared to Carlyle.

Bernhard Severin Ingemann (1789-1862), under the influence of Sir Walter Scott, wrote a number of historical romances, "Valdemar Seier" (1826), "King Erik" (1833) and "Prince Otto of Denmark" (1835). Before these he had published many romantic poems, tragedies, and short tales. His rapidity of production and the religious melancholy of his verse gave him high popularity. He was the author of the national song, "Dannebrog."

Perhaps the only Danish writer who is universally known is Hans Christian Andersen (1805-1875), the prince of story-tellers for children. The son of a poor shoemaker of Odense, he went to Copenhagen and tried in vain to get employment at the theater. He was always fond of travel and his trip to Germany gave occasion for his first book of value, "Silhouettes." After a journey to Italy in 1833 his novel "The Improvisator" gave his impressions of that classic and romantic land. Then came "O. T.," a picture of Northern life. It was not until 1836 that he began to publish the "Wonder Tales," children's stories, forever inseparably connected with his name. In them he gave his fancy free scope, and revealed his child-like heart. The finest story is "The Ugly Duckling" (1845), which is really an allegory of his own career. The most popular of the later volumes are the "Picture Book Without Pictures" and "Tales and Stories." Andersen continued to add to this stock during the rest of his life. In 1837 he published his best novel, "Only a Fiddler," partly autobiographical. His journey to the East is shown in "A Poet's Bazaar" (1842). He was a bird of passage; he never settled down at home till he was past sixty. His "Story of My Life" has been regarded as an imperfect portrait, though it reveals both his merits and his weaknesses. His novels and books of travel show the egotism which constantly beset him. But the children's tales retain their vogue, because they show all things as children see them, living and acting, and tell everything as children wish it to be told.

Wilhelm Bergsøe, born in 1835, was in youth a zoölogist, but having so injured his sight that he was obliged to relinquish such work, he dictated a collection of stories, "From the Piazza del Popolo" (1866), which won general favor. His sight was afterward partly restored and he continued his literary labor. Later works include a romance "From the Old Factory" (1869), "In the Sabine Hills" (1871), stories told in letters; "In the Gloaming" (1876), "The Bride of Rörvig" (1872), and "Who was He?" They show keen observation and vivid imagination and are written in fine style. Some popular works on natural history have come from his pen.

One of the greatest living critics is Georg Brandes, born at Copenhagen in 1842. After a distinguished course at the University he traveled in England, France, and Germany to become acquainted with men of letters and science. The result of his studies appeared in his brilliant and valuable work, "Main Currents of Nineteenth Century Literature" (1872-76). It showed the gradual emancipation of thought through the first half of this Century. His former publications had provoked controversies, but a still greater one arose in 1876 and his opponents prevented his being appointed professor in the University of Copenhagen. Offended at this treatment he left the city and went to Germany. But he had already won a European reputation by "French Æsthetics in Our Day" (1870), "Æsthetic Studies" and "Critiques and Portraits." For some years he resided in Berlin, but he returned to Copenhagen in 1883. Many biographical works have been prepared by him, among them being lives of Tegnèr and Lord Beaconsfield. Among his critical works are "Modern Men of Genius" (1881), "Björnson and Ibsen" (1882). He is industrious, learned, energetic, and brilliant.

NORWEGIAN LITERATURE

Norway had been united to Denmark for four Centuries until Napoleon's wars changed the map of Europe. At that critical period Denmark came into conflict with England in defense of her merchant marine, and in alarm for her own safety, attached herself to victorious France. After the battle of Waterloo the allied powers punished her for this, by forcing her to resign Norway to Sweden. The Norwegians attempted to defend their own independence under a Danish hereditary Prince, but the Swedish army advanced on Christiania, and the brave people were obliged to yield. Norway is still governed by a Swedish King, but has her own Constitution and a separate Parliament. Prior to the year 1814 Norway shared the intellectual life of Denmark. For many years after that writers aimed to celebrate the virtues of the free and independent peasant, and to glorify the rocks and waterfalls of their native land. Two distinct parties were formed, the clash of whose arguments may still be heard.

Henrik Wergeland (1808-1845) was the son of a patriotic clergyman, but had imbibed the views of Rousseau, and his lyrical dramatic poem, "The Creation, Man, and Messiah," was an expression of the fermentation of French ideas of the Eighteenth Century. Though lengthy and tedious, it contained passages of great beauty and majesty; and the author was hailed as the first exponent of a distinctly Norwegian literature. Wergeland had a marked personality, and used his great powers in defending the welfare of the common people, and in waging war against everything having a Danish origin. He became the leader of the political party called Ultra-Norwegians. It was through his influence that the Seventeenth of May, the date of the adoption of the Norwegian Constitution, was made a national holiday. His zealous labors in poetry and politics did not cease till his death in 1845.

Wergeland's opponent was Johan Sebastian Cammermeyer Welhaven, and those who gathered to his standard distinguished themselves as "Intelligence." In 1834 Welhaven, in the preface to a series of sonnets, pointed out that a national literature cannot be constructed from nothing; and that for many years Norway must depend on Denmark for art, culture, and literary style; but that in time she would be able to evolve a distinct culture of her own, based on the study of her antiquities, and on an expression of individual life. These sonnets caused a tremendous sensation. "Intelligence" rallied around Welhaven, while Wergeland and his adherents shouted "Treason!" The violent literary feud which ensued has hardly yet been healed. Welhaven continued his career as author and university professor until his death in 1873. By his lectures on Danish literature, and his romances, founded on popular traditions, he proved himself faithful to those principles which he had advocated as the leader of "Intelligence."

Andreas Munch (1810-1863), professor in the University of Christiania, wrote poetry and dramas which are echoes of Oehlenschläger's, and tales after the fashion of Welhaven. His poems of "Sorrow and Consolation" are dear to all Scandinavians. His prose masterpiece is the "History of the Norwegian People" (1851-64).

The two greatest poets of the North are the Norwegians Björnson and Ibsen. The former is a writer of stories, songs, and dramas for his people; the latter is the author of the most remarkable psychological plays ever portrayed by pen or presented upon the stage. Björnsjerne Björnson, the son of a clergyman, was born among the barren Dovre Mountains in 1832, and removed with his family at the age of six, to Komsdal, the region of all Norway most celebrated for its beauty. To this may be attributed Björnson's magnificent descriptions of natural scenery. In his early years he devoted himself to folk-tales and became a passionate admirer of Wergeland. He commenced his life's work by writing poems and dramas, but his first important book was "Synnöve Solbakken," a story of peasant life which captivated the hearts of his countrymen. It was followed by other tales, poems and dramas in quick succession. The Scandinavians were then setting up barriers between themselves and the thought of Europe. All streams were muddy save the rivers of the pure North. A modern intellectual movement began in Denmark in 1871 and penetrated to Norway, and Björnson was the first to profit by it. He read every variety of work, in every language, and he thus describes the influence on himself: "I am Norseman. I am human. Of late I have been subscribing myself: man." His latest dramas, therefore, are full of the broadest humanitarianism. His modern plays are "The Bankrupt," "The Editor," "The King." The best of his later novels is a profound and exquisitely written story called "Dust." Among all the shorter compositions of Björnson's the most remarkable is the monologue "Bergliot," the lamentations of a chieftain's wife over her murdered husband and son. Björnson's great struggle is for freedom and modern enlightenment. Personally he is a genial giant, with a charming and joyous presence. He has the reputation of being the most eloquent and convincing political orator in Norway.

Henrik Ibsen, the dramatist of pessimism, was born at Skien, in Norway, in 1828. His connections were people of the highest standing in the place, but his father became a bankrupt, and the boy worked in one menial capacity after another. He was twenty-two years old before he had means or leisure for study. His desolate youth, in which he often did not have enough to eat, unquestionably soured his disposition. For many years he toiled unsuccessfully as a newspaper publisher, a theater manager, and a writer of poems and dramas which were misunderstood. Ibsen led a wild life, as a young man, and was disliked and shunned in consequence. At the time of the Schleswig-Holstein troubles in 1864, he fell into a profound melancholy because Sweden and Norway failed to stand by Denmark in her war with Prussia and Austria. Denouncing his countrymen as cowardly, he turned his back on his native land, and has since lived in Dresden, Munich, or Italy, a friendless and isolated man. He is always well received, in a public way, in any city where he happens to reside. His powerful and gloomy dramas have at last brought him fame and fortune; and the North is proud to acknowledge his genius as her own.

His best known dramas are "Brand," "Peer Gynt," "A Model Home" (also called The Doll's House), "The Pillars of Society," "Apparitions," "Hedda Gabler," and "Little Eyeolf." Ibsen would hurl all existing institutions off the face of the earth. Nothing is right. A sense of duty founded upon the conventional claims of others upon us, and our conventional claims on them, he finds intolerable. Like the early Romanticists he insists on each man's right to live, think and act as he pleases, with little regard for others. His dramas have caused an intellectual tumult throughout Europe.

SWEDISH LITERATURE

At the close of the Eighteenth Century Swedish literature had sunk into a depressed state. The French classical style prevailed; didactic and serious poems like those
of Pope and Young were the only kind approved. But
Romanticism was introduced by a group of poets whose
organ was called "Phosphor" (Light-bringer), whence
they were known as Phosphorists. The leader of this
group. Peter Daniel Amadeus Atterbom (1790-1855),
edited the journal, which contained only poetry and critical essays. His lyrical poems called "The Flowers" were
marred by too great fondness for mysticism and allegory.
His most celebrated work is the beautiful drama "The
Fortunate Island" (1823). Another member of this
group, Lorenzo Hammarsköld (1785-1827), published in
1806 "Translations and Imitations of Poets, Old and
New," in the preface of which he condemned the Swedish
classic writers, and commended Goethe and Tieck for imitation. His most important work was a "History of
Swedish Literature" (1818).

The leader of the opposition to these Phosphorists was
the far more distinguished Bishop Esaias Tegnèr (1782-
1846). He was the son of a village pastor and taught
in the University of Lund. In 1808, stirred by the great
events of the time, he composed a war-song which was
welcomed and sung by the people. He then organized a
Gothic League for the study of Scandinavian antiquity.
Its journal "Iduna," so called from the goddess of youth
in Northern mythology, was edited at first by Geijer and
afterward by Tegnèr. In this journal appeared Tegnèr's

romance of "Axel," his beautiful idyl of "The Children of the Lord's Supper," which has been translated into English by Longfellow, and his famous modernization of "Frithiof's Saga." The last consists of twenty-four short cantos or ballads, each having a different form of verse or meter to suit the special subject, and all taken together presenting the finest picture of ancient Scandinavian life.

As a reward for this national epic Tegnèr was made a bishop, though he had not previously been ordained. He discharged his episcopal duties well until his mind gave way. During a temporary recovery he began two epic poems which were left unfinished. The work of his youth, however, has placed him at the head of Swedish literature. As Longfellow has said: "This modern Skald has written his name in immortal runes, not on the bark of trees alone, in the 'unspeakable rural solitudes' of pastoral song, but on the mountains of his native land, and the cliffs that overhang the sea, and on the tombs of ancient heroes, whose histories are epic poems."

The other leader of the Gothic League, Erik Gustaf Geijer (1783-1847), is Sweden's greatest historian. To the "Iduna" he contributed several essays and some songs, whose sweet simplicity and ardent patriotic feeling have made them ever dear to his countrymen. In 1815 he was called to the University of Upsala to give instruction in history, and thenceforward devoted himself to that department. His "History of the Swedish People" (3 vols. 1832-36) brings the subject down to the close of Queen Christina's reign in 1654. Many other historical works and essays were published by him, before failing health obliged him to resign in 1846. They all exhibit correct critical insight and artistic arrangement of material.

Frans Michael Franzén (1772-1847), who was a native of Finland, became professor of history in the University of Abo, and eventually a bishop, was the author of many minor poems full of sweetness and of popular songs. His epics on Sven Sture, Columbus, and Gustavus Adolphus, in spite of beautiful passages, are inferior to his short pieces. His best lyrics sing of domestic joys, the prattle of children and the beauty of the fields.

The most extraordinary character in Swedish literary history is Karl Jonas Ludwig Almquist (1793-1866). In early manhood he gave up an official position at Stockholm and led a colony to wild forest lands to found a primitive community called "Man's Home Association." On its failure he became a teacher and prepared some school text books. After awhile he issued a collection of dramas, lyrics and romances, under the name "The Book of the Thorn-Rose." It contains some of the finest gems of Swedish literature, and quickly made him famous. Then a flood of treatises of all kinds, historical, philosophical, religious, flowed from his pen. With these were intermingled admirable lyrical, epic and dramatic poems. But the unstable author passed from one position to another, and raved about socialism. Suddenly in 1851 he fled from Sweden, and it became known that he was convicted of forgery and charged with murder. It was afterward ascertained that he came to the United States under an assumed name, earned a precarious living, and it is even stated that he was a secretary to Abraham Lincoln. When he was almost within the grasp of the law, his papers were seized and destroyed, but he himself escaped to Europe. He died at Bremen. Almquist put in practice the extreme disregard of morality which some of the Romanticists taught or exhibited in fiction. His books show great keenness of observation, rich humor and strong poetic feeling.

Finland, though now belonging to Russia, is peopled

by Swedes, and has contributed to Swedish literature. Johann Ludvig Runeberg (1804-1877) as a poet, is second only to Tegnèr. He was born in Finland and educated at the University of Abo. His little epic "The Elk-Hunters" (1832) was followed by "Hanna" (1836), a charming idyl in hexameters. Runeberg was now made professor of Latin at Borga College, and from this obscure place sent forth poems which established his high rank. Among them are "Nadeschda," a romance of Russian life, "Kung Fjalar," a cycle of romances in unrhymed verse. His popularity was greatly enhanced by "Ensign Steel's Stories," poems on the War of Independence in 1808. His tragedy "The Kings at Salamis" (1863) shows the true classical spirit. His poems are realistic, yet full of artistic beauty and strong religious feeling.

Another able poet of Finland is Zacharias Topelius, born in 1818. He was editor of a newspaper in Helsingfors until 1860. His poems were collected in book form in "Heather Flowers" (1845-54). His best prose work, "The Surgeon's Stories" (1872-74), relates to the history of Sweden and Finland in the Seventeenth and Eighteenth Centuries.

Of Swedish novelists none is more widely known than Miss Fredrika Bremer (1801-1865). She was born near Abo in Finland, but her childhood was spent at Arsta near Stockholm. In 1821 the family went on a tour through Germany and France. After a year thus spent, Fredrika, to escape the dullness of country life, began to visit the poor and sick. To get money for her charities her brother sold some sketches she had written. When in 1830 "The H— Family" was issued the Swedish Academy awarded her a gold medal. Her career was now determined. Her simple tales of middle-class family life were favorably received in Sweden, and even more so in England and America, when translated by Mary Hewitt. After residing some years in Norway, Miss Bremer visited England and America, and on her return wrote her impressions in "Homes in the New World" (1853). Later visits to Switzerland, Italy, Palestine and Greece, were also pleasantly sketched. The better education of girls and the admission of women to various employments were advocated in her later novels, "Hertha" and "Father and Daughter," but these "purpose" novels were not so attractive as the simpler pictures of family life in "The Neighbors," "The President's Daughters," "Brothers and Sisters," "The Home."

Less widely known, yet almost of equal merit as a novelist, is Mrs. Emilia Flygare-Carlen (1807-1892). She was twice married, her second husband, J. G. Carlen, being a lawyer and poet. Her first novel, "Waldemar Klein," was published anonymously when she was thirty years of age. Its success led her to prepare a long series of similar works, treating all classes and conditions of Swedish life. Her wide experience enabled her to depict not only the well-to-do, but peasants, fishers and smugglers. Among her best books are "The Professor" (1840), "The Rose of Thistelon" (1842), "The Maiden's Tower" (1848), "The Tutor" (1851), "The Trading House" (1860), and her autobiography "Recollections of Swedish Life" (1878). Her novels are graphic pictures rather than studies of character, but they are bright and sparkling.

Abraham Viktor Rydberg (born in 1829) is the most attractive essayist of Sweden. His original work includes æsthetic and historical studies, treatises on the philosophy of religion, and one on "Teutonic Mythology" (1886). His only novel, "The Last of the Athenians" (1859), relates to the struggle between classical Paganism and Christianity.

RUSSIAN LITERATURE

When Alexander I came to the throne of Russia in 1801, he was inclined to peace, but the policy and acts of Napoleon forced him into war, which culminated in the French invasion and the disastrous retreat from Moscow. After the downfall of Napoleon, the influence of Alexander was paramount in the Congresses which settled the affairs of Europe. He was the founder of the Holy Alliance, which was to combine the powers of Church and State in suppressing revolutionary tendencies. But he was also intent on promoting the civilization of his vast Empire. French influence, which during the reign of Catharine II, had prevailed in literature, was supplanted by an effort at a truly national literature.

The historian, Nikolai Mikhailovich Karamzin (1765-1826) was one of the glories of Alexander's reign, and is said to have revealed Russia to itself. His father was an army officer of Tartar descent and wished his son to follow in that profession, but the latter was drawn into literature at St. Petersburg and Moscow. His visit to France and England gave occasion for his "Letters of a Russian Traveler" (1801), but most of his writings were miscellaneous and sentimental tales, until he took up in earnest his "History of the Russian Empire." To accomplish this he had gone to live in retirement, but the Czar, Alexander, learning the fact, invited him to St. Petersburg, and gave him every facility for work. In 1825 his health began to fail, and a year later he died. His History was brought down to the year 1613. It was founded on original research and is written in elegant style, modeled upon Addison. It has been censured for the romantic air cast over the barbarism and cruelty of olden times, and has been called an "epic of despotism." It traced the origin of Russian greatness to Ivan the Terrible and even to his grandfather, instead of limiting it to Peter the Great, as previous writers under French influence had done.

In Russia Ivan Kriloff (1768-1844) holds the same place as La Fontaine in France. He is the national fabulist, and lines from his homely verses are stock quotations among the people. He resembled the French fabulist not only in the style of his writing but in the careless unpractical mode of his life. Born at Moscow, the son of an army officer who died in 1779, he was taken to St. Petersburg by his mother, who hoped in vain to get a pension. Kriloff's earliest writings were for the stage, chiefly translations and imitations, and it was not until 1809 that his first volume of "Fables" was issued. Honors then began to be heaped upon him and he was appointed to a position in the Imperial Public Library. Although he professed indifference to public affairs, his fables were really suggested by passing events, and by idiomatic grace and sound sense caught at once the fancy of the people. Their perfection of style was the result of careful polish. Personally, he was careless in dress, regardless of etiquette, and absent-minded.

The chief representative of Romanticism in Russian literature is Vasile Andréevich Zhukovski (1783-1852). He was the preceptor of Alexander II in his youth, and succeeded Karamzin in editing the "European Messenger" in 1808. His aim was to familiarize his countrymen with the best productions of foreign literature, and for this he translated from Goethe, Uhland, Schiller, Gray, Byron and Moore. He even translated Oriental poems at second-hand through the German. His most famous poems are the ballads in "The Poet in the Russian Camp" which were sung by his fellow soldiers in the War of 1812. Another fine ballad is "Svietlana." His finest tale is "Mary's Grove."

But the most celebrated of Russian poets is Alexander Pushkin (1799-1837) who, like Alexandre Dumas, had some negro blood in his veins. His mother's grandfather was a negro who had been brought from Abyssinia, and by his bravery won the favor of Peter the Great. Pushkin was employed in the ministry of foreign affairs and lived as a man of fashion until a daring "Ode to Liberty" incurred censure and he was virtually banished to Bessarabia, near the Danube, where he held office. Under the influence of Byron he composed "The Prisoner of the Caucasus," a story of the love of a Circassian girl for a captive Russian officer. Another poem was a tale of love and vengeance called "The Gipsies." With this strange people he had become acquainted in his new residence, and their mode of life attracted him. His conduct did not give satisfaction to his superiors, and he was dismissed from the service in 1824. He retired to his father's country place and there became embroiled with his relatives, while he was also under the surveillance of the Government. A product of his retirement was the tragedy of "Boris Gudunoff," in which he departed from the French classical style, and sought to imitate Shakespeare. His "Poltava" is a spirited narrative poem of the defeat of Charles XII by Peter the Great. But a much more original poem is "Eugene Oneguin" which relates the adventures of a Russian in sprightly verse somewhat after the fashion of Byron's "Don Juan." Pushkin had married a noble lady in 1831, and six years later out of jealousy fought a duel, in which he was mortally wounded. His opponent was banished. Pushkin's fame as a poet has steadily increased. Though strongly influenced by Byron, he was not a mere copyist. His subjects and scenery are thoroughly Russian. He excelled in his poetical tales, especially in "Eugene Oneguin," in which humor and satire are well mingled. His few prose tales and his historical novels display dramatic power.

The death of Pushkin was lamented in an impassioned poem addressed to the Czar by Mikhail Lermontoff (1814-1841). He declared that if no vengeance was taken on the assassin Heaven would grant no second poet to Russia. But the Czar was seriously offended and sent the new poet, who was an army officer, to the Caucasus on military duty. Lermontoff, who had visited those mountains in childhood, found there the inspiration of his mature years. He became the poet of the Caucasus, celebrating the courage and other virtues of the mountaineers, as well as the sublime and varied scenery amid which they dwelt. Lermontoff was of Scotch ancestry, as he states in one of his poems, but was born in Moscow and carefully educated. When he returned to St. Petersburg, in 1839, he published a volume of poems and a novel, "A Hero of Our Time." Two years later, like his predecessor, he fell in a duel. Three volumes of his poems were then published, and Bodenstedt translated them into German. Among his poems are "Ismail-Bey," "The Demon," and a remarkable imitation of an old Russian ballad.

As in all other countries of Europe, there arose in Russia imitators of Sir Walter Scott, who endeavored to renew the life of past ages of their country's history. The best of these was Zagoskin, who in "Yuri Miloslavski," took for his subject the expulsion of the Poles from Russia in 1612. But a romantic coloring is given to the narrative, and the characters utter sentiments which belong

to a more refined age than their own. The first really
great and original novelist of Russia was Nikolai Vasilie-
vich Gogol (1809-1852). He was born in Poltava, in
South Russia, and early began writing for the stage. At
the age of twenty he went to St. Petersburg and published
an idyll, which was so severely criticised that he burnt all
the copies he could obtain. Then the recollections of
childhood came back, when his father was regimental
secretary of Cossack troops, and he heard tales of the wild
life of these tribes. These he now undertook to reproduce in a periodical under the title, "Evenings on a Farm
near Dikanka." The novelty and brilliance of the stories
were acknowledged by all critics. Gogol went on to publish "Arabesques," a mingling of stories and essays,
"Taras Bulba," the finest of his "Cossack Tales," and
"The Revisor," a satrical comedy. In the last, a traveler,
who has just arrived in a town, is mistaken for a revisor
or Government inspector, and receives all the attention,
favors and bribes that the town officials intended for the
real inspector. But much more searching and effective
was the exposure made in Gogol's great novel, "Dead
Souls" (1842). A speculator travels around the country, purchasing from landlords the title to dead souls, that
is, serfs who have died since the last census, and then
obtains advances from the Government on this imaginary
property. This plan enabled the author to introduce and
satirize many varieties of provincial Russians. The painful realism of the whole is acknowledged, yet it had
important effect in stirring the Government to redress the
wrongs described. A second part of this work was written when he was in Italy, but he sank into religious melancholy and destroyed most of it. Later he wrote "Confessions of an Author," which showed a mind diseased.
He made a pilgrimage to Jerusalem, but died at Moscow.

Alexander Hertzen (1812-1870), was a political agitator, who in youth was exiled to Siberia, afterward was permitted to return and hold official posts, then in 1847 left Russia, and passed the rest of his life in Geneva, London and Paris. His chief literary work was a novel, "Who Is to Blame?" The story tells how a tutor, having married the unacknowledged daughter of a sensualist of the old type, dull and ignorant, yet kindly, finds his home life troubled by the entrance of a sensualist of a new type, intelligent and accomplished, but callous. The question of the title has reference to the tragical termination. Hertzen's most important political publication was the "Kolokol" (Bell), a periodical printed in London, but vigorously excluded from Russia till after the death of Nicholas I, in 1855. Then smuggled into the country in large quantities, it did much to bring about the sweeping reforms of Alexander II, including the emancipation of the serfs.

A morbid self-analysis is found in many Slavonic writers. This is seen in Feodor Michailovich Dostoievsky (1821-1881), who, at the age of twenty-three, published a novel which won for him the name of "the new Gogol." In "Poor Folk" he revealed the miseries of the poor of St. Petersburg. The power of analysis shown in this work appears also in his later short stories, "The Black Heart," "The Little Hero," and others. In 1849 the novelist was implicated in a socialist conspiracy, and was condemned to death, but at the moment of expected execution, his sentence was commuted to banishment to Siberia. For four years he toiled in the mines, then was allowed to return to St. Petersburg, and published "Recollections of a Dead House," which described his experience. This narrative, revealing the horrors of Siberian prison life, had powerful effect throughout Russia. "Raskolnikoff," another novel, has been translated into English as "Crime and Punishment." In it a weak man is led to murder a woman for a little money, then slowly driven by remorse to admit the crime to a girl friend, and by her friendly sympathy, induced to confess it to the authorities and submit to the punishment of exile. In all Dostoievsky's work the love of the morbid prevails, so as to make the reading of them a painful task.

In novel writing, Gogol had introduced the practice of realism, and Ivan Turgenieff (1818-1883), perfected it. Until the rise of Tolstoi, Turgenieff was the Russian author most widely known. He was born at Orel, of wealthy parents, his father being colonel of a cavalry regiment. In his mother's house French only was spoken, save in intercourse with servants. The serfs were treated with extreme cruelty. From one of these Turgenieff learned that there really was a Russian literature. His mother believed that her son had degraded himself when he began to write in his native tongue. His first sketches that attracted attention were the "Memoirs of a Sportsman," which set various characters of the Russian peasantry in a favorable light and revealed the miseries of their life. The novelist's next production was the pathetic story, "A Nest of Nobles" (1859), which was soon followed by "On the Eve," which showed the generous but indolent youth of Russia. In "Fathers and Sons" (1862), Turgenieff marked the rise of Nihilism, and, in fact, invented that word to express the destructive doctrines then beginning to pervade the educated young men of his country. Their creed was to tear down all existing institutions without caring to substitute anything in their place. During the latter part of his life Turgenieff resided chiefly at Baden-Baden and Paris. At the former he met several Russians exiled for their participation in plots. He came to see that their schemes were mere illusions, and his romance "Smoke" (1867) showed the alteration of his opinions. Though he still retained faith in Russia's final freedom, the Nihilists regarded him as a renegade. Ten years later he published "Virgin Soil," which exposes the futility of Nihilism in action. He was now accused of having been bribed by the Russian Government; yet the book really shows sympathy with the liberty desired by the Nihilists, though condemning the methods they proposed to use in attaining it. Turgenieff produced many short stories, exquisitely finished. All his writings exhibit wide sympathy, close study of the human soul, and pervading all a poetical pessimism.

TOLSTOI

Born of noble family, living the careless and dissipated life of gilded youth, then raised to high honor in war and literature, Count Lyof Tolstoi forsook his early ways to devote himself to the instruction of the emancipated serfs. But his conversion was not complete until, after close study of the New Testament, he humbled himself to become himself a peasant in dress, work and mode of life. In this way he became not only a social reformer in Russia, but an oracle of the civilized world, the prophet of a new religion. Yet his dominion is still in literature, and he is thus the most prominent Russian at the close of the Nineteenth Century.

He was born in 1828 near Tula, and after his father's death was brought up on his mother's estate. For two years he attended the University of Kasan, but left his studies to lead a wild life, becoming a gambler and an idolater of individual force. In 1851 he entered the army and served in the Caucasus, and in the Crimean war took part in the defense of Sebastopol. Having attained the rank of Division Commander, he left the army and married the daughter of a German physician. After publishing "Military Sketches," describing the siege in which he had suffered, he wrote "The Cossacks," portraying the life and scenery of the Caucasus. His first novel, "War and Peace," related to Napoleon's invasion, but had for its chief theme a social complication, in which he showed his repugnance to divorce, even to end the miseries of marriage. Two years later the successful author began to devote himself to the instruction of the peasants, and wrote for them many educational text-books. His next long novel, "Anna Karenina" (1876), shows a growing dislike for Russian society and its conventions. Anna, a gay, impulsive lady, had married Alexei Karenina, an upright, reserved gentleman. The gallant young Baron Vronsky wins her affection, and forms a liaison. When Alexei discovers this he banishes his wife from his house, and seeks a divorce, but becoming aware of her abiding love of their son, he afterward refuses to consent to it. The guilty pair separate, and Anna commits suicide. On the other hand the same story contains an idyll of pure love in the wooing of Katia by Constantin Levin.

Tolstoi had begun to show his new views of the Gospel. He felt bound to adopt a literal interpretation of all the precepts of Christ's Sermon on the Mount. He formed on his own estate a community in which every one capable was bound to engage in manual labor. He himself dressed as a peasant and worked as a shoemaker. His religious views have been set forth in "My Confession" and "My Religion." They approach closely to those of the Quakers. He teaches non-resistance to evil and force, rejects ecclesiastical authority, but does not approve dis-

senting sects, for he holds the spirit to be above all forms
and organizations. He looks on his own past life with
loathing and even regards his novels as monuments of
misdirected energy. Yet, while occasionally issuing
tracts such as "Life," "What to Do," he has still written
some stories, and in the "Kreutzer Sonata" he shocked the
world by seeming to make the institution of marriage
a crime and advocating universal celibacy. But his
friends explain that it is only the abuse of subjecting
woman to man's unstinted lust that is censured. For a
time he appeared to have given up belief in the immortality of the soul, but afterward he regained it. He insists
that the true remedy for the ills of humanity is work, and
points to the peasants, who, even when working against
their will, have peace of mind and soul, while idle nobles
are driven to despair.

Whatever may be thought of Tolstoi's religious views
and practice, it cannot be denied that he is the most forcible
personage in Russian literature. He has carried on the
realistic exhibition of Russian life, commenced by Gogol,
and elaborated by Turgenieff. As Gogol depicted the
owners of small farms, and Turgenieff portrayed the
peasants and the Nihilists, Tolstoi has added representa-
tions of the higher classes and their selfish lives. His
works reveal with the utmost effectiveness all the aspects
of war, the glory of victory, the horrors of the battlefield,
the monotony of sieges, the inspiration of patriotism, the
alteration of the common man into the soldier, with his
peculiar code of morals. He has set forth the evils of
divorce and shown the blessing of pure marriage.
Through all his works runs a strong sentiment of kindness and good will toward his fellow-men, and an intense
hatred of sins which are lightly esteemed, because they are

secret.   His prophetic message has been boldly delivered
not to Russia only, but to the world.   He has called on
every one to work out his own salvation.   There he has
stopped, for he insists on the right of every man to free
will, to choose for himself the way of life or the way of
death.

POLISH LITERATURE

The unhappy Kingdom of Poland came to an end in 1795, when the territories left after two previous divisions went to Austria and Russia. Yet not till after this national extinction did its literary glory arise. Regret for what was irretrievably lost, and vain hope for its restoration, unsealed the mouths of its poets. The first was Adam Mickiewicz (1798-1855), a native of Lithuania. Being involved in political trouble at the University of Wilna, he was ordered to St. Petersburg, where he was well received in literary circles. His poem "Konrad Wallenrod" (1828) described the battles of the Teutonic Knights with the heathen Lithuanians in the Fifteenth Century, but it is easy to see that it was aimed at the wars of the Poles and the Russians. When Mickiewicz obtained permission to travel, he went to Germany, Italy, and finally France. His "Pan Tadeusz" (1832) gives a picture of Lithuania on the eve of Napoleon's invasion in 1812. He ceased writing at the age of thirty-six and afterward his native mysticism grew into a deplorable imbecility. A statue to his memory was unveiled at Warsaw on December 24, 1898, the centenary of his birth.

The second great poet of Poland was Julius Slowacki (1809-1849), who was also a mystic and an imitator of Byron. His mysticism was shown in "Anhelli," which expressed allegorically the sufferings of his native land. His Byronism appeared in "Lambro," a picture of a Greek corsair, and "Beniowski," an adventurer like Don Juan. Sigismund Krasinski (1812-1849), though born in Paris, was a thorough Pole and mystic.   As his father had adhered to the Russian Government, the son concealed his name, and was called "The Unknown Poet."   In his "Undivine Comedy" the woes of Poland were again bewailed allegorically.   His writings seem like a dirge over her extinction.

The most prolific of all Polish authors was Josef Ignacy Kraszewsky (1812-1887), who wrote over 250 works, including epics, novels, romances, histories, and political treatises.   A series of his novels was devoted to depicting Polish history from the earliest times.   Of his other stories, "The Hut Beyond the Village (1855) and "Jermota the Potter" (1857) were the most popular.   The last resembles George Eliot's "Silas Mariner."

But far beyond any other Polish writer, Henryk Sienkiewicz has extended the literary fame of his native land. This has been partly due to the help of the eminent linguist, Jeremiah Curtin, who translated his works into English, yet still more must be granted to the creative genius of the novelist himself.   It enabled him to overcome the opposition of critics in Poland and to win the approbation of all serious judges elsewhere.   Sienkiewicz was born at Vola in Lithuania in 1846.   He was educated at Warsaw and became a journalist.   In 1876 he came to America with a colony led by Madame Modjeska to settle in Southern California.   A year's experience here furnished material for newspaper correspondence and sketches.   In 1884 his novels of Polish history in the Seventeenth Century began to appear.   They comprise "With Fire and Sword," "The Deluge," and "Pan Michael," and describe respectively the Cossack, Swedish and Turkish invasions.   Each has its own hero and its own special interest, the last being the best.   In all of them appears a unique character, Zagloba, somewhat boastful and ridiculous, and yet full of sense and spirit. They are generally regarded as the best historical novels of the last half of the Century. The profound psychological novel of the present day, "Without Dogma" (1890), could not secure the same general attention. But "Quo Vadis" appeared in 1895, and quickly made the author's name familiar throughout the world. It is a story of the persecution of the Christians by Nero, and is founded on a close study of Roman literature of that period. The art of the novelist has reproduced the brilliance of imperial Rome, the waning power of Paganism, and the hopeful courage of the early Christians. The title, meaning "Whither Goest Thou?" is taken from the legend which records that when St. Peter in dismay was leaving Rome, he met his Lord bearing his cross, and asked that question, to which the reply was, "I go to Rome to be crucified." This legend is incorporated in the work. One of the prominent characters is Petronius, who was Nero's master of pleasure, and has left a humorous Latin description of a feast, which is also interwoven in the modern author's work. Sienkiewicz has also displayed his abilities in fine short stories. Those relating to America are not equal to those in which Polish village life is exhibited. The best is "God's Will," a tragical story, relieved at times with humorous scenes.

ITALIAN LITERATURE

In the Eighteenth Century there had been an attempt to reform Italian literature by introducing simplicity in place of the over-wrought rhetoric which had long prevailed. For this purpose the Academy of Arcadia was established at Rome. Its members adopted a style of thought and language supposed to be used in the fabulous Arcadia of the classical poets. But this was far from being a real return to nature such as Wordsworth advocated in English. The Arcadian mode was a palpable sham. The result was a flood of trifling, effeminate sonnets, madrigals and other forms of verse. But the deep-reaching social and political ideas which were circulated in France, and eventually produced the Revolution, made their way also into Italy. The Arcadian school of feeble, languishing poets vanished. The mighty but uncultivated genius of Alfieri was aroused. Inspired with love of liberty and hatred of tyrants, he poured forth twenty-one tragedies, chiefly founded on incidents and characters of classical history. He swept away the foolish trifling that had usurped the place of literature, and directed the intellectual movement to liberal and national aims.

The Italian poets who were excited by the same causes and inspired by his example, looked back to the ancient glory of their land for subjects and to the ancient classics for models of style. Hence they were careful to observe the rules and methods which had long been stamped as classical. In thought they were really modern, full of new ideas of the rights of man and universal freedom, but in form they followed that stiff and antiquated style which the French Romanticists opposed and ridiculed. Yet it must be admitted that the richness and easy grace of the Italian language are seen to advantage in their works.

The most remarkable of these modern classical poets was Vincenzo Monti (1754-1828), who illustrated in his career the frequent political changes which swept over his country. Kindly received at the Papal court, he was early admitted to the Academy of the Arcadians, but provoked his fellow-members by his sharp satire and impatience of criticism. Then he wrote a classical drama in rivalry with Alfieri. In 1793 the murder of the French minister, Basseville, at Rome called forth his splendid poem, "Bassvilliana," written in imitation of Dante. The spirit of Basseville is represented as condemned to wander over France under an angel's guidance, beholding the sufferings brought upon the land by the Revolutionary principles which he had advocated in life. Strange as the subject is, the poem abounds in fine descriptive and dramatic passages, one of which represents the ascension of the soul of Louis XVI to Heaven. In 1796 Monti wrote a poem, "Musogonia," which was favorable to the Papal party, but two years later he altered it to make Napoleon the hero. Still further was this homage to the French general carried in the "Prometeo," another imitation of Dante. Here Napoleon was exalted to Heaven as the impersonation of valor and virtue. After the downfall of the Emperor, Monti sang the praises of the Austrians. This frequent change of attitude is attributed to the mobility of his feelings. He felt keenly the impression of the moment and immediately gave it utterance in vigorous poetry. His only deep abiding passion was for his art. In him the common talent of the Italian improvisator was magnified to a powerful genius. He insisted on making Dante and Petrarch the models of style, and opposed the pretensions of the Della Cruscan school who wished to limit the literary vocabulary to strictly Tuscan words. His influence on the regeneration of Italian poetry was beneficial and permanent.

While the fickle Monti varied in political opinion with every passing breeze, Ugo Foscolo (1778-1827) was ever steady in his love of country, though a man of fierce passions, and apt to quarrel with his friends. He was born at Zante and was proud of being a Greek, yet thoroughly devoted to Italy. His first fame was due to the "Last Letters of Jacopo Ortis" (1799), a tragical love story in imitation of Goethe's "Sorrows of Werther," but also expressing disappointment that Napoleon did not liberate Italy. His finest poem, "The Sepulchers" (1807), rebukes the people of Milan for allowing the poet Parini to be buried in a common grave with robbers, and tells how "the aspiring soul is fired to lofty deeds by great men's monuments." His "Hymns to the Graces" make beauty the source of all high qualities. In all of his poetry the charm lies in the harmonious versification. When made professor at Pavia in 1808, Foscolo offended Napoleon by directing his pupils to seek inspiration in patriotism, and again by his tragedy of "Ajax." Obliged to leave Italy he went to England, where for a time he promoted the study of Italian literature, but afterward by his waywardness lost his patrons and sank into poverty. His prose writings were disfigured by rhetorical vehemence.

A third poet who was a still more ardent classicist was Giambattista Niccolini (1782-1861), born in Florence, where he became professor of history. His first tragedy, "Polyxena," was crowned by the Della Cruscan Academy in 1810. While he imitated Æschylus he allowed his

Muse more freedom than Alfieri. His tragedies show
lyrical power rather than dramatic genius. His subjects
were taken from modern history as well as classical
mythology. One of them, "Giovanni da Procida"
(1830), treats of the expulsion of the French from Sicily
and ends with the Sicilian Vespers. On its presentation,
it was felt to be an attack on Austrian tyranny. The
"Arnaldo da Brescia," founded on the history of the philosopher who proposed Church reforms in the Twelfth
Century, was directed against the Papal power. Although
in dramatic form, it is too long for presentation on the
stage.

Here may be noted, also, a prose classicist who, in his
"History of Italy," imitated the style of Livy, and after
the fashion of ancient writers put into the mouths of his
characters long declamations. This was Carlo Botta
(1766-1837) of Piedmont, who in early life suffered long
imprisonment for an unproved political offense, and thereafter spent much of his life at Paris. His "History of the
War of Independence in America" (1810) is superior to
his other work, and attests his republican principles.
Cesare Cantu (1805-1895), a Lombard by birth, throughout his long life was a diligent writer of history. His
chief work was his "Universal History" in thirty-five
volumes, which has been translated into many languages.
It made no pretension to original research of documentary
evidence, but gave in clear and fluent style the traditional
clerical view of the world's progress.

While the Liberal poets in Italy adhered to the classic
forms in literature, there were others who desired the
literary freedom of the Romantic school. In Milan a
large group of these held firmly the Catholic faith, and
from their general avoidance of political controversy,
were sometimes known as the School of Resignation.

They had for their organ the "Conciliatore," established in 1818. Its very name shows that they were a party of compromise. Some of them longed for national unity, while others looked upon such ideas as chimerical. Minor controversies about purity of language occupied much of their attention. The classicists generally insisted on exclusion of words and forms not belonging to the Tuscan dialect, while the Milanese desired a literary language which should draw from all the dialects of the peninsula. This Milanese or Lombard group is often vaguely called Romantic.

The most distinguished leader of this new school was Count Alessandro Manzoni (1785-1873). He declared that its object was to discover and express historical and moral truth as the eternal source of the beautiful. It has therefore connection with the later realists as well as the early Romanticists. In youth Manzoni had at Paris imbibed the infidelity of Rousseau, but he was converted by the faith of his wife, and became a fervent Catholic, as he proved by his "Sacred Hymns" (1810), which follow the festivals of the Church as in Keble's "Christian Year." Manzoni's noble ode on the death of Napoleon is called "The Fifth of May." His two fine tragedies were criticised for violation of classical rules. But his fame rests on his *"Promessi Sposi"* (The Betrothed) (1827), which placed him at the head of modern Italian literature. The idea of this picture of the past was undoubtedly suggested by Sir Walter Scott's novels, but Manzoni did not confine himself to reproducing history. The plot is slight; Renzo and his betrothed Lucia, simple peasants, are prevented from marriage by the craft and violence of Don Rodrigo and the weakness of the priest, Abbondio. The cruel Innominato assaults Lucia in his castle. Fra Federigo endeavors to rescue the lovers from their perils, and the holy archbishop of Milan is brought to their aid. Don Rodrigo dies of the plague of 1630, which is fully described from contemporary documents. To his famous novel Manzoni added a sequel called "The Column of Infamy." The people of Milan had believed that an inhabitant had introduced the plague by poison and therefore destroyed his house and erected a column to mark the accursed spot. The real value of Manzoni's work lies in its searching analysis of characters. In his later years he so far yielded to the claims of the Tuscan dialect as to revise carefully the diction of his great work. He outlived all his children and died in his ninetieth year.

Another noted member of the Milanese group was the gentle Silvio Pellico (1789-1854), most widely known by his narrative, "My Prisons" (1832). Born of wealthy parents in Piedmont, he associated with Foscolo and Monti and wrote tragedies of which the most famous was "Francesca da Rimini" (1818). He joined the secret society of the Carbonari, who sought the freedom of their country. Being arrested, he was tried, convicted and condemned to death, but this sentence was commuted to fifteen years' imprisonment. In 1830, ten years after his arrest, the Emperor ordered his discharge. Pellico went to live at Turin and wrote there his simple, affecting narrative which attests his piety and charity. This unpretending revelation of Austrian tyranny did much eventually toward winning liberty for Italy.

When Austrian domination was fully re-established in Italy, the lovers of their country expressed their feelings in satire or took refuge in history of its former glory. The noblest of the satirists was Giuseppe Giusti (1809-1850), who in spite of ill health, preserved a sunny temperament. His early verses were romantic lyrics, and had the times been favorable he might have proved himself the restorer of Italian supremacy. As it was, he employed his wit on light temporary themes, and the excellence of his work has caused his admirers regret that his ability was not displayed on grander subjects. He was a Tuscan by birth, and his diction is always in that purest dialect. One of his strongest satires, "The Guillotine," exposes to infamy the bloody tyranny of the King of Naples. Another, "Gingillino," playfully yet pointedly treats of the corruption of treasury officials in Tuscany. Giusti was at first active in the Revolutionary movements of 1847 and 1848, yet afterward was distrusted by his comrades.

Physical suffering, mental gloom and moral despair were united in the person of Count Giacomo Leopardi (1798-1837). This lyric poet of atheism and pessimism remains in the greatest possible contrast with the cheerful Catholic novelist, Manzoni. Yet he represents fairly well the spirit of intellectual Italians under the rigorous, crushing despotism of the Bourbons. His father, an impoverished, bigoted and avaricious noble, lived at Recanati in the Apennines. The sickly, deformed, sensitive boy picked up his education by solitary reading in the home library. He became an expert classical scholar and wrote learned treatises before reaching manhood, but his virtual imprisonment produced deep melancholy, which ended in atheism. His only recreation was in writing poetry, at first in the classical style yet full of the Revolutionary spirit, then realistic descriptions of nature and country life, then the sorrowful cries of agonizing despair. Deprived of companionship, friendship and love, he came to regard all objects of human pursuit and desire as vain illusions. The bright metal of his genius was consumed with rust. When the pale, shy, sickly man ventured to Rome at the age of twenty-four, he was rather an object of ridicule than of pity. He wandered from one Italian city to

another, and settled at a friend's house in Naples. Not
only is his poetry exquisite and limpid, but his prose has
been pronounced among the best that Italy has produced.
It was chiefly in philosophical dialogues and discourses.
His best poems are "Sylvia," "The Last Song of Sappho,"
"The Villagers' Saturday Night," "Brutus the Younger,"
"The Broom Flower," and "The Night Song." All
critics have united in pronouncing him the greatest of
Italian poets of the Century. It has been said that "pain
and love form the two-fold poetry of his existence." So
exquisite is the melody of his verse that it cannot be adequately rendered in translation.

Two historical novels of this period were received with
enthusiasm, "The Battle of Benevento" (1827), and "The
Siege of Florence" (1835). They were written by Francesco Domenico Guerrazzi (1804-1873), a lawyer of Leghorn, who wished to rouse the patriotic feeling of his
countrymen. His activity in political agitation caused
him to be banished more than once. While in exile in
Corsica he wrote "Beatrice Cenci" and other novels, but
none of his numerous later books reached the success of
the early spasmodic novels which for a brief time caused
him to be regarded as the Walter Scott of Italy.

Poet as well as patriot was Aleardo Aleardi (1812-
1878), born near Verona, and educated at the University
of Padua. His "Primal Histories" (1845) is a lofty
rhapsody tracing the progress of the human race through
the Scriptural, classical and feudal periods to the present
age and giving a vision of a glorious future. Another
meditative poem, "An Hour of My Youth" (1858), deals
with his disappointments as a patriot. His later poems,
"Raphael and the Fornarina," "The Three Rivers," "The
Three Maidens," "The Seven Soldiers," are more definite
in scope, finely descriptive, brilliant and impassioned. He

inclined rather to the classicists, and was Christian as well as patriotic.

Francesco Dall'Ongaro (1808-1873) was in early life a priest, but his patriotic feeling brought him into dis-favor with the authorities, so that he abandoned that pro-fession and entered on a varied career as journalist, dra-matist and political agitator. For Madame Ristori he composed the tragedy "Bianca Capello," and for Salvini "Fasma" and "Il Tesoro." For a time he was banished from Italy but afterward returned and held literary pro-fessorships at Milan, Venice and Naples, where he died. As a lyric poet he took high rank.

Giovanni Prati (1805-1884) was best known by his political songs and lyrics but wrote also "Edmenegarda" (1841), a narrative poem in Byron's style, a satire "Satan and the Graces" (1855), and some epics.

CONTEMPORARY WRITERS

Of contemporary Italian poets the greatest is Giosue Carducci, born in 1836. To his example is attributed the marked revival of poetry in recent times. As Leopardi represented the hopeless apathy of Italy under foreign domination, Carducci expresses the joy of the nation in its new life. He is a professor in the University of Bologna. His first work to attract attention was the "Hymn to Satan," published in 1865 under an assumed name. It was really a celebration of the advent of science and free thought, and showed strong love of Hellenic cul-ture. This Paganism is displayed in his other poems, just as it was in the works of artists and poets of the Renaissance of the Sixteenth Century. It interferes with the modern poet's regard for the Christian Dante, whom he otherwise reverences as the supreme master of Italian literature. In his *"Odi Barbare"* (Barbarian Odes) Carducci has endeavored to introduce new meters into Italian. Thoroughly versed in the literary history of his country, he has published some able treatises upon it. Strong national feeling, a thoroughly modern spirit, and a love of art are seen in all his work.

Two writers of later birth have secured more attention abroad—the traveler Edmondo De Amicis, born in 1846, and the novelist Gabriele D'Annunzio, born in 1864. De Amicis had been a soldier, and was a journalist when, in 1869, his volume of short stories called "Military Life," at once scored a success. Other stories from civil life kept up his reputation. But his brilliant books of travel— "Holland," "Morocco," "Spain," "London," "Paris," and "Constantinople," have not only been highly popular in Italian, but when translated into other tongues have attained equal success. They are picturesque, full of enthusiasm, and exhibit the best aspects of every land and people that he has visited. D'Annunzio, born on the Southern Adriatic coast, began his career at the early age of sixteen with a volume of riotously erotic poems, but after some others of similar character, became serious and even pessimistic. French critics were the first to give him full recognition as a master of melodious verse. His first novel, "Pleasure" (1889), was as objectionable as his early poems. His "Giovanni Episcopo" is a tragedy of low life, in which a weak man, long tyrannized over by a brutal companion, at last stabs him for beating his wife and child. In "The Triumph of Death," a sensualist is pursued by the thought of death and at last commits suicide by leaping from a cliff into the sea. In the "Maidens of the Crag," an Italian, wearied with the corruption of

Roman society, retires to his native mountain, and finds three charming sisters. The problem is, Which will he choose? D'Annunzio belongs to the naturalistic school of fiction, but he surpasses its French representatives by the poetic beauty of his style.

SPANISH LITERATURE

When Napoleon in 1808 humiliated Spain by treacherously seizing its King and placing his own brother Joseph on the throne, the intensely proud and loyal people rose in fury against the outrage. Although in open warfare they were soon overcome, they maintained a guerilla struggle for years. This seemingly insignificant trouble proved to be the beginning of the end for the hitherto irresistible Emperor. It might have been expected that this momentous uprising of the nation would have important effects on its literature, which had long been under French influences. But the style of the most ardent patriotic writers remained thoroughly French.

Manuel José Quintana (1772-1857) has been called the Spanish Tyrtæus, from the aid which his popular songs lent to the patriotic cause. His spirited drama, "Pelayo" (1805), and his rhetorical "Lives of Celebrated Spaniards" (1807) were written to incite opposition to foreign oppression. When the Bourbon King, Ferdinand, was restored, Quintana, as a constitutionalist, suffered imprisonment for six years. Later some amends were made for this unworthy treatment, and in 1855 Queen Isabella II crowned with laurel the aged poet who had been her tutor.

The first Romantic poet of Spain was Angel de Saavedra, Duke of Rivas (1791-1865), who held firmly to the national traditions in his epics, "Florinda" (1825), which treated of the Moorish conquest of Spain, and *"El Moro Esposito"* (The Moorish Foundling) (1835). His drama, "Don Alvaro," also maintained the manner of the old theater of Spain. But José de Espronceda (1810-1842) belonged to the cosmopolitan school of Byron. His lyrics are full of fiery defiance to authority. His short life was unsettled and his Liberal politics made him sometimes an exile. During a residence in London he wrote a pathetic elegy "To Spain." An unhappy love affair inspired his "Canto to Teresa." His unfinished "El Diablo Mundo" (The World Spirit) is the story of an old man who receives the boon of immortal youth, but yields to the cynical instruction of a hardened villain, and enters upon a career of crime. In "The Student of Salamanca" Espronceda portrayed the lawlessness of his own character.

Don José Zorrilla (1817-1893) was the next representative of the Romantic school. The legendary history of Spain was ransacked for subjects for his dramas and epics. His "Don Juan Tenoro" (1844) gave a religious turn to that Spanish story. His comedies in the old Spanish style suited the popular taste. He wrote hastily, carelessly and voluminously. He went to Mexico, where he was patronized by the Emperor Maximilian. Before his protector's death he returned to Spain and was assisted by others until the Government granted him a pension. In 1889 he was publicly crowned with gold at Granada. His aim had been to revive national independence in literature. The last dramatist who adhered to the old Spanish style was Manuel Breton de los Herreros (1796-1873), who wrote a hundred comedies.

Like George Eliot and George Sand, the most eminent woman writer of Spain took a masculine pen-name in order to obtain a fair hearing. Fernan Caballero is the assumed name of the lady who was at first Cecilia Böhl de Faber (1796-1877). Her father, a German merchant in Cadiz, had married a Spanish lady of noble family. The daughter, born at Morges, Switzerland, was educated in Germany and traveled much with her parents, but was always passionately devoted to Spain. She was married thrice to Spaniards, lost her fortune, and when past fifty turned to literature for support. Her story, *"La Gaviota"* (The Sea-gull), appearing in 1849, at once made her famous. Other stories followed, but never surpassed the first. They are deeply imbued with fervent Catholicism, devotion to the glories of the past, hostility to all innovations and modern improvements. The poetic side of Andalusian peasant life is especially revealed in her books. She resided in Seville, and had favor at the court of Queen Isabella II. For ten years she was governess of the royal children. In 1859 she published the first collection of Spanish fairy tales. Her object throughout was to sketch with exactness the home life of the people of both higher and lower classes, and thus give a correct view of Spain and its people. Though aiming at realism, as well as morality, her cheerful religious spirit helped to give an ideal color to her sketches.

Another writer who assisted in making the modern novel popular was Telesforo Trueba y Cosio (1798-1835), who emigrated to England in 1823, and wrote there most of his works. He plainly imitated Sir Walter Scott, but drew his subjects from Spanish history. He wrote also historical novels and other works in English.

Among those who strenuously opposed foreign influences was Don Serafin Estebanez Calderon (1801-1867), who collected a vast library of old Spanish literature, especially ballads, now incorporated in the National Library at Madrid. Besides some poems and historical works he published a novel and a pleasing volume of "Andalusian Sketches." In the effort to make his style idiomatic and to avoid foreign words he used rare and provincial terms which obscure his meaning. Calderon was known as "The Solitary." His nephew, the distinguished statesman, Canovas del Castillo, wrote his biography.

The connecting link between the earlier style of novels and the present is found in the writings of Pedro Antonio de Alarcon (1833-1891). In early life he was democratic but he afterward became conservative and was a councilor of state under Alfonso XII. Through most of his career he was an active journalist, and in 1859 he took part in a campaign in Morocco. His diary of this period made a fortune for his publishers. His most celebrated novel, "The Three-cornered Hat," is a quaint and humorous sketch of old-fashioned village life. "The Child of the Ball" is highly esteemed. "The Scandal" and "The Prodigal" are sensational stories. Alarcon was also a poet and critic of no small merit.

CONTEMPORARY WRITERS

The Revolution of 1868 drove from the throne of Spain the profligate Queen Isabella II, who had compensated for her scandalous behavior by allowing the ecclesiastical authorities to control the press. When a more liberal form of government was introduced, the press was granted freedom. This was soon seen in the criticisms of old institutions, and in the expression of modern opinions. In fiction the influence of English, Russian and French writers became manifest. Yet there was also a strong national spirit which led the writers to seek themes at home, either of the present day or the past, not too remote.

The honor of inaugurating the realistic novel in Spain is usually ascribed to José Maria de Pereda, who published

in 1859 sketches of the manners and customs of Santander
the district on the Northern coast, in which he was born
in 1834. His first novel, "Men of Property," which
appeared in 1874, showed the rise of a country grocer, who
is elected to the Cortes, but is afterward cheated out of his
property and falls back into the lower class. In his second novel, "Don Gonzalo Gonzalez" (1878), the leading
character has acquired wealth in the colonies and returns
to enjoy it, but owing to his innate vulgarity finds himself despised and avoided. In other books Pereda
describes with equal force the life of the sea coast and the
mountains of his native province. His style is forcible
and idiomatic. The dialogue is true and racy. His
humor is genuine Spanish of the old type. Pereda is
intensely conservative, an upholder of absolutism. In literature he is opposed to both Romanticism and classicism.

Juan Valera, born in 1827, still holds an eminent place.
He has been a professor of foreign literatures at Madrid,
was secretary of legation in various capitals, and minister
at Washington. Since his return to Madrid he has been
afflicted with blindness. He had distinguished himself as
a critical essayist and translator of poetry before he wrote
his first novel "Pepita Ximenez" (1874). In it he endeavored to portray the conflict in the mind of a devout young
man, who had been trained by his uncle, the dean of a
cathedral, to be a priest, while his father wished him to
marry and inherit his estate. Pepita is a handsome young
widow whose modest charms seize upon his heart and finally control his action. Donna Luz, the heroine of another
novel, also meets an interesting priest, but marries a man
of the world. "The Illusions of Doctor Faustino" (1876)
is the tragical story of a poor and philosophic patrician,
who, finding himself unable to loosen the tangle of worldly
affairs, commits suicide. In "Commander Mendoza"

(1877), a story of the last Century, a Spanish commander having acquired a fortune in Peru, returns to his native land. There he meets Donna Blanca, with whom he had a liaison in Lima, and her daughter, Clara, who is also his child. To enable the latter to marry the man of her choice, the commander secretly sacrifices his wealth. Yet he is rewarded by winning the love of Lucia, his daughter's friend. All Valera's works are of the most polished style; he never introduces imitation of dialect.

Benito Perez Galdos has been a prolific novelist in different styles. He was born at Las Palmas in the Canary Islands in 1845, and at the age of eighteen went to Madrid to study law. After trying the drama to no purpose, he began to write novels and in 1868 published "The Golden Fountain," a Romantic story which told of the rebellion of the young men of 1820 against the reactionary policy of Ferdinand VII. His next book, "The Fearless One" (1872) told the faithful love of a noble maiden for a youth who fell in that Rebellion. But in 1873 Galdos, in imitation of the Erckmann-Chatrian stories, began to issue a series of "National Episodes." They relate to the deliverance of Spain from the domination of the French; and the same characters appear in the successive stories. The first gives the Spanish view of the battle of Trafalgar; the second tells of the baggage which Joseph Bonaparte tried to carry out of Spain. In the "Battle of Salamanca" Gabriel, who tells all the stories, has risen through many adventures to be major and gives important aid to Wellington. In a second series Salvador Monsalud is the principal character. He had been driven by want to take service with the French, but is hated and despised by his countrymen. The "Episodes" are well constructed, graphic in style, full of life and movement. Galdos wrote next some "purpose" novels, of which

"Donna Perfecta," is the best. In this a bright young
engineer who is about to marry his beautiful cousin, finds
unexpected difficulties arise in his way; he shocks the
prejudices and incurs the enmity of everybody in the
village except his true-hearted betrothed; but it is discovered that all these troubles are due to one woman who
wished her homely son to win the prize. Galdos turned at
last to simple realism, setting down the ordinary affairs
of life without any purpose of teaching or surprising the
reader. Yet in these he happens upon the deepest tragedies, as in "The Disowned" (1881), and "Reality"
(1890).

A younger novelist, whose stories have been translated into various languages, is Armando Palacio Valdes,
born in 1853. He excels in rural description and the
portraiture of young women, using sometimes the freedom of French writers, yet adhering to morality. He was
born at Entralgo, near Oviedo, in the northwest of Spain,
and studied law at Madrid. These places and neighbor-
ing towns furnish the scenes of his novels. He became
secretary of the Athenæum at Madrid, and editor of "The
European Review." His first novel, "Senorito Octavio"
(1881) was humorous, sentimental, and somewhat melodramatic. A better one is his "Martha and Mary"
(1883) translated into English under the title "The Marquis of Penalta." Mary, the young and beautiful heroine, gifted with a splendid voice, has become possessed
with so strong religious devotion that she practices the
asceticism of mediæval saints. She also is induced to
believe that placing Don Carlos on the throne will advance
the cause of religion, and therefore engages in a plot which
results in her being arrested. A realistic romance is
"The Fourth Estate" (1888), which tells of the founding of a newspaper in a primitive village. The main plot

shows how a young engineer's engagement with a plain sincere girl is broken by the wiles of her prettier younger sister. In "Sister San Sulpicio" (1889) a gay girl who has been induced to enter a convent finds her true happiness in leaving it for the love of a devoted admirer.

Although political writers are usually excluded from treatment in literary history, an exception is made in favor of Emilio Castelar, whose eloquence as an orator and prominence as a statesman have made his name familiar throughout the world. He was born at Cadiz in 1832, and at the age of twenty-two was conspicuous in the Liberal party. He became professor of history in the University of Madrid. In 1866 he was arrested and condemned to death for participation in a revolutionary attempt, but escaped from Spain. Returning after the Revolution of 1868 he opposed the restoration of monarchy. After the resignation of King Amadeo Castelar was made president of the Spanish Republic, but being unable to suppress the Carlists resigned in 1874 and went abroad. Again he returned and was elected to the Cortes. He now declared that Spain insists on having monarchical government and he accepts that conclusion. Among his numerous works the most noted are "Democratic Ideas" (1858), "Parliamentary Speeches" (1871), "Old Rome and New Italy" (1873).

While the novel has been the most absorbing part of Spanish literature in the Nineteenth Century the drama has not been altogether neglected. In this field there has been the same struggle as in that of romance. Some playwrights adhered strictly to the forms of the old Spanish drama, others drew their inspiration from France. The former wrote in the style of Calderon, the latter in that of the younger Dumas. Zorrilla wrote in the former style, but his rivals seemed to be preferred. But in the contemporary period José Echegaray has been acknowledged as the most vital force in the drama. He was born at Madrid in 1832, and became a civil engineer and professor of mathematics. He took part in the Revolution of 1868 and has thrice been a member of the cabinet. His first dramatic work was "The Check-Book" (1872), but his fame was established by the tragedy of "Madman or Saint?" (1877). In this the hero finds himself unable to induce his friends to accept his view that every man is bound to render obedience to the moral law at whatever sacrifice. The dramatist also insists on the necessary punishment of sin but makes it overtake the innocent as well as the guilty, and in this shows his tendency to pessimism. He is at his best in the exhibition of passion. Several dramas of notable excellence followed, the grandest being "The Great Galeoto" (1881) which exhibits the terrible results of evil speaking, even when no evil is intended. The genius of Echegaray is chiefly tragic, yet he has produced some lighter pieces, the best of which is "A Budding Critic."

With the genuine revival of the novel and the drama in truly national spirit there seems no reason to doubt that Spain has entered on a new literary era, which may be as fruitful as her Golden Age.

AMERICAN LITERATURE

GLANCE AT COLONIAL AND REVOLUTIONARY LITERATURE

At the beginning of the Nineteenth Century American literature had but a small legacy from Colonial and Revolutionary authors. Our forefathers had been compelled to exercise their powers mostly in the development and control of the material and political problems of the New World. And yet much time and attention as they gave to these urgent matters there were two things which most of them prized above all worldly considerations— religion and religious freedom. Pilgrims and Puritans, Separatists and Quakers, Huguenots and Roman Catholics, had all come to this country that they might have a place in which to worship God according to the dictates of their own conscience. Nor were the stout Churchmen, the first settlers of Virginia, less pronounced in their profession of faith. When the British colonists began to realize their actual separation from the mother country, with all its benefits and privileges, they set themselves vigorously to work to supply their needs according to their own estimate of the comparative importance of these. To obtain a learned and godly ministry seemed a prime necessity. Hence the early establishment of colleges—Harvard and Yale in the Seventeenth Century. Though both bear the name of English benefactors, they really depended on the support of the colonists themselves. In loyal Virginia, the ancient William and Mary received more substantial aid from England and bears the name of

392

the sovereigns who granted its charter; yet it has not been able to survive the vicissitudes of later revolutions. King's College, founded in New York City, in the same loyal spirit, afterward entered on a new career as Columbia College, and has commenced a still more promising era as Columbia University. Dartmouth, near the northern frontier of New Hampshire, was a missionary enterprise, intended to benefit Indians as well as whites, but found its work practically confined to the latter. Princeton, in New Jersey, and Brown at Providence, Rhode Island, depended on denominational support, the former from Presbyterians, the latter from Baptists. The University of Pennsylvania is the outgrowth of one of the numerous proposals of Benjamin Franklin for the benefit of his fellow citizens of Philadelphia. In all of these educational institutions a large majority of the graduates before the Nineteenth Century became ministers in various churches. The intellectual activity aroused in the colonies was chiefly directed to religious and theological questions. The few printers that set up their hand presses in the colonies were employed in printing sermons and religious treatises, as well as laws and proclamations, almanacs and handbills. The learned and industrious Cotton Mather is said to have published four hundred works, mostly sermons, solemn and full of quotations from all sources. His ponderous history of New England is called *"Christi Magnalia Americana"* (The Great Works of Christ in America). It treats more of the churches, the ministers, and their little controversies, and their political activity, than of the progress of the people in other matters. The greatest intellect of New England in the Eighteenth Century belonged to Jonathan Edwards, who astonished the philosophers of Great Britain by the metaphysical ability shown in his treatise "On the Freedom of the Will." In his "History of

Redemption" he set forth the unity of all history and thus anticipated the German philosophers, whose speculations were to be so fruitful in that field.

But besides theology Americans were compelled to give attention to questions of government. The revolutions in England produced important corresponding changes in the colonies, and aroused animated discussion from one end of the land to the other. The endeavor to protect the rights of the colonists, inherited or acquired, led to close study of charters, laws and acts of Parliament. The ultimate result was seen in the Constitution of the United States, which was not struck off at one blow, but was framed by careful examination and discussion of many plans already in operation here and there through the country. Enlightened publicists in Europe, who had imagined that the Americans were a rabble of law-defying revolutionists were surprised on reading their political documents to find in them nearly every element of personal and national greatness. Thomas Jefferson takes high rank among the political writers of his time, and the "Declaration of Independence," for literary merit, is not only worthy of the highest enconiums, but stands unmatched in the annals of the world. Benjamin Franklin, who added a few touches to that document, was also eminent as a practical philosopher able to reach the hearts of his countrymen by his pithy proverbs and pointed paragraphs. Alexander Hamilton, James Madison, and John Jay, by their masterly exposition of the Constitution in "The Federalist" have laid the American people under lasting obligations which have been duly acknowledged. John Adams was a writer of state papers not inferior in style to those of his great contemporaries. George Washington, though reserved in speech, and more accustomed and inclined to action, made his Presidential addresses, and particularly his ever-memorable "Farewell Address," models of a pure and effective literary style.

The American Revolution developed not only statesmen and writers of public documents but also orators who possessed the faculty of so presenting the questions of their time as to excite the feelings of the people, to prove to them that the imposition of a trifling tax on tea or a stamp on paper involved the great question of liberty, and to arouse them to action on its behalf. When the great orators from Patrick Henry to Fisher Ames had so moved the hearts of the people, there were responses not only in assemblies and associations, in preparation for war and actual fighting, but in a general outburst of patriotic songs, ballads, and doggerel, which seem to suit well with the Continental fife and drum. The best of all the satires of the Revolution was Trumbull's "MacFingal," a Yankee imitation and perversion of Butler's "Hudibras." It marks well the ludicrous side of the turbulent epoch, and held the Tories up to popular ridicule. Captain Philip Freneau, a mariner of Huguenot descent, was the chief laureate of the Revolutionary War.

It was through the newspapers that Freneau and Franklin and writers of less capacity reached the great public. Newspapers had begun to appear early in that Century. In 1704 the first American newspaper, "The Boston News-Letter," was established. The second, "The New England Courant," was started by James Franklin in 1720. His troubles in connection with it are well known from his younger brother Benjamin's famous "Autobiography." While James by order of the Colonial Assembly was imprisoned for some unfortunate paragraphs the paper was issued in the name of Benjamin, then but a boy. Yet gradually the press worked its way to freedom in spite of stupid governors and assemblies.

In 1765, at the time of the Stamp Act, there were forty newspapers in the British American Colonies.

LITERATURE AT THE DAWN OF THE CENTURY

In the year 1800, gateway to a Century of almost magical national development, the population of the free States was 2,684,616, of the slave States, 2,621,316, making a total of 5,305,932. Philadelphia was the chief city of the Nation. It had been the national capital during the Revolution, though it fell for a time into possession of the British army. Here the Declaration of Independence, the Articles of Confederation, and the Federal Constitution had been framed and signed. Here the Federal Congress met and Washington held his Republican court. Here were the American Philosophical Society, which had grown out of Franklin's Junto; the Philadelphia Library, mother of all institutions of the kind; and the University of Pennsylvania, likewise the outgrowth of Franklin's matchless genius for public enterprise. The first American monthly magazine had been issued here by Franklin in 1741. After the establishment of peace in 1783 other magazines were issued, the principal being the "American Museum." The city therefore was the literary center of the new Nation, though the political capital was in 1800 removed to Washington. Foreigners of distinction still resorted to Philadelphia, whether they came to visit or to settle in the New World. It boasted itself to be the American Athens.

Noah Webster, long regarded as the American authority in orthography, was in other senses a man of letters, and deserves note as a pioneer of literature. He was born in West Hartford, Connecticut, in 1758, being descended from the first settlers. As a young student of Yale in the spring of 1775, he played the fife proudly before the college escort, accompanying George Washington on his way to Cambridge to take command as General-in-Chief of the new Continental Army. After shouldering a gun as a volunteer private in a campaign without a battle, Webster studied law under Oliver Ellsworth, later chief-justice; then fell into his life career as a school teacher, although later admitted to the Hartford bar. In 1782, while teaching a classical school at Goshen, N. Y., he compiled his "Grammatical Institute of the English Language," the germ of his great "Unabridged." He afterward removed to Philadelphia and there taught school and wrote pamphlets in the interest of the Federal party. For twenty-five years the chief support of his family was the penny royalty on his "Spelling Book." Yet he industriously waged his pioneer work for reformed spelling and a New World system of language. In 1806 he gave to America his "Compendious Dictionary." By continued shifts the self-taught dictionary-maker finally developed his nucleus into his "American Dictionary," in two volumes quarto, published in London in 1828. Horace E. Scudder declares in his appreciative biography, "Webster was the prophet of a national independence, in which language and literature were involved as inseparable elements."

Joseph Dennie, then called the "American Addison," had come to Philadelphia, in 1799, as clerk to Secretary of State Timothy Pickering. He had been born in Boston in 1767, had failed to continue a pupil at Harvard, had attempted law, and at last had drifted into his Bohemian career in journalism. In January, 1801, he began the publication of "The Port-Folio" under the sobriquet of "Oliver Oldschool, Esq." He was the most picturesque figure of his day in the then metropolitan city on the banks of the Delaware. The Port-Folio was praised by Josiah

Quincy as the best American magazine of its day, "no whit behind the best English." Dennie himself had a timid reverence for the mother country, and he and his colleagues drew their inspiration from Pope and Addison. "To study with a view of becoming an author by profession in America," wrote Dennie, "is a prospect of no less flattering promise than to publish among the Esquimaux an essay on delicacy of taste, or to found an academy of sciences in Lapland."

Other authors of the Eighteenth Century still survived: John Trumbull, at the age of fifty, author of the Revolutionary satire "McFingal," and chief survivor of the group known as the "Hartford Wits;" Joel Barlow, aged forty-five, whose prodigious epic, the "Columbiad," was issued in Philadelphia in 1807, and dedicated to Robert Fulton, famous for his steamboat; William Dunlap, aged thirty-four, who had written plays, "The Father," and "André," and who was yet to write the "History of the American Theater;" Joseph Hopkinson, aged thirty, whose song, "Hail Columbia"—written in 1798, during the French excitement, to the then popular air of the "President's March"—shared public popularity with the celebrated ode of Robert Treat Paine, Jr., "Adams and Liberty." It was not long afterward eclipsed by the "Star Spangled Banner," the words of which were composed by Francis Scott Key, a Marylander, during the British bombardment of Fort McHenry in 1814.

Philip Freneau did not die until December 18, 1832, when nearly eighty-one years old. This satirical poet of the Revolutionary era had witnessed remarkable progress in his nation and the world. Of Huguenot descent, he was a classmate of Madison at Princeton College, afterward a British prisoner of war, and later a savage satirist. He lent his pen, on the birth of the Republic, to Jefferson and the Democrats, and so bitter were his newspaper attacks upon the administration that Washington has handed him down to posterity in the epithet, "That rascal Freneau." And yet, while this "rascal's" satires and lampoons have faded away, he still deserves indelible credit as the first real American poet. The English poet Campbell did not hesitate to appropriate one of his most effective lines, and Sir Walter Scott did him the honor to borrow, in "Marmion," the final line of one of his stanzas, "They took the spear, but left the shield." Freneau handled effectively Indian themes. "In his verses, says Professor Beers, "appear for the first time, a sense of the picturesque and poetic elements in the character and wild life of the redman, and that pensive sentiment which the fading away toward the sunset has left in the wake of their retreating footsteps." The Indian was already becoming a strange, half-legendary figure to the dwellers in the American towns, and Freneau's "Indian Student" is brought from the remote backwoods:

> "From Susquehanna's farthest springs,
>   Where savage tribes pursue their game
> (His blanket tied with yellow strings),
>   A shepherd of the forest came."

Even in his day he found "the hunter and the deer a shade." In his romantic and poetic appreciation of the American aboriginal, Freneau anticipated, in a mild way, "The Leather Stocking Tales" of Cooper and Longfellow's legend of "Hiawatha."

Of Joel Barlow, it may be noted that he had been one of the "Hartford Wits," earnest patriots in the Revolution. But Barlow deserted Hartford for France, where he wrote his thoroughly American mock epic, "Hasty Pudding," and yet became so plague-stricken a Frenchman that he wrote a song in praise of the guillotine. In 1805 he returned and published in sumptuous style his work, the "Columbiad," in which Hesper fetches Columbus from his Spanish prison "to a hill of vision" where the entire panorama of American—or Columbian—history is unrolled before his eyes. This artificial "Vision," with its machinery borrowed from Milton, and its heroic couplet from Pope, has sunk into oblivion.

Dr. Timothy Dwight's moralizing poem, "Greenfield Hill," descriptive of his own rural parish, gave him contemporary luster as one of the poets of Connecticut. But he is now known only by his "Travels in New England and New York," published posthumously in 1821 and praised by Southey. These descriptions of the Niagara Falls, White Mountains, and the Catskills exerted influence in calling attention to the grandeur and inspiring character of American scenery. James Hall, in his "Letters from the West," had before this written, "The vicinity of Pittsburg may one day wake the lyre of the Pennsylvania bard to strains as martial and as sweet as Scott; . . . believe me, I should tread with as much reverence over the mausoleum of a Shawnee chief, as among the catacombs of Egypt, and speculate with as much delight upon that site of an Indian village as in the gardens of Tivoli, or the ruins of Herculaneum." The first collection of American poems was selected and edited by Elihu H. Smith as far back as 1793, and a second collection, the "Columbian Muse," appeared in the year following.

CHARLES BROCKDEN BROWN

It is necessary to turn now to the true pioneer in the realm of the American novel. Charles Brockden Brown, the first American professional man of letters, as well as first of all Cis-Atlantic writers of fiction, was born in Philadelphia in 1771, was educated in the school of Robert Proud, the historian of Pennsylvania, and would have entered the bar but for ill health. His first published article appeared in the "Columbian Magazine" of August, 1789, and in 1806 he himself became an editor. Perhaps his invalidism put him in peculiar sympathy with those ghostly, ghastly, "clumsy-horrible" English romances before Scott's Waverley Novels—those of "Monk" Lewis, Walpole, and Mrs. Radcliffe. From William Godwin it was that Brown caught the style of his first work, "Alcuin, a Dialogue on the Rights of Women" (1797). Godwin's "Falkland" and "Caleb Williams" furnished the models for Brown's "Wieland" (1798), a story of crime committed by means of ventriloquism, and "Ormond" (1799). Shelley was under the spell of "Wieland," according to his own confession, in writing "Zastrozzi" and "St. Irvyne." Godwin's influence on Brown thus returned upon Godwin's son-in-law. Sir Walter Scott also admired this American novelist, naming the hero of "Guy Mannering" after him, and calling one of its characters Arthur Merwyn. Brown's novel, "Arthur Merwyn" (1799), contains vivid descriptions of the scenes in Philadelphia during the terrible yellow fever pestilence of 1793. Brown's somber genius "for churchyard romance" found a congenial theme in this narrative of the horrors of a plague. His next work, "Edgar Huntley," followed the fortunes of a somnambulist in the mountains of Western Pennsylvania. This curious plot of sleep-walking was as strange as the ventriloquism of the villain in his first novel, which led the hero to believe in spiritual voices and to kill his wife and children; but the incidental descriptions of wilderness scenery atoned for much. Weak as his style now seems, he deserves credit as the first writer to discover the capability of romance in America, its scenery, and its people.

WASHINGTON IRVING AND THE KNICKERBOCKER GROUP

The author who was first to gain for American literature a recognized place in European eyes was Washington Irving. Born in New York City in 1783, the year of the peace between Great Britain and the United States, he was named after the great Commander-in-Chief and first President of the Republic, and, while yet a child, "blessed" by him. His was indeed an international mission to heal to some extent by the sympathetic charm of his style and his personality the breach between the two countries, aggravated by the second war of 1812. He became "the first literary Ambassador of the New World to the Old." Like a loyal son of the soil, he breathed the breath of literary immortality into the traditions of his own country, as well as voyaged to England and began to write about English scenes and associations. Born of a Scotch father and an English mother, he belonged in religion to the conservative Episcopalians. Professor Richardson has remarked, he was "the first conspicuous American author who was neither a Puritan nor a Southron; his local tone is that of New York City and the Hudson." Quick to assimilate the customs and characteristics of other lands, he was the first to make distinctly American themes familiar to the world of letters. The main reason for this lay in his truly Addisonian style, the result of close acquaintance with the English essayists of the Eighteenth Century. Irving, like Bryant and Longfellow after him, studied law, but he found his true bent when he contributed, in 1802, to his brother Peter's newspaper, "The New York Morning Chronicle," a series of letters over the signature of "Jonathan Oldstyle," satirizing the town follies and foibles, and reflecting the theaters and coffee-houses. While he still groped toward his destiny his ill-health gave the decisive turn to his observation. He walked much along the Palisades and in the Hudson region, thus becoming familiar with the scenes he was later to adorn with humorous fancy and romance. In 1804, when he was twenty-one, his persistent ill health led to a sea voyage and a "grand tour" of Europe—then a rare thing—covering two years. To quote Professor Richardson again: "The American author was getting his education; the crude Westerner was becoming a citizen of the world. To see Mrs. Siddons and Kemble; to talk with the greatest of talkers, Madame de Staël; to tread the pavement of Westminster Abbey or St. Peter's; to gaze on Vesuvius and the Coliseum—all this was a new experience for an American. . . . Brockden Brown introduced the weird, the romantic, the appalling, the native American, and made a failure, on the whole; Irving, using the English manner for his treatment of American themes, made one of those happy compromises to which pioneers sometimes owe their success."

After returning to New York, Irving eventually gathered around him a group of friends now known as the Knickerbocker school, which comprised James Kirke Paulding (a connection of Irving by marriage, who afterward became Secretary of the Navy, under Van Buren), and the poets Drake and Halleck. All four were Knickerbockers to the bone. Together with Paulding, Irving now followed up his early boyish letters with the lively "Salmagundi" papers (1807-8). This little paper became the playful satirical censor of that society which dwelt on the island of Manhattan. Behind the mock individualities of such pseudonyms as Anthony Evergreen,

Launcelot Langstaff, and William Wizard, these wits indulged their varied rapier play and thrust of mirth at the provincial town that was yet to astonish the world by its growth in size, riches, and power. It was a spirit of fun akin to that which inspired "Salmagundi," that prompted Irving to that elaborate burlesque-chronicle, Knickerbocker's "History of New York," designed at first as a mere parody of Samuel L. Mitchill's pretentious and then newly-issued "Picture of New York." The book, prefaced by a circumstantial account of the fabulous Diedrich Knickerbocker, and of the way in which the manuscript came into the editor's hands, became in the course of development a jest upon real history, the result being an immortally amusing cartoon of the Dutchman of the original Nieuw Amsterdam. Irving made humorous use of the old Dutch traditions, clustering them about the romantic scenery of the Hudson. Its mock heroic character had at times the coarseness of Fielding. The most familiar episode in the book is the description of the mustering of the clans under Peter Stuyvesant and the attack on the Swedish Fort Christiana. Walter Scott declared Diedrich to be a cousin of Swift and of Sterne. Encouraged by his success, Irving made ten years later a fresh incursion into the Dutch traditions of his native State. The immortal story of Rip Van Winkle, the vagabond of the Catskills, and his twenty years' nap, and the "Legend of Sleepy Hollow," with its quaint picture of the Yankee schoolmaster, Ichabod Crane, gave Irving a new claim to European consideration; as did his later flights in this realm of fiction, such as Dolph Heydiger in "Bracebridge Hall," "The Money Diggers," "Kidd the Pirate," and "Wolfert Weber" in the "Tales of a Traveler;" and the late published "Wolfert's Roost." But Irving simultaneously in "The Sketch Book of Geoffrey

Crayon, Gent.," published in London during his second sojourn abroad, and in "Bracebridge Hall" was the new Columbus to rediscover "Merry Old England"—for Americans. His pleasant description of English country life and its good old Yuletide cheer was also supplemented by such tales of pathos as "The Broken Heart," over which Byron is said to have wept, and "The Pride of the Village." His Westminster Abbey meditation has been praised as equal to that on the same theme in Addison's "Spectator." Irving also opened up for Englishmen as well as Americans a new literary Mecca in Shakespeare's birthplace, Stratford-on-Avon, which has since his time been a favorite point of pilgrimage for the entire English-speaking race. He investigated, too, Shakespeare-land in London, at the Boar's Head Tavern. In the same finished style he wrote his "Tales of a Traveler," which rank high in the second class of American fiction.

From 1842 to 1846 Washington Irving represented the United States as its Minister at Madrid. Attracted by his studies for the "Life and Voyages of Columbus," he found a new field of peculiar interest to Americans in the Iberian peninsula and in the romance of Spain. Truly picturesque are his succeeding books, "The Conquest of Granada," "The Companions of Columbus," and the "Alhambra." His history of "Mahomet and His Successors" was comparatively unsuccessful, but his "Life of Oliver Goldsmith" is a delightful literary memoir. Upon his return to American soil Irving was greeted as the great international representative of the motherland. Having won high honors for American literature abroad, he lapsed into modest retirement at Sunnyside, that now historic home of his on the banks of the Hudson, the river of his romance; and here he lived out, surrounded by friends and enacting the part of a sort of a national literary host, a ripe old age, the influence of which was as sweet and wholesome as his contributions to the world of letters. His "Life of Washington," intended to be the chief and crowning work of his career, is still consulted as an authority. He died at Tarrytown, N. Y., in 1859.

Associated in memory with Irving are the poets Joseph Rodman Drake (1795-1820) and Fitz-Greene Halleck (1790-1867). These two comrades made their début in the Irving style in the "Croaker Papers," a series of humorous and satirical verses contributed to the "New York Evening Post" during the Salmagundi period. In the year that Irving in Europe published "The Sketch Book" (1819), Drake gave America "The Culprit Fay." Three years before this, Bryant had produced his unique "Thanatopsis," and Drake's "Fay," a delicate fairy-tale of the Highlands of the Hudson, was the second best poem then produced in America. As Poe declared, this brilliant poem is fanciful rather than imaginative. Drake's patriotic lyric, "The American Flag," is a spirited national anthem of the first luster. But this promising poet died at the age of twenty-five, lamented by Halleck in the touching elegy, the first stanza of which runs:

> "Green be the turf above thee,
> Friend of my better days;
> None knew thee but to love thee,
> Nor named thee but to praise."

Halleck himself lived half a century longer and witnessed the growth of a new literary New York. His noble ode on the Greek hero, Marco Bozzaris, is worthy to rank in its way with Drake's "American Flag," while his "Alnwick Castle," a playful contrast between mediæval and modern life, has a Praed-like daintiness.

WILLIAM C. BRYANT

William Cullen Bryant (1794-1878), who in early youth wrote anonymously a political satire, "The Embargo," was the first American poet of note. His stately hymn in blank verse, "Thanatopsis," which appeared in the "North American Review" in 1817, was a wonderful masterpiece of precocity, and won him an audience in England. Wordsworth is said to have learned the poem by heart, and in dignity of verse and majesty of style it is certainly still to be recognized as one of the poetical masterpieces of this Century. Bryant, who was born in a little Massachusetts town, became America's great meditative poet of nature, fulfilling what Matthew Arnold asserts to be the peculiar office of modern poetry, and giving to nature its moral interpretation. His "Forest Hymn," "Blue Gentian," "Death of the Flowers," "Green River," "To a Water Fowl," "June," and "Evening Wind" belong to the great anthology of high American verse. Although a country lawyer before he came to New York in 1825, and a hard-worked journalist during his subsequent long career in that busy mart, his heart ever remained in New England, cradled in the Berkshire Hills, and the fruit of his ripe old age, such as "The Planting of the Apple Tree" and "The Flood of Years," is still rosy with the flush of the springtime of his youth. Or rather, we think of Autumnal bloom more than Spring blossom. "Bryant," remarks Prof. Beers, "is our poet of 'the melancholy days,' as Lowell is of June. . . . He is, in especial, the poet of Autumn, of the American October and the New England Indian Summer, that season of 'dropping nuts' and 'smoky light.'" The majesty of "Thanatopsis" was reflected again in his "Battle Field," with its familiar stanza:

"Truth, crushed to earth, shall rise again,
The eternal years of God are hers;
But Error, wounded, writhes in pain,
And dies amid her worshipers."

In the last decade of Bryant's life appeared his blank verse translations of the "Iliad" and "Odyssey," constituting one of the best metrical versions of Homer in the English tongue.

JAMES FENIMORE COOPER

As Bryant may be regarded as the pioneer American poet, and Irving as the pioneer essayist and man of letters, so James Fenimore Cooper may be styled the first American novelist of true distinction. It is the fashion nowadays to criticise Cooper's style—even such a public jester as Mark Twain having taken that office upon himself. There can be no doubt that Cooper was too prolific, too tediously prolix in his style, and actually trashy and insipid in his novels of society. But this should not blind us to the real merits of his greater romances, which far surpassed the writings of Irving in their intense Americanism, and which are almost as fascinating to-day as when they were first published. So great was their appeal to mankind that Morse, the electrician, declared in 1833: "In every city of Europe that I visited, the works of Cooper were conspicuously placed in the windows of every book-shop. They are published as soon as he produces them, in thirty-four different places in Europe. They have been seen by American travelers in the languages of Turkey and Persia, in Constantinople, in Egypt, at Jerusalem, and Ispahan." Cooper was one of the world's great story-tellers, whose defects of style are abundantly compensated by the invention of his narrative in plot and incident. He became, furthermore, the first voice of primeval America, of her virgin wilderness and her aboriginal children. He created the Indian as a life-size figure of literature, impressive even if idealized. And as he originated the novel of the forest, so to a certain extent he originated the novel of the sea. The early childhood of Cooper was mainly passed in the wilderness at the very time, as his biographer says, when "the first wave of civilization was beginning to break against its hills. . . . he was on the border, if he could not justly be said to be in the midst, of mighty and seemingly interminable woods. The settler's axe had as yet scarcely dispelled the perpetual twilight of the primeval forest. The little lake lay enclosed in a border of gigantic trees." When afterward in the first flush of his fame Cooper set out to revive the memory of the days of the pioneers, he said that he might have chosen for his subject happier periods, more interesting events and possibly more beauteous scenes, but he could not have taken any that would lie so close to his heart. The spell of this scenery rests upon the reader of "The Pathfinder" in particular.

Cooper (1789-1851), was born at Burlington, New Jersey, but in infancy was taken to the wilderness of Central New York. Finding his nature unadapted to the college life at Yale, he shipped as a lad before the mast. After an apprenticeship on a merchant vessel he entered the United States Navy as midshipman in 1806. He married and resigned his commission just before the War of 1812. His few years of sea service fitted him to be a great romancer of the salt water. A special expedition to Lake Ontario in 1808 enabled him to draw, as well, that vivid picture of the great fresh-water sea in the novel just cited, and to make the amusing contrast between the old salt and the fresh-water sailors. Mere accident, however, led Cooper to the writing of any kind of novel. At the age of thirty he had written nothing, nor had he collected any material. Writing in itself was distasteful to him. He was one day reading to his wife a novel descriptive of English society; suddenly he laid down the book and said: "I believe I could write a better story myself." The result was a novel (1820) entitled "Precaution." It was not merely a tale of English social life, but it purported to be written "by an Englishman," echoing English cant and even complimenting George III. It was a practical failure, but Cooper resolved to try his hand upon a native theme. John Jay had told him the story of a shrewd, fearless, unselfish spy on the American side in the bitter struggle of the Revolution, in the Highlands of the Hudson. With this inspiration Cooper produced "The Spy, a Tale of the Neutral Ground" (1820). Its best characters are its skillfully drawn hero, Harvey Birch, and the commanding figure of Washington. "The Spy" made Cooper's reputation, both at home and abroad, and he now set about the task that lay near his heart—to describe the frontier life in which he had been trained. Two years later appeared "The Pioneers," itself the pioneer of the five famous romances now known as the "Leather Stocking Tales," of which series it is the poorest. Perhaps the best of the series, the "Last of the Mohieans," was next to appear. The former novel introduced a solitary old white hunter, whose home in the hills is being invaded by the advancing tide of settlement and of that civilization which he loathes. In the latter novel, this hunter had become idealized; he represents the knowledge, mystery and virtue of the silent forest. Cooper's Indians, Chingachgook and Uncas, also became idealized, until it became a joke that "Cooper's imaginary Indians belonged to a tribe that never existed."

But if he gave a prominence to some virtues, real or imaginary, of the Indian race, he was careful not to pass over their vices. Most of the warriors he introduces are depicted as crafty, bloodthirsty and merciless. Throughout the whole civilized world, whether his representation be true or false, the conception of the Indian remains as Cooper drew it in the two tales mentioned and in "The Prairie," "The Pathfinder," and the "Deerslayer," which completed the series. "Leatherstocking," the trapper, scout and backwoods philosopher—or Natty Bumpo, to give the hero his other name—was inspired by the actual personality and career of Daniel Boone, the pioneer of Kentucky. This man of the woods was the first real American in fiction.

Of Cooper's sea tales, the two best were the "Pilot," founded upon the daring exploits of Paul Jones, and the "Red Rover," the introduction of which opens in the harbors of Newport. Cooper's other tales include an Indian story of King Philip's War, "The Wept of Wish-ton-Wish," published in England as "The Borderers" and in France as "The Puritan in America," although the Puritan minister in it bears the repellent name of the Reverend Meek Wolf; "Satanstoe," a picture of colonial life and manners in New York during the middle of the Eighteenth Century, unsurpassed elsewhere and taking rank among his best stories; its sequel, "The Chain-Bearer"; and the "Water Witch."

Cooper's tales reflected to a certain extent the new era of national expansion, for which a motto might be found in Bishop Berkeley's famous line, "Westward the course of Empire takes its way." The westward march and struggle are also dealt with in Irving's "Tour on the Prairies" and in Paulding's "Westward Ho!" as well as

his poem, "The Backwoodsman." It was not long indeed
before the new West was to produce a literature of its
own.

THE EARLY LITERARY MAGAZINES

Meanwhile, in the East, although Irving and his associates had made the practical "retort courteous" to Sydney
Smith's bitter taunt in the "Edinburgh Review": "Who
reads an American book?" it was nevertheless necessary
for professional men of letters to adopt, as Bryant did,
the bread-winning employment of the newspaper. Literature as a profession did not really exist, and such giants
of literary genius as Poe and Hawthorne, not to mention
Lowell and others, belonged to a generation of poorly paid
Bohemians. In the early forties two Philadelphia magazines began to pay their contributors what was then
thought to be a princely munificence. "Godey's Lady's
Book," which had the chief financial success among the
Philadelphia magazines, had succeeded Dennie's "Port
Folio" in the fine personnel of its contributors. It began
in July, 1830, and its circulation grew several years later
to 150,000 a month, largely due to its colored fashion
plates. Somewhat dimmed by these prismatic fashions,
some of the earliest compositions of Poe, Holmes, Lydia
H. Sigourney, Frances S. Osgood, Longfellow, Bayard
Taylor and Harriet Beecher Stowe, appeared in this magazine. Its chief rival was the "Gentleman's Magazine,"
which George R. Graham in 1841 purchased from William
E. Burton, the actor, and renamed simply "Graham's
Magazine." "There is one thing more," said Burton, after
concluding the sale. "I want you to take care of my
young editor." The "young editor" was Poe, who published "The Murderers of the Rue Morgue," "The Masque
of the Red Death," and the poems "The Conqueror

Worm" and "To Helen" and "Israfel" in its various numbers. Later Rufus Wilmot Griswold, of somewhat unpleasant fame, sat in the editorial chair, and Lowell assisted Poe. Longfellow's "Spanish Student," Cooper's "Jack Tier," some of Nathaniel Hawthorne's "Twice Told Tales" appeared in its pages. The Cary Sisters, Charles Fenno Hoffman, Thomas Dunn English, N. P. Willis, W. W. Story, and E. P. Whipple all contributed to it. Bayard Taylor and Charles Godfrey Leland are among the last names associated with it.

Nathaniel Parker Willis came of a race of printers and publishers, and began his literary career by editing illustrated Annuals for Samuel G. Goodrich. He was born in Portland, Maine, 1806, and died on the Hudson in 1867. In 1829 he established the "American Monthly Magazine," later merged in the "New York Mirror," a weekly established by Samuel Woodworth, the printer who wrote that familiar song, "The Old Oaken Bucket." Willis was associated with George P. Morris, also a song writer, but whose only surviving piece is "Woodman, Spare that Tree." Willis had distinguished himself at Yale by his "Scriptural Poems," written in blank verse. In personality Willis was not a Scriptural sort of figure. Though far from handsome, he dressed in the extreme of fashion and affected the dandified manners of a D'Orsay. He was a kindly helper of struggling literary aspirants, however, and as Thackeray, who was helped by him as an unknown, asserted, "It is comfortable that there should have been a Willis." Like Irving, he enjoyed a European tour, which resulted in "Pencilings by the Way" and "Inklings of Adventure," dashing sketches of foreign as well as American life. His style was sparkling and full of melody, but also jaunty and marred by frivolous conceits. He was, it is said, the most successful American magazinist of the second quarter of this Century. His studies of society life at American watering places of fifty years ago are still worth reading, and his "Letters from Under a Bridge" make a charming rural series.

POE

In the Bohemian world of literary newspapers and magazines, Edgar Allen Poe (1809-1849) found his destiny cast. He had been born in Boston, but he never belonged there, though his first volume, "Tamerlane and Other Poems," bore on its title page the words, "By a Bostonian." His father was a Marylander, for whom some biographers have claimed a noble descent, but who was a penniless actor and had married an actress. Early deprived of both parents, Poe was adopted by Mr. Allan, a wealthy merchant of Richmond, Va. For a time he was at school in England and afterward was a student at the University of Virginia, where his irregular nature was nurtured in the old cavalier vices of the South. He drank and gambled, ran in debt, indulged in perverse pride, and was finally disowned by his adoptive father, who had tried to make a soldier of him at West Point. Turning to literature for support, Poe won a prize of $100 offered by a weekly paper for a story. His contribution was "The Manuscript Found in a Bottle." Being brought to the notice of John P. Kennedy, he was made editor of "The Southern Literary Messenger" at Richmond. He married his cousin, Virginia Clemm, in 1836, and a year later went, first to New York, and then to Philadelphia, where he was editor of the "Gentleman's Magazine." When Graham purchased this periodical and changed its title to "Graham's Magazine," Poe was retained as editor, but fifteen months later he left it abruptly. He had in the meantime published "Tales of the Grotesque and Arabesque" (1839), which gave him renown as a prose writer. They were soon translated into French, and since that time Poe's popularity in France has exceeded that of any other American writer. After seven years of literary hackwork in Philadelphia, Poe went back to New York and carried on the struggle for existence there. He was associated with Willis and in 1845 became proprietor of "The Broadway Journal," in which he published "The Raven," the poem which established his fame. His wife died of consumption in 1847, and two years later he himself died mysteriously in a Baltimore hospital, while on his way to Richmond to be married a second time. He had developed signs strangely like insanity, and was picked up senseless in the streets of Baltimore.

There was certainly much in Poe's character and life to call for censure. He drifted from one friend or supporter to another, but never attached himself long to any one. His literary distinction was entirely due to his own genius, yet there was enough of charlatanry in his rodomontade to justify Lowell's sharp couplet:

> There comes Poe with his Raven, like Barnaby Rudge,
> Three-fifths of him genius and two-fifths sheer fudge.

In his "Essay on Composition" he declares that he composed "The Raven" on a strange, artificial principle, but this may be only an ironical hoax, somewhat on the order of his Hans Pfaal mystification. His theories on short poems and on the poetic art in general are often insincere, and yet his critical faculty was strong and his criticisms on his contemporaries were valuable, though not free from prejudice. His imagination was so powerful that it dominated his actual life, producing many prevarications and falsehoods, that still perplex his biographers. But in his literary work this active fancy produced most

remarkable tales, sometimes introducing curious mathematical problems, as in "The Gold Bug," sometimes supernatural incidents, as in "The Fall of the House of Usher,"
and sometimes strangely revolting features, as in "The
Murder in the Rue Morgue." It is hard to believe that
these grotesque and weird stories were the result of delib-
erate calculation of effects, as the author asserted of some
of them. Such combination of mathematical and imaginative powers is unknown elsewhere in all the range of
literature. It must be admitted that the stories are deficient in display of character, that the persons who act in
them are merely pieces in the game, and not really alive
and self-determined. So also it is evident that Poe had
no humor, and that his attempts at it are failures. In the
preface to his "Poems," Poe declares, "Poetry has been
with me not a purpose, but a passion," and though he elsewhere offers a mechanical explanation of his "Raven,"
the poems themselves prove his passion. They spring
from persons or incidents connected with his life, but they
rise into an ethereal region in which the original persons
are idealized and the simple facts are singularly metamorphosed. There is an exquisite fascination and enchanting
melody in his verse that seems beyond the reach of cal-
culating art.

NEW ENGLAND LITERATURE

In the early part of the Nineteenth Century there was in New England a mingled religious and philosophical ferment. There had been some reaction against the rigid Calvinism of the Puritans even before the Revolution, but it was not until Channing arose that Unitarianism took definite shape, and gave rise to a prolonged controversy. It was assisted by influences, direct and indirect, from Germany and France. From these in turn came the New England Transcendentalism, the experiment of the Brook Farm community, the Concord school of philosophy, the Cambridge group of scholars, wits, poets, and romancers, that brilliant era which justified Dr. Oliver Wendell Holmes in declaring Boston "the hub of the universe." It should not be a matter of surprise that New England's literary awakening was due to religious philosophy, for that was precisely the case with the German revival of the latter part of the Eighteenth Century, to which this American revival was much indebted. The philosophy of Kant, Fichte and Schelling found its way to New England as well as Old England and France, and in each country underwent modifications corresponding to its previous intellectual condition. But furthermore the thinkers and writers of Boston and Cambridge had a unique ancestry of ministers and scholars. As Emerson has phrased it, "Man is a quotation of all his ancestors." Emerson's own lineage is a striking illustration in point. Most of his male ancestors in direct line had been Congregational ministers in Eastern Massachusetts, and a maternal ancestor, Rev. Peter Bulkley, had been the first pastor of Concord. Nearly 50 per cent of Harvard's alumni became ministers and cultivated style in their discourses. Even the poets and prose-writers who succeeded this prophetic generation of pulpit orators, though they did not enter the same career, did turn to its kindred institution, the school or college. Amos Bronson Alcott, the patriarch of Concord philosophers, was a schoolmaster of the tribe satirized by Irving in Ichabod Crane. Margaret Fuller, who became Marchioness D'Ossoli, Lydia Maria Child, Mrs. Lydia H. Sigourney, and many more, were teachers.

CHANNING

Distinctive American literature has been said to have been born in "the era of good feeling" which characterized the peaceful administration of President Monroe (1817-1825) when, after the War of 1812, the fierce animosities of Federalists and Democrats had subsided. It owed much to the "beneficial influence of such a creator, critic and stimulating power as Channing." William Ellery Channing (1780-1842) was born at Newport, Rhode Island, graduated from Harvard, and was for a time a tutor in Richmond, Virginia. Chosen pastor of the Federal Street Church, Boston, in 1803, he held this position for the rest of his life. Though he never accepted the name Unitarian for himself, he really gave to the body so called the consciousness of its position. This was especially the result of his sermon preached at Baltimore in May, 1819, at the ordination of Jared Sparks, afterward noted for his American biographies. The controversy which ensued agitated all the churches of New England and gave impulse to later movements affecting literature and politics. Channing proclaimed the essential dignity of human nature, the fatherhood of God and the brotherhood of men. He was a man of intense spirituality, and purity of life, yet resolute in following what he believed to be truth. He became an authority on political and literary as well as religious questions. His essay on "The Character of Napoleon Bonaparte" attracted attention abroad, and one on "Milton" added to his reputation. His literary work was confined to sermons, addresses and essays, all carefully prepared, and beautiful with moral enthusiasm.

The literary organ of the new movement was the "North American Review," a quarterly established in May, 1815. It grew out of a scheme for a bi-monthly magazine by the Anthology Club, an association of young men of Boston and Cambridge, including George Ticknor, Edward Tyrrel Channing, John Quincy Adams, and Richard Henry Dana (1787-1879). Its first editor was William Tudor, and in its general scope it was modeled on the "Quarterly Review," of London. In its first number Dana criticized Hazlitt, and dared to praise Wordsworth. Dana was a melodious and graceful poet, but wrote comparatively little. Between 1815 and 1830 the "North American Review" was edited successively by Willard Phelps, Edward Everett and Jared Sparks. In 1817 it accepted and published the most famous poem—"Thanatopsis"—of William Cullen Bryant, then but a youth. In 1830 Alexander H. Everett became editor, and for the six years that he was in charge Longfellow, Prescott, Bancroft and other distinguished writers were among the contributors. Dr. John G. Palfrey was the next editor, and during his incumbency Ralph Waldo Emerson was a frequent contributor. James Russell Lowell and Charles Eliot Norton assumed control in 1864, and at that time its writers were the most eminent literary men in the country.

EVERETT

Edward Everett (1794-1865), Boston-born and Harvard-bred, returned in 1819 from Germany, where he had spent four years, two of them at Göttingen. He was a Unitarian preacher, and a sermon delivered by him in the House of Representatives at Washington in 1820, gave him a national reputation. In the pages of the "North American Review" Everett unloaded his treasures of German thought. More than a hundred articles came from his pen. In 1824 his address before the Phi Beta Kappa Society of Harvard on "The Circumstances Favorable to the Progress of Literature in America," was a prophetic precursor of Emerson's dissertation on "The American Scholar," delivered before the same society thirteen years later. Everett was noted for his high classical scholarship and for the careful finish of his prose style. But he was not merely a literary man; he was active in public affairs. He represented Boston in Congress for ten years, was Governor of Massachusetts for three years, United States Minister to England for four years, president of Harvard for three years, Secretary of State in President Fillmore's Cabinet for one year, and United States Senator for one year, when he resigned on account of impaired health. Yet afterward he delivered in various parts of the country an oration on Washington for the purpose of raising a fund to purchase Mount Vernon and preserve it intact as a national memorial. His final service was in delivering the oration at the dedication of the National Cemetery at Gettysburg in November, 1863. His speeches were polished to the perfection of classical oratory, and were full of admiring contemplation and thoughtful admonition. But owing to their lack of fervor and to the change in public taste, his fame, even as an orator, has been greatly diminished. During his life-time he was a model in eloquence and a controlling factor in literary criticism.

BROOK FARM

One of the most curious episodes in the history of American intellectual development is the Brook Farm community, which was founded in 1840, and lingered until 1847. It grew out of the Transcendental movement, in which Emerson was a leader. The first meeting of the Transcendentalists was held on September 19, 1836, at the house of Dr. George Ripley (1802-1880), a Harvard graduate and Unitarian preacher. The library in his house in Concord was rich in foreign literature, concerning which he issued a series of books. The organ of the Transcendentalists was "The Dial," a scholarly quarterly. Its teachings, combined with certain notions derived from the French Fourier, led Ripley to propose the experiment of Brook Farm, to be conducted by a semi-socialistic stock company near West Roxbury, Massachusetts. It was to combine agriculture, economical, Unitarian, humanitarian, and educational features. It was hoped that, while life could be supported by honest toil, a high ideal of social and intellectual entertainment might be achieved. Teaching, farming and the milking of cows were to be alternate occupations. Among these intellectual farmers were John Sullivan Dwight, the musical critic, and Charles Anderson Dana (1819-1897), afterward the noted editor. George William Curtis (1824-1896) and a brother, reported by those who knew him to be still more gifted, were pupils in the school. Dana, born in New Hampshire, had been prevented by weakness of sight from completing his course at Harvard, and edited the Brook Farm organ—"The Harbinger." He afterward served an apprenticeship under Horace Greeley on the "New York Tribune," became Assistant Secretary of War, and finally editor of the "New York Sun." Curtis, after travels in Egypt and Syria, became a member of the Tribune staff, published the "Howadji in Syria," an excellent travel-book, "Potiphar Papers," a social satire, and "Prue and I," a delicious series of meditations by a humble clerk, who philosophizes on New York life as he sees it in his daily promenades. Later Curtis had a severe experience, somewhat like Scott's, from a partnership in the publishing business, but finally worked his way clear of embarrassment. He gained a special fame by his "Editor's Easy Chair" in "Harper's Monthly." He was prominent in advocacy of Civil Service reform, and lived to witness it in successful operation.

Margaret Fuller (1810-1850) also joined the Brook Farm community, although she never exactly believed in it. She was regarded by all who came in contact with her as the most learned and highly gifted American woman. She was the daughter of a Congressman, and after his death supported herself as a teacher, conducted "The Dial," afterward became a literary critic of the "Tribune," and lived under Horace Greeley's roof. While on a tour in Europe she met and married Giovanni Angelo, Marquis D'Ossoli, settled in Rome, and entered zealously into the Italian struggle of 1849 for independence. After the capture of Rome by the French army, she sailed for America with her husband and child. The captain of the vessel died at the start of the voyage, smallpox broke out on the ship at sea, and a gale wrecked it off Fire Island beach. The Marquis and his family perished in the sea. The principal work of this remarkable but unfortunate genius was "Woman in the Nineteenth Century," which first appeared in "The Dial." Emerson, Julia Ward

Howe and Thomas W. Higginson have all written biographies of her. She is reflected in the Zenobia of Hawthorne's "Blithedale Romance," which is an idealized and distorted vision of the Brook Farm.

Hawthorne joined the Brook Farm community in 1841 but was not blind to its ridiculous aspects. Emerson, curiously practical as well as sublimely transcendental, stood aloof from it, and humorously called it "a French Revolution in small, an Age of Reason in a patty-pan." With all his idealism and semi-Brahmanism, he had a saving salt of Yankee common sense, that justifies Dr. Holmes' question:

> Where in the realm of thought, whose air is song,
> Does he, the Buddha of the West, belong?
> He seems a winged Franklin, sweetly wise,
> Born to unlock the secrets of the skies.

At Concord he was worshiped in Apollo's two-fold character, as poet and seer. Dr. Holmes again refers to him:

> "From his mild throng of worshipers released,
> Our Concord Delphi sends its chosen priest."

HAWTHORNE

To-day, foreigners probably consider Poe and Hawthorne to contain the most classical elements of any American writers, although they will admit Longfellow's cosmopolitanism, Lowell's scholarliness and Lowell's description of Emerson as "a Greek head on right Yankee shoulders." As Lowell himself declared:

> "There is Hawthorne, with genius so shrinking and rare
> That you hardly at first see the strength that is there;
> A frame so robust, with a nature so sweet,
> So earnest, so graceful, so solid, so fleet,
> Is worth a descent from Olympus to meet.

'Tis as if a rough oak that for ages had stood
With his gnarled bony branches like ribs of the wood,
Should bloom, after cycles of struggle and scathe,
With a single anemone trembly and rathe.
His strength is so tender, his mildness so meek,
That a suitable parallel sets one to seek,
He's a John Bunyan Fouqué, a Puritan Tieck."

Despite a certain delicate humor and playful fancy, which are revealed so beautifully in his "Tanglewood Tales," that feat of "Gothicising" the Greek myths (as he himself described it), he felt the gloomy spirit of Puritanism and became for all time its supreme romantic interpreter.

Nathaniel Hawthorne (1804-1864) was born in Salem, Massachusetts. This old seaport town appealed at the outset to his spirit of melancholy, and its witchcraft associations had a peculiar force for him; for one of his forefathers, Judge Hathorne (so the name was then spelled), had sentenced several of the "witches." Hawthorne himself was a graduate of Bowdoin College in the same class with Longfellow. He was shy and too lacking in self-assertion. As a collegian he served the usual apprenticeship to the Muse and after graduation in 1825 he became a recluse and book-worm, writing by day and night. In 1826 he published anonymously and at his own expense a novel entitled "Fanshawe" in which we can see to-day the real Hawthorne but in which his contemporaries saw nothing. "I passed the day," he afterward said of this time, "in writing stories, and the night in burning them." But some manuscripts, including several of the "Twicetold Tales," were sent to Samuel Goodrich, who published them in "The Token." Peter Parley introduced Hawthorne to literary hack-work as well. The first series of "Twicetold Tales" appeared in 1837 and was reviewed in the "North American" by Longfellow with enthusiasm. These half weird but felicitously told tales marked an epoch in American literature. They were followed by his delightful tales for children from "Grandfather's Chair," in which he first treated New England history. Meanwhile Bancroft, the historian, then collector of customs at Boston, appointed him a weigher and gauger, a place which the Whigs permitted him to retain but two years. He also embarked in the Arcadian Brook Farm experiment. "I went to live in Arcadia," he said, "and found myself up to my chin in a barnyard." Deserting Brook Farm he married and took the historic gambrel-roofed home at Concord, from whence issued the tales collected in the "Mosses from an Old Manse." His second series of "Twicetold Tales" with their Legends of the Province House, added a fresh romantic interest to Revolutionary Boston. Almost noiselessly his shy genius had made itself recognized as a new literary force. He returned to Salem for four years as Surveyor in its old Custom House. After leaving this berth, he gave forth his master work, "The Scarlet Letter," in the preface to which he has told the story of that old Salem institution (1850). Hawthorne afterward observed that "no author without a trial can see the difficulty of writing a romance about a country where there is no shadow, no antiquity, no mystery, no picturesque and gloomy wrong, nor anything but a commonplace prosperity in broad and simple daylight." Yet in "The Scarlet Letter" he had touched even the gloom of Puritanism with the glamour of romance, as well as achieved a world's masterpiece of psychology. He now retired to Lenox, Massachusetts, with Herman Melville, author of "Typee," as almost his sole companion, and wrote the "House of Seven Gables," in which with his peculiar mingling of mystery and melancholy he fairly invested the past-haunted house with a spiritual atmosphere. Hepzibah, sad relic of New England aristocracy, condemned to run a penny store, and stern Judge Pyncheon are masterly delineations of Rembrandt shadow and force. And yet he could turn from this somber tale to his charming "Wonder Book" and parable of the "Snow Image." In Hawthorne's genius there was a remarkable intermingling of delicacy and strength, grave sunshine and beautiful shadow. In the "Blithedale Romance" he figured forth the superb Zenobia, the placid Miles Coverdale, the sweet Priscilla with the same skill as the intensely self-concentrated Hollingsworth, blindly abandoning and ruining himself for a theory. In the "Dolliver Romance" he found theme for his plot in the idea of an elixir of life. In 1853 President Pierce, a life-long friend of Hawthorne, appointed him consul at Liverpool, England. Shortly before his term expired he resigned, and traveled on the continent. The record of his sojourn survives in his charming English, French and Italian Notebooks. In Italy he sketched the tale of "The Marble Faun," in which strange tale a young Italian bears the symbolical tell-tale ears of the Faun of Praxiteles. Here the author treated with the same fascination—despite its change of scene from New England to Italy—the old problem of moral guilt and of passion and sorrow.

LONGFELLOW

Henry Wadsworth Longfellow (1807-1882) had been Hawthorne's fellow collegian at Bowdoin College, became a professor in his Alma Mater and later in Harvard, whence, after some years of a professorial work, he retired and devoted himself to literature. His quality was decidedly academic, as befitted a son of Cambridge. Perhaps the first feature to be here noted concerning him is the influence which he had as a promoter of American culture, a service generally overshadowed by his immense popularity as a poet. In the respect noted he was a lineal successor to Irving, whom he also resembled in his equal treatment of foreign and native themes and legends alike. Such an academic influence as his, broadened and deepened by generous travel abroad to prepare him for his Harvard chair, was certainly needed in the decade after 1830. By his "Poets and Poetry of Europe" he familiarized Americans with the literature and lore of France, Germany, Italy, Spain, Scandinavia and even of old Anglo-Saxon days. His "Outre Mer," a book of travel, has kept a place for itself until to-day. When he came to write his Indian legend of "Hiawatha," his familiarity with the then little known literature of the Northland enabled him to borrow the curious meter, style of imagery, and treatment of the Finnish epic, "Kalevala." As a critic proper, Longfellow possessed more learning than Poe, but was less truly critical, nor had he the satire and penetration of Lowell. But it is as the great poet of sympathy, as America's most popular poet, that Longfellow must be chiefly considered and in the scope of this brief sketch it is impossible to give a systematic account of all his familiar poems. His poetical works include: "The Voices of the Night," "Ballads and other Poems," "Poems on Slavery," "The Spanish Student," "The Belfry of Bruges," "Evangeline," "The Golden Legend," "Hiawatha," "The Courtship of Miles Standish," "Tales of a Wayside Inn," "Flower de Luce," "Christus," "Three Books of Song," "Aftermath," "The Mask of Pandora," "Keramos." Longfellow's conspicuous note as a poet was from the heart and not the head. He touched his readers with such tender poems of common sentiment as "The

Reaper and the Flowers," "The Beleaguered City," "The
Old Clock on the Stairs," and the "Wreck of the Hesperus." He sang, too, like Whittier, inspiring songs of
labor such as "The Ropewalk" and the now hackneyed
"Village Blacksmith," personification of honest toil. He
idealized ambition in "Excelsior," and taught the lesson
of existence in "The Psalm of Life." His national hymn,
"The Ship of State," deserves rank as an achievement of
poetic allegory beside Schiller's "Song of the Bell." This
spiritual symbolism was also admirably attained in "Keramos, the Song of the Potter and His Wheel." Longfellow's mastery of poetic narrative was revealed particularly in the "Tales of a Wayside Inn," which range from
the charming story of "The Birds of Chillingworth"—
"those little feathered minstrels of the air"—to the noble
mediæval legend of "Robert of Sicily," who in his pride
is transformed into a poor court jester while an angel
takes his place for a reformatory spell upon the throne.
The same gift enabled him to treat at such elaborate length
his two notable American epics, "Evangeline," which
depicts the woes of the cruelly dispersed Arcadians in
Gabriel's long and futile pursuit of his wandering sweetheart, and "The Courtship of Miles Standish," which tells
how that sturdy but Cupid-fearing warrior sent John
Alden as his proxy to woo the fair Priscilla. Said Priscilla: "Why do you not speak for yourself, John?" and
the poem ends with the mild clerk and not the fierce warrior as its real hero. In "Hiawatha" he achieved the poetical apotheosis of the American Indian; not such a romantic idealization as that of Cooper's Uncas nor such a
heroic idealization as Simm's Yemassee Chieftain, Sanutee, but an idealization of the Indian's religious spirit,
his sense of the Grand Manitou, his feeling for the mystery and beauty of nature, and his appreciation of those

LONGFELLOW

HOLMES

LOWELL

WHITTIER

gifts of his native soil, as embodied in the myth of the birth of the maize. But perhaps Longfellow's best, ripest, most scholarly achievement in poetry was his translation of Dante's "Divina Commedia," published in 1867. How deeply he lingered throughout this long labor of love under the spell of the stern Florentine may be seen in those sonnets inspired by his work and effectively mirroring on their surface this "mediæval miracle of song." Longfellow's translation is in many respects, such as the metrical and onomatopoetic, superior to that of Doctor Carey.

Two tales in prose by him are "Kavanagh" and "Hyperion," the latter of which with its scenes laid in Europe, is an expression of the ideals of his heart. The serenity of his poetic work as a whole was reflected in his life and especially in his old age. As he himself said in his poem for the fiftieth anniversary of the graduation of his class, the beautiful "Morituri Salutamus:"

> ' And as the evening twilight fades away,
> The sky is filled with stars, invisible by day."

No figure in American literature has gathered unto itself such a wealth of affection as that given to him, and England herself paid her first tribute of memorial honor to an American writer by placing his bust in the Poets' Corner in Westminster Abbey.

LOWELL

Longfellow was succeeded in his professor's chair at Harvard by James Russell Lowell (1819-1888), also a son of Cambridge, a fine New England heritage, and a Harvard student. Lowell, while not entitled to Longfellow's rank as a poet, nor perhaps any more learned than he, was a greater critic and essayist, and may to-day be recognized as the representative of indigenous American culture in the sense that Matthew Arnold was the representative of that of England.   Lowell, who took a deep interest in American politics, was destined to be appointed by President Hayes to the Spanish Mission and to represent his country at the Court of St. James, and to receive the highest degrees from Oxford and Cambridge.   In his youth he was so active in the anti-slavery and other public agitations of the time that in his rollicking and brilliant "Fable for Critics" (1848)—an imperishable landmark of American literature—he satirized himself:

"And there is Lowell, who's striving Parnassus to climb,
With a whole bale of isms tied together with rhyme."

And in that very year he did, indeed, "make a drum of his shell," in his first series of the "Biglow Papers." These poems, prefaced by a delightful parody of old time New England pedantry and even of the new fangled Carlylese, established Lowell as the great typical Yankee wit. His creation of "Hosea Biglow," the Down East poet, full of homely humor, wit, satire, patriotism and idyllicism, is unique in literature.   How well Lowell could write a Yankee idyl he showed in his little poem, "Zekle Crep' up all Unbeknown."   These poems, written in true Down East dialect, with the twang of Down East character as well, were called forth in opposition and satire of the war spirit fomented by the slaveholders eager for new territory.   Lowell held up the contemptible buncombe politicians of the day to merciless ridicule in the figure of the Honorable John Doughface.   He made Congressman Robinson a national butt of laughter in those ludicrous lines:

"John P.
Robinson he
Says they didn't know everything down in Judee."

In the second series he tuned his Down East lyre to the new Northern patriotism, writing Yankee lyrics of the Civil War.

Lowell originally studied for and was admitted to the bar, but the only record of his practice is found in his little story entitled "My First Client." His first volume of poems inspired by his love for her who became his wife appeared in 1841 under the title of "A Year's Life." His earlier "Biglow Papers" were given to the public in the columns of the "Boston Courier" anonymously and edited with its playful learned introduction, notes, glossary, index and "notices of an independent press" by "Homer Wilbur, A. M., Pastor of the First Church in Jaalam, and prospective member of many literary, learned and scientific societies." Before this satire on the Mexican War, slavery and political cant, Lowell had written his exquisite vision of "Sir Launfal," a poem founded on the legend of the Holy Grail, and composed rapidly. Two of his most successful small poems of this time were "The Crisis" and "The First Snowfall." When the Kansas struggle (1856-58) enlisted his sympathies he actually contemplated sending his Hosea Biglow to that "dark and bloody ground" to report in vernacular, but Hosea had to wait for the Civil War. Of all his poems the one most praised for its loftiness and beauty is "The Cathedral." In this poem, despite one unhappy lapse from dignity, Lowell sought to catch that spirit of new-born greatness and sense of human destiny—

"Missed in the commonplace of miracle."

Equally noble is his superb "Ode recited at the Commemoration of the Living and Dead Soldiers of Harvard University, July 21, 1865." This "Commemoration Ode" not only contains a magnificent eulogy of the martyred Abraham Lincoln as the great typical American, but it seeks to give a splendid apotheosis of her whom he apostrophized in the lines—

"Who cometh over the hills,
Her garments with morning sweet,
The dance of a thousand rills
Making music before her feet?
Tis Liberty, fairest of all the daughters of Time and of Thought."

Lowell was not as popular as Longfellow, but his best lines contain that "beauty's acme" described by him as "The wave's poise before it break and curl."

It is, however, chiefly as critic and essayist that he is best known to-day. In his three books of literary criticism and fancy, "Fireside Travels," "Among My Books," "My Study Windows," he proved himself to be America's most scholarly critic. The old English authors Chaucer, Spenser, the dramatists of Elizabeth's reign, attracted his attention particularly. But his catholicity of taste was also accompanied by a catholicity of subjects. In "My Garden Acquaintance," and "A Good Word for Winter," he displayed notable graces of style, and his paper "On a Certain Condescension in Foreigners," was a capital "retort courteous" to the woes inflicted upon America by foreign critics, and continues to be a compensating solace even to this day.

EMERSON

The most potent force in New England thought was Ralph Waldo Emerson (1803-1882). For more than two centuries his ancestors were Congregational ministers. His father, Rev. William Emerson, died in 1811, and his mother was assisted by relatives in providing for her sons' education. William, the elder, went to Germany, and being unsettled in faith, gave up the intention of entering the ministry, and became a lawyer. Waldo studied divinity with Channing and Andrews Norton, and began to preach in 1827. He became assistant to Rev. Henry Ware in the Second Church of Boston, and soon had entire charge. At the end of 1832, being unwilling to dispense the Lord's Supper, he resigned the pastorate. His wife had died in that year, and he resolved to go to Europe. He went to Italy and France, then to England, and found his way to Carlyle's remote humble home at Craigenputtock. The two great thinkers formed a notable friendship which was maintained by correspondence through their lives. Emerson married Lilian Jackson in 1835 and went to live in Concord. He had inherited a modest competence, but later his chief support was derived from lecturing before lyceums, as he continued to do for forty-six years. His first book, "Nature," published in 1836, set forth his transcendental views of man and the universe, in several chapters with little apparent connection. In 1837 his address on "The American Scholar" proved that thoughtful minds were attracted by the new force. His Divinity School address in 1838 on "The Christian Teacher" deeply stirred the Unitarian body and called forth a warm protest from his teacher, Professor Norton, against its radical views. In the controversy which ensued Emerson declined to take part, though his friends

were active. The first series of his "Essays" appeared
in 1841, and met with favor, both at home and abroad.
They enlarged and extended ideas which had been stated
in "Nature." Emerson smiled approval on the Brook
Farm experiment, but took little part in it except to contribute to "The Dial." But he did assist with voice and
pen in the anti-slavery agitation. In 1847 he went on a
second visit to England, which was rich in observation
and effect on his mind. After his return his lectures on
Plato, Shakespeare, Napoleon, Swedenborg, and others,
were published under the title, "Representative Men"
(1850). This proved popular, and still more so was his
"English Traits" (1856). More readers could appreciate
his judgment of great men and nations than could understand his sublime philosophy of the universe.

Emerson had but rarely contributed to periodical literature, but in 1857 a group of his friends—Longfellow,
Lowell, Holmes—arranged in his parlor for the publication of "The Atlantic Monthly," Lowell being editor. For
some years Emerson contributed to it regularly prose and
verse. His essays were collected in "The Conduct of Life"
(1860), "Society and Solitude" (1864), and "Letters and
Social Aims" (1876); his poems in "May-Day" (1867).
He edited a collection of poetry by other authors in "Parnassus" (1874), and a selection of his own "Poems"
(1876). Thereafter he wrote but little, though he revised
and edited his former publications. The projected
"Natural History of the Intellect," on which he had
labored for many years, was never put into a form suitable for publication. In the latter years of his life his
mind and memory failed. After his death his correspondence with Carlyle was edited by Professor Charles Eliot
Norton (1883).

Matthew Arnold shocked his Boston audience when in

1888 he deliberately pronounced Emerson not essentially a poet nor a philosopher, but a seer. Yet in the dozen years which have since elapsed it has been frequently admitted that the critic was substantially right. Emerson himself had said, "I am not a great poet, but whatever there is of me at all is poet." Yet he was aware of his want of facility in metrical expression, and that his poetic faculty was seldom under the control of his will. A single small volume contains all his poetic work. Even in his poetry, though there are often charming lines and melodious passages, the utterances are generally oracular and sometimes enigmatic. When he sang of love, for instance, he was not content to celebrate its rapture, but must elevate it into a divine sentiment and make it a world-mystery.

No more in philosophy than in any other department can Emerson be said to have had a system, but he had intuitions of truth. These are shown in his first book, "Nature," and restated, reinforced, applied and sometimes made clearer in his later essays. He held a lofty idealism or poetic pantheism, such as that of Wordsworth, but was more consistent in applying it than the English poet. Nature or the external world corresponds to the human soul. Nature is the embodiment of God's infinite ideas and is the symbol of the soul. When nature and the soul are brought into proper relations to each other, the highest powers of man will be awakened, and he will behold God. To this rapt state all men are capable of attaining. The idea of nature as a Divine incarnation involved an optimistic view of the universe; it also made natural and spiritual laws identical, and thus gave a religious aspect to everything. To this high ethical conclusion Emerson remained true throughout life and exemplified it in every action. But he did not engage in any strife with others. He avoided all controversy. Having delivered his oracle,

he left it to others to interpret and apply it for themselves.
He was a teacher rather than a leader.   And yet so convincing were his statements that many arose to do as he
had said.   Dr. Holmes declared that his address on "The
American Scholar" was "an intellectual Declaration of
Independence," and Lowell said: "We were socially and
intellectually moored to English thought till Emerson cut
the cable and gave us a chance at the dangers and glories
of blue water."   "The Conduct of Life" has had wide-
reaching effect by giving practical lessons to the young,
and directing them to noble aims.   Like all his other writings it insisted on self-reliance and intense individualism.
His greatest service to his countrymen is to have taught
and exemplified a marked American type of thought and
feeling, not materialistic, but grandly spiritual.

Horace   Bushnell   (1802-1876),   influenced   by   the
teaching of Coleridge, introduced liberal views into
Puritan theology and rendered important service to Christian thought.   He was born at Litchfield, Connecticut,
graduated at Yale College, and in 1833 became pastor of a
Congregational church in Hartford.   After twenty years'
service he resigned on account of ill-health, yet lived and
worked nearly a quarter of a century longer.   His first
publication, "Christian Nurture," insisted on a truly
natural training of children as inheritors of Christianity.
His "Nature and the Supernatural" was an effort to show
the harmony in God's relation to the universe.   "The
Vicarious Sacrifice" was a new explanation of a theological problem, making Christ's sacrifice the measure of
God's love and not his wrath.   "Work and Play," an
oration before the Phi Beta Kappa Society of Harvard in
1848, explained that the highest aim of life is to get free
from the constraint of work and rise to that natural action

of the faculties which may be called play, and that poetry
is the ideal, yet true, state of man's soul. His "Moral Uses
of Dark Things" is a vindication of the Divine government of the world. Bushnell's spiritual interpretation of
nature had profound effect upon the orthodox pulpit, setting it free from the rigid bonds which cramped its
thought.

WHITTIER

John Greenleaf Whittier (1807-1892), born at Haverhill, Massachusetts, was not only the chief Quaker poet,
but the clearest voice of New England country life. Bred
on a farm, he found his first poetic inspiration in reading
the poems of the inspired Scotch ploughman, Robert
Burns. At the age of twenty he had earned enough by farm
chores and shoe-making to secure some instruction at
Haverhill Academy, and then became a district school
teacher. He contributed verse to the "Free Press," and
found a lasting friend in the editor, William Lloyd Gar-
rison, who enlisted him in the anti-slavery crusade. In
1835 Whittier was a member of the Massachusetts Legislature. From 1837 to 1839 he edited the "Pennsylvania
Freeman," at Philadelphia, where his office was sacked
and burnt by a mob. His delicate health obliged him to
return to Amesbury, Massachusetts, where with his sister,
he led a frugal life, contributing chiefly to the "National
Era," published in Washington. Gradually his books of
poems made their way, and when the struggle for Kansas
came, in 1856, he was recognized as the poet of freedom.
These militant poems of a peace-loving Quaker helped to
prepare the Northern people for the Civil War. When the
"Atlantic Monthly" was founded Whittier was a frequent
contributor. His verse celebrated there the emancipation
of the slaves, but in his ballad of "Barbara Frietchie," he

told effectively the story of the old woman of Frederick, Maryland, who waved the Union flag over the troops of Stonewall Jackson, and was gallantly spared by him. This tribute to Northern loyalty and Southern chivalry has become a national classic. In some of his New England poems Whittier told of the persecution of the early Quakers, in others he simply exhibited the homely features of farming life. His "Songs of Labor" appealed to the multitude as combined for general welfare. He revived the legends of his neighborhood. Especially famous is his "Skipper Ireson's Ride," the story of a skipper who, for his neglect to rescue a perishing crew, was tarred and feathered and carried in a cart by the women of Marblehead. And yet more famous is the simple ballad of "Maud Muller" and its dreams of what might have been. The "Tent on the Beach" is an idyl of summer life by the sea, in which Bayard Taylor and James T. Fields listen to a group of tales told by the poet. "Snow-Bound" is the poet's masterpiece, telling of a New England family shut in by a snow-storm for three days. The family was that of the poet's father. After the death of his sister in 1864, his niece took charge of his house till her marriage, then for twenty years he lived alone. Whittier became the most popular American poet, next to Longfellow. This is due to the simple dignity of his character, the homeliness and universal interest of his themes. His anti-slavery lyrics are forgotten, but his pictures of New England life are treasured in the heart.

HOLMES

Dr. Oliver Wendell Holmes (1809-1894), who was the last survivor of the famous galaxy of Cambridge poets, was the cheerful embodiment of the spirit of Unitarian

New Englandism. He was the son of Rev. Abiel Holmes, a Harvard pastor, who wrote "The Annals of America." Having graduated from Harvard in 1829, he studied law and medicine, and spent three years in Europe. He was but twenty-one years old when he made his famous protest, "Old Ironsides," which saved the frigate Constitution from destruction, and not much older when in "The Last Leaf" he combined humor with the deepest pathos. Holmes was professor of medicine at Dartmouth College for a year, but settled in Boston in 1840, and seven years later was made professor at Harvard. Besides lecturing there and on the lyceum platform, he wrote patriotic and entertaining poems for occasions and became the laureate of his Alma Mater, inditing forty poems in her honor. One of these, "The Boys," is the jolliest class poem ever written. Holmes was also the bard of Boston, whose State House he pronounced to be "the hub of our solar system." But his lasting fame was due to the founding of the "Atlantic Monthly" in 1857. Lowell took the editorship only when assured that Holmes would be a regular contributor. The contribution came in a form of a serial, "The Autocrat of the Breakfast Table." When but twenty years of age, Holmes had written for a college magazine two short papers of a similar kind, and at forty-eight he began the new version with the words "As I was saying when interrupted." Then followed a long monologue addressed to some typical New England characters assembled at the table of a boarding house. It consisted of philosophical reflections on things great and small, with occasional "asides" and parenthetical stage directions. Nearly every number contained a poem, graceful, brilliant, or humorous, as suited the Autocrat's whim. Altogether the series was a quaint and happy mingling of wit and good sense, humor and pathos, worldly shrewdness and heavenly aspirations. Among the poems were the comical logical story of "The Deacon's Masterpiece, or the Wonderful One-Hoss Shay," which ran a hundred years to a day, and the mathematical story of "Parson Turell's Legacy," the story of the Harvard President's arm-chair. But the loftiest utterance among the lay sermons of the Autocrat was his own favorite, "The Chambered Nautilus."

At last the ever-grateful monthly series was brought to an end when the Autocrat invited the quiet, sensible school-mistress to take the long path with him. Yet it was renewed, though not with the full vivacity, in "The Professor" (1859) and "The Poet at the Breakfast Table" (1873). Between these came some novels, in which he developed certain physiological theories to account for morbid characters. Thus in "Elsie Venner" the heroine has certain qualities of a snake, the origin of which the story serves to explain. In "The Guardian Angel," the eccentricities of a young lady are similarly explained by heredity. In later years Dr. Holmes wrote pleasant biographies of his friends Motley and Emerson. In 1884 he published "Our Hundred Days in Europe," telling of his observations there fifty years after his first visit. Then in his eightieth year the veteran renewed his conversational contributions to the "Atlantic" in a series called "Over the Tea-Cups," full of the same shrewd sense and tender sentiment as "The Autocrat." He lived to be a "Last Leaf," yet without losing his geniality and optimism, preserving to the last the fresh spirit of youth.

Holmes was small in person, but quick and lively in speech and movement. He belonged to what he called "the Brahmin caste of New England." He was a physician, and his medical studies afforded him both illustrations and theories which appeared in his literary works. Curtis has said: "The rollicking laugh of Knickerbocker was a solitary sound in the American ear till the blithe carol of Holmes returned a kindred echo." Holmes loved the approbation of his fellow-men, and spoke not unkindly of the Boston group as a Mutual Admiration Society. Yet his sturdy independence was shown both in literature and science. His epigrams were often keen thrusts at swollen pretensions; but his best sayings were pithy expressions of general facts of human nature, readily accepted when stated. He penetrated deeply into the character and motives of men, and expressed the result of his research so vividly that all acknowledged its truth. It was his desire, if his name was to live, to have it live in people's hearts rather than in their brains, and his wish has been amply gratified. His wit was never irreverent. His strong religious feeling is shown in many hymns.

The first American writer to devote himself chiefly to literary criticism was Edwin Percy Whipple (1819-1886). Born at Gloucester, Massachusetts, he lived chiefly in Boston, where for over twenty years he was superintendent of the reading room of the Merchants' Exchange. His ability as a critic was first displayed in an able article on Macaulay in 1843. He lectured as well as wrote on his favorite topics. Among his best books are "Literature and Life" (1849), "Character and Characteristic Men" (1866), "Literature of the Age of Elizabeth" (1869), "Success and Its Conditions" (1871), and the posthumous "American Literature" (1887). He was equally familiar with European literature, and exhibited careful judgment in weighing the merits of modern writers and public men not less than the accepted classics. He discussed political and historical questions as well as literature. His penetrating insight was well matched by his humor and eloquence.

Connecticut produced some poets of merit, but of less power than the Massachusetts group. John Pierpont (1785-1866), who graduated at Yale in 1804, after being a teacher, lawyer, merchant, and became a Unitarian preacher in Boston, Troy, and Medford. At the age of seventy-six he was made chaplain of a Massachusetts regiment, but soon exchanged the position for a clerkship in the Treasury at Washington. His "Airs of Palestine and Other Poems" (1816) was intended to show the power of music, combined with local scenery and national character in Palestine and other countries. Most of his other poems were written for special occasions. James Gates Percival (1795-1856), who graduated at Yale in 1815, was an army surgeon, geologist and able linguist. He edited several learned works, assisted in revising "Webster's Dictionary," and made geological surveys of Connecticut and Wisconsin. Throughout his career he published poems, which were finally collected in 1859. His poetry is scholarly and meditative, rather than popular.

THE EARLY AMERICAN HISTORIANS.

In the beginning of the Nineteenth Century a new view of history was developed, as an outgrowth of the Transcendental philosophy inaugurated by the German Kant, and carried out more fully by his successors. History was no longer regarded as a gathering of isolated arbitrary facts, but as the study of the progress of mankind. National history could not be properly considered apart from its relation to the general movement. Each Nation was an actor in a great world's drama. Its contribution was best understood when properly presented in its true connection.

GEORGE BANCROFT

Bancroft was educated in Germany when this new view was introduced and emphasized. His first work was a translation of Heeren's "History of the Political System of Europe" (1828). By such training he was peculiarly fitted to present to the world the significance and importance of the great experiment of democratic government in the New World. For sixty years he continued to labor on his self-appointed task, enlightening his countrymen in regard to the work and intentions of their fathers, and erecting for himself an imperishable literary monument.

George Bancroft was born at Worcester, Massachusetts, in 1800, and died at Washington in 1891. He was the son of a Unitarian minister, was educated at Harvard, and afterward at Göttingen, Germany, where he received the degree of Ph. D. Returning to Massachusetts he founded the Round Hill School at Northampton, to put in practice the best methods of German instruction. But his ambition was to set forth clearly, adequately, and in full detail the foundations of his country's greatness. The first volume of his "History of the United States" appeared in 1834. It started from the discovery of America in 1492, and when completed, in 1888, the work was brought down only to the inauguration of Washington. Colonial History coming down to 1748, occupied about one-fourth. The overthrow of the European colonial system and the American Revolution occupied more than one-half. The remainder, which was issued as a separate work, treated of the formation of the Federal Constitution.

Bancroft's labors on this work were interrupted by his political services to his country. He was an ardent Democrat and was made Collector of the Port of Boston in 1838. When called by President Polk to his cabinet, as Secretary of the Navy, in 1845, Bancroft founded the Naval Academy at Annapolis. He also, in anticipation of the Mexican War, issued orders which helped to secure possession of California. In 1846 he was sent as Minister to England. Returning three years later, he fixed his residence in New York and devoted his time to the history, but occasionally ventured in other fields. During the Civil War he was a firm friend of the Union, and after its close he was sent by President Johnson as Minister to Germany, where he remained until 1874. His later residence was at Washington, though his summers were spent at Newport, where his rose-garden was celebrated.

His great history was the result of conscientious research, careful consideration of authorities, and enthusiasm for the subject. Its style is brilliant, though in the early volumes sometimes discursive and declamatory. There is a tendency to philosophize, to bring forward too

prominently, the underlying principle of the facts recorded. While desirous to give just due to every actor in
public affairs of the time treated, Bancroft offended the
descendants of some, and evoked controversies, which
were humorously called "the war of grandfathers." Overwhelming evidence was required to convince him that he
had been mistaken in his attempt to render the final verdict
of truth. He was slow in composition, and revised the
chapters of his work repeatedly before they were published.
The later editions show still further correction. Probably the best part of his work is the last, written after
the Civil War and the discussion of questions of reconstruction had shed new light on the fundamental principles
of the Union and the Constitution. Though the author
had not historical genius of the highest order, he was
eminently well fitted for his task by a liberal education, by
his capability and disposition to take pains, and by his
judicial insight, which was only occasionally distorted by
partisan bias. Perhaps improperly called the "History
of the United States," the work in its utmost extent tells
only the story of the foundation of the Nation, but it does
point out the sources of its greatness, and sets forth the
virtues of democratic government in a vehement oratorical
way, which rather provokes than disarms criticism. Yet
the whole work, showing at first the exuberant enthusiasm
of youth, and finally the cautious wisdom of age, is a grand
epic of democracy.

HILDRETH

In marked contrast with Bancroft's eloquent declamatory narrative stands Richard Hildreth's "History of the
United States." It is dry in style, judicial in tone, never
aiming at brilliance or entertainment. The author declared his object to be "to set forth the personages of our

Colonial and Revolutionary history such as they really were, . . . their faults as well as their virtues." Three volumes brought the history down from the discovery of America to the adoption of the Constitution. Three more, which surpass the former in interest, carry it on to the year 1821. The author, who had projected his work while a college student, evidently desired to correct the partisan bias manifested in Bancroft's work, and for this purpose it is valuable, though it can never become popular.

Richard Hildreth was born at Deerfield, Massachusetts, in 1807. He graduated from Harvard in 1826, studied law, but after some practice in Boston, became editor of the "Boston Atlas." He was opposed to slavery, and wrote a novel, "Archy Moore" (1837), which was afterward republished under the title, "The White Slave." Another volume, "Despotism in America" (1840), treated of the political, economical and social aspects of slavery. For three years he resided in British Guiana, and there wrote his "Theory of Morals" (1844), and "Theory of Politics," which was not published until 1853. Meantime he had removed to New York and began to publish his History. He was connected with the "New York Tribune." In 1861 he was appointed Consul at Trieste, but when his health failed, he resigned and removed to Florence, where he died in 1865.

Though Hildreth aimed to be impartial, and by his calm, judicial tone, gives that impression, his interest in the politics of the day governed his treatment of men of the past and made him in some cases unjust. Yet in the main his views of the founders of our Government are eminently correct.

PRESCOTT

William Hickling Prescott was not a profoundly philosophical historian, yet he became the most brilliant and famous of our historical writers. This was owing to his judicious selection of romantic themes, in which the American people felt an interest, as belonging to the New World, to his artistic arrangement of the events, and to his captivating style. His works are all the more remarkable because of the serious disadvantages under which he labored. Prescott was born at Salem, Massachusetts, in 1796, grandson of the Captain Prescott who commanded at Bunker Hill. He was educated at Harvard College, from which he graduated with honors in 1814. While a junior in his seventeenth year he was struck in the left eye with a piece of bread thrown in sport by a fellow-student. The sight of that eye was destroyed, and, after his graduation, the right eye was attacked with inflammation, so that it was feared he would lose his sight totally. The sight, however, improved after he had taken a European tour, but for the rest of his life he was practically blind, and subject to frequent inflammatory attacks. Yet undismayed by this grievous affliction, Prescott, who was wealthy, set himself at the age of twenty-six, resolutely to work on a grand historical undertaking. He sought to present for the first time in English an adequate account of Ferdinand and Isabella, who laid the foundation of Spain's greatness. His life was arranged according to an exact programme; his work was performed with the aid of amanuenses and secretaries, and he used a mechanical contrivance for writing. His library was supplied with documents from the archives of Europe. His practice was to have the authorities read to him, then to make a careful mental digest of the material, dividing it into appropriate chapters, and then to shape his thoughts in literary form before the final dictation of writing.

The first installment of Prescott's life-work appeared in 1837, having cost him more than ten years' assiduous labor. It was the "History of Ferdinand and Isabella," printed at his own expense. The romantic nature of the subject, enhanced by the author's dignified yet charming style, gave it a popularity which it has retained to the present day. It was soon translated into several European languages, and caused the author to be ranked the foremost of American historians. In 1843 appeared the "Conquest of Mexico," which had an unparalleled reception, both from the general public and from the highest authorities. It won special praise from Wilhelm von Humboldt, who had visited that country. Four years later the "Conquest of Peru" was published. In 1850 Prescott, who had suffered domestic affliction, went abroad, visiting England and the Continent, and everywhere was received with the highest honor. He never visited the scenes of his histories. On his return he undertook the "History of Philip II," which, unfortunately, he did not live to complete; two volumes appeared in 1855 and a third in 1856. In the latter year his continuation of Robertson's "History of Charles V." was issued. He published also a volume of "Miscellanies," chiefly essays contributed to the "North American Review." Prescott died at Boston in 1859. His life was written by his friend, George Ticknor, the historian of Spanish literature.

As an historian Prescott excels in vigorous and picturesque narrative. His work was based on a thorough study of the original documents, so far as this could be effected by one who depended on the sight of others. Yet there can be no doubt about Prescott's broad and catholic scholarship, his carefulness in selecting facts, and the glowing style, which gives to his history the interest of romance. Prescott criticized his own work and admitted that his style might seem too studied. His rule was to alternate long and short sentences in order to produce harmony. Yet his chief object was to put liveliness into the narrative, believing that if the sentiment was lively and forcible, the reader would be carried along without much heed to the arrangement of periods. Emerson praised Prescott in comparison with other historians for rendering his work of such absorbing interest to his readers, for making them feel its reality, while the others make battles, sieges and fortunes only words. In later years there has been criticism on the value of the authorities which he exhibited so liberally in footnotes, especially in his "Mexico" and "Peru." It must be said in his defense that he used cautiously the evidence of the actors in the events he related. They may have misunderstood what they saw, interpreting it according to European notions of the time. Prescott had not the means of correcting their errors which archæological investigation has since furnished. John Fiske and some English writers have retold the story of the Spanish Conquest of America.

MOTLEY

John Lothrop Motley was a man of high scholarship and varied attainments, but was late in concentrating his labor on the historical work which was to give him fame. He was born at Dorchester, (now part of Boston) Massachusetts, in 1814. He was partly of New England Puritan descent, and partly Scotch-Irish. He was educated at Bancroft's Round Hill School and at Harvard College; after his graduation he went to Germany and studied at Göttingen and Berlin, forming a memorable student-friendship with Bismarck. On his return to Boston he studied law. His first book, "Morton's Hope" (1839), a novel of Revolutionary times, was unsuccessful, but his second, "Merry Mount" (1849), a story of the founding of Boston, had greater favor. Meantime he had contributed some historical articles to the "North American Review," and had determined to write a work on the revolt of the Netherlands from Spain in the Sixteenth Century, and was encouraged in his undertaking by Prescott. Finding it essential to his purpose to consult the European archives, he went abroad in 1851. So great was the labor that his "Rise of the Dutch Republic" did not appear until five years later. But it immediately won fame by its impetuous, graphic style, its enthusiastic love of liberty, its masterly exposure of Spanish misrule, tyranny, and religious persecution under Philip II and the Duke of Alva. The great hero of the work is William the Silent, and in the portrayal of this great statesman and others on both sides of the struggle, the ability of the author was finely displayed. The whole work was characterized by vivid description and dramatic force. After a year's interval, spent in travel, Motley continued his historical labors, and published in 1860 the "History of the United Netherlands," which was marked by the same general character as the former work. While the great hero was missing, the scene was greatly enlarged, and much attention was given to English and French affairs. It was an inspiring recital of the story of a brave little nation conquering for itself a place in the world's affairs.

When the American Civil War broke out, Motley wrote to the London "Times" an elaborate letter explaining the cause of the war and the nature of the Union, which was misunderstood in Europe. He was appointed by President Lincoln Minister to Austria, where he still exerted himself in behalf of his country's interests. The concluding volumes of his "History of the United Netherlands" were also issued, bringing the narrative down to 1609. Motley resigned his ministerial position in 1867, owing to some complaint by an American traveler, which should have been disregarded. President Grant sent Motley as minister to Great Britain in 1869 at the request of Senator Sumner, but afterward, when the President and Senator quarreled, recalled him. Motley was deeply hurt and never recovered from the effects of the blow. In 1874 he published "The Life and Death of John of Barneveld," a continuation of his history, giving a view of the primary causes of the Thirty Years' War. Motley had hoped to bring his narrative down at least to the peace of Westphalia in 1648, but his health failed, and he died near Dorchester, England, May 29, 1877.

It cannot be denied that Motley wrote his histories as a partisan, as an enthusiastic, eloquent advocate of the great cause of liberty. Nowhere could he have found a more inspiring theme than in the uprising of a gallant and determined people, with few natural resources, against the crushing, bloody despotism of Spain, enriched with the spoils of two worlds. But the method of historical writing has been changed and in treatment of great movements perfect objectivity is now insisted on. Yet Motley's works retain their high mark and popularity, owing to their thorough research and splendid delineation of an important period in the progress of humanity. Froude, who is the English historian most akin to Motley in spirit and manner, pronounced his first work "as complete as industry and genius can make it."

PARKMAN

Another historian, who, like Prescott, labored under the affliction of partial blindness, and yet achieved memorable results, was Francis Parkman. Descended from the earliest settlers of Massachusetts, he was born in Boston in 1823 and was educated at Harvard College. He studied law, but he had already determined to devote his life to an adequate presentation of the great conflict between the French and English for the possession of North America. In order to understand the background of the subject fully, he resolved to examine the manners and customs of Indians as yet unaffected by contact with the whites. For this purpose in 1846 he explored the wilderness toward the Rocky Mountains and lived for several weeks among the Dakota Indians in that region then just becoming known. Although previously strong and fond of exercise, the privations which he endured rendered him an invalid for life. The immediate results of his observations and experiences were given in his picturesque book called "The Oregon Trail" (1849). The next was "The Conspiracy of Pontiac" (1851); chronologically it treated of a later episode of his historical series, called as a whole, "France and England in the New World." This series comprised "The Pioneers of France in the New World" (1865); "The Jesuits in North America" (1867); "La Salle and the Discovery of the Great West" (1869); "The Old Régime in Canada" (1874); "Count Frontenac and New France under Louis XIV" (1877); "Montcalm and Wolfe" (1884), which was issued in advance of the one chronologically preceding it; "A Half-Century of Conflict" (1892). Parkman paid several visits to France to examine the archives. He gave considerable attention to horticulture, and for a time taught that branch

in the Agricultural School of Harvard. He published also
"The Book of Roses" (1866). Ten years earlier he had
published his only novel, "Vassall Morton." He died in
1893, having completed his main work, though his ill
health had seemed likely to prevent its consummation.

It is an evidence of Parkman's genius that he observed
and selected a grand historical subject, practically unex-
plored, though the material was rich and accessible. The
real grandeur of his subject can only be estimated by considering that it was not merely a story of exploration and
colonization of a vast wilderness, but an important part
of a conflict which extended over the world in the Eighteenth Century. This was the great question at issue, Was
France or England to become the foremost factor in ruling and civilizing the outlying world? The outcome of
the struggle for Canada decided that England was to be
supreme in the empire of the world. Parkman not only
possessed rare insight into the causes and effects of large
events; he was also an excellent judge of character, and
treated all the actors in the great drama with which he
was concerned, whether French, English or Indians, with
even and exact justice. His personal reputation is
enhanced by the fact that his arduous and delicate work
was done fairly and impartially in spite of the physical ills
which steadily beset him. His history is a permanent
monument reflecting credit on himself and on New England.

MRS. STOWE

It was given to a New England woman to write the
most widely circulated book of the Century, one which
had even greater political effect than literary power.
"Uncle Tom's Cabin" excited both in North and South

that impassioned feeling which culminated in bloody strife
and did not cease till slavery was abolished.   Yet the book
was written by a woman who had never been in the slave
States, though she had lived on the border and had learned
much of the working of the slave system from fugitive
negroes and from newspapers.   Her strong imagination,
humanitarian sentiment and reforming spirit had supplied
whatever was necessary to make the fiction more powerful than fact in overthrowing an institution protected by
legal and constitutional bulwarks.

Harriet Beecher Stowe was the daughter of Rev.
Lyman Beecher, the leading orthodox Calvinistic minister
of his time.   Her brother, Henry Ward Beecher, became
even more noted in his time, being as active in the political strife as in the theological field.   Other brothers and
sisters were prominent in Church and educational matters.   Harriet was born at Litchfield, Connecticut, in
1811, and grew up in a strongly religious atmosphere.
She was a pupil and afterward teacher in her sister Catherine's school.   In 1832 the Beecher family removed to
Cincinnati, and there Harriet was married to Prof. Calvin
E. Stowe, of Lane Theological Seminary.   Her first book
was "The Mayflower" (1849), slight sketches of New
England life.   Professor Stowe was called to Bowdoin College, at Brunswick, Maine, and there his wife wrote
"Uncle Tom's Cabin, or Life Among the Lowly."   It
appeared first in the "National Era," an anti-slavery
paper published at Washington, but excited no sensation
until it came out in book form in 1852.   When its revelations of slavery were called in question, Mrs. Stowe
published a "Key to Uncle Tom's Cabin," containing
extracts from Southern newspapers and other testimony
in vindication of the truth of incidents in her story.   As
that book had shown the working of slavery in Kentucky

and Louisiana, she went on to describe the system in Virginia in "Dred, a Tale of the Dismal Swamp." Being raised to affluence by the income from her books she went to Europe, where she was received with high honor. In 1864 the family removed to Hartford, Connecticut, where she kept her residence until her death in 1896. She made several visits to Europe and for many years spent her winters in Florida. After the Civil War Mrs. Stowe wrote several tales of New England life, including "The Minister's Wooing," "The Pearl of Orr's Island," "Oldtown Folks," "Poganuc People." In these appeared a new development of the Puritan spirit, turning away from the logical discussion and devoting itself to the cultivation of kindness and immediate social duty. Sam Lawson, a shrewd, talkative Yankee, was made responsible for several stories. In "My Wife and I" and other tales, Mrs. Stowe undertook to teach young married people the proper way of living. But while these didactic stories were attractive to a large class, they never reached the wide popularity of her anti-slavery novels.

NEW YORK AUTHORS

The growing commercial and political importance of New York, its increase of wealth, and the enterprise of its publishers, both of books and periodicals, tended to make it a literary center before the close of the first half-century. Among the writers drawn thither were some who had been connected with Brook Farm, including Dr. George Ripley (1802-1880), who had first suggested that experiment. Ripley became literary critic of the "New York Tribune," which had been founded by Horace Greeley (1811-1872). Ripley was also the chief editor of "Appleton's American Cyclopædia" (1858-61; revised edition, 1875). In this he was assisted by Charles Anderson Dana (1819-1891), a native of New Hampshire, who had also been a member of the Brook Farm community, and edited its organ, "The Harbinger." Dana became assistant editor of the "Tribune," and during the Civil War assistant Secretary of War, but his chief distinction is as editor of the "New York Sun," which under his management became the model in style for American daily newspapers. George William Curtis (1824-1892), who had been a pupil at Brook Farm and a student at Berlin, went on a tour in Egypt and Syria, which furnished material for his entertaining books of travel, "Nile Notes of a Howadji" (1851) and "The Howadji in Syria" (1852). He joined the "Tribune" staff, and afterward was editor of "Putnam's Magazine." In it appeared his social satirical "Potiphar Papers" and his charming "Prue and I," in which a clerk philosophizes on New York social life as he sees it in his daily walks. Partnership with a printer

who failed involved Curtis in debts which embarrassed
him for many years. After some contributions to "Harper's Magazine" and "Harper's Weekly," he became editor of the latter and the writer of the "Editor's Easy
Chair" for the former, and retained these positions to the
end of his life. Thirty-five years were thus spent in constant literary work of a high order, but no books were
issued except the novel, "Trumps," which had been a
serial in the "Weekly." The "Easy Chair" touched
lightly, gracefully, but wisely, all the questions of the
time, and contained tributes to many prominent personages. Curtis was also widely known as a lecturer and
political orator. He was especially active in behalf of civil
service reform, and may be regarded as the champion of
that movement.

TAYLOR

Bayard Taylor (1825-1878) achieved wide fame, yet
never reached the distinction at which he aimed. He was
renowned as a traveler and descriptive writer, was much
sought as a lecturer, but he wished to be known as a great
poet. He was born at Kennett Square, Pennsylvania, of
Quaker parents, learned to set type, and early showed
strong desire for travel. At the age of twenty, after publishing a poem called "Ximena," he set sail for Europe,
and supported himself during two years' wandering by
writing letters to American newspapers. His "Views
Afoot, or Europe Seen with Knapsack and Staff" (1846)
proved very popular. It led to his success as a popular
lecturer, and to an engagement as writer for the "New
York Tribune." On behalf of this paper he went on new
travels to California, Russia, Syria, Central Africa, the
Land of the Midnight Sun, India, China, and Japan. Ten
more books of travel followed the first, besides "Rhymes

of Travel," "California Ballads," "Poems of the Orient."
His novels, "Hannah Thurston" and "A Story of Kennett" were intended to exhibit the scenery and life of his
native Chester county in his own day and in the Revolutionary period. "John Godfrey's Fortunes" is partly autobiographical, showing his early experience in New York
city. But all the while Taylor was cherishing his ambition
to be a great poet. He published altogether thirteen volumes of verse in a great variety of styles, from ballads to
dramatic romances. His most laborious undertaking was
the translation of Goethe's "Faust" in the original meters,
and in this he was successful beyond the utmost expectations of critics. He married as his second wife a
German lady and had indeed become perfectly saturated
with German ideas. He wished to realize in himself the
noble intellectual life of Goethe. When he was appointed
American Minister to Germany in 1878, it seemed that his
desire to write adequate biographies of Goethe and Schiller would be fulfilled, but his health had already failed
and he died in Berlin in December of that year. His two
great poems are "Prince Deukalion," which recites dramatically the progress of civilization, and "The Masque
of the Gods," which shows vast movements in human
affairs. His long narrative poem, "Lars," is a pastoral
of Norway. But he was at his best in short lyrical pieces,
whether relating to his native Pennsylvania, or to the
distant Orient.

STODDARD

Richard Henry Stoddard is a connecting link between
the early New York period and the present. He was born
at Hingham, Massachusetts, in 1825. His father, a sea
captain, was lost at sea while the poet was a child. Removing afterward to New York, Stoddard worked for some

years in an iron foundry. But the iron did not enter into his soul to the exclusion of poetry. In 1849 he brought out a volume called "Footprints," but he afterward destroyed the edition, and issued a riper volume in 1852. For many years he was employed in the Custom House in New York, and in the Dock Department. Yet he did not abandon writing, nor did the Muse forsake him. His "Songs of Summer" (1857) abounded in a tropical luxuriance of feeling and delicate fancy. For ten years Mr. Stoddard was literary editor of the "New York World," and has since held the same position with "The Mail and Express," though partly disabled by impaired sight. He is a just and discerning critic. Among his best poems is "Abraham Lincoln: a Horatian Ode," a noble tribute to the martyred President. His fancy has been attracted by Persian poetry, and he published in 1871 "The Book of the East." He has also written some tales for the young, and edited various collections of English and American poetry. While he has written much prose, his poetry represents his best literary efforts. He excels in lyrics, showing delicate feeling and wide sympathy.

Died May 12, 1903.

HOLLAND

Dr. Josiah Gilbert Holland did good work in editing the "Springfield Republican," and founding "Scribner's Monthly," which became the "Century Magazine." He was born at Belchertown, Massachusetts, in 1819, and in spite of poverty and ill-health, won a doctor's degree from Berkshire Medical College at the age of twenty-five. Yet he was obliged to turn to teaching and other employment until in 1839 he became editor of the "Springfield Republican," just founded by Samuel Bowles. To this paper, under the name Timothy Titcomb, he contributed "Letters to Young People, Married and Single," which by their moral earnestness, sprightliness and good sense, obtained wide popularity, especially when published in book form. In 1870 Dr. Holland assisted in founding "Scribner's Monthly," which was intended to be (like "Macmillan's Magazine," then just started in England) unobjectionable to religious readers and at the same time of high literary quality. Its success was very great from the start. Afterward, on a change of proprietorship, it became the "Century Magazine," Dr. Holland remaining editor until his death in 1881. His best writing is in his short lyrics and his mixed narrative and dramatic poems of American home life, "Bittersweet" (1858), "Katrina" (1868), and "The Mistress of the Manse" (1881). His novels, "Arthur Bonnicastle" (1873), "Sevenoaks" (1876), and "Nicholas Minturn" (1877), did not attain popularity. In all his writings a high moral aim was manifest.

SOUTHERN AUTHORS

In the South, before the Civil War, literature was not generally favored. Men of intellectual ability there became statesmen, ministers, orators and jurists. Yet some of these gave occasional attention to literary work, and a few devoted themselves to it almost entirely. William Wirt (1772-1834), of German descent, and famous as a lawyer, published in 1803 "Letters of a British Spy," describing the scenery and prominent persons of Virginia, and contributed to the volume of essays, called "The Old Bachelor" (1812). His best known work is the "Life of Patrick Henry" (1817), which preserved the fame of that orator.

John Pendleton Kennedy (1795-1870), born in Baltimore, became a lawyer, member of Congress, leader of the Whig party, and in 1852 Secretary of the Navy. His chief literary work was "Swallow Barn" (1832), in which he sought to do for Virginia country life what Irving had done for the Hudson, and some novels, of which the best are "Horse-shoe Robinson" (1835), a story of the Revolutionary War, and "Rob of the Bowl." He wrote also the "Memoirs of William Wirt."

SIMMS

But the principal literary figure of the Old South was William Gilmore Simms (1806-1870), who was born in Charleston, South Carolina, where his father had come from the North of Ireland, shortly after the Revolution. Left a motherless boy, he was apprenticed to a druggist,

studied law under difficulties, but early showed devotion
to the Muse. His father had gone to settle in the Territory of Mississippi and fought in the Florida campaign
under Andrew Jackson. The son joined the father, and
with him made long journeys through the backwoods,
visiting the Creek and Cherokee nations. This experience
laid the foundation for Simms's later work. He was admitted to the bar in 1827 and became editor of a Charleston paper which opposed nullification, and was thus
reduced to poverty. He had already written fair verses in
Byronic style, and "The Lost Pleiad" showed Wordsworth's influence. His eccentric drama, "Atalantis,"
describes a sea-fairy who is persecuted by a demon, but
rescues herself and marries a mortal lover. The scenes
take place at the bottom of the sea, on an enchanted island,
and on the deck of a Spanish bark. Simms went North
and lived for a time in Massachusetts. His first novel was
written under the influence of Godwin, but his second,
"Guy Rivers" (1834) introduced his readers to new personages of romance, the Southern backwoodsmen, the
squatters and Indians, the North Carolina mountaineers,
and the Yankee peddler. This was the beginning of a long
series which showed not only the heroism of the settlers of
Carolina and the Southwest, but the bravery and virtues
of their Indian foes. Simms did not make his redskins
as noble as those of Cooper, nor as devilish as did Dr.
Robert M. Bird in "Nick of the Woods." In the tragical
story of "The Yemassee" (1835), the chief Sanutee, the
soul of the uprising of the Indians against the whites,
his wife Mattawan, a lovely character, and their unfortunate son, Oconestoga, perish in their defeat. "The Partisan" (1835) was a story of Marion's men, and may be
ranked with Cooper's "The Spy." Its Lieutenant Porgy
is one of Simms's best characters. His "Wigwam and

Cabin Tales" contain thirteen short stories of pioneer and Indian life. "Grayling" has been praised as one of the best. Simms wrote historical, geographical and didactic or reflective works, but he lives only in his novels. Even these are full of faults, but the rapidity of action and the vigor of the narrative gave them popularity. They are in the style of Scott and Cooper, but never reach the enduring qualities of those masters. In the latter part of his life Simms lived on a plantation at Midway, South Carolina.

Augustus Baldwin Longstreet (1790-1870), born at Augusta, Georgia, became a judge and president of the University of Mississippi. His chief literary work was the humorous "Georgia Scenes" (1840) and "Master William Mitten" (1858).

Albert Pike (1809-1891), born in Boston, and educated at Harvard, went to St. Louis in 1831. Thence he set out on an expedition to Santa Fé, and finally settled in Arkansas, becoming editor and proprietor of a newspaper, and afterward a lawyer. During the Mexican War he served as a volunteer. In the Civil War he organized a force of Cherokee Indians on the Confederate side, and with them fought at the battle of Pea Ridge, in March, 1862. In 1867 he became editor of the "Memphis Appeal." Later he resided in Washington, practising law. His "Hymns to the Gods" (1831) were for their force and beauty republished in "Blackwood's Magazine." "Buena Vista" is a war ballad; other poems showed high lyric power. Collections of his poems were made in 1873 and 1882.

John Esten Cooke (1830-1886) undertook to do for Virginia what Simms had done for South Carolina. After some stories and sketches he published the novel "Leather

Stocking and Silk" (1854), which was soon followed and surpassed by "The Virginia Comedians" (1854), probably the best Southern novel written before the war. Others of his early stories were "The Last of the Foresters" and "Henry St. John, Gentleman." During the Civil War Cooke served on the staff of various Confederate Generals. Afterward he retired to his farm near Winchester, and wrote biographies of Lee and Stonewall Jackson, and several novels relating to the great conflict. Among those were "Mohun, or the Last Days of Lee and His Paladins" (1868), "Hilt to Hilt, or Days and Nights in the Shenandoah" (1869).

Paul Hamilton Hayne (1831-1886), bearing a name famous in the annals of South Carolina, was the finest poet of the South. He was a native of Charleston, and edited literary periodicals there until the war, when he served on the staff of General Pickens. His house and property were destroyed in the bombardment of Charleston, and after the war he settled at Copse Hill, Georgia, where he pursued literary work till his death. Among his best poems are "The Pine's Mystery," the ballad "The Battle of King's Mountain," "The Lyric of Action." His war lyrics are thrilling and his descriptive and meditative verses are exquisite in music and thought.

Henry Timrod (1829-1867), also born in Charleston, suffered from ill-health and poverty, yet wrote poems full of ardent devotion to the South and its lost cause. His war lyrics, grand and impetuous, won for him the title of "the Tyrtæus of the South." His poems were edited by P. H. Hayne.

Abram Joseph Ryan (1840-1886), born of Irish parents at Norfolk, Virginia, was equally devoted to the Southern cause. He was a Catholic priest, and served as chaplain in the Confederate army. After the war he edited religious and literary papers in New Orleans and Knoxville, and had charge of a church at Mobile. In 1880 he published his "Poems, Patriotic, Religious, Miscellaneous." He died at Louisville, Kentucky, in 1886. He is best known by his lament over the defeat of the Confederacy, "The Conquered Banner," and the spirited tribute to the Southern leader, "The Sword of Robert Lee." Other fine poems are "Erin's Flag," "Sursum Corda."

Charles Etienne Gayarré (1805-1892) was born in New Orleans of Creole stock, and became a lawyer and judge. His chief work was a "History of Louisiana" (3 vols. 1854-57), but he wrote also a history of "Philip II of Spain" and two historical novels, "Fernando de Lemos" (1872) and "Aubert Dubayet" (1882).

LANIER

The most remarkably original singer of the South was Sidney Lanier (1842-1881), who was chosen to write the cantata for the opening of the Centennial Exhibition at Philadelphia. He was descended from a long line of musicians, and distinguished his poetry by the intermingling of musical effects. He was born at Macon, Georgia, and studied at Oglethorpe College, until the war broke out, when he entered the Confederate service. He was captured on a blockade-runner, and held prisoner for five months. The hardships of war developed consumption, and the rest of his life was a courageous struggle with that disease. In 1873 he went to Baltimore to be a musician. He had already published a novel "Tiger Lilies" (1867), founded on his war experiences. His fine poem, "Corn," which appeared in "Lippincott's Magazine" in 1875, was the first to attract attention to his name. For support of

his family he wrote a "Guide-Book to Florida" and edited
for boys "Froissart," "King Arthur," "Percy's Reliques"
and the "Mabinogion." In 1879, he was appointed
lecturer on English literature in Johns Hopkins University. His "Science of English Verse" (1880) is an elaborate study of the metrical structure of English poetry,
in which he held that time was as important as in music.
"The English Novel and the Principle of Its Development" (1883) was the first treatise in which the growth
of fiction was fully considered, historically and philosophically. Lanier's "Poems" were not collected until
1884, three years after his death; but since that time his
fame has steadily risen. All of his work is marked by his
strong feeling for music, and many of his pieces are really
songs, "Song of the Chattahoochee," "A Song of Love."
His "Psalm of the West" is a grand expression of true
Americanism. "The Stirrup Cup" is a friendly challenge
to death. "A Ballad of Trees and the Master" is a mystical expression of the sympathy of nature with the sufferings of Christ. Many others of his poems give a striking
personality to the products of nature, as "Corn," "Clover,"
"Tampa Robins," and "The Dove." His dying swan-
chants are found in "Hymns of the Marshes." Though
his art was too fine and high for general appreciation, Lanier must be regarded as one of the greatest American poets.

CABLE

More than a dozen years after the Civil War there
began to appear in "Scribner's Magazine" a series of short
stories, revealing singular types of character, and a peculiar civilization, surcharged with a delightful atmosphere,
admirably adapted to the purpose of romance. They were

found in the limits of the United States, and yet belonged to a reserved aristocratic French and Spanish community. This revelation of the Creoles of New Orleans, hitherto secluded from general observation, was made by George Washington Cable, who had lived familiarly among them, and had the artistic sense necessary to set them properly before the world. He was born in New Orleans in 1844, the son of a prosperous merchant, who failed a few years later. On the death of his father, young Cable left school and became a store clerk. At the age of nineteen he entered the Confederate army, and served till the close of the war. Thereafter he led a checkered life, as clerk, member of a surveying expedition, reporter and contributor to the New Orleans papers. The stories of Creole life published in "Scribner's Magazine" proved still more popular, when issued in the volume "Old Creole Days." In 1880 appeared "The Grandissimes," his first long novel, followed soon by "Madame Delphine" and "Dr. Sevier." This remarkable trio of novels has given Cable a unique place in American literature. No rivals have entered his field; he stands alone as a truthful delineator of a remarkable civilization. His scenes were laid in a former generation, thus giving better scope for his fancy, while his thorough knowledge of the conservative society and its environment prevented his going astray in depicting it. Of course the sensitive, tender-hearted Creoles, jealous of their caste and their privacy, resented the exposure of their lives, however sympathetic the relation. Part of his picturesque stories related to the Quadroons, and the mixture of these with the others gave serious offense. There were later sketches of the descendants of the Acadians, who found refuge in Louisiana, when dragged into exile from Nova Scotia. The volume, "Bonaventure," includes three of the best stories.   Mr. Cable wrote also a "History of New Orleans," in connection with the census of 1880. He afterward removed to Massachusetts and engaged in religious work.   One more novel has been added to his list, "John March, Southerner."

THE LATER HISTORIANS

According to the method which long prevailed in the study of history, attention is confined to wars, battles, sieges, changes of dynasties, actions of rulers and intrigues of courts, while the condition and desires of the mass of the people were disregarded. But in recent years the latter has come to be considered not only an essential element but the chief material of true history. It was probably first exemplified in a single notable chapter of Macaulay's "History of England." It was afterward fully presented in J. R. Green's "History of the English People." Its chief American representative is J. B. McMasters' "History of the People of the United States," which aims to exhibit the social growth of the American people from the adoption of the Constitution in 1789 to the outbreak of the Civil War in 1861. The first volume appeared in 1883, and four more have been issued, bringing the history down to 1821.

John Bach McMaster was born in Brooklyn, New York, in 1852, and graduated from the College of the City of New York in 1872. He became instructor in civil engineering at Princeton College in 1877, and after the publication of the first volume of his history in 1883 was called to the University of Pennsylvania as professor of American history. Besides his chief work, he has published "Benjamin Franklin as a Man of Letters" (1887) and "With the Fathers" (1896), a series of historical portraits. He is thoroughly democratic in spirit, and objects to the hero-worship which has occupied so much space in records of the past. He believes that the true vitality of a nation consists in the general welfare of the plain people, whose combined efforts make the commonwealth.

John Fiske was noted as a linguist, an exponent of evolution, and a synthetic philosopher, before he devoted himself to writing the history of his country. He was born at Hartford, Connecticut, in 1842. His father was Edmund Brewster Green, but the son at the age of thirteen took his present name from one of his mother's ancestors. His extraordinary facility in acquiring languages was early displayed. He graduated from Harvard in 1863, and studied law, but soon devoted himself to literature. For some years he was assistant librarian at Harvard. Intending to prepare a work on the early Aryans, he wrote "Myths and Myth-Makers" (1874), but afterward laid the project aside, finding it necessary to know more about the barbaric world. In his "Cosmic Philosophy" (1874), the system of Herbert Spencer is fully expounded. His other philosophical writings are "Excursions of an Evolutionist" (1883); "The Destiny of Man" (1884); "The Idea of God as Affected by Modern Knowledge" (1884). The last were originally delivered as courses of lectures. Mr. Fiske holds that the Darwinian theory of natural selection, so far from lowering man in the scale of organic life, exalts him and his spiritual part as the goal toward which nature has been tending. Original sin is the brute inheritance from warring ancestors. Mr. Fiske declares his belief in a future life and the existence of God, maintaining that there is no necessary conflict between science and religion.

Another course of lectures was called for in aid of the preservation of Old South Meeting House, in Boston. Mr. Fiske then discussed "American Political Ideas" (1885), and since its delivery, he has given attention chiefly to American history. In the "Discovery of

America" he treated fully the condition of the aborigines
found by Columbus and his successors, and traverses much
of what Prescott had written on the authority of the Spanish explorers. His other historical works are "The Begin-
nings of New England," "The American Revolution,"
"The Critical Period of the American Revolution." All
his writings are characterized by clearness and fluency.
His vigor and skill are best displayed in the romantic incidents and dramatic crises.

Edward Eggleston had attained popularity as a writer
of stories of Western life before he undertook to relate in
a series of books the history of social life in the United
States. He was born at Vevay, Indiana, in 1837, his
father having come from Virginia. In youth he suffered
from ill-health and went to Minnesota on this account.
Here he became a Methodist preacher, and soon began
writing for newspapers. In 1870 he was made literary
editor of the New York "Independent," and afterward he
edited "Hearth and Home." In this was published "The
Hoosier Schoolmaster," his most popular novel. It was
soon followed by others, "The End of the World," "The
Mystery of Metropolisville," "The Circuit Rider,"
"Roxy," "The Graysons." These were chiefly founded
on his experiences in Indiana, but the last related to an
incident in the life of Abraham Lincoln. Meantime Mr.
Eggleston published a series of sketches of "Life in the
Colonial Period," and a school "History of the United
States" as preliminary to his larger work, which was not
intended to be strict history, but descriptions of individual
and social life at successive periods. The first volume,
"The Beginners of a Nation," appeared in 1896. It treats
of the various experiments in colonization, the various
motives influencing the leaders, and the unexpected outcome of the several ventures. Mr. Eggleston's industry

of research and realistic imagination are shown in these picturesque sketches. His style is simple, vigorous and natural. A strong moral enthusiasm is manifest in all his writing. In treating of the founders of New England he condemns their religious intolerance, and while admiring Roger Williams' noble plea for soul-liberty, does not conceal his scruples about insignificant trifles.

The Adams family has always been prominent in the history of the United States, and its diaries and other records are part of the national archives. Henry Adams, son of Charles Francis Adams, who was the American Minister in England during the Civil War, has devoted himself specially to historical writing. He was born in 1838, graduated from Harvard in 1858, and served as his father's private secretary in England. He was afterward editor of the "North American Review" and professor of history at Harvard, where he introduced the new methods and inspired his pupils with enthusiasm for research. Besides many essays, he has written valuable biographies of Albert Gallatin (1879) and John Randolph (1882). But his most important and characteristic work is his "History of the United States, 1801-17" (9 vols., 1889-91). To this subject he was drawn by the fact that while President John Adams had been the head and front of the Federal party, his son, John Quincy Adams, who also became President, went over to the Democratic party. The History presents an explanation, if not a justification, of the change. In preparation of it the author spent much time in Washington, London, and other foreign capitals, examining archives and studying every subject necessary for a complete understanding of the questions involved. The result is a remarkable reconstruction of a period long supposed to be perfectly understood. The account of the War of 1812, for instance, is entirely different from that

of former historians, except in the general outline. As
a work of art, the History deserves high praise for orderly
arrangement and clear statement of a vast number of particulars, without obscuring the general effect of the whole.
Every statement is carefully fortified by array of authorities. The author has enforced by example what he had
before taught by precept.

Theodore Roosevelt has been so prominent as a maker
of history that it excites wonder that he has also been diligent and productive as a writer. He was born in New
York city in 1858, his father being a successful merchant.
He graduated at Harvard in 1880, and three years later
published his "Hunting Trips of a Ranchman." His direct
interest in the West led to his study of its dramatic development which is shown in "The Winning of the West"
(4 vols., 1895). These volumes exhibit careful investigation of original documents, as well as thorough sympathy
with the subject. But they did not exhaust his energies.
He wrote also lives of Thomas H. Benton (1887) and
Gouverneur Morris (1888) and a "History of New York
City" (1891), besides two or three new books on hunting.
Yet during this period of book-making, the author was
also busy in politics; he was member of the New York
Assembly, 1882-84, United States Civil Service Commissioner, 1889-95, president of the New York Board of
Police Commissioners, 1895-97, and Assistant Secretary
of the Navy until the declaration of war with Spain. Then
he resigned, raised a regiment of Rough Riders, went to
Cuba, distinguished himself at Santiago, and returned to
be elected Governor of New York. Throughout his
career he has been conspicuous for stalwart independence,
and a leader in behalf of civil service reform and the puri-
fication of politics. His thoroughly American spirit is as
conspicuous in his writings as in his public life. His style

is fresh, vigorous and manly. He is an honor to American literature as to American public life.

An epoch-making work in history was Captain Alfred Thayer Mahan's "Influence of Sea Power Upon History" (1890). This treatise was the first adequate literary statement of the importance of a navy, and even of the real meaning of its existence. It shows the precise force which maritime strength has had upon the fortunes of each nation from 1660 to 1783. The revelation has had profound effect in every civilized country, and when the author visited Europe in command of the Chicago in 1893, he received many public honors in acknowledgment of his services. Captain Mahan was born in New York City in 1840, and entered the Naval Academy at Annapolis in 1856. He was made lieutenant in 1861, and served in the blockading squadrons during the Civil War. In 1872 he was made captain and he was President of the Naval War College at Newport in 1886-89 and 1890-93. Before publishing his great work he had written "The Gulf and Inland Waters" (1883). Afterward he wrote a "Life of Admiral Farragut" (1892), and continued his great work in the "Influence of Sea Power upon the French Revolution and Empire" (1893). From various magazines he has gathered his essays on "The Interest of America in Sea Power, Present and Future" (1897). His latest publication is an admirable "Life of Nelson" (1897) which has been received with the warmest welcome in England. The chief object of Captain Mahan's labors has been to prove that the interests of the United States require a departure from the traditional policy of neglecting the navy. He appears to have converted the whole world to his central idea, if not to its intended application.

Henry Cabot Lodge, United States Senator from Massachusetts, has been as active and distinguished in

historical, as in political work.   He was born in Boston
in 1850, and after graduating from Harvard, edited the
"North American Review" and "International Review."
He served in the Massachusetts Legislature two years, in
Congress eight, and was elected to the Senate in 1893.
He published "Life and Letters of George Cabot" (1877),
as a defense of New England Federalism; also lives of
Alexander Hamilton, Daniel Webster, and Washington;
also "Studies in History" (1884), "Political and Historical Essays" (1888), "Certain Accepted Heroes" (1897).
Mr. Lodge is a painstaking investigator and brilliant
writer, but somewhat disposed to inject into controversies
of the past feeling derived from political conflicts of the
present day.

NATURE-ESSAYISTS

Several writers of this Century have devoted them-selves almost entirely to the literary treatment of natural history. Perhaps the first of the Nature-Essayists was Henry David Thoreau (1817-1862), who was born and died at Concord, Massachusetts. The son of a farmer, he was educated at Harvard, and for a time taught school. But after a while he took up his self-appointed work of minute observation of nature. He attached himself to Emerson, who always showed him friendly regard. In 1845 he built himself a hut on the shore of Walden Pond, and lived as a recluse in communion with nature. His experiences and observations were embodied in "Walden, or Life in the Woods" (1854). He had already published "A Week on the Concord and Merrimac Rivers" (1848). Thoreau was an apostle of plain living and high think-ing, and practiced what he preached. His life was a pro-test against all forms of superfluous comfort, and an effort to reach harmony with nature, as the basis of true hap-piness. After two years' experience of hut life, he left the woods because he had "several more lives to live, and could not spare any more time for that one." He never entered a church, but he was thoroughly imbued with Pantheism, and had a devout spirit. His individualism was carried so far that he refused to pay taxes and was imprisoned on that account, but was released when Emer-son, against his wish, paid them for him. But the world's indebtedness to him is for the love of nature manifested in his books. Besides "Walden" he wrote "Excursions" (1863), "The Maine Woods" (1864), "Cape Cod" (1865), "A Yankee in Canada" (1866), "Summer"

(1884), "Winter" (1888), "Autumn" (1892). These posthumous publications were made up from his daily journal begun in 1835.

Wilson Flagg (1805-1894) also deserves a place among the American nature essayists. Born at Beverly, Massachusetts, he was educated at Phillips Acadamy, Andover, and studied medicine. He was a keen observer of outdoor life and natural phenomena. His writings were contributed to Boston newspapers and to the "Atlantic Monthly." His best known works are "Halcyon Days," "A Year With the Trees," and "A Year With the Birds."

Another man who took delight in the portrayal of outdoor nature with the pen was William Hamilton Gibson (1850-1896). He was also an artist and book-illustrator. He was born at Sandy Hook, Connecticut, and after studying went to New York, where he was engaged in making illustrations of botany and natural history for various publications. Soon he began to write on these subjects, and to illustrate his own books. Much of his time was spent in study of the night life of plants and insects. But in his popular books he gave literary form to his observations. These include "Camp-Life in the Woods," "Highways and Byways, or Saunterings in New England," "Happy Hunting Grounds, or a Tribute to the Woods and Fields," "Strolls by Starlight and Sunshine."

But the best known of the nature-essayists and most genial successor of Thoreau is John Burroughs, who was born at Roxbury, New York, in April, 1837. As he says in an essay, "I think April is the best month to be born in; in April all nature starts with you." His boyhood was spent on a farm, and after receiving an academic education, he taught school and became a journalist. For some years he was a clerk in the Treasury Department at Washington, and afterward a bank inspector. In 1874 he settled on a farm at Esopus, New York, and gave his leisure time to friendly study of nature. Among his books are "Wake-Robin," "Birds and Poets," "Locusts and Wild Honey," "Fresh Fields," and "Signs and Seasons." Burroughs, like Thoreau, has written of travels and literature, but his chief interest is in nature. In his essays the charm of out-door life is reproduced. His readers are initiated in wood-craft and bird-lore, and are not inveigled into mysticism and metaphysics. He is a single-hearted lover of nature, endowed with sympathy for everything that lives.

Donald Grant Mitchell is well known by the pen-name "Ik Marvel," under which he wrote his most popular books —"The Reveries of a Bachelor," and "Dream Life." Born at Norwich, Connecticut, in 1822, he was educated at Yale College, and became a lawyer, but has given much attention to farming. His first books were the results of travel in Europe, "Fresh Gleanings" (1847), and "The Battle Summer" (1848), and the more popular books, named above, followed in 1850 and 1851. The "Reveries," to use the author's statement, consist of "such whimsies and reflections as a great many brother bachelors are apt to indulge in, but which they are too cautious or too prudent to lay before the world." "Dream Life" sketches a career from the cradle to the grave, from the aspirations of boyhood to the reminiscences of age. In 1853 Mitchell was made United States Consul at Venice, and on his return settled on his farm, Edgewood, near New Haven. Here he has written a series of delightful books on the practical and æsthetic aspects of rural life, "My Farm at Edgewood," "Wet Days at Edgewood," "Rural Studies." Later he has treated, in a fresh and lively way, the history of literature in "English Lands, Letters and Kings," and "American Lands and Letters."

WHITMAN

The most startling and debatable contribution to
American literature is that made by Walt Whitman (1819-
1892). It claimed to be the true voice of Democratic
America, and while the claim has been admitted by a
scholarly few here, and acknowledged by an equal number of scholarly poets in Europe, there is no evidence that
it has been so accepted anywhere by the people. Longfellow and Whittier they know and respect, Whitcomb
Riley and Will Carleton they quote, but Whitman they
care nothing for. Nor does there seem any likelihood
that the few enthusiastic admirers will be able to infuse
their warm feeling into the apathetic masses. Yet respect
must be paid to the high endorsement which this singular
poet has obtained from critics of high rank.

Walt Whitman was born at West Hills, Long Island,
in May, 1819. His father was an English carpenter, his
mother Dutch, and there was a strain of Quaker blood in
him. While he was a boy the family moved to Brooklyn, where he attended the common schools and became a
compositor. He began to write for newspapers and in
1838 to publish a weekly paper at Huntington, Long
Island, but after two years' experience returned to the
printer's case. He cultivated familiarity with workingmen of all classes in New York city. In 1846 he was
editor of the "Brooklyn Eagle" and afterward set out
on a long tour through the Western and Southern States,
until he reached New Orleans, getting employment as
compositor or editor in various places. Then he returned
in the same way to Brooklyn and engaged in building
small houses. In 1855 he published his "Leaves of
Grass," having set most of the type himself. Rhyme
and the old regular forms of verse were discarded. Lines

of various lengths were joined in stanzas quite as abnormal. Slang and uncouth phrases were used, and a bold egotism was everywhere manifested. "Toward all" exclaimed the author, "I raise high the perpendicular hand —I make the signal, to remain after me in sight forever, for all the haunts and homes of men." The book met with little but ridicule until Emerson, ever generous and alert for new genius, wrote the author a letter of praise. This letter was published in an enlarged edition of the "Leaves," containing matter much more objectionable than anything in the first. Whitman's thought was a singular outgrowth of the strong individualism of the Transcendental School, but Emerson was repelled by its later manifestations. The Pre-Raphaelites in England hailed the author as the type of the new American. In New York city Whitman became the hero of a Bohemian club of young "cameradoes." Then came the Civil War and Whitman went to Washington, where for a time he had employment as a clerk in the Department of the Interior, and afterward devoted himself to visiting the wounded in hospitals. The war experiences inspired his volume of lyrics, "Drum-Taps" (1866), mournful rather than exhilarating. From 1865 to 1873 Whitman was a clerk in the Treasury Department, then, having had a stroke of paralysis, he removed to Camden, New Jersey, where in a whitewashed cottage he was supported by the generosity of a few friends. His tastes were simple, his wants few. The evening of his life was passed in cheerful serenity. Most of his poems were gathered in late editions of his "Leaves of Grass," but he added "November Boughs," "Specimen Days and Collect," and "Good Bye, My Fancy." Whitman's aim was to set forth in poetic spirit, if not recognized poetic form, American manhood. At times he presents himself without conventional

disguise, "hankering, gross, mystical, nude;" at times he
calls attention to the swarming multitude around him,
with all their various movements and desires, and refuses
to pronounce any common or unclean; at times, he
describes as the goal of American progress a grand personification of free and pure Humanity.

LATER WRITERS

HARTE

Bret Harte was born at Albany, New York, in 1839. After receiving an ordinary education he went to California in 1854. There he taught school, worked in the mines and in a printing office, and wrote for the press. In 1867 he published "Condensed Novels," clever parodies of the leading English and American novelists. From 1864 to 1870 he was secretary of the Mint at San Francisco, and during this time wrote his poems, "John Burns of Gettysburg," "The Pliocene Skull," and "The Society upon the Stanislaus." In 1868 the "Overland Monthly" was started with Harte as editor, and in it appeared his tales of frontier mining life. "The Luck of Roaring Camp" was instantly hailed as the evidence of a new genius. It was soon followed by "Miggles," "Tennessee's Partner," "The Outcasts of Poker Flat." In 1871 Harte removed to New York, and became a contributor to the "Atlantic Monthly." In 1878 he was appointed United States Consul at Crefeld, Germany, and in 1880 was transferred to Glasgow. His time, however, was chiefly spent in London, where he became a social favorite. He still lives in England, and writes stories usually of California life.

The first success of Harte's poems and stories was due to their vivid revelation of strong characters living amid strange surroundings which brought out in bold relief their good and evil qualities. The stories showed dramatic power, keen insight and glowing humor. Within a small compass these men and women were swiftly and clearly portrayed so as to be easily understood and recognized. And yet, however real the characters and incidents appear, there is an artistic idealism thrown over the whole which stamps it the work of genius. Harte did not succeed so well in his novel "Gabriel Conroy," which relates to early California civilization. Though it has fine descriptions and humorous scenes, it is a succession of episodes, not wrought into an organic whole. Harte's best poems are dramatic monologues in dialect. The one most widely known as "The Heathen Chinee," but properly called "Plain Language from Truthful James," is an historical landmark.

HOWELLS

William Dean Howells, born at Martinsville, Ohio, in 1837, is descended from Welsh Quakers. His father was a printer and published local newspapers. The son learned the same business and at nineteen went to Columbus, the State Capital, to become correspondent and editor. With his friend, John James Piatt, he published a volume of verses, which showed poetic talent. A campaign biography of Abraham Lincoln helped to procure for the young journalist an appointment as Consul at Venice. His four years' sojourn in the romantic Italian city of the sea gave opportunity for his graphic sketches of "Venetian Life." On returning to the United States, he settled in New York and wrote for the "Tribune" and "Nation." In 1871 he became assistant editor of the "Atlantic Monthly," and for it wrote "Their Wedding Journey," a pleasant portrayal of American character. In this mode of sketching actual life he went on with "A Chance Acquaintance" (1873) "A Foregone Conclusion" (1874) "The Lady of the Aroostook" (1878) "Dr. Breen's Practice" (1885). But his strongest work was

"The Rise of Silas Lapham," a realistic description of the success of a country-bred man who acquires wealth by the discovery on his farm of a substance from which mineral paint is made. He and his family are brought into contact and contrast with cultured Boston people with resulting comedies and tragedies. The story abounds in humor and shows kindly sympathy with the actors. In 1886 Howells became connected with "Harper's Magazine," having charge of "The Editor's Study," and in it explained and inculcated realism as the proper method of fiction. Sensationalism and every species of Romanticism are entirely banished, as giving false ideas of life. People are sketched and characters revealed in ordinary incidents. Howells has exemplified this in his later work, as "April Hopes" (1888), "Annie Kilburn" (1889), "A Hazard of New Fortunes" (1890), "The World of Chance" (1893). In the romance "A Traveler from Altruria" (1894), he has set forth the contrast between the actual life of American people and their ideals. His interest in social problems and the relations of labor and capital is shown in several stories. But in general he is content to exhibit pictures of ordinary life, leaving the moral to suggest itself. He has been called the apostle of the commonplace. Some of his stories have been dramatized, and he has shown skill in writing parlor dramas and farces. Many essays in criticism and on social questions have come from his pen. He has especially been the interpreter and advocate of the ideas and methods of the Russian Tolstoi, whom he regards as the greatest novelist of the Century. "Modern Italian Poets" (1887) is an instructive review of the Italian literature of this Century. "Stops of Various Quills" (1895) is a collection of his poems, showing brotherly interest in the movements of humanity.

HENRY JAMES

Henry James, noted as an essayist, sketch writer and novelist, was born in New York city in 1843. His father, bearing the same name, was a scholarly Swedenborgian and wrote much in advocacy of his belief. The son, on account of delicate health, was educated at home. Both as boy and man he has spent much time in Europe. He entered early on a literary career, and after publishing some sketches, issued in 1875, "Roderick Hudson," in which he displayed the two motives that appear in most of his work—the contrast between Americans and Europeans, and the contrast between the artistic and the average human character. These contrasts were brought out still more strongly in "The American" (1877), in which Christopher Newman is the hero, but the pathetic short story, "Daisy Miller" (1878), impressed them most effectually on the public. James has written with great care and deliberation other short stories and studies, and has had much effect on the style of other writers, though he has never become a really popular novelist. He treats of polite society and cares little for plot. His object is to reveal character, and this is done in dialogue and preliminaries tending to action rather than in action itself. He has written descriptive sketches of men and places, minor travels, and essays on social topics. With Sir Walter Besant he prepared "The Art of Fiction" (1885) and he has made translations from the French. One of his best short stories is "The Madonna of the Future" (1879); others are "The Lesson of the Master" (1892), and "What Maisie Knew" (1897). "The Portrait of a Lady" (1882) is deservedly the most popular of James's longer stories. "The Princess Casamissima" (1886) is a kind of sequel to "Roderick Hudson," introducing again

one of his finest characters, Christina Light.   It is more
serious and somber than the earlier part.   "The Tragic
Muse" (1890) is a long complicated novel of English
characters, who are made more attractive than his Americans.   James has been a close student of Turgenieff and
the modern French school, and has written excellent criticisms of those novelists.   He is a realist, yet not in any
offensive sense.   He never descends to the vulgar or
impure.

WALLACE

Lewis Wallace had won distinction in other fields than
that of literature before he became known to the world
as the author of "Ben Hur," but this distinction has
eclipsed his former fame.   He was born at Brookville,
Indiana, in 1827, the son of the Hon. David Wallace,
who was at one time Governor of Indiana.   At the beginning of the Mexican War he was studying law, but left
his books to take the field.   After serving with credit he
returned and was admitted to the bar.   He was in the
State Senate for four years and when the Civil War
began received command of a regiment.   After brilliant
service both in the West and the East, he was mustered
out in 1865 with the rank of Major-General of Volunteers.
He resumed the practice of law at Crawfordsville, Indiana.
From 1878 to 1881 he was Governor of Arizona, and was
then sent as American Minister to Turkey.   Before writing "Ben Hur" he had published "The Fair God" (1873),
a story of the Spanish conquest of Mexico.   "Ben Hur,"
a romantic setting of the life of Christ, appeared in 1880,
and soon obtained a wider circulation than any previous
American work, except "Uncle Tom's Cabin."   This is,
of course, due to its religious character, as well as its literary merit.   The hero is a noble Israelite, whose eventful

life has brought him in contact with the Savior. The Oriental scenery was accurately depicted from vivid imagination, before General Wallace had ever visited the East. The description of the chariot race is justly regarded as one of the most stirring chapters of an historical romance. The author's style is not free from faults, but these seem not to have interfered with his popularity. General Wallace has since written "The Boyhood of Christ" (1888), founded on the apocryphal Gospels, "Commodus, a Tragedy" (1889), and "The Prince of India" (1893). The last is an historical novel, dealing with the capture of Constantinople by the Turks. The Prince is a finely drawn character, whose career bears some resemblance to that of the Wandering Jew. General Wallace in 1897 published an Oriental narrative poem in blank verse, "The Wooing of Malkatoon." *Died Feb. 15. 1905.*
His last words were, "I am ready to meet my Maker"

HALE

Among the most busy and productive leaders of Boston for nearly half the Century has been Edward Everett Hale. Born in 1822, he was educated at the Latin School and Harvard College. For ten years from 1846 he was pastor of a church in Worcester, and then took charge of the South Church in Boston. By personal effort as well as by his writings he has helped to organize societies for doing good in manifold ways. One of his enterprises was the magazine, "Old and New," which was finally merged in "Scribner's Monthly;" another was "Lend a Hand," which represents organized charity. Besides these he has written a pile of books, including histories, novels, poems and short stories. All of his books were written for instruction, some for spiritual or moral purposes. The most famous is "The Man Without a Country" (1862), a story intended to inculcate loyalty to the Federal Government. Though pure fiction, it was told in such a realistic way as to be taken for fact. Other stories illustrate his power of making impossibilities appear real, as the comical "My Double and How he Undid Me," and "The Skeleton in the Closet." "The Brick Moon," is in the style of Jules Verne. Among the other stories which have had wide effect for good are "Ten Times One Is Ten," and "In His Name." The novels include "Philip Nolan's Friends," "Mr. Tangier's Vacations," and "Ups and Downs." Several books of travel are grouped together under the general name, "A Family Flight." The story of his early days is told in "A New England Boyhood." All his books show a true literary instinct, good sense and sound morality.

MILLER

In 1870 the "Songs of the Sierras," published in London, and describing California scenes, produced a literary sensation in England, and gave the author temporary fame as the long-expected truly American poet. The author's name was given as Joaquin Miller, but it was originally Cincinnatus Hiner Miller, the name Joaquin being borrowed from a Mexican brigand. Miller was born in Indiana in 1841, but when he was a boy his parents emigrated to Oregon. After working on a farm he went to seek for gold in California, and began to write verse. Unsuccessful as a miner, he led a wandering life in California and Nevada, and went with the filibuster Walker to Nicaragua. On his return to Oregon in 1860, he studied law and was for a time a county judge. In 1870 he went to England, and having there obtained a reputation as a poet, came back to America to seek work

as a journalist. In 1887 he settled at Oakland, California.
His poetical works include "Songs of the Sunlands,"
"Songs of the Sierras," and "Songs of the Mexican
Seas." His best known prose works are "The Danites in
the Sierras," " '49, or the Gold-Seekers of the Sierras," and
"The Destruction of Gotham." Miller has not hesitated
to appropriate some of the work of others, and yet he
has originality and force. He cares little for accepted
laws of literature. He is able to represent vividly the wild
life and grand scenery of the Pacific slope.

STEDMAN

Edmund Clarence Stedman has done immense service
to American literature by his poems and criticisms, and
by his editing the "Library of American Literature" (11
vols. 1890-92), the "Victorian Anthology" (1895), and
a complete edition of "Poe's Works" (1895). He was
born at Hartford, Connecticut, in 1833, and was educated
at Yale College. For twelve years he was a journalist
in the country, at New York and with the army. In 1864
he became a broker in New York, yet he has steadily kept
up a connection with literature. His poems were collected in 1884 and a later volume was added in 1897. His
important critical work is seen in "The Victorian Poets"
(1875) and "The Poets of America" (1880). In these
books the chief poetical productions of the Century are
subjected to careful, discriminating and suggestive inspec-
tion. His own poems are chiefly lyrical, celebrating
events of the time in appropriate and memorable verse.
Among the notable pieces are "How Old Brown took Harper's Ferry," "The Hand of Lincoln," "Pan in Wall
Street."

ALDRICH

Thomas Bailey Aldrich is a writer of polished, delicate poetry, and of quaint humorous stories. He was born at Portsmouth, New Hampshire, in 1837, but entered on mercantile life in New York at the age of seventeen. Soon he turned to literature and in 1866 went to Boston to be editor of "Every Saturday." After a tour in Europe in 1875 he published "From Ponkapog to Pesth," a charming book of travel. In 1881 he was made editor of the "Atlantic Monthly," and held this post for nine years. He has since made a journey around the world. His poetry is mostly in short pieces, expressing single emotions or describing special scenes. His most noted poem is "Babie Bell," which relates tenderly the birth and short life of a child. "Friar Jerome's Beautiful Book" has met with wide favor. "Judith" and "Wyndham Towers" are narratives in blank verse, but the most striking piece in this form is "The Unguarded Gates," crying out against unrestricted immigration as threatening the stability of American institutions. In his short stories Aldrich has shown a fondness for elaborate mystification, as in "Marjorie Daw." His longer novels "Prudence Palfrey," "The Queen of Sheba," are more serious, yet involve a quaint humor. "The Story of a Bad Boy" is an autobiographical record of his youthful pranks, which has been welcomed by old and young.

CRAWFORD

So competent a critic as Andrew Lang has pronounced Francis Marion Crawford the "most versatile and various" of modern novelists. His novels cover an immensely wide range and introduce to the reader a great variety of character as well as environment. He has great adaptability and suppleness of mind and is equally facile and free of touch in dealing with life in modern Rome or New York, in India or rural England, at the court of the ancient Persian Darius or in Sicily of the present day. Liberal education and wide travel have furnished a rich variety of knowledge, which his native genius has been prompt to utilize.

Francis Marion Crawford was born in Italy in 1854, his father being the celebrated sculptor, Thomas Crawford, whose statue of Liberty surmounts the dome of the Capitol at Washington. When a lad he was sent to St. Paul's school at Concord, New Hampshire, but afterward returned to Italy, and then entered Trinity College, Cambridge, England. For some years after graduation he traveled on the Continent, and then going to India joined the staff of a newspaper at Allahabad. The result of his Indian experiences was shown in his first novel, "Mr. Isaacs," in which an educated Mohammedan merchant pays court to a typical English girl. Crawford has since been an exceedingly prolific writer, and his stores of accumulated knowledge have stood him in good stead, being illumined by a vivid and picturesque imagination. His thorough knowledge of the upper classes of Italian society has enabled him to present it in a satisfactory way to English readers. He has perhaps reached his highest mark in his trilogy of novels of Roman life, "Saracinesca," "Sant' Ilario," and "Don Orsino." Among his other novels may be mentioned "A Roman Singer," "A Tale of a Lonely Parish," "Marzio's Crucifix," "Greifenstein," "The Three Fates," "Casa Bracchio," and "A Rose of Yesterday." To these he has added a remarkably brilliant description of Rome in various ages, under the title, "Ave Roma Immortalis."

CLEMENS—("MARK TWAIN")

The most distinguished exponent of American humor is Samuel Langhorne Clemens, known universally as Mark Twain. He was born at Florida, in Missouri, in 1835, and became a pilot on a Mississippi steamboat. Here he got the name "Mark Twain" from the cry used to signify that the water was two fathoms deep. In 1862 Clemens went to Nevada, engaged in mining, and wrote for the newspapers. At the suggestion of a friend "The Jumping Frog and Other Sketches," were published in New York in 1867 and set the public in a roar of laughter. Clemens then went on a tourists' excursion to the Mediterranean and the Holy Land and gave the voyage wide fame in his "Innocents Abroad." In his next work, "Roughing It," he described in the same grotesque style his mining experiences. He joined with C. Dudley Warner in "The Gilded Age," to satirize the modern race for wealth. Clemens fixed his residence at Hartford, Connecticut, and continued his sketches and stories of Western life in "The Adventures of Tom Sawyer" and "Huckleberry Finn," but hoping for more ample pecuniary returns from book-publishing, he joined a firm which after a few years' success became bankrupt. Clemens had in the meantime been writing some romances, dealing with history in a novel way. "The Prince and the Pauper" was a reconstruction of the story of Edward VI of England. "A Yankee at King Arthur's Court," was a mingling of things old and new in fantastic style. Then the story of Joan of Arc was retold seriously as if written by a personal attendant. Though this was published anonymously, the authorship was soon disclosed. Meantime Clemens, in his effort to get rid of debt, had gone to lecture in Australia and India, and afterward to Austria, whence he sent humorous sketches of his observations. He is a bold caricaturist of human peculiarities, national and individual.

STOCKTON

Among American writers of fiction Frank Richard Stockton holds a unique place. He was born in Philadelphia in 1834 and learned wood-engraving. He began his literary career by writing for children "Roundabout Rambles" and "Tales out of School." But his peculiar position was established by his "Rudder Grange" (1879), a picturesque humorous exposition of American life. His peculiarity consists in treating odd, and even impossible, events as if they were perfectly natural. Over the improbabilities of character and incident there is shed a pleasant humor, which beguiles and reconciles the reader. "The Casting Away of Mrs. Lecks and Mrs. Aleshine," and its sequel "The Dusantes," are full of amusing impossibilities, yet told in such a straightforward manner as to enchain the attention. "The Lady or the Tiger?" is a short story which ends like a riddle, leaving the reader to give his own answer. "The Adventures of Captain Horn" (1895) and its sequel, "Mrs. Cliff's Yacht" (1897), are full of absurdly romantic incidents, related in a clear and charming style.

HARRIS

A remarkable contribution to American literature was made by Joel Chandler Harris in his negro dialect fables, popularly known as "Uncle Remus." Harris was born in 1848 at Eatonton, Georgia, learned the printer's trade and studied law before he settled down to journalism. While editing an Atlanta paper, he prepared for it the sketches which were afterward published in book form as "The

Folk-Lore of the Old Plantation" (1880). The welcome with which this was received led to "Nights with Uncle Remus" (1883), "Daddy Jake the Runaway" (1889), and many more sketches. The four-footed hero of these new fables is Brer Rabbit, who, weak as he is, manages by his shrewdness to get ahead of the fox, the wolf and the bear, and other smart and strong folk. In his book, "On the Plantation," Harris tells his early experiences, and in other books he shows his affectionate feeling for the negro as well as the white.

FIELD

Eugene Field (1850-1895) was a remarkable combination of a book-loving scholar, a wide-awake journalist, a Western humorist, and a tender-hearted poet. He was born at St. Louis, studied at more than one college, graduated from the University of Michigan and traveled in Europe. After his return he was a journalist in Denver and other cities, but finally settled in Chicago. Here he found congenial work in contributing daily to the press whims and fancies in prose and verse. Some of his poems were in Western dialect and described vividly rude frontier life. But he also had especial fondness for children and some of his most pleasing work was lullabies, little folk's stories, and "Love Songs of Childhood." His classical scholarship was shown in his translations from Horace. After his death his works and plays were collected in ten volumes, and his friends testified their regard in affectionate praise.

James Whitcomb Riley is the popular Hoosier poet. He was born at Greenfield, Indiana, in 1852, and early contributed to local papers, chiefly in verse. He belonged for a time to a strolling company of actors, for whom he recast plays and improvised songs. Then he obtained a place with the "Indianapolis Journal." He has also been a popular lecturer. Among his publications are "The Ole Swimmin'-Hole and 'Leven More Poems," "Pipes o' Pan at Zekesbury," "Rhymes of Childhood," "Poems here at Home." Though most of his poems are in dialect, he has written also in serious style, and has touched the hearts of people, seldom reached by the loftier poets.

Another poet who has won favor with the masses of the people is Will Carleton. He was born at Hudson, Michigan, in 1845, graduated at Hillsdale College, and engaged in newspaper work in Detroit and Chicago. His numerous poems of rural life and incidents have been collected in "Farm Ballads," "Farm Legends," "Farm Festivals," and a similar series relating to the city. The best known of his poems are "Betsey and I Are Out," "How Betsey and I Made Up," "Over the Hills to the Poor House," and "Gone With a Handsomer Man." Though not ranking high from a literary point of view, they deserve commendation for their correct moral tone.

John Boyle O'Reilly (1844-1891), a native of Ireland, entered the British army for the purpose of propagating Fenianism. Detected, tried and convicted, he was transported to Australia, but managed to escape to an American vessel. He settled in Boston, where he became editor of "The Pilot." Besides a narrative of his adventures, he published some volumes of poetry and a novel, "Moondyne." He was, above all, a poet, and utilized his knowledge of remote lands and seas in both poetry and prose.

Richard Watson Gilder, born at Bordentown, New Jersey, in 1843, belongs to a literary family. In 1869 he became associate editor of "Scribner's Monthly" and when the title was changed to the "Century Magazine," in 1881, he was made editor-in-chief. His own books have been poems, artistic and mystical. They include "The Celestial

Passion," "The New Day," "The Poet and His Master" (1878), and "Lyrics" (1885).

No more vivid picture of the condition of Virginia just before and during the Civil War has been given than in the dialect stories of Thomas Nelson Page. These humorous and pathetic tales are put in the mouth of an old negro, who looks back with regret to the vanished blessings of patriarchal slavery. "Marse Chan" appeared in the "Century Magazine" in 1884, and was soon followed by "Meh Lady," "Ole Stracted," and "Unc' Edinburg's Drowndin'." Page was born in Hanover County, Virginia, in 1854, was educated at the University of Virginia, and became a lawyer at Richmond. He has sketched his own boyhood in "Two Little Confederates" (1888). Other stories of Virginia war life are "On Newfound River" (1891), "The Burial of the Guns" (1894). In "Red Rock" (1899) the troublous times of reconstruction and carpetbaggers are dealt with from the Southern point of view.

The novelist who has best succeeded in reproducing the atmosphere of Kentucky country life before the war is James Lane Allen, who was born at Lexington in that State in 1850. He had been engaged as a teacher before he devoted himself to literature in 1885. For "Harper's Magazine" he prepared sketches of the Blue Grass Region, and afterward used these studies as the background of his stories. "The Choir Invisible" is an enlargement of a tale of pioneer times originally published as "John Gray." "With Flute and Violin" is a pathetic story, founded on the life of a minister of Lexington. One of the "Two Gentlemen of Kentucky" is an old negro preacher. "King Solomon" is a tribute to the self-sacrificing heroism of an outcast. In other stories historical events and personages are freely introduced. "Summer in Arcady," though full of local color, is poetical and spiritual.

The American novelist of socialism was Edward Bellamy (1850-1898). Born at Chicopee Falls, Massachusetts, he was educated in Germany. He was chiefly engaged in journalism, and for a time resided in Hawaii. Returning to his native State in 1877, he founded the "Springfield News." His earlier novels were "Six to One; a Nantucket Idyl" (1878), "Dr. Heidenhoff's Process" (1880). But his name was made widely known by his novel, "Looking Backward" (1888), in which a person enjoying the public comforts and manifold inventions of the socialistic era of A. D. 2000 describes the inconvenience and troubles of life in the Nineteenth Century. Such was its effect on the public mind that societies were formed in all parts of the country to promote the ideas of the work, especially the single tax on land. After some years of labor in this cause, Bellamy's health failed, but he added another work, advocating the same ideas, "Equality" (1897). His great merit is that he put into literature the ideal community of the vast mass of the American people, whether to be realized in the way he proposed or not.

Julian Hawthorne, son of Nathaniel, was born in Boston in 1846, and went with his father to England in 1853. He returned to Massachusetts for his education, but left Harvard on the death of his father in 1864, and went abroad. After further study in Germany he became a civil engineer, and was employed as such in New York City. In 1872 he took up journalism and literature and since that time has been constantly engaged in contributing to periodicals and newspapers. For some years he resided in London and contributed to "The Spectator." His "Saxon Studies" consists of pleasant sketches of German life. Among his best short stories are "Bressant," "Idolatry," and "Archibald Malmaison;" among the longer novels are "Garth," "Sebastian Strome," and "Fortune's Fool." He has also written a biography of "Nathaniel Hawthorne and His Wife."

John Hay at one time seemed to be the rival to Bret Harte, but the wealth acquired by his marriage seems to have diverted him to other pursuits. He was born at Salem, Indiana, in 1838, graduated at Brown University, and entered on law practice at Springfield, Illinois. Abraham Lincoln, when elected to the Presidency, chose John G. Nicolay and Hay as his private secretaries, and during the war employed the latter on missions of importance. For faithful service in the field he was brevetted colonel of volunteers. When Lincoln died, Colonel Hay was at his bedside. Afterward he was in the diplomatic service at Paris, Vienna and Madrid. In 1870 he became an editorial writer on the "New York Tribune." His "Pike County Ballads" (1871), at once took the world by storm; "Jim Bludso," the pilot who stuck to his post when the steamboat was on fire, and "Little Breeches" were the first dialect poems in which the humorous and heroic were blended. At the same time Colonel Hay published "Castilian Days," giving his impressions of the romance and beauty of Spain. The style is graceful, and the book shows both humor and fancy. A notable novel, "The Breadwinners," describing the struggle between labor and capital, has been ascribed to Hay, but he has never acknowledged it. His most important literary undertaking has been the "Life of Abraham Lincoln" (10 vols., 1890), prepared in conjunction with Nicolay. It portrays the martyred President in public and private life and gives full details of his surroundings in all parts of his career. In 1897 Colonel Hay was appointed Minister to England, and in 1898 he was called to be Secretary of State.

One of the strangely attractive writers of recent times is Lafcadio Hearn. He was born in the Ionian Islands in 1850, of an Irish father and Greek mother. He was educated in England and France, but came to America, and was employed on newspapers in Cincinnati and New Orleans. After publishing "Chita, a Memory of Last Island" (1889), he was sent to the West Indies to describe the natives. This was done in "Two Years in the West Indies," and in "Youma," a tale of the fidelity of a black nurse to her infant white charge during an insurrection. Hearn then went to Japan, where he has become a teacher, learned the Japanese language, accepted the Buddhist faith, married a Japanese wife and taken a Japanese name, Y. Koijumi. His books include "Glimpses of Unfamiliar Japan" (1895), "Kokoro; Hints and Echoes of Japanese Inner Life" (1896). His style is highly picturesque, vividly expressing the beauty of the distant land in which the wanderer has fixed his abode.

Charles Dudley Warner is a delightful essayist, humorist, and companion in travel, and an accomplished editor. He was born at Plainfield, Massachusetts, in 1829, graduated at Hamilton College in 1851, was a surveyor in Missouri, and a lawyer in Chicago. In 1860 he removed to Hartford, Connecticut, and became editor of the "Courant." He has had charge of the "Editor's Drawer" in "Harper's Magazine" since 1884. After various contributions to magazines, he became known as a humorist by "My Summer in a Garden" (1870), a book full of quiet but irresistable fun. "Back-Log Studies" (1872), mingled graver thoughts with mirth. Warner was associated with Mark Twain in "The Gilded Age" (1873). His books of travel in Egypt and the Levant, and in the Western and Southern United States, are among the best of their class, brisk, bright, and stimulating. Warner has

also written much on literature, one of his best books being
"The Relation of Literature to Life" (1896).   He has
published biographies of Captain John Smith and Washington Irving.   He was chief editor of the "Library of
the World's Best Literature" (1896-8).

Having earned a high reputation as a newspaper correspondent, Harold Frederic (1856-1898) was coming
into fame as a novelist when death suddenly cut short his
career.   He was born at Utica, New York, of an Irish
father and New England mother.   Taken from school at
twelve, he found his way to a newspaper office.   As a
reporter he went to Albany and New York, and in 1884
was made London correspondent of the New York
"Times."   His ability was soon widely recognized.   Amid
his journalistic labors he found time to write stories and
novels of more than average merit.   The first that
attracted notice was "Seth's Brother's Wife" (1887), a
"purpose" story.   "In the Valley" was a story of colonial
times along the Mohawk River, contrasting scenes of peace
and war; "The Copperhead," a somewhat similar story
of the Civil War.   But "The Damnation of Theron Ware"
(1896), challenged public attention by its startling title
and manifest power.   A weak, imperfectly educated
Methodist minister is brought into unexpected contact
with the strong faith and impressive ritual of the Roman
Catholic Church.   Swayed from his religious moorings
by admiration and love of an intellectually robust girl, he is
morally shipwrecked.   Carefully as the story is wrought,
and exact as it is in separate scenes, the whole is not consistent.   The signal ability displayed in the first part is not
maintained to the end.   In later stories Frederic turned
to England for scenes and themes.   His last, "The Market Place" (1898), is equal to any of its predecessors.
Yet the testimony of his associates is that in none of his

works did he exhibit the full measure of the powers they believed him to possess. In particular, humor, which was a marked characteristic of his conversation, is absent from his writings.

Literature for juvenile readers has been almost exclusively an American invention. There had been some English precursors in "Evenings at Home," "Sandford and Merton," and Miss Edgeworth's "Moral Tales." Even Goldsmith and Charles Lamb wrote some children's stories. But the first who devoted himself with success to instructive books of this class was the American Samuel Griswold Goodrich (1793-1860), best known as "Peter Parley." More than two hundred volumes were prepared by him, historical, biographical and instructive. So popular did his pen-name become that more than seventy volumes were issued under it without his authority. Jacob Abbott (1803-1879) wrote almost an equal number of instructive story books, including the "Rollo Books," the "Franconia Stories," and the "Marco Paul Series." William T. Adams (1822-1897), a teacher in the Boston public schools, became, under the name "Oliver Optic," a favorite writer for boys. He wrote several series, "Young America Abroad," "Lake Shore," and "Army and Navy." Other superior writers of this class are Hezekiah Butterworth, born in 1839, who has written "Zig-Zag Journeys" in many countries, many excellent stories and ballads; Horatio Alger, born in 1834, who has written "Luck and Pluck," and more than fifty similar books, urging boys to self-support, besides biographies of Lincoln, Garfield, etc.; Horace Elisha Scudder, born in 1838, who has written the "Bodley Books," biographies of Washington and Noah Webster, some histories, and literary essays; Willis John Abbot, born in 1863, who has written boys' books on the Navy in each of the American wars.

To the same class may be added Charles Carleton Coffin (1823-1896), best known as a war correspondent, who wrote for boys the "Story of Liberty" (1878), and a series of books on the Civil War.

Dr. S. Weir Mitchell, after attaining international reputation as a specialist in nervous diseases, began, at the age of fifty, to write stories, sketches, and literary essays, with increasing success until in "Hugh Wynne, Free Quaker" (1897), he produced a powerful historical novel of Philadelphia in the Revolution. He has, however, done injustice to the Quakers and their mode of life. Earlier novels were, "In War Time," and "Far in the Forest." Later came "The Adventures of François," a tale of the French Revolution. François was a foundling, who became a thief, juggler and fencing-master. The tale is artistically constructed, but has not the same direct interest as its predecessor. Dr. Mitchell has also written poems which were collected in 1896. In his dramatic pieces he has displayed especial vigor. Dr. Mitchell was born at Philadelphia in 1829, the son of a distinguished physician. He was led to his study of nervous affections by his experience as an army surgeon.

The most successful American soldier novelist is Charles King, born at Albany, New York, in 1844, but taken to Wisconsin a year later. He is a graduate of West Point, but resigned from the army in 1879, and was for a time professor of military science at the University of Wisconsin. In the Spanish-American War he was made a general of volunteers, as his father had been in the Civil War. His literary work consists of narratives of his own experience, as "Campaigning with Crook" (1890), and "Famous and Decisive Battles of the World" (1884), and a long series of novels describing army and frontier life. Among the best are "The Colonel's Daughter" (1883),

"Kitty's Conquest" (1884), and "Captain Close and Sergeant Crœsus" (1895). Two of his stories relate to the Civil War, and one of these, "Between the Lines" has had special success.

WOMEN WRITERS

The popular story, "Little Women" (1868), was an idealized transcript of the author's family life. Never was there a more humorous and pathetic contrast than between the self-sacrificing devotion of the author and her mother and the unworldly wisdom of her unpractical father, "the sage of Concord." Yet family affection united this household in enviable harmony. Louisa May Alcott (1832-1888), was born at Germantown (now part of Philadelphia), but in infancy was taken to Boston, where her father taught school. From the age of seventeen she was busily occupied in helping to support the family, by teaching, sewing, and writing stories. In 1862 she was a hospital nurse in Washington, and wrote "Hospital Sketches." In 1866 she became editor of a magazine for children, and was thus led to her successful family story. This was followed by "An Old-Fashioned Girl" (1869), and by "Little Men" and "Jo's Boys," as sequels to her "Little Women." For the "No Name" series she wrote "A Modern Mephistopheles." Her popularity brought her fame and comparative wealth, yet for the family's sake she toiled on until she died on the day of her father's funeral. Children of all ages are attracted by the unaffected humor of her books, which teach, by lively examples, the duty of work and loving service of others. The rapidity with which she wrote for support of her family excuses the carelessness of her style. Some of her best work was done before she was in demand as a writer for children.

The mountains of Eastern Tennessee and their peculiar inhabitants have been made familiar to American readers by the genius of Miss Mary Noailles Murfree, who writes under the name Charles Egbert Craddock. She was born at Murfreesboro, Tennessee, in 1850, but on account of ill health, which has rendered her permanently lame, she spent much time in the mountains. When her stories first appeared in the "Atlantic Monthly," they were supposed to come from a man, and the editor was much surprised when, in 1883, she presented herself in person. Her writings are free from expression of the author's feelings, and show full understanding of masculine life. They abound in picturesque descriptions of scenery, grand mountains and romantic streams, brilliant sunshine and variegated clouds, gloomy woods and sylvan glades. Against this background are depicted hardy, taciturn men and lonely reserved women, and the strange phases of their isolated life. "In the Tennessee Mountains" (1884), the first collection of these sketches, proved popular, and was soon followed by "Where the Battle was Fought," and "In the Clouds" (1886). "The Story of Keedon Bluffs" (1887), "The Prophet of the Great Smoky Mountains" (1888), and "Down the Ravine," are further specimens of her artistic skill in her familiar region.

Under the initials "H. H." an American woman won high regard as a poet, and afterward showed brilliant descriptive power in prose. Later, when her name was fully disclosed, she took up the cause of the Indian and in history and a popular novel pleaded in his behalf with the Government and the people of the United States. Helen Fiske was born in 1831 at Amherst, Massachusetts, where her father was professor in the college. At twenty-one she was married to Captain Edward Hunt of the United States army and wandered with him in different parts of the country. When he was killed by the explosion of a mine and her daughter died, Mrs. Hunt was plunged in the deepest grief. After some time she began to write meditative and descriptive poems which attracted attention by their strong feeling, and vivid fancy. Sometimes they took the form of parable or allegory, but they were best when they painted out-door nature. Mrs. Hunt then wrote prose descriptions which were collected under the title "Bits of Travel," and proved attractive to even a wider circle of readers. They abound in humor as well as pathos, and show the delicate insight of women. Other books of the same class followed. Two novels in the "No Name" series are known to have been from her pen—"Mercy Philbrick's Choice," and "Hetty's Strange History." The stories published under the pen-name "Saxe Holm" have also been ascribed to her. After she was married to Mr. William Jackson in Colorado, she became fully aware of the gross wrongs done to the Indians, and exerted herself to secure justice for them from the nation. For this purpose she studied the full history of Government dealings with the red men and summed it up in "A Century of Dishonor," making a passionate appeal for removal of the national disgrace. This was followed by the powerful story "Ramona," written shortly before her death in 1885. This expiring effort of her genius is perhaps its fullest illustration.

Another woman writer who has won popularity is Elizabeth Stuart Phelps Ward. She was born at Andover, Massachusetts, being the daughter of the distinguished professor, Dr. Austin Phelps. Her book, "Gates Ajar" (1868) was an attempt to depict the future life as in many respects resembling the present. This idea was continued in "Beyond the Gates," and "The Gates Between" (1887). In other books, as "The Story of

Avis" (1877), and "Doctor Zay" the conflict in woman's nature between love and professional ambition is shown. In 1888 she was married to Herbert D. Ward, and with him she has written some stories and essays. To her "Old Maids' Paradise" (1879) they added a sequel "The Burglars Who Broke into Paradise" (1897).

Frances Hodgson Burnett is best known by her story, "Little Lord Fauntleroy," in which a boy brought up in poverty in New York brings English aristocratic life into humiliating contrast with democratic equality, when he is restored to his rights as heir to a dukedom. She was born at Manchester, England, in 1849, and lived there till she was sixteen. Then the Hodgson family, having suffered losses, removed to Knoxville, Tennessee. Frances began early to write stories for magazines, but did not reach success till after her marriage to Dr. Burnett, in 1873. With him she settled in Washington in 1875. "That Lass o' Lowrie's" appeared in "Scribner's Magazine" in 1877, and made her name known. Joan Lowrie had been abused since infancy and was compelled to do a man's work as a pit girl in an English coal mine. Her father is a vicious brute, but she develops such noble virtue as to win the regard and love of Derrick, the educated engineer. The contrast between this pure soul and her grim and repulsive surroundings is dramatically brought out. Other novels sustained the high reputation now awarded the author. Among them were "Haworth's" (1879), "Louisiana" (1881), "Esmeralda" (1882), "A Fair Barbarian" (1882). "Through One Administration" (1883), was a bright picture of Washington society. Then came "Little Lord Fauntleroy" (1887), which won greater triumph in a new field. In "The One I Knew Best of All" (1893), Mrs. Burnett sketched her own career. In "A Lady of Quality" (1895), and its sequel "His Grace of Osmonde," she seems to have departed from the high moral tone of her previous works. She has since separated from her husband.

Octave Thanet is the pen-name of Miss Alice French, who has written good short stories of Trans-Mississippi life. She was born at Andover, Massachusetts, about 1850, and was educated there, but her father had settled at Davenport, Iowa. She has a plantation in Arkansas, and her stories generally relate to that State or Iowa. They are marked by strong dramatic quality, truth in dialect, character, and scenery. Some of her collections are "Knitters in the Sun," "Otto, the Knight," "Stories of a Western Town," "Stories of Capital and Labor."

New England life is by no means exhausted as a quarry for the novelist in search of characters and types. Several women writers have done good work in this direction and have brought to light some striking specimens. Among these is Sarah Orne Jewett, born at South Berwick, Maine, in 1849. Her first book, "Deephaven" (1877), was in the form of an autobiography, revealing life in fishing villages. Her chief novel is "A Country Doctor," but most of her work has been in short stories, which Howells has pronounced masterpieces. Among them are "The King of Folly Island" (1888), "The Country of the Pointed Firs" (1896).

Another successful explorer of this field is Mary Eleanor Wilkins, born at Randolph, Massachusetts, about 1855. In her first book, "The Adventure of Ann" (1886), and other collections of short stories, "A Humble Romance," "A New England Nun," and "Young Lucretia," she deals with plain country folk, and especially the old maids. "Giles Corey, Yeoman" (1893) is a play depicting colonial times. In her later novels, "Jane Field" (1893), "Madelon" (1895), and "Jerome, a Poor

Man" (1897), there is more attempt to introduce roman
ticism. "The Long Arm" (1895) won a prize as a detective story.

Still another who deals with New England life is Mrs.
Annie Trumbull Slosson, born in Stonington, Connecticut,
of the well-known Trumbull family. She has, however,
directed her attention chiefly to peculiar characters, such
as are "cracked" or "a little off." Seven of her sketches
were collected under the title, "Seven Dreamers" (1891).
The best is "Fishin' Jimmy."

Another writer of this class is Mrs. Sarah Pratt (Mc-
Lean) Greene, who had the unpleasant experience of being
tried for libel for her "Cape Cod Folks" (1881), and had
to alter the story. She has since written "Towhead, the
Story of a Girl" (1884), and "Lastchance Junction"
(1889).

Mrs. Burton Harrison's maiden name was Constance
Cary, and she was born at Vancluse, Virginia, the residence of her maternal grandfather, Thomas, ninth Lord
Fairfax. She was married to Burton Harrison, who had
removed from Virginia to New York after the war. Her
first story was "Golden Rod" (1878), relating to Mount
Desert. It was followed by "Helen Troy" (1881), a
story of New York society and the Berkshire Hills. Then
came an "Old-Fashioned Fairy Book" (1884), and "Bric-
à-Brac Stories" for children. But the work by which
she attracted special attention was "The Anglomaniacs"
(1889), a brilliant and witty exhibition of certain phases
of American society. "A Bachelor Maid" treated of
social questions of the day; "An Errant Wooing" (1895),
embodies material gathered in a tour in Spain and Italy.
Other stories related to the South before and during the
war. Among them is "A Son of the Old Dominion"
(1897).

Frances C. Tiernan, born at Salisbury, North Carolina, has written, under the pen-name, Christian Reid, a large number of excellent stories. The first was "Valerie Aylmer" (1870); others are "A Daughter of Bohemia" (1873), "A Question of Honor" (1875), "Hearts of Steel" (1882). In "The Land of the Sky" (1875) the scene is laid in the Allegheny Mountains.

Mrs. Frances Courtenay Barnum was born in Arkansas in 1848; her maiden name was Baylor. Besides many short stories and essays, she has written "On Both Sides," an international novel, and "Behind the Blue Ridge."

Louise Chandler Moulton, born at Ponfret, Connecticut, in 1835, has been active as a writer of children's stories, poems, sketches, essays, and novels. Among her sketches are "Ourselves and Our Neighbors" (1887), "Some Women's Hearts" (1888).

Blanche Willis Howard, born at Bangor, Maine, in 1847, has by marriage become Mrs. von Teuffel, and lives in Germany. She has published several popular novels, "One Summer" (1875), "One Year Abroad" (1877), "The Open Door" (1889), "No Heroes" (1893).